Negotiating the New Ocean Regime

Negotiating the New Ocean Regime

by Robert L. Friedheim

University of South Carolina Press

Written under the auspices of the Center for International Studies, School of International Relations and the Sea Grant Institutional Program, University of Southern California.

University of Southern California

Published in Columbia, South Carolina, by the
University of South Carolina Press

Manufactured in the United States of America

Library of Congress Cataloging-in-Publication Data

Friedheim, Robert L.
   Negotiating the new ocean regime / by Robert L. Friedheim.
     p. cm.
   Includes bibliographical references and index.
   ISBN 0–87249–838–7 (hard cover : acid-free paper)
   1. Maritime law. I. Title.
JX4411.F75 1993   92–23764
341.7′566—dc20

Contents

Tables

Figures

Preface

The United Nations Convention on the Law of the Sea (UNCLOS III) was open for signature in Montego Bay, Jamaica on December 10, 1982. It was composed of 320 articles and seven major annexes (containing over 300 more articles). The Convention touched on virtually every major issue of ocean use—coastal jurisdiction and management in territorial seas, contiguous zones, and a 200-mile exclusive economic zone (EEZ); marine transit passage and overflight through straits and archipelagos used for international navigation; a special status for archipelago states; management of fisheries under the high seas and EEZs; coastal- or flag-state jurisdiction over vessels for the purpose of preventing environmental insults; the general ocean environmental obligations of states; the right to conduct ocean science; and the creation of a system for managing what had not been done before—the exploitation of deep seabed minerals. The Convention took over fifteen years to negotiate through the United Nations General Assembly, an Ad Hoc and Permanent Seabed Committee and eleven sessions of the U.N. Law of the Sea Conference. UNCLOS III was the longest continuous international negotiation held in modern times.

During and after the years of the UNCLOS III negotiations, its substance and processes were subject to comment and analysis by generalists, specialists, pundits, observer-participants, international lawyers, political scientists, economists, ocean managers, bargaining analysts, representatives of interest groups ranging over the entire political spectrum, U.N. and national government officials, common property and regime theorists, and many others. UNCLOS III was clearly an international event of great importance. In thousands of articles and dozens of books, most writers have emphasized single aspects of an international interaction that has meaning and impact at many levels. Usually, they were concerned with either the substance or the process, rarely both. They tended to see what UNCLOS III meant in terms of law, ocean policy, cooperation or bargaining theories, or national or various stakeholders' interests. What insights they provided often were isolated from the larger context of the negotiation. These works rarely treated the negotiations comprehensively, nor were many of them useful in developing theoretical insights.

The underlying premise of *Negotiating the New Ocean Regime* is that the meaning of UNCLOS III cannot be truly understood without linking process (bargaining) to substance (statics)—that the law of the sea negotiations have to be viewed in their totality to understand how the international community has addressed and will be likely to deal with ocean law and policy problems. It has contemporary importance as potential precedent. How UNCLOS III was negotiated and judgments as to what it accomplished are now shaping the way governments are approaching the resolution of other commons problems such as global change. For all these reasons, it is important to see how the process shaped the outcome.

To analyze UNCLOS III in its totality required an approach worthy of the task. Insights from any single discipline or method would not do. The approach chosen was to use history and law as background, bargaining and cooperation theory to analyze process and regime theory, and resource economics to analyze substance. The process of the negotiation was analyzed using a bargaining model, and the data presented in a visual manner that should be understandable to the nonmodeler. A multiattribute utility model was used to evaluate the treaty through the eyes of the major stakeholders.

A study of this size, scope, and methodological requirements has occupied many years of my time. Indeed, it sums up my long involvement with oceans and negotiation. That involvement began serendipitously but appropriately at the end of my graduate training at that "wet" university, the University of Washington (Seattle). I was seeking a doctoral dissertation subject to be completed under the supervision of a crusty old international lawyer, Dr. Charles Emmanual Martin, then president of the American Society of International Law. He suggested that I do a legal analysis of the recently completed First United Nations Conference on the Law of the Sea (1958).

Since I was a refugee from law school the subject sounded acceptable (although I knew little about it), but not the method. My first lesson in negotiation had begun. I came back with a counterproposal: how about a study of the politics of international law-making? It was accepted. As happens frequently, I came away from the experience having learned not only what I expected to learn, but also what I did not expect to learn or appreciate. I came to have a high regard for law or formal rules and rule-based social institutions. I gained an appreciation of how difficult it is to coordinate the actions of multiple parties who must arrange satisfactory outcomes on multiple issues, especially in what some of my international relations colleagues are fond of calling an "anarchic" system. I also learned how intractable were the allocation problems when many claimants used a resource that was in joint supply and there were few or no mechanisms for closing entry.

In 1966, after five years of teaching in the landlocked Midwest, I joined the professional staff of the Center for Naval Analysis (CNA) in Arlington, Virginia, then affiliated with the University of Rochester. It was a period of great ferment on ocean policy issues and, of course, the U.S. Navy was an important stakeholder. A presidential commission—the "Stratton Commission"—was trying to develop a coherent ocean policy for the United States. In order to respond to the informational and analytical demands of the Commission, the Navy asked CNA to perform studies in a wide variety of ocean law, policy, and science problems. I became involved with these efforts. Many of the studies performed by the study group were later published as *The Navy and the Common Sea* (1972). In addition to learning about the substantive problems, the experience also allowed me to rub elbows with the ocean movers and shakers of that day and learn the intricacies of policy-making in Washington, DC.

The middle-to-late 1960s was also the period in which the United States had to make up its mind on whether the rules promulgated at the First United Nations Conference on the Law of the Sea (UNCLOS I) were adequate or whether there should be another attempt by conference to put together a more workable set of ocean rules. Other states, most notably the Soviet Union, were also pushing for reopening some of the issues that UNCLOS I ignored or failed to resolve, or where the negotiated outcome was proving unworkable. I went to work on some of those issues. But discussions as to whether to go back to the bargaining table, what issues should be on the table, and who should be invited to the table were made moot by the dramatic 1967 speech to the U.N. General Assembly of Dr. Arvid Pardo, Maltese Ambassador to the U.N., United States, Soviet Union, and Canada. Although it took several years of discussions and preparatory work in an Ad Hoc and the Permanent Committee on the Seabed to see Pardo's initiative to fruition, it was obvious early on that all ocean issues would be on the table in a universal U.N.-sponsored conference.

In 1969, Charles DiBona, president of the CNA, offered my services as analyst and forecaster to Vice Admiral James Doyle, Joint Chiefs of Staff representative to the Seabed Committee discussions. Since the task to be undertaken was large (how large we did not realize at the time!), a study group was formed under my direction. To overcome my methodological limits, I sought help from Dr. Joseph (Jay) Kadane, a consultant to CNA from Carnegie-Mellon University. He was largely responsible for putting the project on a sound modeling basis. Over the years we have jointly published a number of papers using the methods developed, and I could not have written this book without what he taught me.

The Law of the Sea Forecasting Project provided services from 1969 to 1975 not only to the Navy and the Joint Chiefs, but also under contract to the U.S. Department of State on behalf of the entire U.S. delegation to the Law of the Sea Conference. During that period, I had the help of many fine analysts and support persons. Most notable was Karen Sherif, analyst and computer programmer extraordinaire who took pages of elegant Kadane concepts and turned them quickly into Fortran programs. William Durch and John Gamble, Jr. also made major contributions. Since the data base we gathered was assembled using content analysis techniques, scores of coders were needed. They all did splendid work, but are too numerous to mention by name.

I returned to academia in 1976 when offered a joint appointment by the Institute for Marine and Coastal Studies and the School of International Relations, University of Southern California. The Law of the Sea Forecasting Project was terminated. Since UNCLOS III entered a different phase, our data collection methods would have had to have been revised and therefore it was a good time to shut down. In the later 1970s, Dr. James Sebenius, using different techniques for a different stage of the negotiation, was providing analytic services to the U.S. Delegation. I did not go to Southern California alone. In creating an ocean policy program, I had the assistance of Arvid Pardo, the "father" of the Law of the Sea negotiations. Like many others before him in political life, after his government was defeated, he took up an academic appointment. A gracious, helpful, and sagacious colleague adored by our students, he helped improve this work in many ways in discussions held over the years as well as through comments on this manuscript.

Many others contributed to my effort to correctly portray the UNCLOS III negotiations and understand its consequences. I. William Zartman not only read and critiqued the manuscript, but also provided me an opportunity to show others what could be learned using the methods that Joseph (Jay) Kadane and I developed. Book chapters evolved from the papers I wrote for a project Bill managed for the Overseas Development Council and for his seminar at the School of Advanced International Studies, Johns Hopkins University. At these seminars I had the opportunity to receive the advice and criticism of the Honorable Elliott Richardson, head of the U.S. Delegation to UNCLOS III, and Tommy T. B. Koh, president of UNCLOS III and the United Nations Conference on Environment and Development.

Undertaking a large book project often means badgering friends to provide ideas, engage in discussion, or read first drafts. While my friends and colleagues were remarkably generous with their time, doubtless my hectoring put them to a great deal of trouble. This would have been a much poorer work without the comments of William Burke and Edward Miles, whose knowledge of ocean law and policy are encyclopedic. If this book has any conceptual merit, it is because of the debt I owe to Oran Young. My grasp of economics was improved by the detailed comments of Ross Eckert. No one in the world understands fisheries economics better than Francis Christy, and some of that store of knowledge has been incorporated in my fishing chapter. After I thought that chapter was ready to go, it was improved further by Jon Jacobson, editor of *Ocean Development and International Law Journal,* who published the improved version as an article.

Moritaka Hayashi, whose position in the United Nations puts him at the center of world ocean policy, helped improve my inadequate characterization of the U.N. system. John Odell's advice on bargaining theory and Mark Zacher's comments on regime theory and marine transportation were very helpful, as was Bob Smith's geographic expertise. In chapter eight, I borrowed a technique—multiattribute utility technology—from one of the method's originators, Ward Edwards, and used it in a manner not found in his MAUT texts. Harry Scheiber, historian of law, and Chris Stone, environmental lawyer, were very enlightening. A university press book does not get published unless it is "vetted" by readers. One of those was Chris Joyner. Not only am I grateful that he liked the work well enough to make a positive recommendation, but also because he provided a long list of detailed recommendations for amendments and revisions, most of which I took.

No publishing organization can alleviate all of an author's anxiety, but the people associated with the University of South Carolina Press did their best to mitigate it. I was privileged to work with Warren Slesinger, acquisitions editor; I also would like to thank Marvin Sooros, series editor, and Charles Kegley, member of the Press's editorial board, for their help.

The "other" USC, where I hold my appointment, also helped get this work into print. The work was completed under the auspices and with the financial support of the University of Southern California Sea Grant Institutional Program and the School of International Relations and its Center for International Studies.

Saving my greatest debt for last, I acknowledge the efforts of my most persistent and consistent critic and helper—Robin Friedheim, *uxor* and professional editor.

The final ritual of a preface is to absolve from the author's failings all of those who helped in trying to put the author on the right path. I do so willingly. I am responsible for what is said, and what is displayed, having drawn all the graphs and tables based on the data collected by the Law of the Sea Forecasting Project.

Negotiating the New Ocean Regime

PART I

Regimes and Multilateral Bargaining

1

The Regime of the Ocean:
Where We Were and Why We Had to Change

The thing is most practicable, for
its success all that is lacking is
the consent of Europe and a few
similar trifles.

Frederick the Great on Abbé de Saint-Pierre's
Projet de Paix Perpetuelle

In the last third of the twentieth century, the problem of inducing consent
via a collective decision is no less difficult than it was in the reign of Frederick the Great. Consent rather than an expectation of obedience to authority
is necessary whether one considers the world system "anarchic"[1] or merely
a weaker system than the domestic system in which to play out the relationship between ruler, rules, and ruled.[2] Moreover, the means of inducing consent are limited—coercion, historical accretion, and negotiation.[3]

With the transformation of the European state-centered system into a
world system of nation-states, making collective decision processes work effectively has become even more difficult. We have experienced the growth
not only in sheer numbers of independent states but in the variety of stakeholders' perceptions, values, and interests.[4] And even, if unanimous consent
can be achieved, the process of unanimity "does not assure that all efficient
outcomes will occur."[5]

The margin of safety within which statesmen operate in the latter half of
the twentieth century has narrowed considerably. Thus consent, preferably
given without coercion, has become more important to the survival of the
international system, its members, and their citizens. Wars using modern
weapons—nuclear, chemical, biological—threaten the world as we know it
with potential destruction. War in the Clauswitzian sense, "a continuation of
politics by other means,"[6] or the ultima ratio of international society, looks
less attractive as a means of establishing rules that all would obey, even if a
hegemon or a superpower were willing to impose them upon others.[7]

The margin of safety has also narrowed because the five billion people of
planet Earth consume more than ever before, and unrelentingly stress the

3

areas we share in common, such as the ocean and the atmosphere. If the scramble for resources and the overwhelming of the carrying capacity of the world's commons are not to lead to chaos, some norms or rules that bind all of the world's states to less destructive practices must be adopted.[8] But can we wait for spontaneous recognition by the world's statesmen or their citizens that certain practices are more desirable or less destructive? Recognition over a long historical period of the unacceptability of certain practices is too slow a process to solve many of the problems of our age.[9] Thus, we are left with the necessity of negotiating with each other to try to craft outcomes that will make us all better off; and even this mode of international decision-making is considered by some observers as too slow.[10]

Gaining consent is difficult when only two parties attempt to work out arrangements that would leave them better off.[11] It becomes increasingly difficult when more parties and more issues are added.[12] With numerous parties, it becomes especially difficult to reach a consensus, since the variety of interests that must be served and the costs of information rise measurably.[13] When the problems concern virtually all states in the international system, and all insist that they will not obey rules they have not participated in making, the negotiating process reaches an apogee of complexity. How can the 150 + states of the modern world political system (even assuming they are "unitary actors") negotiate simultaneously with each other?[14] In the language of economics, it would appear that the "transaction costs" (the costs in time and money of interacting with each other) are likely to be high.[15] This is particularly true if the agreements sought are expected to reconcile or integrate the parties' interests and provide a significant benefit to all of them.[16]

One answer is that states can seek to keep their transaction costs low by unilaterally solving as many problems as possible. If a problem looms that they cannot solve exclusively through the application of their own resources, they can seek to resolve it with the smallest number of negotiating partners necessary to address the problem. One partner would be best. But transaction costs are often not unacceptably high with a small group of partners. As the group grows, however, the time and effort needed to satisfy all parties grows.[17]

Unfortunately, many problems cannot be resolved by unilateral action or ad hoc agreement between two or a small number of parties. This is especially true for rules relating to the use of a physical common or area in which all potential users have a right of access.[18] If a state allows the discharge of pollutants into the ocean or atmosphere, it cannot guarantee that the pollutants will be contained within its territory, or that arrangements with one or a few neighbors will resolve spillovers.

More than 140 states have ocean-fishing industries.[19] Although some of the problems can be resolved ad hoc, or even on a bilateral or regional basis, many fish are highly migratory, and solutions to some potential problems— especially allocation problems—may not be found among a small group of states. In the related area of marine transportation, if a vessel owner or his flag-state sponsor must negotiate with 145 separate coastal states concerning potentially idiosyncratic pollution control rules, manning levels, or construction standards before he can be permitted to sail his vessel near the coasts of those states, the transaction costs may be very high indeed. Moreover, because the ocean is susceptible to claims of multiple use, the claimants representing a variety of functions will find their individually preferred outcomes are interdependent with each other. In sum, many ocean issues exhibit "issue density" because they are closely linked with one another.

For problem resolution in subject areas that exhibit issue density, it is useful to have a regime develop "where the costs of making *ad hoc* agreements on particular substantive matters are higher than the sum of the costs of making such agreements within a [different] framework . . . "[20] But arranging agreements within a different framework when the consent of many parties is required creates its own transaction costs, and they are often substantial. Nevertheless, there are a number of problems that cannot be effectively solved without universal or near-universal consent. To gain that consent, universal participation in a formal multilateral negotiation may be necessary.

The Third United Nations Conference on the Law of the Sea (1967–1982) is an example of one type—indeed, the largest type of large-scale multilateral negotiations that has operated under decision rules characterized as "parliamentary diplomacy." The Third United Nations Conference on the Law of the Sea, or UNCLOS III, has been described as the largest, most technically complex, continuous negotiation attempted in modern times.

Negotiating the New Ocean Regime

The task of the Third United Nations Conference on the Law of the Sea was to create a new ocean regime. This required gaining consent from 150 + states, all of which had some voice in the decisions. Many observers (some even after the Conference ended in 1982) expressed concerns about both the process and the substance of the mammoth negotiation. They feared that the transaction costs of trying to resolve the ocean-use problems between states in universal conference would be too high in general, or for some key states, or that the conference would fail completely.

Many observers feared that a new ocean regime negotiated under conditions of parliamentary diplomacy could not adequately address and resolve the many equity and efficiency questions that arise in devising a scheme to manage the commons we call the world ocean.[21] These critics feared that the solutions likely to be chosen via large-scale negotiation would be least-common-denominator solutions—political solutions if you will—and therefore, at best, "good" solutions, but not the "best" solutions.

Finally, some observers feared that the outcome would be "distributive," that it would divide the limited resources of the ocean among the ocean states of the world in such a way that some would win benefits, but only at the expense of others. If this were to happen, they claimed, some members of the world political system, especially the small and the weak, would have "bad" solutions imposed upon them, solutions that would increase tensions because the burdens arising from these decisions would be shared disproportionately.[22]

This book will undertake an examination of two questions: (1) how well, and at what cost, did the process of parliamentary diplomacy engender consent among large numbers of participants; and (2) how adequate was the outcome—the rules embodied in the Third United Nations Convention on the Law of the Sea—for managing the oceans under modern conditions?

Answers to both questions are vital to any assessment of the shape of the human and nonhuman dimensions of the future state of the world. It is hoped that, although a case study with a sample of only one, this analysis may contribute to a better understanding of international relations.

In order to understand the new ocean regime, we must first review the nature of international regimes in general and international resource regimes in particular, including their legal, political, and economic dimensions. Since the purpose of the UNCLOS III negotiation was not to create principles, norms, or rules de novo, but to replace existing obsolete "international legislation," it is essential to survey the traditional law of the sea and discover why it needed to be supplemented, reformed, or replaced. Chapter 2 will offer a short narrative history of UNCLOS III to help the reader navigate the more detailed analytical chapters that will follow. Chapter 3 will present a guide to the special methods of analysis developed to examine large-scale multilateral negotiations of the parliamentary type. Those methods will be used in chapters 4 through 7 to try to understand both process and outcome on all major issue areas dealt with in UNCLOS III. Chapters 8 and 9 will summarize the finding on the ocean regime adopted, and the process by which it was adopted.

Regimes—Their Legal and Political Dimensions

If one is convinced that rules matter—that they influence, shape, and constrain behavior of decision-makers, even those acting on behalf of the collectivities we call nation-states—then one must be concerned with both the content of the rules and the process by which rules are created. Content and process are inextricably intertwined: one's belief in the aptness of a rule is related to one's belief that the process by which it was made was fair and appropriate. One does not have to be a Dantean idealist[23] or even a strict Grotian to believe that, without at least a minimum set of rules to shape the expectations and behavior of the participants, the life of man in this world might well be as Thomas Hobbes described: "solitary, poore, nasty, brutish and short."[24] One does not even have to be convinced that rules need be substantively perfect or perfectly applied to appreciate the values of rules as guides and constraints on human behavior.

Rules are but one portion—though the most visible one—of a larger social institution that recent international relations scholarship has labeled a "regime." The notion of regime, borrowed from legal scholars, is helpful in explaining why, despite the lack of an authoritative central institution, one can safely anticipate that most international actors will converge around outcomes in areas of interest, and accept and implement those outcomes. There are many reasons nations obey rules. Some do so for reasons of self-interest or political power. Others obey because they agree with the underlying normative standards, because they are caught up in the routinized behavior of custom, or because they are pulled by the liberating force of new ideas. In sum, where the expectations of nations converge, there is at least minimum order in international intercourse.[25] Sometimes, expectations converge merely because coordination of national actions is found to lower individual transaction costs. At other times, expectations converge because only collective action will achieve a desirable outcome.[26]

The circumstances of our case are open and evident. We will examine the negotiation of an international legal regime whose purpose was to establish widely accepted rules for managing ocean resources and uses.[27] From this we should learn some useful lessons about how, and whether, the process of regime formation (or as we shall see, regime reformation) produced a guide to future behavior that world decision-makers will actually use in shaping their conduct toward ocean resources and uses, and therefore, by inference, whether the process is a worthy candidate for shaping other international regimes.

We do not have to hunt for "patterned behavior" through all of the acts of states in an issue-area to find, say, a food or security regime.[28] The overtness of the international ocean regime is useful analytically for several reasons. First, despite a long tradition of debate within the legal profession as to whether international law is law, most lawyers, and most states in the international system, treat international law as law.[29] There is a substantial record of compliance with international law by nation-states; its significance as an operative legal regime to international decision-makers is established. Second, international legal regimes meet all the criteria set by recent scholarship for international regimes. We therefore do not have to establish the place of our endeavor in recent international relations scholarship. Many works by regime theorists cite aspects of the ocean regime to bolster their cases.[30]

The ocean regime is relatively self-contained. Although it goes beyond the UNCLOS III Convention negotiated in New York, Caracas, and Geneva, that convention (characterized by many observers as a "constitution" for the ocean) is so comprehensive that it is reasonable to assume that what was negotiated was in fact the regime of the ocean, and that the output of the Convention, in the form of acts implementing or rejecting provisions of the Convention, will be reflected in future diplomatic notes, court cases, and the acts of administrative structures. While we will occasionally refer to these other sources of the ocean regime, mostly we will confine the analysis to the making of the 1982 UNCLOS Convention.[31]

Examining the ocean regime also provides clues to the nature of the international system. While the titles of many of the issues specifically address management of ocean problems, the issues themselves raise first-order questions about the nature of statehood and the international system, such as national authority and territoriality. Even if the specific substantive rewards of one formula over another were small for some states at UNCLOS III, their decision-makers paid attention to the negotiation to better establish national sense of self. (Sometimes consciously, at other times unconsciously following the author's biases, this analysis will be state-centered and liberal in orientation, but hopefully will not play down regimes as arenas for conflict.)[32]

Here it is worth citing, as one commentator has noted, the "canonical"[33] definition of international regime propounded by Stephen Krasner. For the purposes of this analysis, I accept Krasner's notion of an international regime as the "principles, norms, rules, and decision-making procedures around which actors expectations converge in a given issue-area."[34]

While rules often take the form of commands, of prescriptions or proscriptions,[35] they may also be permissive, that is, they may authorize establishment of conditions to enhance the likelihood of their being obeyed voluntarily.[36] In negotiating international regimes, negotiators seem to focus on the language of the rules. Control of what is said in the documents to which the parties are asked to consent is ostensibly what the negotiation is all about. However, even rules drafted by clever negotiators or members of their staffs are not picked out of thin air. Specific rules in an issue-area must refer back to principles, reflecting beliefs of fact, causation, or rectitude, and to norms, standards of behavior defined in terms of rights and obligations widely shared. Moreover, the belief that the process by which decisions are made is legitimate is critical to the propensity of parties to comply with the outcome.

One cannot understand properly the process of negotiating an international regime by concentrating exclusively on the proposed wording of draft rules. Often the underlying struggle is about establishing the operative principles or norms in the given situation. These principles or norms become "referents" or "the secondary or underlying values that give meaning to the items under discussion."[37] The referents, in turn, become the core of a formula. Usually, after a diagnostic phase, agreement is achieved in two further steps—first, through acceptance of the operative principle or norm in a general formulation, and second, through working out detailed rules. Often what occurs in the final phase of bargaining is an attempt to protect—or undermine—the operative principle or norm through manipulation of the language describing the rule. We will examine this process in detail in Part II.

Although this work will concentrate on one of three processes used to create international regimes, we must take into account other related regime types, whose rules were formed by different processes, as part of the context of the negotiation process. Rules are rarely negotiated in a political vacuum. Many ocean rules have existed for so long that one could deal with them as if they had arisen spontaneously[38] (despite debates in the international legal community as to their origin and present applicability). Once such spontaneous regime rules are the entrenched rules that members of the international system are seeking to alter in a negotiation; we shall treat them as the operative regime rules unless they are altered by the negotiators.

Imposed regimes also must be accounted for by evaluators of the process of negotiating new rules in a bargaining arena. Laws or rules relating to rights and obligations most often protect the rights and interests of those parties already well established in the system.[39] Regimes, or bundles of rules in a given issue-area, may be forced by the powerful on the less powerful. When a single "leader" state imposes a regime or "order" on others, it acts as a "hegemon." While we do not wish to enter the debates on (1) whether the very notion of regime implies imposition[40] or (2) whether it is essential to have a single strong state act as a hegemon in order to create an international regime,[41] some aspects of the traditional regime of the ocean have been fostered and supported by the powerful. This too is part of the context of UNCLOS III as a negotiating arena. Indeed, the evidence we will present will show a lively concern on the part of some of the assembled states to avoid the influence of a purported hegemon, or at least of a superpower or coalition of powerful states, and a concern on the part of the powerful not to be considered merely as individual voters in a formal decision system based on a one-state, one-vote formula. This made it particularly difficult for a consistent pattern of leadership to emerge in UNCLOS III and was one of the causes of its high transaction costs.[42]

What was negotiated at UNCLOS III was a resource regime. Rights, rules, and decision procedures relating to the allocation of scarce resources and space in the international common we call the ocean were made in subjects that had not been treated before, or remade where a traditional regime rule was under assault. The assembled states were attempting to decide upon an appropriate mix of rights and rules. Often the issue was a matter of private versus common property rights—whether a particular nation-state could appropriate to its own citizens the right to use and enjoy the resources in question or whether other potential users also must be allowed rights to use and enjoy the resources. In legal terms, many of these issues were framed as questions of jurisdiction.

Issues at stake

What states or international organizations were permitted to do within areas of their jurisdiction constituted the portion of the negotiation concerned with use rules. The negotiators were laboring to provide guides to the manner in which a resource or area could be enjoyed, and the types and levels of liability required of any public or private users. UNCLOS III also had extensive sets of regulations under negotiation. Third World delegates hoped that in areas of ocean use where they could not completely reverse the advantages enjoyed by the developed states, they might limit those advantages by a regulatory approach. This was particularly true in the negotiation concerning access to the minerals of the deep ocean floor.

To foster agreement in rule-making where the proposed allocations were not to their liking or benefit, states were expected to sacrifice their preferred outcome in an issue-area of lesser importance or salience in order to gain acceptable outcomes in areas of higher importance. Within a "losing" issue-area, dissatisfied states were commanded to obey, although the "winning" negotiators had few sanctions they could apply against "losers."[43] However, great faith was placed in a package approach as a decision mechanism.[44]

Finally, in constructing a new "constitution" for the ocean, the delegates had a choice between finding integrative or distributive outcomes among the regime rights, obligations, use rules, and liabilities. The agreement on the new regime could increase the benefits of all participants before they were divided between them, or they could struggle over developing rules that would benefit some participants, often at the expense of others.[45] While perhaps the new regime for the deep seabed (Part XI of the Convention) was intended to have an integrative outcome, we noted an overwhelming preference for distributive outcomes among the delegates as they shaped a new constitution for the ocean.

The Grotian Ocean and Its Challengers

There has been a regime of the ocean for millennia. Despite numerous challenges and, some charge, significant backsliding by the leading states expected to enforce it, rights and obligations of ocean users have been defined under the principle of freedom of the seas since, in a phrase some publicists or international legal theorists favored, time immemorial. This concept was not invented by the seventeenth-century Dutch legal and political scholar Hugo Grotius (Hugh de Groot), but has been associated with Grotius's name since the publication of his *Mare Liberum* (*The Freedom of the Seas*) in 1608.[46] This was a chapter of a larger work—*De Jure Praedae* (*The Law of Prize*)—that was not discovered until 1864.[47] Grotius deserves credit for codifying an international regime whose rules remained consistent to the principles and norms he set out so that the expectations of international actors would converge.

The ocean regime credited to Grotius essentially lasted for more than 370 years and served humankind well.[48] Not only was it doctrinally consistent, it was also congruent with human needs and the technological conditions of the times. However, many observers, even some current supporters of the basic Grotian approach, concede that enormous changes in technological circumstances, and thus in human needs, have resulted in the obsolescence of many Grotian ocean rules, and perhaps even of the principles that justified obedience to them.[49] Opponents since the publication of *Mare Liberum* have contended that Grotius's work was incorrect and inappropriate in its entirety. Their modern successors contend that the regime of the Grotian ocean cannot be merely patched or reformed, but must be replaced.

Grotius posited that all potential users, and the states which claimed political control of their behavior, should have equal access to the ocean and its resources beyond a narrow band of state jurisdiction directly off the coast. The only limitation to the general right of access to the ocean was that the user not interfere with the rights of others (an implied liability rule).[50] Open entry to the ocean meant that no individual user could claim an area of the ocean under the notion of private property and therefore monopolize entry into that area, or use of the area's resources. Nor could a state claim an ocean area distant from its coast under the notion of sovereignty. For centuries, it made sense to keep open access to the ocean because, with the primitive technological means of transportation and exploitation available, claimants could not "effectively occupy" areas they might claim beyond the coastal zone. They could not consistently exclude others' vessels from transiting through such areas, nor consistently stop them from taking "fugitive" living resources.[51] The ability to prevent "adverse possession" over the centuries has been a political, and sometimes a legal, test of whether alienation of property and resources would be accepted by states.[52]

What could be possessed to the exclusion of others was a narrow band of water off a state's coast. For most states, that narrow band—the territorial sea—hardened into a three-mile zone. There has been a vigorous debate in the first half of the twentieth century over whether this narrow limit resulted from the "cannon-shot rule" popularized by van Bynkershoek (cannon of the seventeenth and eighteenth centuries had a maximum range of three miles and therefore a state could claim possession of what ocean territory lay under the control of its coastal artillery).[53] We will note merely that the cannon-shot rule is clearly based on one interpretation of adverse possession. As their cannons improved and the area from which they could consistently exclude others expanded, some states looked to expand their jurisdiction.

Learned specialists in international law and economics have long debated whether the vast area beyond national jurisdiction (or much of the 71 percent of the earth's surface that is salt water) was to be characterized as *res nullius* (belonging to no one) or *res communis* (belonging to all). Although the debate had no practical bearing until the late twentieth century, it raised an important question: if all have a right to use the oceans, how could a specific claimant justify extracting the resources of the ocean and consuming or disposing of them? Even if no claimant could rightfully claim ocean space beyond the territorial sea as territory, claimants have been taking fish from the open ocean for thousands of years. The answer is they have done so under the law of capture: the resource uncaptured in its native waters remains free and available to all, but the fisherman who captures some of them gains a legal title to them when he brings them to the deck of his ship.[54] Whatever the correct theory, we have treated the living resources of the open ocean as if they belonged to no one and therefore could be taken by any claimant, thereby solving one of the chief allocation questions of a Grotian regime of the oceans.

The detailed rules of the Grotian ocean were remarkably scant.[55] Few were needed since, except within limited regions, there was no overall scarcity of ocean space or resources. Only when the situation became one of economic scarcity, or physical crowding of two or more maritime states in a small region (e.g., England and the Netherlands sharing the North Sea), was it likely that the parties would target the same resources and begin a serious quarrel.[56] It was far cheaper to switch than fight. While on the open ocean, vessels using the right to transit or fish were subject to rules governing their conduct. Essentially they carried their own rules with them, their own national laws, the laws of the flag state. This is akin to the notion of the law of the wandering tribe. Obviously, when the tribes clashed, decision-making procedures to help them resolve their quarrel were needed.[57]

Over the centuries, the ocean regime that operated under the principle of the freedom of the seas did not go unchallenged. There were claims of property rights to all of the world's oceans. Some less ambitious states merely tried to have their jurisdiction creep from close to their coasts to somewhat farther offshore, or to swallow up a particularly coveted area rich in fish. Ocean enclosure (*mare clausem*), or the creation of a property right for a particular claimant, and right of that "owner" to choose whether to exclude other users, has been an attractive alternate regime notion for as long as social and legal theorists have understood the value of exclusive rights.

On May 4, 1493, Pope Alexander VI proclaimed the division of the world's oceans between Spain and Portugal. The boundary was established 100 leagues west of the Azores. The enclosure was confirmed in the Treaty of Tordesillas and vigorous attempts were made to impose this regime on other states. Hired by the Dutch East Indies Company to refute the claims of what would be called today a "limited access" regime, Grotius did so powerfully.[58]

Refutations of Grotius were, in turn, powerfully argued by Seldon in his *Mare Clausem* (1635), by Welwood in *A Scottish Abridgment* (1613) and *De Dominio Maris* (1615), and by Seraphin de Freitas in *De Justo Imperio* (1625). Seldon and Welwood's arguments resonate in our own time: by proposing that, under the notion of effective occupation, a state could extend its maritime borders to monopolize offshore regions or resources if it could exclude others, they provided an intellectual justification for the process of enclosure.

In defending Spanish imperial ambitions, De Freitas appeals to those who see a continuous stream of Spanish jurisprudence from the Spain of 1493 to the Latin America of the twentieth century.[59] His defense of total ocean enclosure did not help Spain and Portugal enforce total ocean enclosure against the likes of Sir Francis Drake and Sir John Hawkins. Indeed, the costs of trying to exclude other users from the vast areas of the oceans that the two countries claimed helped ruin their economies. Paul Kennedy has noted that "try as they might, Spain and Portugal simply could not keep their papally assigned monopoly of the outside world to themselves."[60]

Spain and Portugal also failed because they were attempting to carry out a mandate gained from the Pope, whose moral authority and universal dominion were under attack. As F. J. C. Hearnshaw has noted: "The idea of a united Christendom had completely passed away, and had given place to that of a family of nations."[61] Grotius's concept of the state was consistent with the then-modern notions of the independence of states and the contractual or "contractarian" origin of political association: "the state is a complete association of free men, joined together for the enjoyment of rights and for the common interest."[62]

Until recent times, freedom of the seas was the least-cost regime for managing human interactions on the world's oceans. But Grotius's regime rested upon three fundamental assumptions: first, that the ocean was so large as to be, for all practical purposes, infinite and could therefore be treated as an undifferentiated whole since it was too difficult to divide; second, that the ocean's resources were inexhaustible, and therefore claimants had no need to curb their exploitative appetites since there would always be more in other areas of the ocean or in a new season; third, that the ocean would remain perpetually unpolluted since human beings could not more than temporarily affect its purity.[63]

It is unlikely the conditions Grotius posited ever fully existed—he created an ideal model—and they certainly do not exist today. The fundamental condition facing us today is scarcity. And that scarcity exists in an area humankind has treated as an unowned commons with open access to all.

Like the airspace above us and outer space beyond, the ocean is a physical commons. As Elizabeth I was said to have defined it: "The use of the sea and the air is common to all; neither can a title to the ocean belong to any people or private persons, forasmuch as neither nature nor public use and custom permit any possession thereof."[64] Because of its physical attributes or nature, it is extremely difficult to enclose or reduce the ocean to territories from which claimants can easily exclude others. It is impossible to brand a fish, or demand that sand transported down a "domestic" river not enrich the continental shelf of an adjacent state, or to contain pollutants carried by air or water strictly within the boundaries of the party that created them. As a result, these are considered "fugitive" resources or attributes.

Means appropriate for enclosing physical commons become easier to construct with sophisticated technology. But sophisticated technology is costly, raising the question of the net gain in relation to costs. Until recently we could treat physical commons only as legal commons. For reasons of "public use" or "custom," as Elizabeth I noted, some groups, clans, tribes, and states have deliberately chosen to enjoy their landed property in common.

But we will, for the most part, exclude those areas held communally as a matter of choice from our discussion.[65] Areas that are communally owned can avoid many of the problems associated with "commons" (where the word is taken to mean pertaining to all) since they are not owned by all. Communal property implies ownership by members of a recognizable, limited community of persons who can restrict entry to the area or its resources, as well as assign rights to members, enforcible by formal internal rules or social mores. These can help avoid the inefficiencies of universal ownership or nonownership and prevent overexploitation.[66]

Our modern dilemma over the ocean commons originates in the virtual impossibility for earlier claimants—whether individuals or states—to effectively occupy ocean space and requires rethinking now that it is indeed possible for some to do so.[67] If ocean space cannot be reduced to ownership under the notion of territoriality, then the resources of the ocean commons must be treated as if they were available to all humankind. Common or unowned resources have four attributes: (1) they must have economic value; there must be a reason people want to capture them; (2) they must be, for all practical purposes, indivisible or in "joint supply," as previously discussed; (3) they must be usable by, and of interest to, all potential claimants; and (4) they must be open to all, so that "no single user, can exclude others from participating directly and simultaneously in the same use."[68]

If unowned resources can be captured by all, then there is no market price for the resource per se. The price of an ocean fish to a consumer includes only the cost of capture plus profit. This makes ocean resources very attractive as objects of exploitation, though commercial fishing is the last form of major food production where the food producer has no control over the reproduction of his stock. Under open entry, if an exploiter discovers a rich ocean resource, he has little incentive to conserve. Since the resource is fugitive, what he leaves today may be taken tomorrow by other claimants. Therefore, he tries to leave as little as possible since his "opportunity cost" is virtually zero.[69] Fortunately, in the past, the methods used for exploitation were primitive, and much of the resource could not be captured by exploiters with the means available. In the case of a renewable resource like fish, enough survived to spawn again and renew the stocks.[70]

Until fairly recently, it was not a major concern of social policy to alter the incentives of those who exploited the wandering resources of the commons. They could not do enough harm to have a permanent systemic effect. To be sure, world history has recorded many incidents of local depletions, but there were few threats of biological extinction or of outright ruination of the commons. That was to change as fishermen used nets of manmade fibers, gained heavy lifting capabilities with power winches, developed refrigerated holds that could store large quantities of fish, and roamed the ocean in ever more efficient vessels. Scientists provided fishermen with sonar and radar, which made it difficult for an adequate number of fish to escape to guarantee a sustainable yield at a relatively high level. By the middle 1950s, economists began to recognize that many fisheries were boom-and-bust industries involving considerable economic waste.[71] More labor and capital were being expended than the economic returns justified.[72] Grotius's inexhaustibility of supply was rapidly coming to an end.[73]

Other technological changes were also imperiling Grotian ocean-management principles. Soon after World War II, the search for petroleum extended to the sea bottom of nearshore areas. Placer mining for hard rock minerals also began under shallow water. As the exploitative technologies improved, the search for and capture of nonliving resources occurred further from shore. Under Grotian principles of open access, any attempt to exploit nonliving resources should have been based on a first-come, first-served principle. No claimant could be excluded. But this would promote a Gold Rush atmosphere and encourage the development of a resource at an uneconomic rate, as well as a high level of conflict over sites for fixed resources. Geographically fixed resources are best managed when a single rights-holder has the right to control access. This was understood by the manganese nodule miners. They preferred—indeed, insisted upon—exclusive right to exploit a specific area and clear title to the resource.

We now know that, under present conditions, freedom to use the ocean commons may also be the freedom to destroy it. Another fundamental assumption of Grotius, the perpetual purity of the ocean, is under attack. If everyone is allowed access to the commons, no one is responsible for its preservation. As a result, again largely because of technological change, users can produce public "bads"[74] and deposit them in the oceans at the expense of all of us. To quote Kenneth Boulding: "The laws of gravity make [the oceans] the natural sinks for societies' wastes."[75] Since there is no market price for using the commons, storing wastes there can be treated as external to the cost of production. Because use of the ocean or the atmosphere is a free good, those who produce "bads" in using these commons do not pay the full social cost. If the commons belong to all (res communis), we all share in the costs of the "bads." As Allen Kneese explains: "It is well known that unhindered access to such resources leads to overuse, misuse, and quality degredation. Market forces, while marvelously efficient in allocating owned resources, work to damage or destroy common property resources."[76]

Indeed, some claim that if we do not eliminate open entry to the resources of the ocean, we will suffer a "tragedy of the commons," through an inexorable process of destruction.[77] If each user is allowed to increase his use of the commons, he will benefit in the short run, but ruin the commons in the long run. Unfortunately, the individual user has little incentive to forgo short-run benefits since unless all, or virtually all, users simultaneously forgo those benefits with him, the commons will be ruined anyway. Cooperation is possible but difficult, because of the information costs of coordinating a large number of exploiters.

The short-run benefits that tempt the potential user to overutilize labor and capital are akin to those available to players in a theoretical "prisoner's dilemma" game.[78] The prisoner is given a choice: (1) confess and implicate comrades and get off with a warning; (2) do not confess and if your comrades do not confess or implicate you, you will be released because of lack of evidence; or (3) do not confess, but if your comrades do and implicate you, you will bear the brunt of the entire group's misdeeds. To keep the game pure, the prisoners are kept in separate interrogation cells so that they cannot collude. The best long-run alternative—(2)—will work only if all players mutually adopt the strategy. But all players fear the possibility of (3), the "sucker's payoff," for being socially "good" while others are socially "bad." Therefore, they most often choose (1) when circumstances make it difficult to cooperate and "the shadow of the future" is dim.[79]

Grotians, already reeling under critics' assault on the grounds of inefficiency, were further set back by the assault upon their doctrine on the grounds of equity. They considered open access, the right of all to enjoy the commons as equals, to be inherently equitable. But, in 1955, when poor, Third World states were first admitted in large number to the United Nations, open access meant equal access to the valuable resources of the commons in name only. Only those with the technological means to exploit the commons could make full use of their right to exploit. Competition over scarce resources in the ocean was limited to developed states and their legal entities. Worse, according to spokesmen for the developing states (or Group of 77), "freedom of the seas" was merely a mask, a disguise to justify not only the exploitation by the developed in seas off their own coasts, but also the rape of resources off the coasts of developing states. Under open access, the developing states feared, little would be left to capture by the time they acquired the means to exploit the commons on an equal footing with the developed states.[80]

Francis T. Christy, Jr., captured well the policy dilemma faced by ocean decision-makers in the latter half of the twentieth century:

Ode to the Grotian Ocean

Good gracious, dear Grotius
Your law is atrocious,
Your *mare liberum* must end.

The cannon shot rule
Is a rule for a fool
In these days of the ICBM.

Van Bynkershoek's wishes
Aren't good for the fishes
When everyone has his own fleet.

Economists smirk
At McDougal and Burke
'Cause their freedom's a right to deplete.

The maritime powers
Have long had their hours
In using the ocean for free.

Now the 77
Are in 7th heaven
Repealing the law of the sea.

And Seldon is seen
As fully redeemed,
With nodules increasing the stakes.

Dear Grotius, my gracious!
The oceans aren't spacious,
They're nothing but coastal states' lakes.[81]

Modifying the Grotian Regime

Evidence mounts that the Grotian regime is inadequate for managing human uses of the ocean in the twentieth century. Four policy approaches therefore suggest themselves: (1) deny that there is a problem and stand fast on Grotian principles; (2) admit that there is a problem and attempt to revise the basic Grotian principles so that they will more adequately address emergent problems; (3) modify some of the details of Grotian principles in order to resolve particular problems that could then be treated as exceptions to the general framework; or (4) replace Grotian principles completely with new principles. All have been espoused, but only the latter two have proved to be practicable approaches.

States like Japan whose interests were best served under the Grotian regime tried for a time to hold back the flood of change by engaging in what critics called an "except-one policy," vehemently defending all aspects of a Grotian worldview after most other traditional defenders had partially or fully abandoned it. Eventually, Japan too was forced to abandon unrestricted support for freedom of the seas.[82] As the Christy poem humorously shows, some observers saw Myres McDougal and William Burke's attempt to revive and modernize Grotian principles[83] as an unsuccessful response to the depletion of common-property resources through potential misuses of freedom of the seas.

The politics of the mid-twentieth century stepped up the attack on Grotian norms and principles. Third World spokespeople said often and loudly that the ocean regime of freedom for all helped perpetuate their subjugation. The very principles of Grotius were anathema to them. Only a transformation of the world system into one governed under a "New International Economic Order" would satisfy their needs. They sought to define their notion of "order" as a framework broader than a regime[84] in many fora. Their attempts to create regime principles consistent with the New International Economic Order pervaded virtually every aspect of negotiations at the UNCLOS III Conference and, to a lesser extent, negotiations at the predecessor conferences of UNCLOS I and UNCLOS II.

Much of the process of making claims in the twentieth century pushed aside considerations of principle in favor of solving specific problems. In particular, it focused on the transformation of rules. Unilateral extensions of national jurisdiction—through new national rules—were attempted by the score. These purportedly were intended by the coastal states to solve particular problems in their offshore regions—control of fishing or smuggling; fiscal, sanitary, security, or transit problems—and were often touted as mere exceptions to the rules.[85] Some states pushed exclusive claims as appropriate for dealing with new problems arising since the Grotian framework was adopted; they did not intend to undercut the Grotian framework, merely to supplement it.

Finally, among those making unilateral claims to ocean space were states which stoutly maintained that they had never consented to be bound by Grotian rules in the first place, or that Grotian rules did not apply to them because of historical claims, or that they were deliberately undermining the Grotian framework of world ocean management by adopting rules that flouted Grotian principles. In particular, west coast Latin American states claimed sovereignty over a 200-mile territorial sea—a deliberate challenge to the Grotian framework that spontaneously spread to other Latin American and African states.[86] Still other states, such as Canada, which defined their interests in purely coastal terms, saw themselves as in the "vanguard [of] unilateral action."[87]

Beyond the individual actions of states, the process of making claims was often a deliberate effort to define new regime principles, such as when the Latin American group attempted to create a distinctive regional framework, the "patrimonial sea," as a core concept of a new regime.[88] Whatever a state's specific claim, when it had exercised its rights under that claim for a period it deemed sufficient, it could justify the claim under the concept of customary international law.[89] The result of many of these spontaneous transformations was confusion and, where new claims purportedly terminated prior-use rights of other states, conflict.

States with domestic stakeholders who ardently supported Grotian principles, norms, and rules as the most appropriate for protecting their interests, were being pressed to turn away from Grotianism by new groups of domestic stakeholders who found that Grotian rules did *not* protect theirs. The result was that major ocean-using states were forced to make particular claims which they hoped would not threaten the general principles of freedom of the seas—but which could not help threatening them. The United States found itself in this situation.

In 1945, fresh from its victory in World War II and still unaccustomed to its role as leader of the free world, the United States made two important particularistic claims. President Truman issued two proclamations, over the objections of some State Department officials responsible "for the creation of a new liberal international economic order in the postwar period," who understood how the proclamations would undermine that order.[90]

The first proclamation made claim for the United States to control coastal fisheries on certain areas of the high seas.[91] In areas "contiguous to the coasts of the United States" but not specified by miles or other geographic coordinates, the United States claimed the right to establish "conservation zones," in which fishing would be "subject to the regulation and control of the United States Government." It would establish the zones unilaterally in areas where American fishermen alone had fished, and in cooperation with other states in areas where Americans and non-Americans had fished. Supposedly the high-seas character of these zones would not be changed by what appeared to be a claim to use rights.

The second proclamation dealt with seabed minerals.[92] In what was meant to resemble a use claim and not a property-rights claim, the United States claimed "as subject to its jurisdiction and control . . . the natural resources of the subsoil and seabed of the continental shelf beneath the high seas but contiguous to the coasts of the United States."[93] In an accompanying press release, the United States indicated that the 100-fathom line was an appropriate limit line for its claim.[94] However, if the new claim overlapped with that of an opposite or adjacent state, the United States proposed that the boundary be adjusted according to "equitable principles."

The genie was out of the bottle. The race was on, not to match the United States, but to surpass it in unilateral claims. The caveats of not establishing zones affecting the rights of others without their consent or adjusting conflicting boundary claims by equitable principles were forgotten in a torrent of new claims under the notion of sovereignty. Ann Hollick noted that, in 1945, the United States could probably have secured the rights to manage its offshore areas in a multilateral forum.[95] Instead, it chose the process of unilateral claim, and set in train a bifurcated policy—simultaneously attempting to enforce its new claims to exclusive use of its near-shore waters and its old claims to "free and unimpeded navigation" in near-shore waters everywhere—that continues to the present day.[96]

Some might argue that the United States' policy of making limited near-shore claims while opposing the claims of others that go beyond its own, and of enforcing its right to navigate anywhere outside a narrow territorial sea, was an attempt to impose a regime upon all other states in the world in a period of American military and economic superiority. Others might argue that the United States was merely exercising "entrepreneurial leadership." Whether one favors superior power or entrepreneurship as the motive behind American regime-making depends upon whether one views the United States as acting only in its own interest or as "supplying public goods that are enjoyed by other members [of the international system]."[97]

The ocean regime was also transformed by negotiation. International lawyers recognize two major tasks in creating a comprehensive document to describe the state of an international regime in an issue-area. The first is codification—assembling the rules that have been and will continue to be enforced by those willing to be bound by the document. The second, as western international lawyers say, is "progressive development"—developing new rules on subjects not yet regulated by international law, or not sufficiently developed in the practice of states.[98] Or, as Third World representatives insist, new rules based upon a new set of principles. In many major regime negotiations, it is difficult to separate what is being codified from what is being progressively developed, since by the time states assemble to deal comprehensively with an issue-area, there has already been a good deal of state practice on the record, though much of it is recent and unilateral. Nevertheless, conference diplomacy is never merely a matter of tidying up the obvious. It is always messy and highly political.

Four attempts were made in the twentieth century to deal with the Grotian ocean regime in comprehensive diplomatic conferences. The first three attempts failed to affirm the basic thrust of Grotianism—restriction of national jurisdiction to a narrow band off the coasts of states. The Conference for the Codification of International Law sponsored by the League of Nations in 1930 foundered on an attempt to set a definitive breadth for the territorial sea and produced no convention on the territorial sea, not even one "reflecting what the existing law was understood to prescribe."[99]

By 1949, it was obvious to all interested parties that the ocean regime needed more than codification of its Grotian-based rules. The United States had emerged from World War II as immensely powerful, with its productive machinery intact and in possession of the atomic bomb. While playing an external leadership role, it also tried to satisfy domestic economic ocean stakeholders that their interests were being protected. Hence, the U.S. government had issued the two Truman proclamations on the continental shelf and fisheries, much to the dismay of Grotians and naval officers, an alliance of odd political bedfellows that was to last many years. Meanwhile the Soviet Union was attempting to solidify its hold over Eastern Europe, develop its nuclear prowess, and vie with the United States for world leadership. Until the USSR had developed its own blue-water navy, merchant marine, fishing and oceanographic fleets, its attitude toward ocean law was primarily defensive. It used exceptions to Grotian standards such as "historic bays" and idiosyncratic interpretations of "innocent passage" to keep foreign intruders as far from its shores as possible.[100] The Soviet Union also advocated allowing coastal states to fix the outer limit of their territorial sea as far as twelve miles from shore, an unacceptable distance to Grotians and Western naval authorities. The Cold War was in full swing everywhere, the oceans included.

During the late 1940s and early 1950s, much of the so-called civilized world was attempting to recover from the devastation of the war. Some of the efforts restored prewar rivalry for scarce fisheries resources. By 1948, as a result of an American decision to make Japan as self-sufficient as possible in food, Japan regained access to the waters from which she had taken more than 80 percent of her prewar catches.[101] And there were stirrings among people of the European colonies in Africa and Asia that they ought to become free and independent. In 1955, a number of newly independent ex-colonial states joined the ten-year-old United Nations and brought with them their own agenda.

These events were reflected in the work of the International Law Commission (ILC) established within the United Nations system in 1949. The ocean regime was one of the Commission's early principal agenda items. In that year, the ILC's legal experts began to develop draft articles for a future conference on ocean law. By 1956, the Commission published four draft treaties on the territorial sea and contiguous zones, the high seas, fishing, and the continental shelf.[102]

The First United Nations Conference on the Law of the Sea (UNCLOS I) convened in Geneva on February 24, 1958. By April 1958, the 86 states represented had produced four conventions for signature and ratification. The process used by delegates to UNCLOS I was typical of conference diplomacy. It was an early version of what matured in UNCLOS III into what we have called "parliamentary diplomacy."[103] Since so many states were represented, it was impossible to negotiate in classic bilateral monopoly style.[104] It was necessary to form coalitions and negotiating groups to conduct business. Work had to be parceled out to committees and working groups. The decision process of UNCLOS I and UNCLOS II was a curious blend of features associated with international negotiation (parties were not bound without their consent) and with domestic legislatures (decisions were taken by majority vote, and interests aggregated through coalitions).

Two key decision attributes, prominent in 1958 and 1960, did not carry over to UNCLOS III. First, decision was by vote with no attempt to reach consensus. Two-thirds of those present and voting won on substantive issues in plenary sessions. The voting process was orderly, since strict parliamentary procedure was followed—first amendments to amendments were put to the vote, then amendments, then articles, then sections of the treaty, and finally the treaty as a whole. The drafts prepared by the ILC were the substantive positions of the conference; their provisions, except where amended or defeated, became the core of the new convention.

Since ocean law was being decided upon in a world riven by Cold War and North-South rivalries, it should come as no surprise that the voting on the major issues was characterized by bloc politics. Most prominent was the division between North and West, on one side, and South and East, on the other, over the issues of the territorial sea and contiguous zone followed by a strict North-South division over altering Grotian rules governing fisheries, and over whether the thrust of ocean law should remain multilateral or be changed to favor unilateral initiatives.[105]

The broad coalition led by the United States had the best record overall (voting with the majority 82.7 percent of the time) and dominated the process of drafting and getting amendments adopted, since, with reasonable discipline, it had an automatic majority. The developing states (voting with the majority only 57.2 percent of the time), together with the Soviet bloc (voting with the majority only 42.6 percent of the time), could only play the role of spoiler.[106]

The four conventions produced by UNCLOS I in 1958 altered the Grotian basis of the ocean regime as little as possible; it was hoped that new problems such as the continental shelf might be resolved by an exception to the general thrust of a Grotian regime. While the general bargaining strategy of UNCLOS I worked on most issues, it failed to resolve one key issue. Like the League of Nations' Codification Conference, neither UNCLOS I nor UNCLOS II (called in 1960 to resolve the one issue on which UNCLOS I failed), was able to get a positive decision on the question of the breadth of the territorial sea.

Only three proposals on the territorial sea at the First Committee of UNCLOS I had a reasonable chance of passage: a proposal by the United States to expand the territorial sea to six nautical miles and to allow creation of a 12-mile fisheries contiguous zone with residual rights to foreign fishermen who had fished the outer six miles in recent years; a proposal by Canada for a 6–12 formula, but with no residual rights for foreigners; and a proposal by India and Mexico to allow states with a territorial sea of less than 12 nautical miles to establish a fishing contiguous zone of 12 nautical miles from the baseline of their territorial sea. All failed, although the Indian-Mexican proposal came close to adoption. Revised versions and a straight 12-mile territorial sea proposal also failed in plenary session votes. This resulted in a Territorial Sea Convention with a wide range of carefully specified rights and duties of states, but with uncertainty as to where these rights and duties could be applied.[107]

Two other problems spoiled the sense of accomplishment of the UNCLOS I delegates who came away from Geneva believing they had successfully defended the Grotian approach to ocean management. The first was the virtual worthlessness of the solution they reached for managing the fisheries. The second was the open-ended nature of their definition of the legal continental shelf. The measures adopted simply did not solve the underlying problems, forcing reconsideration in the middle 1960s of the entire range of Grotian rules of ocean management.

While the fisheries regime was drafted with great care, it was based upon a false premise. It attempted to conserve the stocks of fish without attacking the core problem—the allocation of a scarce resource. The intent of the drafters was clear: to preserve the right to fish on the high seas (Article 1) and to encourage cooperation among states in the conservation of the stocks (Articles 3–8). All participants in a fishery were to have rights. Coastal states would have only one superior right to a heavily pressed coastal fishery—the right to impose unilateral conservation measures six months after a failed negotiation with the other states whose fishermen fished the region (Article 7). Even that unilateral right was subject to settlement by a special commission (Article 9).

The problem of the fisheries was to be resolved by cooperation rather than allocation. The framers of the Convention on the Territorial Sea and the Contiguous Zone were convinced that the objective was to conserve based upon the principle of "optimum sustainable yield (Article 2)." "Optimum sustainable yield," usually expressed as "maximum sustainable yield," was a biological standard that made no sense to fisheries economists, who pointed out that maximizing the physical yield usually produces significant economic waste.[108] The core problem was that the convention did not say who should get what. The measures called for, even if they worked as intended, would merely determine how much could be caught, not who could do the catching. The ocean is a commons that is imperfectly divisible, and as long as there is no property right in the fish, fishermen have an incentive to take as much as they can, and no incentive to conserve. The Territorial Sea Convention simply ignored this problem.

The Continental Shelf Convention was also fundamentally flawed. The delegates to Geneva attempted to bring the general rules of the Truman Proclamation on the Continental Shelf into a codified document, and much of what they did was useful in defining a key portion of the ocean regime; but they muddied the waters through carelessness or greed.[109] Indeed, coastal states were granted "sovereign rights" (a step beyond the "exclusive rights" preferred by the United States) over the continental shelf "for the purpose of exploring it and exploiting its natural resources (Article 2)." This was an allocation measure. Coastal states had the right to make the rules concerning the conditions under which potential exploiters could gain access to the continental shelf for the purpose of creating wealth. It was clear that the continental shelf was a limited-purpose zone. Coastal state sovereignty over wealth-producing activities did "not affect the legal status of the superjacent waters as high seas (Article 3)."

Unfortunately, the 100-fathom line suggested by Truman was transformed into a formula that undercut the very idea of a definitive geographic line to limit national jurisdiction on the seabed. While a depth of 200 meters (the rough equivalent of 100 fathoms) could be used to delimit the "seabed and subsoil of the submarine areas adjacent to the coast but outside the area of the territorial sea (Article 1)," it was but one of two potential criteria for defining the outer edge of the legal continental shelf. Any state using the 200-meter criterion would rob itself of an opportunity to expand its jurisdiction as technology improved, since the second criterion for delimiting the continental shelf allowed it to claim any area "where the depth of the superjacent waters admits of the exploitation of the natural resources (Article 1)." This merely encouraged a race to possess all areas of potential economic value, whether a state itself possessed the capability to exploit or had to charter that capability from others.

Despite the gradually accumulating ratifications, some states wondered whether the four conventions were up to the task of managing the oceans into the 1960s and beyond. In addition to the continued deterioration of the fish stocks and the uncertainty about jurisdiction on the seabed, evidence was mounting that the ocean environment was being degraded. In the summer of 1967, the Soviet Union approached the United States and proposed reopening a number of ocean issues, most notably the 12-mile territorial sea and fishing contiguous zone. To achieve settlement on those and other open issues, especially fisheries beyond 12-miles, the United States recognized that it might be necessary to agree to a new United Nations Conference on the Law of the Sea. By 1969, the United States was circulating an aide-Mémoire among its friends, inquiring whether they wished to hold a new conference and whether the agenda could be restricted to a limited number of issues.[110] As it turned out, it was not possible to limit the agenda. What resulted was the longest, largest and most complex formal negotiation ever attempted—the Third United Nations Conference on the Law of the Sea.

2

A Short History of UNCLOS III

The Diagnostic Phase (1966–72)

When the Second United Nations Conference on the Law of the Sea failed in 1960, the need for a third soon became apparent.[1] The negotiators demonstrated that they could not reach agreement on the only major agenda issue— the breadth of the territorial sea. Much of what the first conference had agreed to was revealed to be, after analysis by governments and scholars, ineffective in solving the major problems of ocean utilization. Fisheries, under a slightly modified Grotian regime, were to be no better managed after UNCLOS I than before. No provisions were made to solve the ocean management problems of archipelagoes. Environmental degradation was largely ignored, other than an exhortation in the High Seas Convention to states to prevent oil pollution and ocean dumping.[2] UNCLOS I did codify practice reducing the uncertainty over whether the new (since the Truman Proclamation[3]) legal continental shelf belonged to coastal states. But it muddied the waters by providing three potentially contradictory delimitation standards.

In the early to mid-1960s, states were considering ratification of the four conventions signed in 1958. They were also considering whether it might be necessary to do more than develop implementing decrees or domestic legislation. Many states were still engaging in unilateral acts of enclosure, extending their national jurisdiction by decree.[4] Others were selectively ratifying one or more of the conventions, but with reservations which vitiated the impact of the agreement upon them.[5] Still others wrote implementing legislation that ideosyncratically reinterpreted the rights granted under one or more of the conventions.

In short, responsible bureaucrats in many governments realized that the agreements did not meet their national needs. Scholars and publicists recognized that the conventions were not leading to the orderly international system they thought desirable.[6] Slowly, many parties began to realize that, in essence, they might have to start over again, and that they might be better off with a new comprehensive agreement than with ratifying and patching the Geneva four.[7] The process of diagnosis that would lead to the Third United Nations Conference on the Law of the Sea (UNCLOS III) had begun.

UNCLOS III was a conference that virtually all stakeholders wanted, but for different motives. Near unanimity was necessary to get them to the table, but their differences in motivation made agreement difficult. For diehard Grotians, a third conference represented a last chance to avoid disaster and to convince the international community of the necessity of maintaining freedom of the seas. For newly empowered (largely African and Asian) and established (Latin American) anti-imperialist forces of the Third World, a new conference was an opportunity to press their northern opponents to accept enclosure decrees that would push imperialist vessels farther from their shores. They also had a larger agenda into which enclosure seemed to fit—to get the developed states to accept a New International Economic Order. Others, often small new states and their intellectual supporters, adopted a more Kantian perspective[8] and looked at the new conference as an opportunity to convince the assembled states to accept a true *res communis* and permit a new international organization to manage the oceans on behalf of the peoples of the world. States or groups of states such as the landlocked or archipelago states who did not fare as well as they had hoped at UNCLOS I looked forward to reopening their agenda at a new conference.

In light of the trend toward enclosure in national ocean policy evident in the period, some—notably major developed states with navies and merchant marines—were less concerned with doctrinal purity than with protecting privileges such as transit rights and flag-state jurisdiction over vessels. A new conference, in which these states might promote trade-offs to retain what they wanted might be the best method of protecting their interests.[9] Coastal fishermen were left with little to catch after foreign factory fleets, exercising capture rights under freedom of the seas, fished their waters. Their plight made them amenable to a new conference, in which they might convince their governments to protect their interests.

The 1960s saw the first flowering of modern environmentalism with the passage in the United States of the Air Quality Act (1960), Water Quality Act (1965), and National Environmental Policy Act (1969). Worldwide interest culminated in the Stockholm Conference on the Human Environment (1972).[10] Newly created environmental agencies in a number of governments could be expected to welcome a new conference, since it gave them an opportunity to inject their issues into the overall mix. Other new stakeholders were also emerging, such as ocean miners. While the scientific community had known about manganese or polymetallic nodules for about a hundred years, the 1960s gave rise to the first efforts to plan and develop the technology to extract them from the deep-ocean floor.[11]

The increasing number of stakeholders made ocean policy discussions in the 1960s resemble a Tower of Babel.[12] Reform was demanded. The idea that there should be a "national ocean policy," begun mostly in the United States, spread quickly to other states.[13] New institutions were formed to create the desired coherent outcomes.[14] The United States Marine Sciences Council (1966), chaired by the Vice President, forced government departments and agencies to justify their bureaucratic and domestic needs, and to create a national position on all major ocean issues.[15]

In short, the time was ripe for general reconsideration of many of the rules of the ocean regime. But why go to a universal law-making conference? Why not let states individually solve their own problems through their own exclusive efforts? Or, if that was insufficient, why not arrange to have states negotiate bilaterally, or regionally, with their neighbors?

In the mid-1960s, many governments initiated studies on a large number of the ocean-use problems,[16] many of which required more than unilateral acts for solution. In dealing with particular problems—fisheries, the continental shelf, pollution—shipping and naval rights analysts often recommended technically sound solutions which they hoped could be achieved unilaterally, bilaterally or regionally. They recommended going to a universal conference only if unilateral, bilateral, or regional efforts had failed, or were likely to fail, and they preferred returning to a universal forum only if the issues could be grouped into "separate packets."

Nevertheless, Third World states seized upon the right moment to push for a universal conference. Concerns expressed by William T. Burke[17] and others in the developed world about the efficacy of a universal conference were overtaken by two events:

In the summer of 1967, the Soviet Union sent a diplomatic note to the United States' and other governments requesting reconsideration of the territorial sea and straits transit.[18] This triggered an American aide-mémoire[19] adding straits to the discussions. The major states discussed what might be done to make up for the failures of UNCLOS I and UNCLOS II, and these discussions were widely known in the ocean policy community. This knowledge helped trigger the second event.

In a three-and-a-half-hour speech to the 21 September 1967 meeting of the First Committee of the General Assembly, Dr. Arvid Pardo, Ambassador from Malta to the United Nations, captivated his fellow diplomats, the audience, and reporters. He argued with great erudition, that imminent exploitation of deep-seabed manganese nodules would lead to the enrichment of a few developed states and would encourage national claims to the oceans; further, that newly available technologies would encourage using the seabed for military purposes. Instead, he proposed that the United Nations declare the seabed beyond national jurisdiction, "the Common Heritage of Mankind," and create an international agency to control exploitation of deep-seabed

resources. In short, he proposed enclosing the deep seabed (or operational-
izing *res communis*) on behalf of the people of the world, especially for the
benefit of the developing states.[20]

The United States' and other developed states' governments, legislatures,
and interest groups had mixed feelings about turning over the seabed to the
United Nations.[21] Still, Pardo's dramatic speech could not be ignored. Es-
sentially he seized the initiative on behalf of those who wanted the United
Nations to play a central role in developing rules for ocean use. As a result,
in December 1967, the General Assembly created the 35-member Ad Hoc
Committee on the Peaceful Uses of the Seabed and Ocean Floor Beyond the
Limits of National Jurisdiction.[22] As a harbinger of the future, the Ad Hoc
Committee conducted its work on the basis of consensus.[23]

No agreement was reached on a Declaration of Principles to guide the future negotiations in the Ad Hoc Committee; in December 1968, the General
Assembly created the Permanent Seabed Committee to continue the discussions.[24] Two different sets of principles, one supported by the Group of 77,
and the other supported by the United States and its Western European
friends vied for support. It was not until 1970 that a Declaration of Principles emerged that was widely supported (108 votes for, including the U.S., 0
against, and 14 abstentions).[25] In the meantime, the Group of 77 and its
friends put further pressure on the developed states by successfully passing in
the General Assembly a Moratorium Resolution which stated that all states
were "bound to refrain from" all seabed exploitative activities and that no
national claims to the international commons would be recognized.[26]

The United States voted for the 1970 Declaration of Principles, even
though some American ocean stakeholders were uncomfortable with its
"common heritage" provision. Then, in the name of President Richard M.
Nixon, it introduced a Draft Convention on the International Seabed Area
that was remarkably liberal.[27] This would have ended national jurisdiction on
the seabed at the 200-meter isobath, giving coastal states the right to explore
and exploit resources in a "trusteeship zone" beyond, but requiring revenue-
sharing with international institutions financing development, and authoriz-
ing an international agency to grant mining access to the seabed to state and
private corporations under license.[28] If adopted, the draft convention might
have provided substantial sums for development, since the prospect for finding oil in many trusteeship zones was good, and it would have avoided an
international monopoly of mineral resource exploitation, under the "common heritage of mankind." U.S. oil companies and all those concerned with
American economic interests were aghast that the Nixon Administration had

proposed such a scheme. They needn't have worried; the proposal was ignored by Third World delegates.

By 1971, the General Assembly Seabed Committee had 91 members, virtually a committee of the whole. It divided itself into three subcommittees: Committee I, with oversight of the seabed beyond national jurisdiction; Committee II, with oversight of the territorial sea, straits used for international navigation, archipelagoes, fisheries, the continental shelf, and exclusive economic zones; and Committee III, with oversight of the environment and ocean science.

The Seabed Committee's proceedings were acrimonious, and serious questions were raised in some national capitals as to whether states would be better off trying to resolve ocean problems in a U.N. conference or in some other venue. States with fundamentally different approaches to the issues, despite extensive contacts, were not negotiating with each other; instead, as Edward Miles explains, they were "trying to aggregate interests, build coalitions, and define positions on the issues."[29] During the Seabed Committee sessions there was also a shift in the general thrust of the negotiation, away from a strict focus on seabed issues to a growing emphasis on consolidating claims to national jurisdiction and creating a new economic zone.

The preparatory phase ended without even an agenda for a major diplomatic conference, much less a draft treaty prepared by experts that could be amended in the usual orderly progression, as in previous major diplomatic conferences. Instead, the Seabed Committee at its third preparatory session in February 1972 produced a "List of Subjects and Issues," 150 strong, organized in 23 groups.[30] The contentiousness of interactions between states during the preparatory work, the shift of emphasis, and the inability of states to agree upon an agenda and bargaining documents, made it clear that UNCLOS III was to be long, complex, and controversial.

The Formula Phase (1973–75)

Two critical tasks faced the delegates attending the early sessions of the Third United Nations Law of the Sea Conference in New York, Caracas, and Geneva: (1) establishing the rules of interaction and decision, and (2) establishing a formula that would underlie a comprehensive treaty.

In order to foster agreement on substantive issues, it is necessary to identify core ideas with which all major parties can agree and which can then form the basis of a formal treaty. These shared ideas must be a "coherent bundle of referents" that can be shaped into a formula.[31] They are principles of justice. While there is a strong flavor of substantive agreement in the notion of a formula, it can be still be accepted by a party who disagrees as long as there are positive or negative compensations for acceptance, and perhaps agreement over the adequacy of the process by which the formula is reached. When there are 150 issues on the agenda, there will be more than one formula idea, but there cannot be too many and they cannot be described in too great detail or a sense of direction will be lost. If a wide variety of interests must be satisfied, the core ideas that will emerge will spring from trade-offs and be assembled in a package.

However, the first order of business when the Conference met for a short session in New York in December 1973 (to fulfill the obligation to hold the Conference formally in 1973) was to organize itself. Hamilton Shirley Amersinge, Sri Lanka, Chair of the Seabed Committee, was elected President of the Conference. The three subcommittees of the Seabed Committee were converted into the three main conference committees with the same subjects on their agendas. In accordance with normal U.N. General Assembly practice, leadership posts were distributed on a regional basis. An African, Paul Bamela Engo (Cameroons) became First Committee Chair, a Latin American, Andres Aguilar (Venezuela) Second Committee Chair, and Alexander Yankov (Bulgaria) Third Committee Chair. Vice-chairmanships and rapporteurships were distributed with equal care for group representation. The major permanent members of the Security Council became vice presidents of the conference, and two of them—the United States and the Soviet Union—became members of the important Drafting Committee.[32]

Delegates could not agree to rules of procedure and decision during the first formal session. When they met in Caracas for the first substantive session in June 1973, they spent the first week deciding how to decide. The fear was that, if delegates operated by traditional decision rules of two-thirds-majority vote and voted each amendment, phrase, article, and then the treaty as a whole, the Group of 77—by then over 100 states—would have an automatic majority and could create a treaty tailor-made to its interests. But the treaty would have been one from which most of the developed states would have defected; therefore, a consensus-based approach was chosen.

Because voting could not be completely avoided, delegates were committed by a gentlemen's agreement to "make every effort to reach agreement on substantive matters by way of consensus and there should be no voting on such matters until all efforts at consensus have been exhausted."[33] Rule 37 provided for a "cooling off" period to delay voting even if the question was called. Finally, in an attempt to promote a more widely supported treaty, the conference modified the usual two-thirds-present-and-voting rule to require "that such a majority shall include at least a majority of States participating in that session of the Conference."[34] (A consensus-decision rule gives disproportionate weight to the opinions of the naysayers and is therefore very expensive in time and effort.)

Even after the rules were adopted, the proceedings at Caracas moved slowly. Though virtually all participating states had put their opinions on record in the Ad Hoc and Permanent Seabed Committees, because Caracas was the opening of a plenipotentiary conference, they felt it necessary to do so again. It took five weeks to get through the formal speeches of 115 delegations in plenary session. That left only four weeks to begin serious negotiations in working groups, and between regional groups and common-interest groups, some of which were extensions of the same groups in the U.N. General Assembly, while others were specially formed to protect ocean interests.[35]

There was much that was new that would impact the outcome. Both the United States and the Soviet Union recognized that under the basic consensus rule the treaty would have to be a package, and they would therefore have to offer trade-offs on issues of lesser salience to get favorable outcomes of issues of higher salience. Both announced their willingness to accept a 200-mile Exclusive Economic Zone (EEZ)—a step toward ocean enclosure—in return for a 12-mile territorial sea and the right of transit through straits used for international navigation. These became the core of the formula ideas that made up a "single negotiating text" in the next conference session. Progress, while slow, was made on seven issue-areas: territorial sea, straits, fishing, the EEZ, deep-seabed mining, ocean science, and pollution.[36] The conference president and the chair of the U.S. delegation were confident of a successful outcome.

Two related matters, however, should have tempered optimism. The first was the efforts of the landlocked states to exact a price for their acquiescence in enclosure. African landlocked states, meeting in Kampala, Uganda, issued a declaration demanding access to the resources of the economic zones their coastal neighbors were about to absorb under the 200-mile EEZ notion, as well as a strong role in the powerful Seabed Authority.[37] Less well known at the time was the internal turmoil within the U.S. delegation, not merely over bargaining tactics but over the basic U.S. approach to the negotiation, and indeed, over whether a large-scale multilateral negotiation was the most effective means for achieving American objectives.

In the wake of the OPEC embargo in the 1972 oil crisis, staff members from the U.S. Treasury Department began to realize that the resources under negotiation at UNCLOS III were valuable and might be bargained away or, at least access to them made subject to Third World whims. They demanded and got an economic review of the U.S. position. Even though eighteen important public-choice-based papers were produced,[38] they lost this first round. U.S. negotiating instructions remained as before. But they had not been permanently defeated.

The third meeting of the Conference in Geneva (March 17–May 9, 1975) was critical for developing the core formula ideas that eventually led to a comprehensive ocean treaty. They were embodied in a "single negotiating text," or SNT, as it came to be called. Since there was no model convention text, or even agenda, it was necessary to develop a common document as "an appropriate starting point for further negotiations."[39] The negotiating texts were to be prepared by the main committee chairs, reflecting where consensus had been reached or where, in the chair's opinion, it might be reached. In theory, this was to be a "negotiating" text, not a "negotiated" text, but in fact, the SNT became the first draft of the treaty. It was released on the last day of the session and therefore not subject to review.

Considerable progress was made on the Committee II issues. The basic trade-off of a 200-mile EEZ for a relatively narrow 12-mile territorial sea and the right of transit passage through straits held up, although many specific issues remained unresolved—details of the EEZ, landlocked rights, archipelago status, highly migratory fisheries, opposite and adjacent states' rights, and the continental shelf. Less progress was made in Committee III; the chair's report showed that a serious quarrel on ocean science was looming.

From the developed states' viewpoint, the SNT was viewed as a retrogression on the deep-seabed-minerals issues. Some of the key issues concerning the conditions of exploitation and the design of a regulatory system were negotiated in a working group chaired by Christopher Pinto (Sri Lanka). It appeared that negotiators agreed to a "contractual joint ventures" approach.[40] But Pinto's report was ignored by First Committee Chair Engo.[41] Instead, he submitted his own articles based on a draft treaty introduced by Group of 77 members in the Seabed Committee. Engo's articles demanded a monopoly on access for an international enterprise, excluding private and state enterprises, and would have created a governance system controlled strictly by majority vote. Some claimed he took his seemingly arbitrary action to save the negotiations since he could not get Group of 77 support for the Pinto text. In any case, the "radicals"—Algeria, Tanzania, Mauritania and China—were in control of the Group of 77.[42]

Whatever consensus, or lack of consensus, was reflected in the articles developed by the three committee chairs, they became the focus of further negotiation—indeed, years of further negotiation. In the remaining years of the conference, the basic concepts were either refined or, in the process of working out details, undermined.

The Detail Phase (1976–81)

Little did supporters or detractors of the SNT realize that it would take seven more years of negotiations to turn the basic formula ideas into a treaty. In this final, detail phase they had to look at the detailed implications of the general formula and refine it so that it was acceptable to all, or virtually all.[43]

Not all the formula ideas would survive. Some parts of the SNT, in what supporters viewed as backsliding, were radically altered; other parts would be transformed as fundamentally, but in more subtle ways, by changes in their details. Formula ideas did not always mean what they were originally intended to mean, at least according to the supporters of the original ideas. Agreement also had to be brought about by making trade-offs on other issues that were not part of the core package in order to bring a number of states into acquiescence. In addition, there was much technical drafting to be done in putting together a new regime for the oceans. This was a long and often tedious process with few dramatic interludes.

The first dramatic development came in the next, or fourth, session (March 15–May 7, 1976) of the Conference. Dr. Henry Kissinger, U.S. Secretary of State, intervened in hopes of breaking the logjam on the deep-seabed issue. In a speech to an American audience that was widely distributed to the conference delegates, Kissinger proposed a "parallel" system as the way of getting around the monopoly of access proposed by the Group of 77, or the unlimited licensing system preferred by the developed. Under the parallel notion, a miner sponsored by a state, consortium, or private enterprise would propose two equally valuable mining sites. He would be awarded one of them, and the other would be "banked away" for future exclusive use of the International Enterprise.

A revised version of the SNT (RSNT) was produced at the end of the session. Progress was made in Committee I. The scope of the Seabed Authority's powers no longer was over the area itself but only exploitative activities in the area. The text also indicated that state and private corporations might have access to mining sites. However, it also included quotas for mining sites, and required production controls. In an article-by-article review in 53 informal meetings, Committee II refined many of the major articles under its jurisdiction. The chair was able to fend off most efforts to radically amend the articles. There was, therefore, reason to hope that most of Committee II's text would be widely acceptable. Committee III worked on vessel-source-pollution articles, adding enforcement rights for port states. The consent rule for research in the EEZ drew even more support.

The fifth session (Summer 1976) was essential for absorbing Kissinger's proposals. Committee I needed certain matters clarified and extended—such as an American promise to arrange financing for the International Enterprise in exchange for "assured access . . . to deep-seabed mining sites by all nations and their citizens."[44] It also had to deal with some radical Group of 77 states' attempts to reject any effort at compromise on the system of exploitation. Much of this was done in a workshop, which was virtually a committee of the whole. Although Committees II and III were able to work in open-ended negotiating groups and to make progress on the details of the issues, the seeming impasse in Committee I made many participants and observers gloomy about the prospects for overall success.

The sixth session (May–July 1977) confirmed the gloomy prognosis. An Informal Composite Negotiating Text (ICNT) was produced that contained seabed articles less acceptable to the developed states than those of the Revised Text (RSNT). The new U.S. Representative, Elliott Richardson (who had extensive internal U.S. Government experience with law-of-the-sea issues) expressed his "considerable frustration" over what transpired.[45] There was a major attempt to craft a compromise on seabed issues. The Working Group of the Whole, under the leadership of Jens Evensen (Norway), was appointed to bring all sides together in open discussion. The developed considered the text it submitted unsatisfactory. They had problems with provisions on assured access, technology transfer, production limits, and contractor financial burdens. But the Evensen text was at least a negotiated document. Chairman Engo ignored it, and after private consultations with some Group of 77 advisers, produced the seabed articles of the ICNT, which mandated joint ventures and gave the Seabed Authority broad, open-ended power over all aspects of seabed mining.

Richardson was frustrated by Committee I's failure, and also because the accomplishments in Committees II and III made overall success seem tantalizingly close. Various negotiating groups were refining the language of articles that confirmed the major trade-off made in 1973—a 200-mile Exclusive Economic Zone (EEZ), in return for a 12-mile territorial sea and the right of transit passage through straits used for international navigation. In particular, the legal status of the waters in the EEZ was clarified for non-resource-related activities there. Environmental rules also were sharpened—during straits transit, and for coastal states in their own territorial sea. There was even some progress on clarifying coastal consent for ocean science. Discussions on delimitation of the continental margin got more intense, with a group of broad-margin states—the margineers—pushing to extend national jurisdiction further offshore (see chapter 4). Since consensus had not emerged on the latter problem, no provision on this subject was included in the ICNT.

Something had to be done to salvage the negotiation. After the sixth session, Richardson recommended to President Carter that "our government must review not only the balance among our substantive interests but also whether an agreement acceptable to all governments can best be achieved through the kind of negotiations which have thus far taken place."[46] As a result, the seventh session (March–May, August–September 1978) was dominated by efforts to get the negotiations back on a consensus basis and away from the arbitrary decisions of individual committee chairs. A resolution was adopted making it mandatory that changes in the ICNT be the collective responsibility of the president and the main committee chairs, in consultation with the chair of the Drafting Committee and the rapporteur-general.[47] It also became clear that the seabed mining provisions of the ICNT were not even minimally acceptable to the industrial states. The key task was to bring them back aboard. Since the developed states did not have the numbers to force decision by vote, they had to recognize that, if they stayed in the negotiation, the best they could expect was to force opposing states to modify their formula ideas.

Forward movement was slowed by a procedural wrangle. The government of Sri Lanka fell, and as a result H. S. Amersinghe lost his credentials as a delegate. After three weeks of intense negotiations and a fierce fight within the Group of 77, Amersinge was confirmed by vote as conference president despite having no credentials. In the remaining weeks, progress was made in the working groups on keeping closed issues thought by many to be settled (such as transit passage through straits used for international navigation), as well as developing new initiatives on marine pollution articles. Although a new version of the ICNT was not produced, informal articles on seabed mining inched toward minimum acceptance by the major industrial states, though some Group of 77 members feared that too many concessions had been made to keep the developed states in the negotiation.

A revised ICNT emerged from the Eighth Session (March–April, July–August 1979). Extensive intersessional consultations made it possible to begin substantive negotiations on the first day of the session. Even though there was still a good deal of North-South rhetoric, "most active developing and developed country representatives demonstrated a seriousness of purpose throughout the session" and considerable progress was made.[48] Seven negotiating groups were appointed to work on core issues.[49] While many Third World delegations were still concerned as to whether the parallel system proposed by the United States would work to their disadvantage, it was included in the draft on the basis of a U.S. promise to fund the International Enterprise. More compromises were made on other First Committee issues such as production controls and powers of the Seabed Authority and principal organs. In addition, the idea of a Preparatory Commission for the regime was introduced. That seemed to help get around the constant tension between developed states, who wanted to negotiate all details before agreement, and the developing states, who preferred to endow a new international agency with broad powers and not to deal with details, where they feared they would be outmaneuvered.

While the conferees held onto the basic thrust of most Committee II and III articles, problems arose over the delimitation of the continental shelf. After the basic trade-offs on the territorial sea, international straits, and the EEZ were accepted, a group of major coastal states began caucusing—the so-called margineers—who wanted to extend national jurisdiction as far out as they could reach. Their preferences were summed up in an "Irish formula," for which they lobbied strongly. But the Soviet Union was adamantly opposed. Finally, an attempt to preempt the Conference and to split the texts into two treaties was beaten back. There was also evidence that the United States, under severe domestic pressure to have Congress pass unilateral legislation on seabed mining, might be losing patience.

Although negotiations in the Ninth Session (February–April, July–August 1980) were laborious and detailed and progress seemed slow, it was solid. Many delegates thought that all but a few major issues had been resolved, and that a final treaty draft could soon be turned over to the Drafting Committee for polishing.

In Committee I, despite another attempt by its chair to impose his preferences on the issue of decision-making authority of the Council of the International Seabed Authority, many issues had been refined to the satisfaction of the major contending parties. Elliot Richardson believed that only four major issues remained to be resolved on the treaty, of which three (the "three P's") concerned the seabed portion—participation, the Preparatory Commission, and preparatory investment protection.[50] The major problem remaining in Committee II was delimitation of the margin; the committee successfully resisted a number of attempts to make substantive changes on the core issues of the territorial sea, international straits, and the EEZ. Although there were some difficulties involved in finding the precise words for describing coastal states' rights to withhold consent for research on the margin beyond 200 nautical miles, the issues in Committee III also seemed to be on the way to final resolution.[51]

Crises, Convention, and Present Status (1982–)

Over the years, UNCLOS III had weathered several crises in which one or more states or groups of states had threatened dire consequences or even defection if their demands were not met. Crises in negotiation often force the negotiators into recognizing that they are at a turning point that will lead, after further interactions, either back to stability, or to breakdown.[52] Delegates to the tenth session had to weather two crises—the death of the conference president and an 18-month hiatus in American participation. Both events were considerable traumas to delegates so close to successfully producing the most complex written document ever under a consensus-decision rule.

H. S. Amersinghe's death in December 1980 occasioned a struggle over his succession between members of the Group of 77 and between the Group of 77 and other stakeholders. Fortunately, the problem was resolved when two rival Asian candidates (the presidency being considered an Asian position) knocked each other out of contention, and a third, Tommy T. B. Koh (Singapore), emerged as a widely supported compromise candidate.

In January 1981, the new administration of President Ronald Reagan announced it required a period to review the United States' position. The UNCLOS III delegates were stunned and as the U.S. Delegation Report put it, reacted with "bewilderment and frustration."[53] Their frustration was understandable, since the delegates wanted to complete the treaty quickly; they were tired, and afraid that, if they delayed, those wanting to reopen specific issues would succeed, and thereby unravel the entire convention. Group of 77 members, so long rigid on seabed issues, had been compromising in the recent sessions and were now in no mood to make further concessions to the United States.

Those who watched the United States' performance in the negotiations were not as bewildered. Signs of discontent had been present in domestic politics at least since the economic review in 1973, and were manifest in the Republican party platform, in interagency task force proceedings, in Congressional hearings, and in industry fora. Elliot Richardson resigned as head of the U.S. delegation with the expectation that he would be succeeded by his deputy, George Aldrich. But in March 1981, Aldrich was abruptly dismissed and replaced by James Malone. For all practical purposes, the United States dropped out of the negotiation.

Attempts to reopen Committee II issues were resisted, and essentially the text was closed. When the Tenth Session resumed work in summer 1981, it concentrated on delimitation of maritime boundaries, preparatory investment protection, and the Preparatory Commission (Prepcom). While progress was made, a draft treaty could not be finalized because of the United States' nonparticipation.

The U.S. review was completed in time for the Eleventh Session (spring 1982). But U.S. demands grew from the six announced by President Reagan to ten, and then to still another demand (contained in the "Green Book") to completely rewrite the seabed portion of the Convention (Part XI). While the United States stated that this last demand was not an ultimatum, it was so treated by most delegations.[54] They viewed it as either a demand for surrender, a document to justify the U.S. scuttling of the Conference, or at least prolong it indefinitely. A Group of 11—mostly middle-sized developed states—was formed to bridge the gap. But the U.S. rejected the Group of 11's compromise proposals and the Group of 77 would not negotiate any portion of Part XI not contained in the Group of 11 draft. President Koh made a number of personal efforts to alter the Part XI text on composition of the Seabed Council, the requisite voting majority in treaty amendments (three-fourths instead of two-thirds), and production controls. Other last-minute efforts, for example, between Alvaro de Soto, the Group of 77 coordinator, and Leigh Ratiner, new deputy head of the U.S. delegation, and between former delegation members and mining industry representatives came close, they claimed, to success.[55]

But the United States called the question. After the mandatory, but now irrelevant cooling-off period, 130 states voted in favor of the Convention, 4 voted against (Ecuador, Israel, Turkey, and the U.S.), and 17 abstained (the Soviet bloc and many major industrial states). While a resumed eleventh session was necessary to take care of a number of Drafting Committee refinements, it was over. Most states preferred a comprehensive UNCLOS III Convention without the participation of the United States and perhaps other major industrial states—or, as the President of the United States put it, without the consent of states producing more than 60 percent of the world's gross national product and 60 percent of the contributions to the U.N. budget[56]—to no convention at all.

As of this writing, the Convention has not come into force. But 43 of the required 60 ratifications have been deposited with the United Nations.[57] Nine sessions of the Preparatory Commission have been held. After the election of the Bush Administration, there were intensive efforts to find a way around a treaty that was not subject to amendment or reservation, to find a "fix" that would allow the United States to adhere to the Convention.[58] Although the United States "had an opportunity to discuss [its] objections with a number of states," there was no sign that the Bush Administration was interested in becoming a signatory.[59]

3

Methods of Analyzing the Negotiation:
Modeling Parliamentary Diplomacy

This work is a study of collective action and its consequences in a specific historical setting. To conduct the analysis, appropriate analytical and evaluative methods had to be assembled by building upon previous work, or developed de novo. This chapter is about those methods, how they were borrowed, assembled or developed, and used to assess the process of collective action. Its purpose is to assist the reader in following the analysis that follows, and in evaluating the adequacy of the methods used.

Chapters 4 through 7 concern the details of bargaining within the Third United Nations Conference on the Law of the Sea (UNCLOS III) over a 15-year period. Chapter 8 evaluates the outcome, the UNCLOS III Convention; in judging whether the Convention met the needs of the stakeholders and whether the new regime for the oceans is likely to solve critical substantive problems, Chapter 8 also discusses the methods used for dealing with these matters of "comparative statics."[1]

General Approach

The puzzle that this work attempts to solve is whether 150+ stakeholders can negotiate or interact concerning 150+ issues and achieve a positive-sum outcome. More particularly, how well did the UNCLOS III process work in producing one particular type of positive-sum outcome, namely, unanimity? Did the outcomes reached satisfy the stakeholders' perceived needs and are they likely to solve the substantive problems that brought the stakeholders to the negotiating table in the first place?

This study has five goals: (1) to understand how parliamentary diplomacy as a bargaining process worked to achieve collective decision; (2) to estimate the present and future quality of the outcomes achieved; (3) to judge whether the effort was worth the resources devoted to it (whether such a process of policy formation and resolution is worth considering for future use, and under which particular circumstances); (4) to assess the fate of the oceans in the evolving world political system and the contribution the new ocean regime has made in helping to shape that system; and (5) to improve the basis for

41

theory development concerning bargaining in general, and large-scale multilateral negotiations in particular.

As is not uncommon in a large study, the goals are varied. In a similar context, Alexander George has noted that a blend of knowledge, values, and action are often characteristic of forecasting studies.[2] This study began as a forecasting effort. Goals 1 and 2 seek to discover regularities in observations. Goal 3 partly reveals the author's values, as does goal 4 in assessing the impact of the UNCLOS III Convention on the fate of the oceans. (Comparative statics are not value-free.) Finally, although goals 3 and 5 seek to improve theory about human decision-making, at least in Harry Eckstein's heuristic sense of "stimulat[ing] the imagination toward discerning important general problems and possible theoretical solutions,"[3] this is not a theoretical work, but an empirical one. It attempts to provide data from which others may generate and confirm hypotheses respecting the phenomena examined.

A Case Study

This analysis is a case study, albeit a very large single-focused one. It examines one diplomatic encounter over a 15-year period. It does not attempt to formally compare the process or outcome in this case with other known cases of large-scale multilateral negotiations, although it employs general questions to guide the data collection and analysis in the historical situation. Although its methods are different, its intent is similar to that recommended by Alexander George.[4]

There were theoretical and practical reasons for choosing the approach taken. The most compelling was the author's belief that UNCLOS III was a crucial case for demonstrating parliamentary diplomacy's supposed benefits and limitations.[5] While similar bargaining techniques were used in other conferences, and in some respects in the United Nations General Assembly, UNCLOS III was seen by many as a test case. If 150+ states could come up with an acceptable outcome over 150+ issues, statesmen in the future would have less to fear from Frederick the Great's warning. The modern version of the consent of Europe could be achieved without prohibitive cost.

UNCLOS III was a contract negotiation resulting in a formal convention that may be binding upon most nation-states of the world for years to come. Its policies, frozen in the words of the convention, were intended to govern human uses—and perhaps abuses—of 71 percent of the earth's surface. Although considerable negotiating for effect took place over the 15-year encounter, more on some issues than others, the principal outcome sought was not recommendations, resolutions, or advisory opinions, but rather contracts concerning state power, jurisdiction, and wealth.

Practical considerations compelled me to restrict the study to a single case. The resources required for tracking the stakeholders, the stakes, the bargaining groups, the arena, and the substantive concepts through the 15 years of preparatory work and debates in the General Assembly, Ad Hoc and Permanent Seabed Committees, and 11 formal sessions, were immense.

The size and complexity of the encounter compelled other decisions. The basic approach used in this study was inductive. No preliminary hypotheses were developed and then tested on the data generated in the case. The study attempted to gather data in a systematic manner and to model the negotiation, but it proceeded inductively because it was a study of a real-world problem. UNCLOS III may have been a crucial case, but it was no laboratory. It sprawled, and it was not possible to develop systematic controls for testing causality. Too many alternative explanations for outcomes were possible. Too many processes going on at the same time made it difficult to separate out the independent effect of different variables.[6] With the methods outlined below, regularities will be discovered. These in turn, may suggest possible causal explanations, but they should not be treated as definitive.

History of Methods Development

The reader may find the methods used in this study a bit more understandable if the historical context that shaped their development is presented first. In addition, the history of the author's involvement with the study will help the reader in assessing the author's biases.

I first became acquainted with bargaining over ocean subjects when searching for a doctoral dissertation subject. I settled upon an analysis of the First and Second United Nations Law of the Sea Conferences (1958 and 1960).[7] A decade later, while on leave from academia and working at the Center for Naval Analyses (a federal contract research center), I was asked to do analytic work that would help prepare the U.S. Navy for the major changes on ocean policy occurring in the late 1960s, including preparation for possible U.S. participation in the Third United Nations Law of the Sea Conference (UNCLOS III).[8] Soon thereafter, I was asked to direct the U.N. Law of the Sea Forecasting Project, which would provide analytic and forecasting capability, first, to the U.S. Navy and Department of Defense representatives on the U.S. Delegation at UNCLOS III and, later, to the entire delegation.[9] The project lasted from 1969 to 1975, when I returned to academia.[10]

As this short personal history makes clear, the project (1) was policy-oriented; (2) was designed to create a forecasting capability; (3) had to operate in "real time"; (4) was backed by substantial resources, so that a large body of data could be collected and appropriate models developed; and (5) was U.S.-biased. Doubtless there are remnants of all of these attributes in the facts reported, and the judgments made, in the chapters to follow. Although much original work was contributed by the project's participants, the existing literature on game theory, decision theory, microeconomics, voting theory, collective choice theory, and theory of legislative behavior was mined so that the project's methods could build upon previous work.[11]

The methodological and conceptual work of the U.N. Law of the Sea Forecasting Project had to be supplemented to produce this volume.[12] When the project ended in 1975, UNCLOS III had completed the second of three phases typical of international bargaining. While the project's data and analytic methods were adequate for those two phases, others were needed to analyze the third phase. Still other methods had to be developed to analyze the substantive outcome and to assess its acceptability to stakeholders and its adequacy for solving substantive problems.

Attributes of Parliamentary Diplomacy

As I. William Zartman has noted, the most obvious central characteristic of large-scale multilateral negotiation is its complexity.[13] In the case of parliamentary diplomacy, this is an understatement. It is bewilderingly complex, combining elements of diplomacy, where participating states may choose to defect if what is being negotiated does not seem to make them better off, with elements of legislation, where the interests of individual states aggregate into group positions, and ultimately into a collective decision.

When the project began in the late 1960s, much of what was known about parliamentary diplomacy was based upon observations of behavior in the United Nations General Assembly and a few earlier U.N. law-making conferences,[14] all still dominated by a U.S.-led majority. After the first mass admission of Third World states into the U.N. in 1955, new rules of the game began to evolve. Analysts could understand where some of these changes were going, but not all. Parliamentary diplomacy has changed so much that the earlier and later forms seem almost like separate phenomena. Commentators have described it as a "process in flux."[15]

With the extraordinary range of complex interactions among its participants, parliamentary diplomacy shares attributes with several types of social-choice mechanisms—especially legislation—yet, for all of its borrowings, it remains, at its core, bargaining. Parliamentary diplomacy is exercised in a mixed-motive situation: its participants have both conflicting and common goals.[16] These goals can best be reached by finding outcomes in which the parties are better off with agreement than without. Put another way, the outcomes sought are non-zero-sum or positive-sum. If a positive-sum outcome cannot be found and a participant believes it could be better off under the status quo, it can defect. While in the bargaining arena, the parties function with imperfect information, and the process of interaction is sequential, that is, it consists of offers or proposals followed by counteroffers or counterproposals. In short, parliamentary diplomacy has parties, values, movement, and outcomes.[17]

Complicating factors added to the basic bargaining situation create the distinctive personality of parliamentary diplomacy. For instance, the need to aggregate the positive-sum outcomes expected by many parties makes it necessary for a bargaining system governed by parliamentary diplomacy to take on some of the trappings of a legislature. Yet the choice mechanisms characteristically used by legislatures do not normally provide positive-sum outcomes to all participants. Legislatures tend to pit majority against minority, to create winners and losers. Legislative decision works best where a social compact is present; where it is understood that a minority will accept the decisions of the majority and that the majority will not use its powers to oppress the minority. Such a social compact does not yet exist in the United Nations or in the world community, where defection, or refusal to accept a decision, is still within the power of a nation-state. Consequently, although in many respects a United Nations plenipotentiary conference resembles a legislature, it has moved away from voting as the basic decision mechanism (although there is a requirement to confirm a decision by formal vote), and toward consensus.

Before drawing conclusions about parliamentary diplomacy as a bargaining system, we should review the attributes of our case example, UNCLOS III. First, the number of negotiators was large (150+) and their values and interests were heterogeneous. Second, the list of issues to be negotiated was voluminous; after 15 years of interaction negotiators promulgated a convention with 320 articles and 9 annexes, containing a further 126 articles.

Third, the interactions were based upon a formal structure. The Conference had an elected leadership (a Conference president, main committee chairs, vice-chairs, and rapporteurs, a credentials committee chair and members, a drafting committee chair and members). Plenary sessions were held to record official state positions and to confirm decisions worked out in subordinate units. Main committees were responsible for subsets of the conference's issues and reported their progress to the plenary sessions. Formal working groups were also established.

Fourth, formal rules of procedure outlined the decision process that was to be followed. Formal decision required a favorable vote by the requisite ma-

■ SIZE
    Many parties, many issues
       150+states,150+issues
■ FORMAL PROCESSES
    Parliamentary organization
       Elected leadership
       Plenary sessions,speeches,etc.
       Committees,formal working groups
    Formal decision system
       Decision by vote of requisite majority
       One state-one vote formula
       Delayed voting (gentlemen's agreement)
       No reservations allowed
       No mechanism for forcing adherence to convention
■ INFORMAL PROCESSES
    Many bilateral small group negotiations, often simultaneous
       Bilateral interactions
       Contact groups
       Negotiating groups
       Compromise groups
       Secret groups
    Informal decision processes
       Single Negotiating Text(SNT)
       Trade-offs on single issues; between issues
       Convention a giant package of trade-offs & subpackages
    Informal decision rule
       Consensus or near-consensus
■ PARTIES,COALITIONS & LEADERSHIP
    Blocs & caucusing groups act like political parties
    Coalitions shift between issues
    Bargaining within delegations
    Bargaining between like-minded, as well as, opposing groups
    Informal entrepeneurial leadership
    Mediation efforts by formal & informal leaders
■ ISSUES
    Technically complex issues
       Ocean management,common property, natural resource & security
       Types: mix of distributive & integrative issues
■ TIME
    Little time pressure,took 15 years
    Few outside forcing events(external crises)
    Continuity of participants, many General Assembly veterans,
      only two leadership changes

Table 3.1:   Parliamentary Diplomacy Characteristics

jority. Each state—large, small, powerful or weak—had one vote. In order to avoid "premature" voting that would cause the attempt to achieve consensus to collapse, a delay was required before voting (often called the "gentlemen's agreement"). The rules did not allow for reservations by a participant to any provision of the treaty. It was all or nothing, at least in terms of formal commitment. On the other hand, no formal mechanism existed to force acceptance of the outcome, or to punish a defecting state.

Fifth, a rich set of informal procedures developed to manage the interactions of states as they sought positive-sum outcomes. Frequent bilateral negotiations occurred. Contact groups, negotiating groups, and compromise groups met to narrow the gaps between their members. The objective in the early stages was to create an informal "single negotiating text" (SNT) to express a set of formula ideas agreed by consensus that would be the basis of final negotiations. These were to be assembled by the chairs of the main committees.

When consensus could not be reached, the chair was expected to indicate where he thought it might be found. This put considerable authority in the hands of main committee chairs. The chairs did not merely proceed issue by issue. Each chair's section of negotiating text was expected to be a package composed of trade-offs that would attract the largest number of states to support the negotiating document. In turn, the trade-offs in one section of the SNT (and ultimately the convention) were expected to allow states to balance off losses in that section of the overall package with gains in other portions of the draft document. Consensus was the preferred mode of decision.

Many informal mechanisms were used in order to aggregate interests. States that had similar interests in arenas beyond the conference often worked together in fixed caucusing groups that resembled political parties in domestic legislatures in order to negotiate with opponents from a common position. Since UNCLOS III concerned issues that were not always perfectly expressed by fixed caucusing groups, states with common ocean interests also formed common interest groups that lasted for the life of the conference. The existence of caucusing groups, common interest groups, and other interaction groups created many opportunities for complimentary (overlapping) and contradictory interests (cross-cutting cleavages).[18] As much time was spent on negotiations within delegations between delegates representing conflicting internal stakeholders, or between representatives of like-minded states, as was spent on negotiations between states with major differences between them. Sometimes entrepreneurial delegates gave impetus to the negotiations. At other times, well-regarded individual delegates attempted to mediate between opposing groups.

Sixth, the nature of the issues themselves played an important role in shaping the negotiations. They were complex and technical. Specialists in ocean law, ocean mining, marine transportation, ocean science and environment, fishing, fisheries law and economics were needed to aid the generalist delegates. On occasion, this allowed negotiators to use the tactic of deferring to expert opinion to overcome a political impasse without appearing to have made politically painful concessions.[19] But the issues negotiated in UNCLOS III were also the bread and butter of political negotiation. Often what was under negotiation was not merely a formula that promised to solve a transnational problem, but a political principle that would create a shift in national authority. Delegations treated any increase or decrease in their authority over territory as a matter of supreme importance, often allowing little bargaining room. This was particularly true if the proposal under negotiation would require altering their domestic constitutions or would cause major dissension in their domestic ratification process. Such concerns created considerable tension within the negotiation. On substantive grounds, the technically best solution on many issues could be arrived at only if the delegates agreed upon an integrative outcome (increasing the size of the pie by cooperative actions); on political grounds, the easiest solution was to arrange a distributive outcome (cutting the existing pie into slices so that one negotiator's gain was another's loss).[20]

Finally, continuity was a notable attribute of UNCLOS III. It took 15 years (1967–82) from the time the conference was first proposed in the United Nations General Assembly to the time Conference negotiators produced a convention for signature. The Ad Hoc and then the Permanent Committee on the Seabed had to be created to prepare for a full-scale conference. The conference required 11 sessions, some divided into two sets of meetings. Yet, during all that time, few outside events changed the timetable for the conference or forced delegations to alter their positions. There were only two major leadership changes in 15 years; many of the same delegates participated in many or all of the sessions.

Complexity And Disaggregation

For modeling purposes, the notion that the most important characteristic of large-scale multilateral negotiations is complexity is troubling. It is one thing to realize that "multilateral negotiations as a complex system . . . needs to be analyzed as a problem in managing that complexity." It is another to try to encompass that complexity in a single analytic construct.[21] Creating an operational model that would weave together all the strategic factors, tactical moves, structural opportunities and constraints, personality types, behavioral skills, contextual factors, and history of law of the sea negotiations was judged too difficult.

Instead we chose to suboptimize—to capture some of the major characteristics that were most salient for understanding one level of the negotiation. By restricting what was to be modeled, some richness of analysis was lost, but by choosing the most salient features, an accurate model of the proceedings, at least at the strategic level of analysis, could be produced.[22]

A central focus had to be chosen. The movement toward or away from agreement by 150+ states on 150+ issues (which were reduced to 20–25 key issues) was chosen for analysis and forecasting. To do that, it was necessary: (1) to understand the individual issues on which bargaining was taking place and assess where all participating states stood on these issues, especially over time; (2) to trace the linkages between the issues and understand the aggregation between issues and issues and parties; (3) to capture the existence, internal integrity and movement of coalitions formed and interacting at UNCLOS III; (4) to forecast small packages (trade-offs) and the overall package (Convention) that emerged, and compare them to known preferred packages of major states and groups that participated; and (5) to posit the "best" package that might emerge if states had "better" knowledge of their own and others' positions.

To perform such an analysis, disaggregation, then aggregation was necessary—going from one to many. The task had to begin with an issue-by-issue analysis.[23] One issue was then built into many with a packaging model. The central phenomena of interest were the many states, many issues, and the variable saliences between issues exhibited by states, and the concomitant trade-offs and packages that led to a multilateral treaty of considerable complexity.

Models and the Phenomenon to Be Modeled

As noted, UNCLOS III was a genuine negotiation; however, it possessed, as well, many attributes characteristic of legislation, adjudication, and other social decision processes that, for the purpose of theory development, analysts normally try to separate.

In order to model UNCLOS III, certain of these attributes had to be made operational, while others had to be dropped. Knowledge of other approaches or attributes of negotiation, legislation, or adjudication was used in interpreting the results.

I. William Zartman has identified five schools among writers on multilateral negotiation.[24] This work does not fall into any single school, but it tends to follow a concession or convergence approach more than any other. Zartman claimed that a convergence approach to the analysis of multilateral negotiations is a weak analytic reed to rely upon because it can view this multidimensional process in only two dimensions.

To a degree, that problem was overcome with the approach chosen. It was possible to build from one to many, once matters were understood issue by issue. What could not be traced in detail issue by issue were tactics. With the data assembled, it was also not possible to determine whether certain personalities might have done better or worse in bargaining with each other, or to suggest whether mediation might have been called for in a particular phase, or to determine what might have caused the movement that was observed. What we tried to keep in mind was that real people were negotiating with each other issue by issue.

Modeling Parliamentary Diplomacy

Forecasting the way states would behave in a large-scale law-making conference requires information about participants' preferences. The information had to be in a form that could be manipulated on a computer, drawn from a primary source so that the interpretive role of the information collectors was reduced to a minimum, and collected in a reliable manner.[25]

A data collection, recording, and storage system had to be created. A thematic content analysis was performed on the official records of the U.N. General Assembly, its Ad Hoc and then Permanent Seabed Committee, and the Third United Nations Law of the Sea Conference.[26] Although well-developed systems of content analysis existed at the time the project began, none collected the type of data wanted, or collected it in a way that was conducive to the analytical needs of the project.[27] Great care was taken in collecting, recording, and storing data. I personally recoded 10 percent of all data collected to test reliability; other project members did formal tests of reliability.[28]

Coders looked for statements of preference by delegates on the major issues under negotiation. Simple statements of preference, as well as contingent statements (e.g., "My state would accept X if the conference put Y in the agreement"), were collected. The differences between types and degrees of preference were dealt with in a separate step. Our content analysis produced over 40,000 observations of preferences of all participating states on some 40 major issues (later reduced to 20–25 key issues).

Modeling the Issues

Next, the preference data were made usable for modeling. The problem was to model conflict on issues under negotiation; to determine whether or not states found an acceptable collective outcome through interaction. The underlying concept framing the issue under negotiation had to be understood, as well as the particular proposals that states put forward to solve the conflict.

To do this, "conflict issues" were created by scaling, a technique widely used in the social sciences: the expressed positions of states were arrayed along a spectrum with an underlying dimension.[29] Below is a typical conflict issue in international resource allocation and management:

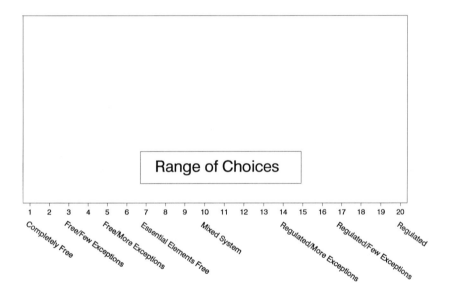

Figure 3.1:   Scaling of Bargaining Preferences

On this issue, the underlying dimension was the degree of control a rightsholder might be able to exercise over other possible rightsholders in the area under negotiation. It ranged from no control at rank 1 (on the left) to complete control over the activities of others at rank 20 (on the right). Fallback positions for advocates of a complete freedom position (rank 1) are located at ranks 3 and 5. Negotiators who begin at the total regulation position (rank 20) might fall back to positions at ranks 17 and 14. In the middle is a mixed system (rank 10), which purports to arrange a compromise between freedom and regulation.

Some of the rank numbers listed are unused where the scalers felt there was something more than a mere order involved in the scale. Thus, for example, the scalers thought that accepting the exceptions to freedom (shown at rank 3) was more of a loss of policy benefits for a complete freedom advocate than could be represented by a mere fallback of one rank (to rank 2). This form of interval scaling was dubbed "policy spacing." Scaling was done in this manner because that was the way the project's U.S. Government clients viewed the issues. Conflict variables were scaled experimentally using both an ordinal scale and an interval scale. When tested formally at the needed level of precision, the results were found to be approximately the same.[30]

Understanding Where States Stood on the Issues

To create meaningful data, all states speaking on an issue were placed on the scaled variables. If a state said it supported completely free use of an ocean area, its position or national score was at rank 1. Often states would indicate a fundamental preference for one or the other core concepts underlying an issue, and then make conditional statements indicating a willingness to accept a fallback (e.g., to a position supporting free use, but with a number of exceptions, or rank 5). A national score for that state would be derived by calculating a weighted average.[31] For example if the hypothetical state mentioned rank 1 five times and rank 5 twice, it was reasonable to assign that state a national score of 2.1.

Unfortunately, not every state in the UNCLOS III spoke to every issue. But all were entitled to participate, and if consensus or near-consensus was the decision mode, their preferences had to be taken into account. The missing data were estimated by doing a linear regression with the statements made by members of interest categories as the dependent variable; the independent or predicator variable was some 58 interest categories composed of group membership, and data about the political, economic, and ocean interests of the concerned states.[32] The national scores and the estimates were combined into a "preferred position," which summed up where a state was believed to stand on an issue at a given time.[33] This allowed examination of the bargaining issue by issue.

Using this method, data sets could be produced showing where all states were, or were estimated to be, on all major issues over a series of time periods. The movement of a specific state by issue over time or more detailed products could also be prepared from the descriptive data. However, the most useful issue-by-issue products were in graphic form, showing the distribution of all state preferences over single or multiple time periods—where states were on the issue at various points, and whether there had been any movement over time. These graphic representations of the negotiation showed the results of the bargaining, but did not purport to show the process of bargaining. Figures 3.2(a) through 3.2(f) illustrate typical distributions. Figure 3.2(a) displays a typical issue early in the negotiation. There is no discernible pattern.

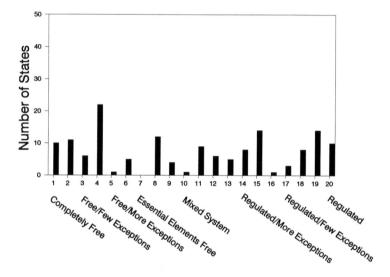

Figure 3.2(a):   Modal Distributions: No Pattern

Figure 3.2(b) does display an interpretable pattern. Here a typical bimodal distribution can be seen, with two camps centered at rank 4 (a free-use position with some exceptions) and at rank 18 (a regulation position also with some exceptions). It is obvious what has transpired.

Figure 3.2(c) shows a different stage of a typical parliamentary diplomatic negotiation—a unimodal distribution with a tail. Here one strong camp exists with scattered, but still relatively strong, opposition. Only about two-thirds of the states favor a moderate regulatory position. The remaining one-third

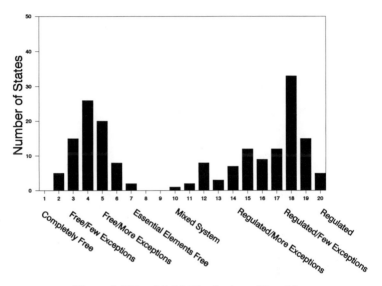

Figure 3.2(b):   Modal Distributions: Bimodal

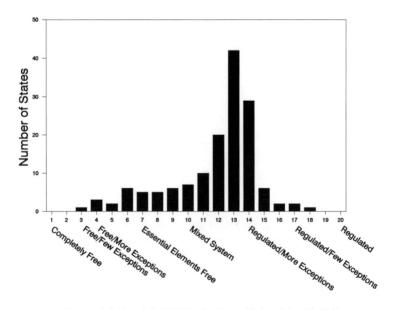

Figure 3.2(c):   Modal Distributions: Unimodal with Tail

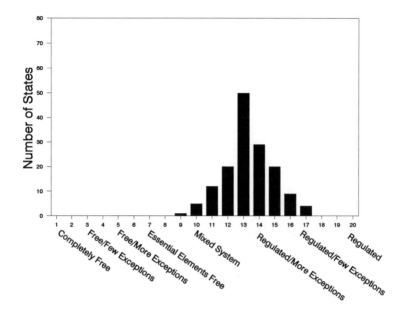

Figure 3.2(d):   Modal Distributions: Consensus or Near-Consensus

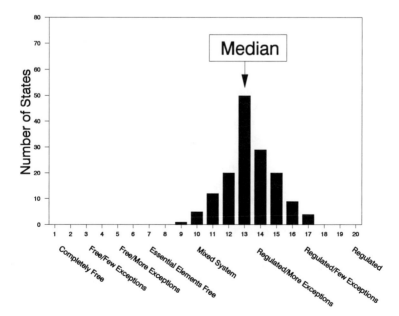

Figure 3.2(e):   Modal Distributions: Median

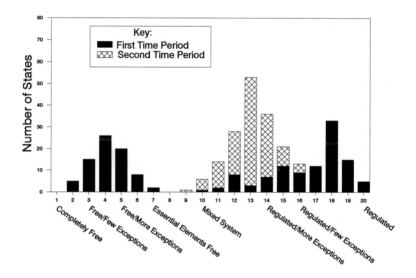

Figure 3.2(f):   Modal Distributions: Movement over Time

do not favor that position but have no strong core to rally around. It seems likely that, with further negotiations aimed at refining their proposal in the next stage of negotiation, the proponents of regulation could pull the states at ranks 7–11 into their camp. That might create a near-consensus or, with further refinement, a true consensus.

Consensus or, at worst, near-consensus is shown in figure 3.2(d). Here a unimodal pattern with *no* tail is shown. (At this stage the data may not be sufficiently refined to make a precise interpretation without looking at supplemental evidence, especially over time.) This is a probable winning position. If this were an issue to be settled by voting, as seen in figure 3.2(e), where rank 13 is the median, a forecast would predict the position at rank 13 as the winner. Voting theory posits that the median is the position against which no amendment could succeed.[34] The median was interpreted cautiously because the conference deliberately chose to work toward consensus and used a single vote only to confirm formally that a treaty was achieved. In a different distribution, the interpretation of the median would also be different. For example, if a median for the situation in figure 3.2(a) had been calculated, an analyst could say only that the median confirmed that it was a situation not ripe for decision.

Finally, figure 3.2(f) puts two time periods of data on a single figure showing the movement from no pattern in the first time period to consensus or near-consensus in the second. Graphs are a powerful device for demonstrating to readers the state of play on the issues.[35]

Bargaining Theory and Parliamentary Diplomacy

It was easy to see when the majority of the parties (1) elected to stand fast, (2) continued to negotiate, or (3) chose to defect. If project members decided to interpret the data in the light of Fred Ikle's work on negotiation, they had a simple convergence model to use as a guide.[36] But with the data and methods that were developed, analysts could see more than three steps in the negotiation process and, as figure 3.3 shows, many more moves toward or away from convergence in the negotiation. While this figure does not exhaust all

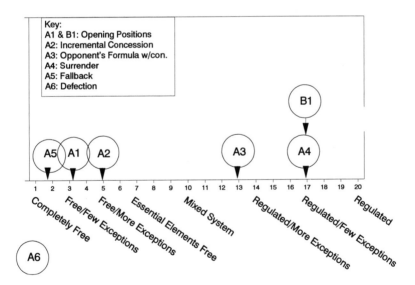

Figure 3.3:   Available Moves for One Party in Negotiation (Convergence)

possible moves, opening positions (A1 and B1) can be shown (thereafter, to simplify the discussion, only the moves of one party [A] will be shown):

incremental concessions (A2), moving to the opponent's "formula" (more on this term later) after he makes concessions (A3), surrender to the opponent(A4), falling back from an earlier position to a tougher position (A5), and finally defection or the decision to break off negotiations on the issue (A6).

As the UNCLOS III negotiations moved into the middle 1970s and the 1980s, even more useful guides became available to help interpret the data the project generated. We turned to concepts developed by Zartman, especially the notion that political negotiations largely involve "a search for agreeable referents of a joint decision," which Zartman defines as "principles of justice on which both parties can agree."[37] Fit into a coherent framework, these principles become a "formula" for agreement. Zartman is quick to point out, however, that a convergence approach makes many types of political bargaining appear too incremental and mechanical, that "most negotiations are not of the incremental type, that only lesser details within a larger context of a different type are handled incrementally, and that even then the negotiations follow a different pattern."[38]

Convergence and Parliamentary Diplomacy

Observing UNCLOS III, we concluded that a purely incremental convergence approach, assuming tit-for-tat moves and countermoves, would not be productive. In multilateral negotiations of the parliamentary diplomatic type, all parties do not, as a rule, search for a single, mutually acceptable formula (although there are analysts like Gilbert Winham who argue that they do).[39] Rather, in the early stage, parties form into rival camps to support rival formulas. Each side tries to convince the other to accept its fundamental approach, with the winners often adjusting their approach to make it more palatable to the losers through trade-offs or packages, or both.

Phase I Negotiations

There are three phases to a major negotiation. In the real world, the borders between the phases blur, and backtracking can take place, but generally negotiations go through (1) a diagnostic phase, (2) a phase of identifying the formula idea which will be most influential in molding the outcome, and (3) a phase of refining the formula idea, polishing the language, and bringing the recalcitrant on board.[40]

The sorting out process of Phase I is reflected in the scaling of the issues. Scaling attempts to replicate the substantive ideas thrown into the hopper, and also the process negotiators go through in trying out substantive ideas on each other. It also reflects how negotiators in a parliamentary diplomatic setting look around for allies, make judgments concerning opposing ideas and states, and work out trade-offs, if necessary, between internal stakeholders.

Figure 3.1 illustrates a typical UNCLOS III issue, scaled with the concept of freedom at one end of the spectrum and regulation at the other, rival notions in their purest forms. UNCLOS III had many real-world examples of rival conceptual frameworks that were considered in the negotiations—narrow versus extended territorial sea, limited versus exclusive coastal-state control over resources, freedom versus coastal-state control of transit through straits, freedom versus coastal-state control of science, and so on. In sum, most of the main issues at UNCLOS III were viewed as problems of dispute settlement and not as problems of developing common perceptions in a situation of mutual learning. After the first several sessions of Phase I negotiations, which were devoted primarily to exploration, the delegates had to deal with rival formulas.

Phase II Negotiations

Rarely did a candidate formula idea get through the negotiations unscathed or unmodified. But how much can a formula idea be modified and still retain its conceptual core? A "zone" or range of variations on most major rival approaches that still retained the core of their approach to solving a problem can be seen in the changing distributions over time. No precise method of determining the width of the zone at UNCLOS III was developed. It was a judgment call whether the original adherents (always concerned that their preferred position was being sold out) would view a modified formula idea as sufficiently coherent to retain their support. A formula idea can move outside its zone and enough away from its pure core that some of its supporters are no longer happy with it, as in figure 3.5, even if it is better than its rival.

Formula zones showing what was happening in Phases II and III were constructed with more art than science, based upon in-depth work on the negotiations. Consider the modal problem of freedom versus regulation, as shown in figure 3.4 The zone was drawn for the freedom formula from ranks 1–5 and for the regulation formula from ranks 15–20. In the analysts' judgment, freedom supporters, at least in an early phase, think that the position shown at rank 7 (essential elements free) requires so many concessions that it falls outside of an acceptable formula zone. The same would be true for the regulation supporters, who would not support the many exceptions to regulation found at rank 14.

Figure 3.4 also does double duty, showing a later phase of the negotiation, where data bunched toward the center and the median at rank 10 reflect the outcome of a mixed system. This splitting the difference (the classic

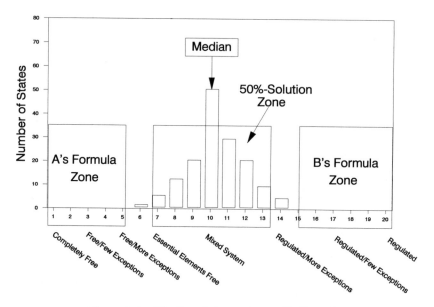

Figure 3.4: The Search for an Acceptable Formula

50-percent solution) shows a third formula idea—a genuine compromise that manages to blend the original rival ideas into another, unique formula. Such outcomes occur in parliamentary diplomacy, but in our experience, they were rare at UNCLOS III.

More common was the array of states shown in figure 3.5, where one of the basic conceptual frameworks is chosen over the other. Such a distribution indicates that Phase II of the negotiation might soon be over; that a substantial number of states have chosen a candidate formula idea. This pattern was visible most often after a single negotiating text (SNT) was promulgated by the committee chairs on the instruction of the conference chair, but it could come earlier, later, or not at all. The familiar single-peaked preference with a tail is shown here. One set of proponents of a formula has begun to gather about a particular formulation of the formula. There is no longer a negotiable rival formula, only scattered, though stubborn, opposition from nearly one-third of the delegations. The forces supporting freedom (rank 3) have to move further to one edge of the formula zone than the proponents of regulation, who do not have to adjust their original position as much to get to the other edge of the formula zone, where the final stage of the negotiation will take place.

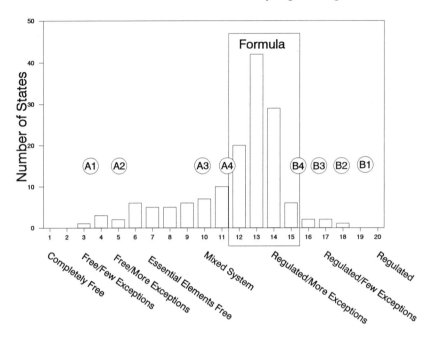

Figure 3.5:   Phase II —The Process of Finding a Formula

Phase III Negotiations

The main task from this point forward in the negotiation is to refine a general formula on the issue at hand into an acceptable deal. In our example of a single-peaked preference with a tail, there is much hard bargaining to be done in Phase III. Sometimes a single-peaked preference with no tail was discovered at the end of Phase II. It usually (but not always) meant that Phase III would mostly involve refining the language of the general formula with little further adjustment of its core idea.

What was the principal function of the Phase III of parliamentary diplomacy? The third phase of UNCLOS III took roughly seven years from the issuance of the Single Negotiating Text (SNT) in 1976, through the Revised Single Negotiating Text (RSNT) and the Consolidated Text (CT), to the UNCLOS Convention in 1982. What were the delegates doing in all that time? They were adjusting the details of the formulas supported by substantial majorities to make them minimally acceptable to the losers.

Getting the losers reconciled to accepting formulas they did not initially approve was difficult. In parliamentary diplomacy, there are three ways to get losers to accept their losses: (1) side payments; (2) wins on other issues of higher salience (trade-offs); and (3) continued negotiations to soften the impact of the winning formula on losing stakeholders.

At UNCLOS III, heads of delegations usually handled trade-offs, packages (sets of interrelated trade-offs), and side payments, since they were responsible for overall strategic decisions. Often it was their staff members, specialists in particular issues or the work of particular committees, who had to soften the impact of an obnoxious formula. To accept the opposing formula was not only to lose on the issue in the abstract sense, but also to embarrass oneself before one's clientele. Often on larger delegations that clientele's or stakeholder's representatives were part of the delegation as advisors. That was incentive enough to struggle as hard in Phase III as in Phase I and II.

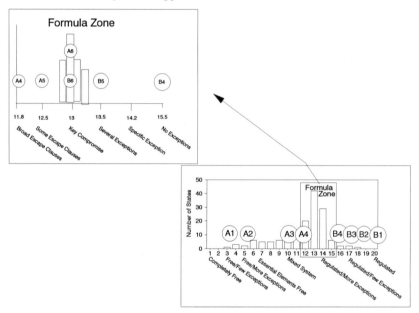

Figure 3.6:   Phase III—Bargaining: Negotiating the Deal/Refining the Language

In the lower right corner of figure 3.6 is the situation at the end of Phase II: the formula is identified, but not finally agreed to. In Phase III (upper left), the opposing parties usually begin at the edges of the formula zone, and work to find agreement (shown at A6, B6).

As is usually the case, the parties that began at ranks 1–3 and 16–20 in Phase II, have kept the same relative position in Phase III, at ranks 11.8 and

15.5. The "regulation" forces are trying to find ways to bring their opponents to accept the regulation formula and limit the concessions they must make, but will make concessions as necessary. Their opponents attempt to gut the regulation formula if possible, leaving in the core concept underlying the formula, but omitting operational language to carry it out. If that doesn't work, they may attempt to promote escape clauses for their domestic clients, exceptions to the prevailing general rule, or make the rule apply only in certain circumstances, or its language so vague that it can later be interpreted favorably, or so precise that it excludes their clients.

Movement over Time

At all phases of the negotiations, one could tell, using the techniques developed, where the participating states stood on major issues. In the analytical chapters to follow, the pattern of state preferences on the major issues will be shown in two "snapshots." The first (T-1) will measure the state of play from the informal beginning of the negotiation in the 1967 U.N. General Assembly session to the fourth preparatory session of the Permanent Seabed Committee in 1973. The second (T-2) will measure from the fifth preparatory session (also 1973) of the Permanent Seabed Committee to the third session of the Conference (1975). For purely practical reasons, it was too laborious to track 150+ states individually, but the bargaining positions of major states were followed.

Showing the movement of major negotiating groups over time proved even more useful. Since the general setting was quasilegislative, it was helpful to know where groups stood that actively participated as bargaining units. It was also helpful to know how fervently members of the group espoused common positions. The movement, and discipline, of these groups over time could be examined by calculating the means and standard deviations of members' preferred positions during certain time periods. To do this, T-1 and T-2 will be broken down into P-1 (beginning to 1970 Ad Hoc Committee meeting); P-2 (1971–73 Permanent Seabed Committee meetings); P-3 (1973 fifth Permanent Seabed Committee meeting to 1973 Conference session); and P-4 (second and third Conference sessions, 1974–75).

On this sample issue, in figure 3.7(a), most component groups of the Group of 77 started the negotiation with a reasonably common position. The outlier is the Arab group, later supported by the Asian Group. The data indicate that the Arab group was showing some internal dissonance in the second time period (or there was "noise" in the data), but that they came together by the fourth time period in quite disciplined fashion. Figures 3.7(b) and 3.7(d) show geographic groups that do not have common interests with each other, and demonstrate that the landlocked states (LL) opposed the

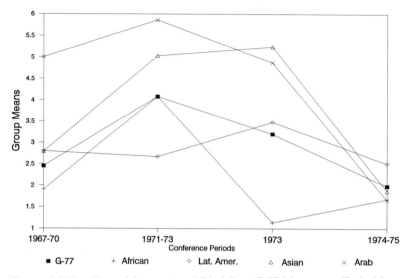

Figure 3.7(a):   Group Movement and Discipline: G-77 Means on a Typical Issue

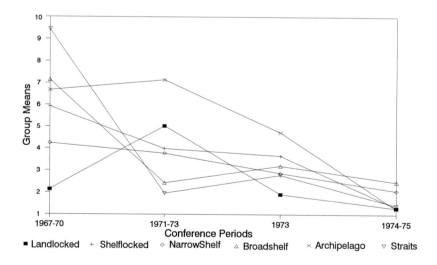

Figure 3.7(b):   Group Movement and Discipline:
Geographic Groups Means on a Typical Issue

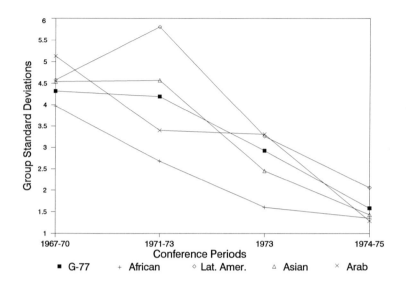

Figure 3.7(c): Group Movement and Discipline:
G-77 Standard Deviations on a Typical Issue

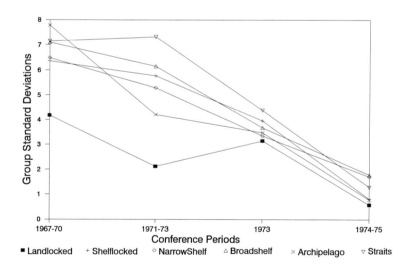

Figure 3.7(d): Group Movement and Discipline: Geographic Groups Standard
Deviations on a Typical Issue

position of the straits states (STR). Though there is a substantial gap between them, the straits states might (and did) look to the broad-shelf states (BS) for a working relationship on this issue during the middle periods of the negotiation. All coalesced at the end.[41]

Packages and Trade-offs

We needed a method to forecast and analyze the packages and trade-offs that promoted collective decision in Phase III. We built such a model in two steps: (1) a utility model for forcing decision on an individual issue; and (2) a packaging model to test the probable outcome of forcing states to choose one known package over another. The operation of the utility model is shown graphically in figure 3.8. Underlying this model is an explicit assumption—

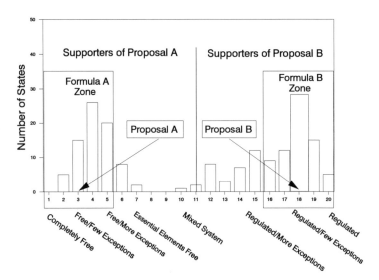

Figure 3.8:   Utility Model: Decision and Intensity of Choice

that delegations in a multilateral negotiation, after an initial stage of considering a large variety of possible proposals, will focus on a limited number that have a base of support. When it comes time to choose, delegations will be forced to support one of two formula concepts. Reducing the number of realistic choices began to emerge in the latter portion of Phase I and dominated Phase II. Therefore it was reasonable, near the end of Phase II, for analysts to force that choice in order to forecast the outcome of Phase III. In figure 3.8, support for proposal A (rank 3) is measured against the support for proposal B (rank 18). Since a decision is being forced, a logical place to divide supporters and opponents would be halfway between the opposing positions. Halfway between 3 and 18 is 10.4, so one could estimate that all states falling between 1 and 10.4 would support proposal A, and all those falling between 10.5 and 20 would support proposal B.

There are important differences in the intensity of choice among some states that were forced to choose. From the distribution, it is evident that not all states were equally enthusiastic about the choices they were forced to make. Those at ranks 6–10.4 seemed a bit reluctant to support proposal A, though from their general situation, it was a better choice than proposal B. Similarly, supporters of ranks 10.5–15 seemed hesitant to support proposal B. The data reflect not only their choice but also the degree of reluctance.

Usually proposals were chosen for testing because they represented the core positions of rival formulas, or reasonable fallback positions from one or both of these core positions. This allowed us to test bargaining strategies. For example, if we wanted to estimate what would happen if the sponsors of proposal B moved from rank 18 to rank 16, but the sponsors of proposal A stood fast, we could just vary the first set of assumptions to run—a minor task. Throughout the project, this part of the analytic arsenal was more useful for strategic planning than for forecasting the outcome of the UNCLOS III negotiation.

Useful in issue-by-issue analysis, utility pairs were crucial building blocks for trade-offs and package analysis. Here, one more essential piece of information was needed to supplement knowledge (or regression-based estimates) about the preferences of states on the issues; namely, salience, or the comparative importance to each state of one issue as compared to others.[42]

Virtually all states in multilateral negotiation, however small their power base or foreign service, and however limited their interests, learn about the issues during the preliminary stages of the negotiation. The starting package for most states was often a maximum preferred package, or collection of maximum preferred positions, on each of the issues.

How can the analyst judge what package states will accept after bargaining? What will they trade off on one issue or set of issues in order to gain an acceptable outcome on other issues, or in the convention as a whole? Presumably they will trade off a favorable outcome on an issue of lesser salience in order to achieve a favorable outcome on an issue of greater salience. A package they could support provides favorable outcomes on more salient issues and concedes less favorable outcomes on less salient ones. Such a package might include only two issues or, if the overall shape of the negotiation is to be tested, it might include up to 20–25 issues.

The indicator of salience used was frequency of mention of a theme or themes. It worked well because UNCLOS III continued over 15 years. Many participants remained with the negotiations over much of the life of the conference. A consistent, reliable body of raw data was available—the U.N. record—from which information about state preferences could be extracted; our data-collection scheme minimized duplication of data. Over time, states would speak and defend most vigorously what was most important to them, and therefore frequency of mention provided an accurate indicator of what was salient to them. The large size of the database helped overcome a possible problem of tactical misrepresentation. At times, delegates tried to deceive others, but they revealed their true position over time, or they could never have found a winning position. Although not appropriate for all bargaining modeling, the method we used to account for salience worked for this project and gave us the necessary means to deal with packages and trade-offs.[43]

The packaging model requires two steps as reflected in figure 3.9.

Consider the preference of state A in step 1 of a two-issue package. On issue 1, state A's preference is at rank 5, but there is no provision in the package at rank 5, only at rank 1 or rank 15. State A must choose between them. Since its preferred position is at rank 5, if it were to choose only on the basis of issue 1, it would prefer package 1, whose position on issue is at rank 1, or four ranks away from A's preferred position, to package 2, whose position, at rank 15, is ten ranks away. However, we get the opposite result on issue 2. Here state A's preferred position is at rank 16, or four ranks away from the package 2 position on the issue, while package 1's position, at rank 6, is ten ranks away from state A's preferred position. In other words, state A faces a dilemma. If it opts for package 1, it wins on issue 1 and loses on issue 2. But are both issues equally salient to state A? Usually not.

The problem is resolved in step 2. Here state A made ten remarks about its preferences on issue 1, and five remarks about its preferences on issue 2. If state A is forced to make a trade-off, it would choose package 1, in order to gain a favorable outcome on the more salient issue 1, and sacrifice its preferred outcome on the less salient issue 2.

To try to simulate that real world, packages were constructed for some of the major participating states and many of the known bargaining groups. A procedure was followed similar to what was done on scaling: preliminary versions of the packages were assembled by the research team, based upon sub-

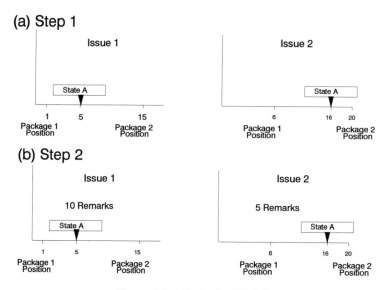

Figure 3.9:   Packaging Model

stantive knowledge of the negotiation, and fine-tuned by members of the U.S. delegation. Over the course of the project, the study group modeled more than 160 potential large, and many smaller, packages.

In the overall state of the negotiation, which package seemed the most acceptable? Since the data were available on the degree of preference by states and groups for each package, we could see who were strong and who were weak supporters of particular proposals; we could judge who was likely to stand firm, who might be subject to persuasion if the right trade-offs were offered. "What if" analyses also could be performed, e.g., what if our side traded off a bit more on issues less salient to us, and stood firm on more salient issues in the face of movement or no movement by opponents.[44]

PART II

Analyzing
the Negotiation

4

Committee II:

Attempting to Create "Agreement in the Large" via Trade-offs

To many observers of the ocean negotiations in the United Nations General Assembly, its Ad Hoc and Permanent Seabed Committees, and the first session of the Third Conference on the Law of the Sea (1967–73), the proceedings must have resembled the Tower of Babel. In these meetings more than 150 states took the floor to express their preferences on the more than 150 issues that comprised the "List of Issues." To understand where all states stood, one would need to know the content of more than 22,500 decision cells. And it got worse before the UNCLOS III Convention was finally produced in 1982. The convention contained 320 articles and nine appendices with more 126 more articles, representing more than 66,900 cells.

Complexity was the most obvious characteristic of UNCLOS III. There were many issues, and the conference chose consensus as the mode of decision. (Formally the decision was by vote, but only after consensus, or at least near-consensus, had been achieved.) That meant that 150+ entities we call sovereign and equal states had to converge on 150+ issues in 446 articles. How could a negotiator, or even a large negotiating team from a well-prepared major state, deal with 150 to 446 issues simultaneously, keeping track of not only its own preferences and stated positions and goals, but those of 149+ of its negotiating partners?

Simplifying devices were needed—and found. Arranging agreement first on key issues that set the general direction of the new regime was the principal method. There was often wide divergence of opinion on these critical issues, so it was unlikely that consensus would be reached if negotiations proceeded strictly on an issue-by-issue basis. The key issues had to be arranged in a package which included enough favorable outcomes on issues of greater salience to a state or group of states that they would accept less favorable outcomes on other issues of lesser salience.[1]

The package approach allows states to accept trade-offs as long as the overall outcome is positive; that is, as long as they feel they would be better off with than without an agreed outcome.[2] When it works, this approach allows states to accept losses gracefully in international negotiation. This is much more difficult in practice than in theory. It is not always easy to get domestic elites to accept the losses arranged by negotiators representing them. Nor is it simple to find a clearly less salient issue to trade off. Therefore, at times, an unfavorable outcome on a slightly less important issue must be traded off for a positive outcome on a slightly more important issue. This can be painful. And the complex process is very time-consuming, with possible changes of government during the negotiation. A trade-off accepted by a delegation from a previous government can evaporate if a new government claims that, not having been party to the understanding, it is not bound by any prior arrangement.

The first task at UNCLOS III was to identify the key issues whose resolution could be the foundation of a complex treaty acceptable to all, or almost all, the states represented. The preliminary negotiations, noisy as they were, played an essential role in helping to identify the issues that clearly had to be settled first, so that there would be a recognizable and acceptable core to the new regime for managing the oceans of the world. This created a double burden—first, identifying the issues that must be settled and finding a means of settling them, and then, settling them in a workable manner. This chapter is about finding and resolving some of the key issues so that "agreement in the large" might be achieved.

As it happened, agreement in the large at UNCLOS III was almost achieved.[3] The Conference would not have achieved whatever success it did without the resolution of most of the core issues. Chapter 7 deals with the issues, mostly relating to deep-seabed manganese-nodule exploitation, on which agreement in the large, largely achieved in Committee II, was lost.

Three Key Issues

It became evident during the preliminary negotiations that the three key issues which had to be resolved so that the remainder of the issues could be negotiated were enclosure of near-shore ocean resources, preservation of movement rights, and access to deep-ocean resources.

Two of these issues, both negotiated in Committee II, were linked historically. Movement rights and access to deep-ocean resources beyond a relatively narrow territorial sea were linked under a framework of ocean law "since time immemorial," as some lawyers described it, or at least since the 1608 publication of Hugo Grotius's *Mare Liberum*.[4] If states had a right to use the oceans beyond a narrow territorial sea as they pleased, so long as they did not interfere with the rights of others, management of movement and extraction of resources were regulated by the same doctrine.

During much of the twentieth century, the Grotian approach was under vehement attack by those who believed it was both inequitable and inefficient. Critics, claiming it was necessary to expand the territorial sea on, over, and under which coastal states would be sovereign, proposed to turn the Grotian regime on its head. Where the Grotian scheme granted freedom over most of the ocean and exclusive rights over only a small portion—a narrow territorial sea—the anti-Grotians expanded the notion of the territorial sea to enclose or put under coastal-state sovereignty virtually all ocean space with present value for navigation or for extraction of living and nonliving resources. Freedom would, therefore, be exercised only over the much-reduced deep ocean, and that freedom would be further restricted by excluding from free exploitation the only deep-ocean natural resource with known potential—the so-called manganese or polymetallic nodules. As long as the assault on the Grotian regime was conducted in general ideological terms, and in a manner which seemed to accept no compromise, the Grotian regime was defended vehemently by major developed states.

As beneficiaries of some important aspects of the Grotian framework, the developed states had little reason, in terms of their own short-term self-interest, to acquiesce in an all-out assault upon it; however, they had mixed feelings about many of its specific rules. In truth, the Grotian regime was failing under the pressures of modern technology.[5] Congestion was growing, and the supply of ocean resources did not seem to be able to keep up with demand.[6] It did not make sense to manage fixed as well as wandering resources under the law of capture (a corollary of Grotian freedom of the seas). Since the Truman Proclamation of 1945, no state has managed its offshore oil and gas resources under a first-come, first-served rule, fearing that chaos would result from common-pool problems.[7] Similarly, environmental goods were being threatened because, with near-shore areas treated as a commons, there was no responsible party to force consideration of the general good and to keep abusers polluting the commons from imposing systemic costs on all.[8]

As a result of these pressures, bureaucracies and interest groups in developed countries responsible for energy development, environment, and near-shore fisheries had been pushing to modify the existing legal system.[9] Naval establishments, ministries of marine transportation, and bureaucrats and representatives of distant-water fisheries had been just as vigorously resisting change.[10] Until the late 1960s, the forces resisting change had been dominant, even if they were essentially losing ground.[11] Everyone was looking for a formula, preferably embodied in an international treaty, that would allow the two sets of interests to coexist and continue to serve their domestic constituencies.

The developing states that led the charge in challenging the rules of the Grotian regime had their own problems.[12] In planning their assaults on the existing Grotian framework, they had a tactical dilemma. Some, particularly the "territorialists" (Chile, Ecuador, Peru, and some Central American states), had mounted what many developed states considered an all-out assault. Other developing states observed that all the territorialists' efforts accomplished by the early 1970s was stiffening the resistance of the major developed states to unilateral territorialist acts. Tactically, the territorialists' demand of sovereignty out to 200 nautical miles made little sense if they wished those who resisted enclosure to acquiesce to a negotiated solution.

Sovereignty was useful but not essential for most states deciding to pursue enclosure. Control of the natural resources, living and nonliving, was essential, especially those found in near-shore areas. Near-shore waters comprise almost 40 percent of the world's oceans and are the most economically productive. A concept was needed that claimed for the coastal state the right to control resources out to 200 miles, but which did not claim jurisdiction over all activities, especially those of movement of ships and aircraft. For bargaining purposes, it had to be a concept that opponents of the 200-mile territorial sea might consider sui generis, and therefore acceptable ideologically and practically. That concept was called a 200-mile Exclusive Economic Zone (EEZ).[13] Since it was separable from the questions of delimitation of the territorial sea and right to control transit through straits used for international navigation, all three concepts could be packaged together. Developing states saw developed-state stakeholders who resisted change and not the domestic forces in those states favoring change. As a result, developing states were pleased to purchase resource control with the coin of a narrow territorial sea and a right to transit straits.

But developing states also had a substantive dilemma. Some Latin American and African states preferred sovereignty out to 200 miles, which would allow them to control all activities off their shores, but many developing states felt they would not necessarily be well served by turning the oceans into national lakes. Like the major developed states, they had an interest in retaining elements of the old Grotian skeleton in the new regime. They realized it was important to preserve the oceans as open highway. Some, although they publicly complained that Grotian rules were imposed upon them,[14] were also aware of the possible usefulness of superpower gunboats being available to rescue them if their domestic regimes faltered or they were threatened by regional enemies.[15] Considering themselves potential participants in the world economy, they looked to develop movement rules that did not give other states, particularly neighboring ones, substantial degrees of control over how, when, at what costs their goods got to market. In many cases, least-cost means of ocean transportation would be available only if ships serving their ports could transit straits or move freely beyond relatively narrow territorial seas. Developing states, especially the landlocked and shelf-locked, had little incentive to turn over control of large ocean spaces or the right to transit straits to potentially hostile neighbors. So the developing, too, had sufficiently mixed motives to give the negotiators a chance to work out the trade-offs necessary for bargaining success.[16]

Trade-offs that were arranged in the Second Committee of UNCLOS III essentially mixed elements of the traditional Grotian regime with those of its opposite, the regime of enclosure. If a sui generis "exclusive economic zone" (an EEZ) were created to provide the coastal state ample economic powers out to 200 miles, they could live without sovereignty over a substantially enlarged territorial sea. Thus, a 200-mile EEZ and a moderately enlarged territorial sea—out to 12 nautical miles—became key elements in a basic trade-off that was arranged in 1974 as states prepared for the first substantive session of the UNCLOS III at Caracas. But if a moderate expansion of the territorial sea were sanctioned, some major straits used for international navigation would come under exclusive national jurisdiction. A new "right of transit passage" had to be created. In many respects, this was new in name only, having incorporated most attributes of the Grotian freedom of movement. These three issues were the linchpins of the new law of the sea. Since one major participant—the United States—defected, the conference did not achieve "agreement in the large" (defined as consensus), but it came close. Some claimed that the major developed states agreed to a fourth linchpin—a New International Economic Order outcome to the problem of allocating and managing deep-seabed manganese nodules, although the evidence is weak. These four, they said, comprised the overall core of the UNCLOS III Convention.

We will examine here the first three linchpins and associated issues, such as whether the EEZ would interfere with movement rights, or whether within the EEZ, distant-water claimants would have residual rights after their establishment. We will look also at whether the concept of the legal continental shelf should continue to exist in an era of EEZs. The continental shelf concept provided a perfect vehicle for an end run around attempts to restrict the geographic scope of coastal-state jurisdiction. It was the only major issue in

Committee II's deliberations that we shall examine not directly tied to the early trade-offs, and the only one where positions shifted substantially in the later stages of the negotiation.

Because of the early arrangement of trade-offs, we shall see patterns typical of trade-off situations. Between the first substantive session in 1973–74, when the package of trade-offs was announced by the major states, and the 1975 creation of the Informal Single Negotiating Text, there was not much movement toward consensus. Essentially, the bargaining stopped on these issues (or moved backwards) and the formula was adhered to rigidly, while most of the parties turned their attention elsewhere. These were decided issues, even if a substantial number of states would have voted against the accepted outcomes if the issues had come to a vote issue by issue. Indeed, that is precisely why UNCLOS III—unlike UNCLOS I and UNCLOS II—chose not to use voting as the mechanism for deciding outcomes. UNCLOS III used voting formally only to confirm the outcome of a consensus-based process.

The Territorial Sea

Although resolved at UNCLOS III with seeming ease, territorial-sea delimitation is an especially interesting bargaining problem. UNCLOS III was the fourth conference in the twentieth century to place the problem on the agenda, and the first to resolve the problem. Three times previously, negotiators failed to establish a uniform breadth for the territorial sea—at the League of Nations Codification Conference in 1930, the First U.N. Law of the Sea Conference in 1958, and the Second U.N. Law of the Sea Conference in 1960.[17] Although the earlier efforts fell short of success by only a small margin, there is no reason to believe that, if the issue had been framed at UNCLOS III as it had been at earlier conferences, the prospects for success on the territorial sea would have been bright. The importance of the territorial sea as an issue was reduced considerably by the development and successful negotiation of the two related concepts of transit passage and an exclusive economic zone. The former robbed the territorial sea of a good part (but not all) of its importance for security purposes, and the latter robbed it of much of its importance for economic purposes. Once its importance had been reduced, it was a candidate for trade-off.[18]

The territorial sea is one of the most ancient concepts in the law of the sea.[19] Even under the strictest Grotian interpretation of freedom of the seas, all countries have for many generations conceded that the coastal state may exercise sovereign rights over airspace, surface, water column, seabed, and subsoil in a narrow band off the coast. The coastal state's law runs throughout the territorial sea, but the coastal state cannot deny foreign users the right to innocent passage through the waters of the territorial sea.[20] There have always been quarrels as to what constitutes innocent passage, and who has the right to establish the criterion of innocent passage for any particular voyage through the territorial sea.[21] While many of the major maritime states long claimed that three miles was the standard delimitation of the territorial sea (perhaps under that mythical standard of the cannon-shot rule), the question of its breadth was subject to differing interpretations throughout the twentieth century.[22]

Politically, an important assault on the three-mile rule came from the coalition of Soviet-bloc and Third World states attending UNCLOS I and UNCLOS II.[23] For them, a 12-mile territorial sea was the preferred standard. Not only was this a traditional Russian delimitation, but it was also seen as a deliberate assault on freedom of the seas. At that time, the Soviet Union was still not a major shipping, fishing, and naval power. Its perceptions were those of a second-class ocean power hoping to use formal rules to push strong and potential hostile users of near-shore waters farther away.[24] These perceptions were shared by the limited number of newly emergent nations participating in UNCLOS I and II.[25] To avoid head-to-head confrontations on the territorial sea between two powerful, diametrically opposed voting groups at the two conferences, the forces of compromise introduced a split-the-difference proposal—establishment of a uniform territorial sea of six nautical miles over which the coast state would exercise sovereignty, with a fisheries contiguous zone of another six miles over which the coastal state would exercise more limited rights for specific purposes. Neither side was satisfied, so the proposal failed, though in one instance by only one vote.[26] At UNCLOS III, the comprehensiveness of territorial sea jurisdiction was reduced in importance by shifting some rights to the EEZ, making the problem of agreeing to uniform delimitation much easier. As figure 4.1 shows, the range of the alternatives was obvious.

There has been a steady erosion of support for the three-mile territorial sea throughout the twentieth century, with proponents of four, six, and nine nautical miles, as well as even greater distances. Nevertheless, three nautical miles was the delimitation distance supported by the United States, United Kingdom, Japan, and other important traditional users of the ocean, and it was still their preferred delimitation distance in 1973, when UNCLOS III began its formal deliberations.

Leaving aside some of the proposals for four, six, or nine nautical miles, or idiosyncratic limits like 130 nautical miles (Guinea), the real contest was

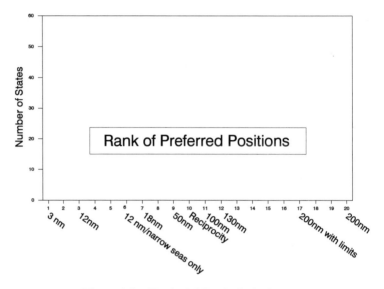

Figure 4.1:   Territorial-Sea Delimitation

between 3 (rank 1), 12 (rank 3), and 200 nautical miles (rank 20). Although three nautical miles had powerful supporters, it had failed three times previously and, as a result of creeping jurisdiction, was very likely to fail a fourth time. At best, supporters of three miles could hope to produce a stalemate, or later demand an important trade-off or side payment for conceding. Or they could indicate early on that, although they remained firmly in support of three miles as the *existing* legal standard if no consensus was reached, they would support a 12-mile territorial sea if the right of transit through straits used for international navigation was guaranteed. Most of the three-mile group (minus Japan, who continued to support Grotian positions long after other major maritime states had abandoned them)[27] chose this second strategy at UNCLOS III. This was done after advanced consultations between the Soviet Union and the United States.[28]

At UNCLOS I and II, the Soviet Union championed a 12-mile territorial sea as an expansionary enclosure move, and also because it was the traditional Russian standard. In the late 1950s and early 1960s, the Soviet Union saw itself as a coastal state surrounded by more powerful maritime enemies. By the later 1960s, the strategic situation had changed. When the Soviet

Union approached the United States to reopen the issues which failed to be resolved at UNCLOS I and UNCLOS II, it did so as a major maritime power. Thus, the standard the Soviet Union espoused—a 12-mile territorial sea— was now a relatively moderate one, and it was not difficult for the United States to convince the Soviet Union to tie the territorial sea and straits passage together, since over 100 straits classified as international waters would come under national control if the territorial sea on both sides of the straits expanded to 12 nautical miles (or 24 nautical miles in all), without other arrangements being made.[29]

Although the superpowers indicated early in the preliminary negotiation that they would prefer to negotiate these issues in separate packets from the economic issues, it was fortunate that they were included on that marvelous hodgepodge of items called the "List of Issues" that served as a primitive agenda for UNCLOS III. Trade-offs would have been much more difficult to arrange if security and sovereignty issues alone were on the agenda. Nevertheless, the United States and its Western friends were not happy with the juxtaposition of security and economic issues at the beginning of the conference.

At the opposite end of the scale was a proposal to create a territorial sea of 200 nautical miles. This was the preferred outcome of the so-called territorialist states of Latin America—Chile, Ecuador, Peru, Brazil, and some of the Central American states. There has been a long debate as to whether territorialist sovereignty claims meant sovereignty as understood in Anglo-American jurisprudence or were more in the nature of claims to economic rights.[30] However, at UNCLOS III the point was moot, since the term they used in their proposal was "sovereignty" and was therefore treated by its opponents as a full-sovereignty claim. It was also attractive to those African states wishing to push the industrialized states as far away from their coasts as possible and to make themselves the final arbiter of all economic activities off their coasts, though no African state claimed a 200-mile territorial sea when UNCLOS III began. Fortunately for UNCLOS III, while many states were unhappy with a three-mile standard, they had not made up their minds as to what they would accept before they entered the negotiations.

Uncertainty for many and the commitment of a few states can be observed in figure 4.2, our first attempt at measuring where states stood in 1967–73, (or time period T-1).

Three centers of support seem to be evident early in the debate about the territorial sea. The first is located at rank 1. It is composed mainly of Western ocean-using states and landlocked states. There is also a large, rather amorphous, and unfocused group spread out between ranks 3 and 12 that

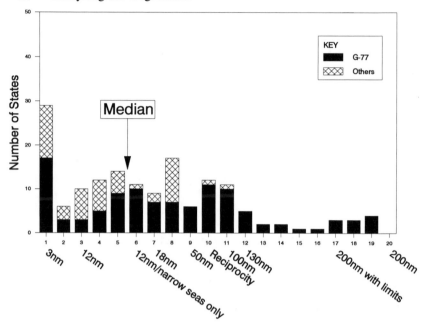

Figure 4.2:   Territorial-Sea Delimitation (T-1)

seemed to be seeking a moderate solution. Finally, there is the smaller, but ardent 200-mile club at ranks 17–19. There was a great deal of uncertainty early in the negotiation, probably because the trade-offs had not yet been pinned down, and many states were still exploring their options. But a few tentative conclusions can be drawn.

First, if the median (5.7) is a useful indicator of the state of negotiations in 1973 and where they were likely to go, the probable outcome would be moderate, closer to a 3-mile than a 200-mile standard. In fact, by 1973 it was already close to a 12-mile outcome. There was little hope that without a truly dramatic reversal, the conference would approve a 200-mile territorial sea. Second, the territorial-sea issue was not a North-South issue. Large numbers of developing countries in column 1 were primarily landlocked, and to some degree shelf-locked, states. As a result, the territorialists were not able to mobilize the Group of 77 on this issue. But only one non-Group of 77 state is shown on the figure beyond rank 10. The territorial sea may have been a North and East issue, but it was not a South issue. Our third tentative conclusion flows from the above—the territorialists were isolated on this issue.

By the second time period, which ended in 1975, events moved quickly on the territorial-sea issue. By then, all states were aware of the trade-offs which associated a modest territorial sea with transit passage through straits and the creation of the 200-mile EEZ. As a result, the median was very close to the eventual outcome, 12 nautical miles. Since it remained the outcome and got into the convention, we may conclude that negotiations on this issue had effectively terminated by 1975.[31]

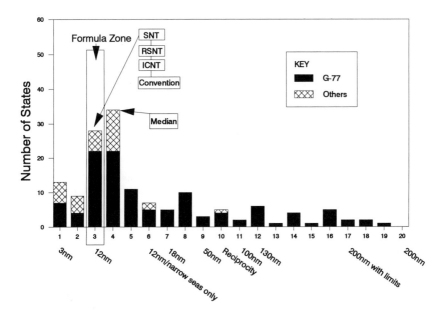

Figure 4.3:   Territorial-Sea Delimitation (T-2)

As figure 4.3 shows, the pattern in T-2 was unimodal with a tail. The territorialists did not like it, and only near-consensus, rather than true consensus, was reached (or indeed would be achieved), but a 12-mile territorial sea would be an integral part of the UNCLOS III Convention. That provision, using virtually the same language, was included in all of the so-called negotiating texts—the SNT, the RSNT and the ICNT. This may present a policy dilemma for some of those territorialist states that claim that a 200-mile territorial sea is part of their domestic constitutions and therefore not negotiable. It will be interesting to see whether, if they ratify the treaty, they will try to change their constitutions, interpret the treaty to fit the constitution, or merely ignore the issue.[32] As in T-1, all of the non-Group of 77 states supported the outcome in T-2. This could be expected since West and East were united on this issue.

The Right of Transit through Straits Used for International Navigation

For the United States and its maritime Western allies, the key trade-off fostering agreement on a 12-mile territorial sea provision was inclusion in the same document of an assured right of transit through straits used for international navigation. The Soviet Union and the Eastern Europe group also very much wanted an assured right of transit through straits (though they would not concede more than they already had—a 12-mile territorial sea—to get what they wanted).[33] This made for a formidable coalition at UNCLOS III.

There was also strenuous opposition to granting (or as some put it, reconfirming) existing rights favoring straits transitors over coastal states. If handled poorly, negotiated strictly on its own merits and not in the context of a trade-off, the straits issue could have split the UNCLOS III negotiations wide open.[34] Fortunately, the issue was well managed, and a balanced set of rights and obligations was created on a functionally related set of issues.

The reason that controversy shifted from the territorial sea to straits was, in fact, the tied promise on the part of the coalition to accept a 12-mile territorial sea. If a uniform world standard for the territorial sea was set at 12 nautical miles, straits less than 24 miles wide would be put under national jurisdiction.[35] Then if the coastal state was arbitrary, it could close off a strait to all, or to a particularly unfavorable transitor. Fear of arbitrary behavior by a coastal state had to be tempered by the awareness that even in a territorial sea, a transitor had rights under the doctrine of innocent passage. However, innocent passage does not cover certain modes of transit, among them overflight and submerged transit, and for generations there has been considerable controversy over such questions as who defines what is innocent behavior, whether a coastal state, merely because it is sovereign, can deny passage "without cause," and what is "cause."[36]

Problems of defining innocent passage, and of who has the right to make authoritative determinations concerning transit rights, are not new. Solving these problems was less important when major transitors accepted as national territory territorial seas of three miles on either side of a strait. Straits wider than six miles were assumed to have a channel down the center in which high-seas rights prevailed, including transit in a mode preferred by a transitor. However, if territorial seas were extended to 12 nautical miles, over 100 international straits that were less than 24 miles wide would be enclosed, including the English Channel, and the Straits of Gibraltar, Malacca, and Hormuz.[37]

Was there a real threat to transit through straits in the 1960s and 1970s? Naval staffs thought so. No doubt some of their concerns were based upon worst-case scenarios, which naval staff planners are obliged to use as a planning method. Under a worst-case scenario, assuming compliance with an adverse ruling on straits transit by a coastal state, plans to engage in major naval activities in the Mediterranean Sea, the Indian Ocean, the East China and Yellow Seas, among others, could have been seriously imperiled.

But naval staffs could also point to some real-world indicators which made them nervous. For example, Spain, although an ally under a security treaty with the United States, was making claims to Gibraltar directed primarily at the United Kingdom. However, if circumstances changed, Spanish claims might have been used to control access by the U.S. Sixth Fleet to the Mediterranean. For another, at least three major straits separating the Japanese main islands, without special arrangements could have come under the Japanese Constitution and the Three Non-Nuclear Principles of Japanese law, thereby possibly restricting transit of nuclear-powered vessels and aircraft, or those carrying nuclear weapons.[38]

Finally, in the late 1960s there was a serious concern with threats to transit through the Strait of Malacca.[39] As the pace of oil shipment by sea quickened in the 1960s, the threat and actuality of oil spills emerged as a major issue for coastal states, especially for those on frequent used routes strewn with natural hazards. The 500-mile-long Strait of Malacca is sufficiently shallow in some critical locations that a small mistake in navigation could result in a major ecological disaster. In that period, developing straits states complained about the careless and arbitrary behavior of major oil carriers and their state protectors, and also about the stingy behavior of many of the same states in providing development assistance. There was speculation in the press, fueled by comments from officials, about how much the Malacca Straits states could earn if they turned the strait into a binational canal and charged tolls for its use. This almost turned into a diplomatic incident. In 1972, the Soviet Union approached Japan and the United States to stage a joint demarche to the Straits states, but was rebuffed. Instead, the Soviets brought their concerns to UNCLOS III for solution.[40]

Ironically, the Soviet Union had to turn to the United States for diplomatic assistance in optimizing its strategic naval position. In any comparative evaluation of the naval positions of the superpowers, the geographically disadvantageous position of the Soviet Union shows up clearly. The Soviets are trapped in their continental bastion by narrow seas and straits.[41] To reach the open sea, most Soviet ships in the Far East (except those from ports on the Kamchatka Peninsula) must pass through straits separating the Kurile Islands, the Korea Strait, or the straits between and past the islands of Japan. Soviet ships from Black Sea ports must go through the Dardanelles (for which there is a separate legal regime under the 1936 Treaty of Montreaux[42]), and either the Suez Canal or the Strait of Gibraltar; those from Baltic ports must traverse the Skagerrak and Kattegat.[43] The Soviet northern fleet, based on the Kola Peninsula facing the Barents Sea, cannot reach the North Atlantic without penetrating the so-called G-I-UK (Greenland-Iceland-United Kingdom) gap. Although under no legal definition would the G-I-UK gap be considered a strait, strategically, the Soviets face the same dilemma of a "choke point" there that they face through true straits.

United States naval authorities were aware that, abstractly, unrestricted right of transit straits would be of greater advantage to the Soviet Union than to the United States; but, to achieve its own relatively unfettered right to move naval and air units to all the major oceans of the world through and over straits used for international navigation, the United States had to concede the same rights to others under the doctrine of reciprocity inherent in international law. Given the long tradition of Mahanian thinking in the U.S. Navy (which demands control of the sea), any alternative would be almost unthinkable.[44]

U.S. decision-makers had to go beyond mere acquiescence in the right of the Soviet Union to move both civilian and military vessels and aircraft through straits. They had to collude with them at UNCLOS III to see that a transit regime acceptable to both superpowers had a good chance of getting in the final treaty. American and Soviet delegates met frequently throughout the negotiations. According to Bernard Oxman, who participated on the U.S. delegation for the entire negotiation, relations became strained in later years on some issues where interests began to diverge. But on straits the superpowers saw eye to eye for the entire negotiation.[45] This was an interesting example of the necessity of making bargaining alliances in a multi-issue negotiation so that the bargaining partners could maximize their hostile positions in another arena.

The driving concern behind the straits-transit question was military transit. Theoretically, civilian vessels carrying the world's commerce could also become hostages to the strait states, but the merchant marine ministries of the developed states or the lobbying groups that represented vessel owners or shippers didn't worry much about the "robber baron on the Rhine" scenario[46] (despite some evidence, such as the Malacca incident of 1972, that might have given them pause).

Three sets of rights might be at peril if coastal states attempted to exercise sovereign rights over the major straits of the world: air transit, submerged transit, and surface transit. Only the third is partially protected by a "right of innocent passage." Air transit over national territory, including the territorial sea, has been completely controlled by the state over which an aircraft passes since the 1944 Chicago Convention on International Civil Aviation.[47] The 1958 Convention on the Territorial Sea is unequivocal: to qualify for innocent passage, a submarine must transit on the surface flying its correct flag.[48] The military authorities of major states were not willing measurably to reduce their rights to use any of the three modes of transit.

The issue was joined between users of straits transit rights and continental coastal states such as Spain that bordered straits, and also between transitors and states whose territory was composed of islands. Waters between the islands of oceanic archipelagos can be defined as straits. Archipelago states claimed they had a special problem of holding their separated territories together, and therefore the ocean areas between their islands should not be viewed either as normal territorial seas or, where distances between the islands were substantial, as high seas. To deal with their special problem, they insisted that they needed a special archipelago status in international law. In its classic form, archipelago status required the drawing of a straight baseline around the outermost geographic points of all islands grouped together as a nation-state. This line would become the baseline for the territorial sea. Within the line, all waters would become "internal waters." Since transit through internal waters is completely under the jurisdiction of the coastal state, the existing right of transit through the waters of archipelagos would be reduced to a privilege to be granted by the archipelagic state.[49] The problem of straits transit in general could not be solved without simultaneously solving the problem of the status of archipelagic straits.

In the early stages, as preparations were being made for UNCLOS III, the question of straits transit was discussed vigorously in the United States not only within the delegation, but also by the public and the scholarly community. At that stage, the Department of Defense indicated that the well-known U.S. position (unrestricted military right of transit through all international straits) was based on the need for strategic mobility so that the U.S. Navy could perform its deterrent role. The right to have strategic missile-carrying submarines (SSBNs) transit through straits was claimed to be vital to the maintenance of the strategic balance.

In 1974, Robert Osgood contended that the U.S. position rested on a weak reed if the major reason for a right of straits transit was the maintenance of strategic mobility.[50] Except for ballistic missile-carrying submarines operating in the Mediterranean until the middle 1960s (stationed there because the relatively short-range missiles of that era could not reach southern and middle Soviet targets from accessible open seas), it made little strategic sense to station supposedly invulnerable second-strike deterrent units in narrow, often shallow, seas reached only by straits. The SSBNs might be especially vulnerable during the very act of transiting straits. Improvements in the range of missiles made a right of transit less valuable strategically. For deterrence purposes, it was obviously better to station SSBNs in the deep ocean, where they could retain their "invulnerability" to possible Soviet anti-submarine warfare, than in shallow seas.

Nevertheless, the straits-transit debate is instructive as an attempt to legitimize a set of rights both domestically and internationally. Maintaining deterrence and strategic stability is easier to sell to domestic and friendly foreign elites than many other reasons a navy might desire to use straits. But with hindsight, we can see that a right of transit through straits used for international navigation has not been critical to maintaining deterrence and strategic balance between the superpowers.

In domestic discussions and UNCLOS III debates both proponents and opponents consistently underplayed the subject of air transit rights, although it may have been the most important of transit rights to straits transitors. In any case, during the more than ten years of UNCLOS negotiations, it proved to be a critical right in a major military conflagation. In the 1973 Arab-Israeli war, the United States made a major effort to resupply the hard-pressed Israelis by air. When its European allies denied the United States the right of overflight of their territories for this purpose, resupply flights from the continental United States, air-refueled over the Atlantic, reached Israel via transits over the Strait of Gibraltar.[51]

While the underplaying of air-transit rights is somewhat mysterious, the underplaying of the right of surface transit is not. Transit of naval units through straits is most often associated with what has been come to be known as gunboat diplomacy, the stationing of naval vessels or fleets off the coast of a state, which the naval power uses to deter the coastal state from taking some form of unacceptable action.[52]

Gunboat diplomacy has been a difficult subject for many states to deal with in public, especially in a multilateral context. There were vociferous protestors among the delegates at UNCLOS III, especially from Third-World states that played a leadership role in the Nonaligned Movement. In strong language, they vigorously opposed putting in a universal treaty provision that would protect the rights of gunboat users. Other developing states preferred to ignore the issue, to deal with it behind the scenes, or to treat it as a subject to trade off. Some Third World states had formal alliances with First or Second World states or were their informal clients. Even where no prior arrangements had been negotiated, many leaders of smaller, or weaker Third World states feared treaty restrictions that might prevent their preferred superpower navy from rescuing them if domestic circumstances or foreign neighbors turned against them. Thus, the debate on the straits issue began slowly in the first time period (1967–70), with the merits of the issue downplayed. This was also the preference of the naval members of the superpower delegations.

Although treated here as a separate issue, straits transit is closely tied into the key trade-off of UNCLOS III. Many developed states—especially the superpowers—were explicit about straits being part of a three-way trade-off: a satisfactory regime for straits in return for acceptance of a 12-mile territorial sea and a 200-mile Exclusive Economic Zone. This triad was the linchpin of the entire UNCLOS III Convention. It was worked out as early as 1974 at the first substantive session at Caracas. Many leaders of developed states explicitly insisted on the three-way trade-off as the cornerstone of the agreement.[53]

The nature of the key package raises several intriguing questions. In theory, a trade-off involves accepting less than optimal outcome on one or more issues of lower salience in return for a more favorable outcome on one or more issues of higher salience. But the package the major maritime states insisted upon—12-mile territorial sea, unrestricted transit through straits, and a 200-mile Exclusive Economic Zone—has no issues of low salience. As we shall see, the big winners under the 200-mile EEZ regime are mostly major maritime states. So the first question is, what did these states give up to get what they wanted?

A second interesting question arises. Was the United States bound under an implicit trade-off to accept the International Seabed Agency as a further price for the explicit trade-off of straits transit and territorial sea for 200-mile EEZ? Even the most ardent advocate of such an idea would be hard put to find any explicit promise by the United States to accept major provisions in a comprehensive treaty that it abhorred.[54]

Before we can deal with the more tangled bargaining questions, we must understand the situation issue by issue. On the right of transit through straits used for international navigation, the range of alternative outcomes, as shown in figure 4.4, was wide.

The debate began predictably, with the introduction of opposing conceptual frameworks as candidates for the formula notion: free transit through straits used for international navigation versus complete coastal-state control.

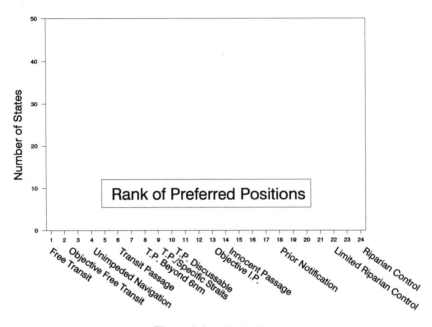

Figure 4.4:   Straits Transit

These polar positions, although too extreme to be negotiable in their starkest form, helped to frame the debate.

At rank 1, transitors would have the same rights in transiting straits used for international navigation that they had on the high seas. Frequently, those rights were left unspecified. What transitors were after was complete freedom of movement.

On the other side, proponents simply wanted to swallow up straits as part of an expansion of their national territory; most implied that straits would not even be subject to the usual protection of innocent passage. They wanted a full-consent regime (rank 24), in which transitors could use a national strait only with the permission of the coastal state, which presumably would have a right of refusal.

Some of the harshness implicit in a complete riparian control scheme is mitigated by the fallback at rank 22. Consent would still be required, but the coastal state would have to specify particular categories of acts or military systems (often nuclear-armed or powered fleet units) subject to exclusion.

At ranks 14–17, proponents would have the traditional right of innocent passage through the new water territory coastal states would acquire if a 12-

mile territorial sea was established as a worldwide uniform standard, thereby putting straits less than 24 miles wide under the jurisdiction of one or more coastal states. At rank 19 were proposals requiring prior notification of a transit before it could be considered innocent, a position considered extreme by supporters of transit rights. To soften the opposition of those claiming that a prior notification rule might give coastal states arbitrary powers, some states proposed that objective criteria for innocent passage be developed to guide coastal states.

The fear of arbitrariness was not confined to one side in this debate. Many states, whatever their ideology, were concerned that allowing vessels, under the doctrine of "free transit," to go where, when, and how they pleased could injure the rights not only of straits states, but of third parties as well. Some states, particularly from the Third World, had as much difficulty with the terminology—"free transit" and "unimpeded navigation"—as they had with the exercise of the rights they implied. Such concepts raised the specter of the Grotian framework for ocean law, which many Third World states rejected as an imposed regime.[55] At the very least, supporters of transit rights had to assure coastal states that transitor vessels would not pollute, or if they did, the transitors would accept liability.

A new set of descriptive terms was needed to describe what proponents of transit rights wanted, without using words such as "freedom" or "unimpeded." "Transit passage" was perfect—and eventually became the core concept of Article 38 in the UNCLOS III Convention. Here placed at rank 6, "transit passage" was construed to mean that all transitors—vessels and aircraft alike—should be allowed to transit in their "normal mode." Since aircraft can transit only by air, there was never any question that they had to transit in their normal mode if they were to transit at all. This was not the case for submarines. Submarines can transit on the surface. However, in that mode they are a hazard to surface transitors, since they are low in the water, provide a very small radar profile, and are not very maneuverable. Thus, Article 39 allows submarines to transit in their normal mode—submerged.

There was an attempt to balance rights under the new transit passage concept. On the one side, transitors were assured that coastal states could not suspend the right of transit passage (Article 44). On the other, the right of transit passage was restricted to continuous and expeditious passage (Article 38) and ships had to refrain from delays, threats to the coastal states, or acts other than incidental to normal mode, and they had to comply with international regulations concerning safety at sea and the prevention of pollution (Article 39). They could not conduct research while in transit without the prior authorization of the coastal state (Article 40). States bordering straits

could create sea-lanes (Article 41), regulate the safety of navigation, pollution, fishing, and punish customs violations so long as the rules were not discriminatory (Article 42).

Closer to the center of figure 4.4 were proposals accepting transit passage
with modifications to protect the coastal state a bit more. At rank 8 was a
proposal to exempt narrow straits, even if used for international navigation,
from the requirements of transit passage. More restrictive still was a proposal, at rank 10, to apply the transit passage regime only in a limited number
of specified straits.

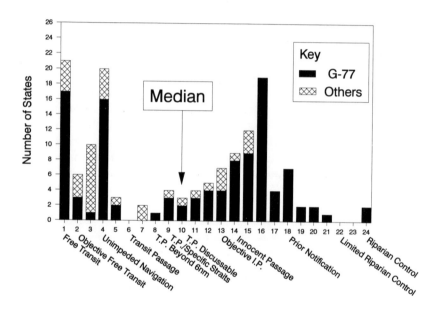

Figure 4.5:   Straits Transit (T-1)

As shown in figure 4.5, the distribution of state preferences up to 1973–74
is essentially bimodal. This pattern of opposition did not form immediately at
preliminary stages of negotiations, but took some time to show up publicly.
In the early United Nations First Committee debates, the issue was kept low-
key because the superpowers were reluctant to discuss the issue openly. It was
put on the Conference agenda only as part of a package, and only over the
protests of the superpowers, who wanted to negotiate the many disparate is-

sues in separate packets.[56] That effort failed. Many members of the Group of 77, as well as a variety of smaller developed states who were dependent upon or in an alliance relationship with the superpowers, were reluctant to speak openly on the issue of straits transit, since any defense of "freedom" or "unimpeded transit" was seen as tantamount to approving gunboat diplomacy by many of their caucusing group members as well as elites back home. Thus, much of our data in T-1 was taken in the later part of the 1970–73 period.

During the early debates, the two reasonably strong contending forces were those who supported unimpeded navigation (ranks 1–4) versus those who supported innocent passage (ranks 14–19). Although few states wanted to give the coastal state unfettered control of straits, there *was* strong sentiment for increasing the coastal state's control of straits at the expense of transitors. The median of rank 10 is at the "hole" in the middle of the figure. It indicated early that a compromise had to be sought to settle this issue. Yet, since the median was slightly nearer the free transit side of the midpoint, it gave the transit forces some hope that a satisfactory solution could be found, despite the rhetoric of coastal enclosure that permeated the conference.

Straits transit was not principally a North-South issue. Time-series analysis shows that, although the North clustered toward the freedom pole and the South toward the coastal control pole, both groups were split on this issue.[57] Members of both groups were cross-pressured by their other interests and affiliations. For example, in T-1, the Arab group as a whole favored coastal control of straits because of their position vis-à-vis Israel's right to transit through the Strait of Tiran.[58] Later they would find this a double-edged sword because of their fear of Iranian control of the Strait of Hormuz, first under the Shah and later under Khomeni.

Other caucusing groups were equally divided. For example, unity of the Western European and Other (WEO) group was shattered on the straits question by the strong and explicit antitransit stands of its two straits state members at the opposite end of the Mediterranean—Spain and Greece. Belgium (another straits state) and Austria (a neutral landlocked state) also wanted relatively strong controls of transit. Canada, Japan, and the Netherlands favored a general right of transit passage, but were in ranks 8–10, supporting a right of transit carefully circumscribed to forbid the coastal state from control of transit activities they consider injurious to their interests. Canada's position was largely driven by concern over potential transit through the so-called Northwest Passage between Canada's Arctic Islands.[59] This was partially assuaged by including in the treaty a special provision in Article 234 for ice-covered areas.[60] Japan, an island country divided by straits often used by both superpowers, worried that both friend and foe might violate the Three Anti-Nuclear principles of its constitution. The Netherlands worried about heavy marine traffic entering the Strait of Dover off its coast.

By 1974–75, a significant shift had occurred, as shown in figure 4.6.

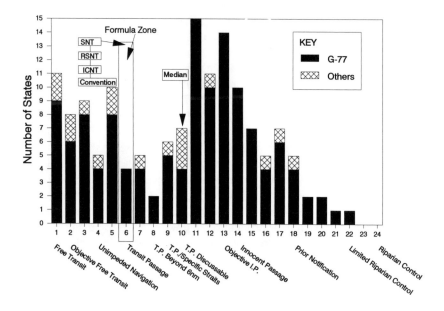

Figure 4.6:   Straits Transit (T-2)

Although the distribution has shifted markedly, the median still sits in a "hole" at rank 10, with relatively little support on either side. The only conclusion as of 1975 was that the straits issue was not close to resolution; distribution was still bimodal—there were still two camps. However, the median did show that the two camps, while still intact, were not as far apart as previously. Some convergence had taken place.

The outcome adopted—transit passage—was not close to near-consensus, much less at true consensus, by the time the Single Negotiating Text was promulgated. But the issue was essentially resolved when the chairman of the Second Committee included a transit passage provision in his section of the SNT. The formula zone remained solidly on the transit passage position shown at rank 6. Through subsequent revisions of the negotiating text, the underlying formula concept, and even the language remained the same. SNT,

RSNT, ICNT, and convention transit passage provisions remained remarkably solid over the entire period of the negotiation.

Did the LOS Study Group miss a shift of positions of a majority of states that made transit passage a winner? Or did a shift occur after the period on which the study group collected data on states' preferences at UNCLOS III? Neither was true. The study group correctly captured what states would prefer on the issue if the outcome was to be reached on the merits of the issue alone. Transit passage was adopted as part of a set of trade-offs. Figure 4.6 is typical of a major issue about which there are strong and variable preferences, and which therefore can be resolved only by trade-off. A resolution was possible as long as there were other issues in the package on which a favorable outcome was so salient to opponents that they would tolerate transit passage as the operative rule for transiting straits in international navigation. That issue was the extension of national jurisdiction over economic exploitation of living and nonliving resources out to 200 nautical miles—or enclosure. After the first phases of negotiation, some opponents of enclosure who conceded its adoption as part of the package reanalyzed their interests. They came to realize that they could reap enormous benefits from the issue they supposedly conceded away by their switch of negotiating stances on enclosure. They could win on both straits and resource jurisdiction. As a result, there was more convergence over 200-mile Exclusive Economic Zone (EEZ) than over straits.

Though consensus had not been reached by 1975, the United States delegation thought that "a clear majority of states participating in the debates favored a regime of unimpeded transit of straits, with a significant number of states endorsing the principle."[61] Although not much more than a majority expressed a positive preference for transit passage, the confidence of the U.S. delegation was justified. The pattern of movement of groups over three time periods between 1967 and 1975 also made them optimistic that the issue would ultimately be dealt with successfully as part of the overall package. The data reinforced the observation that the United States did not face a solid phalanx of opposition from the Group of 77 on the issue.

National Enclosure of the Oceans

By 1973–74, the 200-mile Exclusive Economic Zone was an idea whose time had come. It was the core of the package that was central to the UNCLOS III Convention. While the UNCLOS III Convention could not have been negotiated without a 200-mile EEZ provision, the fact that such a provision is now in the treaty may not help in promoting the treaty's ratification. Since the superpowers accepted the EEZ concept in early 1974, many states have enacted domestic legislation to promulgate and enforce a 200-mile economic zone.[62] Pundits, commentators, and some international law specialists have claimed that the 200-mile EEZ is already a part of customary international law, and that national rights being exercised under the concept are not necessarily tied to the signature and ratification of the UNCLOS III Convention.[63] If states continue successfully to make claims under the EEZ concept without ratifying the Convention, states that supported the 200-mile EEZ at the UNCLOS III negotiation reluctantly, and only as a trade-off, may find that they got little in return for what they gave.[64]

Why is the 200-mile EEZ important? Because it solves a conceptual problem in ocean management that has divided states for much of the twentieth century, namely, how far is the reach of the coastal states over ocean space off their coasts, and what type of rights can these states arrogate to themselves under that reach? In recent years there has been a contest between states favoring expansion of national jurisdiction over ocean space and those favoring its restriction to "traditional" distances.

In addition to the question of how far out is out, state representatives have been testing each other to define the nature of the rights being claimed. States preferring little or no expansion of national territory in the ocean have usually also attempted to limit the nature of the rights claimed. If they failed to stop enclosure in its tracks, their fallback was to oppose the expansion of general-purpose rights, and, if a further fallback became necessary, to accept limited claims to special-purpose rights.

The territorial sea as an ocean management concept is inherently difficult because it conveys to the coastal state general-purpose jurisdiction, or sovereignty. Ever since Jean Bodin invented the concept in the late sixteenth century, there has been a problem with the comprehensiveness of jurisdiction embedded in sovereignty.[65] As it applies to the territorial sea, true comprehensiveness is not achieved because of the right of innocent passage, but outsiders have virtually no other guaranteed use rights there. If the area of the territorial sea expands, those who previously used ocean areas being absorbed as national territory potentially lose existing rights. Hence they resisted change. On the other hand, comprehensiveness was the most attractive feature for many coastal states in making sovereignty claims. Sovereignty meant the right to decide upon *all* rights and rightsholders for the ocean area; no statesman who made a sovereignty claim could therefore be accused by domestic opponents of selling out to wily foreigners.

Nevertheless, selling out was what many leaders of claimant countries had to do. Sovereignty claims engendered strong opposition from other states who would have lost rights. The path of less resistance was to claim "special purpose" rights—rights to regulate immigration, customs, fiscal, or sanitary matters in contiguous zones or to allocate claims and regulate economic activities on the continental shelf. Here, the coastal state merely claimed for itself the right to control the ocean area *only* for the purpose of managing a special problem.

Frequently, a claimant state made such a special-purpose claim because it wished to reduce not only foreign objections to its demands, but also domestic objections. Some major states had interests that would have preferred expansion of domestic jurisdiction and restriction of foreign access to their near-shore waters, but they could not achieve both simultaneously as a result of the reciprocity required by international law. As a result, the history of the law of the sea since World War II has been one of creeping jurisdiction. While major claims to general-purpose jurisdiction were successfully resisted, claims to special-purpose jurisdiction were not, and many states were not comfortable with the accumulation of these piecemeal national actions.

To break the deadlock required a new concept, but one that would not unduly favor either pro-enclosure forces or anti-enclosures forces. A concept was needed to convey economic rights over offshore resources to coastal states while retaining high-seas navigation rights. The Exclusive Economic Zone (EEZ) had about it a well-thought-out conceptual framework that earlier claims to special-purpose jurisdiction lacked. The earlier claims were viewed, with some justification, as no more than a bundle of ad hoc adaptations; compared to them, the EEZ was easier to define and defend.[66]

The EEZ, or as some Latin American theoreticians dubbed it, the "patrimonial sea," was explicitly designed to help solve the disagreement between some Latin American, North American, and European states that threatened to make convoking another universal conference on ocean law futile. It was designed as much to solve a problem in bargaining as a problem in ocean management. The 200-mile territorial sea proposed by some Latin American states was interpreted by the United States and others as a sovereignty claim that would essentially terminate all foreign user rights in waters out to 200 miles, so it was nonnegotiable. An idea was needed that would give the coastal state some of the specific rights it wanted but would protect non-resource rights of outsiders to use the waters and air space within 200 miles. The 200-mile Exclusive Economic Zone was that idea.

If an exclusive economic zone could be agreed to, and its outer boundary placed further away from the coast than a territorial sea, then the problem of the delimitation of the territorial sea was solvable. This threw the burden of finding an acceptable solution on a definition of straits, one that would protect the right of transit without eliminating protections for straits or archipelago states. All three issues therefore had to be treated as part of an integrated functional whole—a package. Even if there were no other pressures to use a package approach as the major mechanism for resolving the core issues of the Conference, the linkage between the near-shore economic and security issues dictated that such a bargaining tactic be used.

After the conference, there was much concern about the U.S. refusal to sign the UNCLOS III Convention over an issue, which from the point of view of contemporary substantive ocean management was trivial—management of deep-ocean minerals. This made many overlook the centrality of the EEZ to the overall treaty. It was by no means assured that the states assembled in numerous sessions in Caracas, New York, and Geneva would find their way out of the triangular dilemma they faced when law of the sea discussions began in the General Assembly in 1967. Many major maritime states were content merely to update the details and patch the holes in the 1958 Continental Shelf Convention as it related to coastal-state economic jurisdiction. Landlocked states were reluctant to negotiate any increase in coastal state jurisdiction, tending to view the situation in zero-sum terms.[67] But the concept of the EEZ pushed all parties to a new level of discourse.

The alternatives that emerged from the debate are shown in figure 4.7.

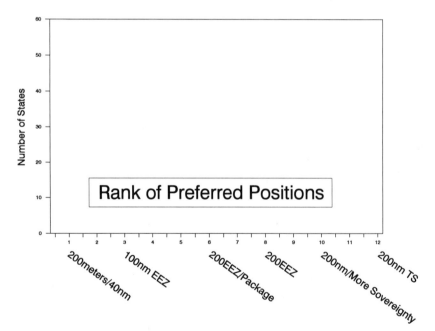

Figure 4.7:   National Enclosure of the Oceans

Before the superpowers fell into line as supporters of a 200-mile EEZ, the choices for dealing with coastal economic jurisdiction were limited, but the policy distance between alternatives was wide. While there were a number of ideas introduced in the exploratory stages, most were only straw-man proposals. The real choices were restricted to a formula for retaining a narrow zone of national economic jurisdiction on the seabed such as out to a depth of 200 meters or to 40 miles, with an intermediate zone beyond that (rank 1), a compromise formula like the EEZ, perhaps applied only out to 100 miles from the coast, but with a clear extension of jurisdiction over activities like fishing (rank 3), a full 200-mile EEZ (rank 8), a 200-mile EEZ with some rights over movement activities (rank 10), or a full 200-mile sovereign territorial sea (rank 12).

In the early negotiations, as shown in figure 4.8, the forces supporting limits on national jurisdiction appeared to have the situation reasonably well in hand.

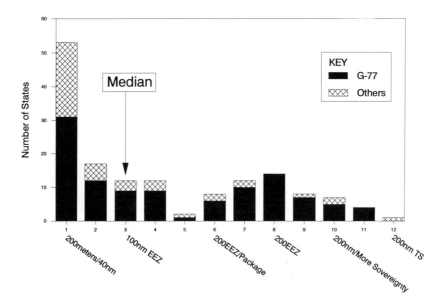

Figure 4.8:   National Enclosure of the Oceans (T-1)

The distribution is unimodal, but with a long, strong tail. Supporters of limiting national jurisdiction on the seabed seemed to favor an early U.S.

proposal to limit jurisdiction, which would have set the boundary of national jurisdiction at the 200-meter isobath or 40 miles from the coast, with an intermediate zone in which the coastal state would have authority to issue regulations, but from which it would have to share revenues with the international community.

While the conservative position was strong—in fact, a majority position—there was also strong but disunited opposition. T-1 showed the first signs that the real alternative to narrow jurisdiction would be a 200-mile EEZ (at rank 8). Of the active caucusing groups, only the Latin American, Caribbean, and archipelago states had mean scores clustered around the 200-mile EEZ position. On the other side, we can find the landlocked, shelf-locked, African, Eastern European, Western Europe and Other states, as well as a number of common interest groups such as the distant-fishing states and major merchant-marine states, supporting or clustering around the 200-meter/40-mile standard.

The EEZ was not driven by the early lineup of forces. With a median of 2.85, the narrow-jurisdiction forces seemed to be at a significant advantage; on the economic jurisdiction issue, states were quite firm in their positions. The debate was extensive, and all groups were remarkably well disciplined in the early going. Yet the outcome shifted dramatically once states gathered at Caracas for the first substantive session of UNCLOS III in 1974.

A rethinking of conference strategy occurred as states prepared for Caracas. The conservative forces probably would have won on the seabed delimitation issue if they had continued to press for something like a 200-meter/40-mile/intermediate zone idea, but UNCLOS III might have collapsed. The coalition that supported restricting national economic jurisdiction was fragile—the major maritime, the landlocked, and the shelf-locked states. Only the landlocked and shelf-locked states were relatively united internally on the question of enclosure. There were strong pressures within some maritime states to expand national jurisdiction. Some of these pressures had been held in check by the claim that expanded jurisdiction might threaten security interests on the oceans. Thus, the security specialists among delegations from industrial states altered their position on restricting economic jurisdiction to enhance the odds of passing a package that included issues directly concerning them.[68] Economic jurisdiction out to 200 miles was traded off for transit passage through straits and a moderate increase in the territorial sea. The three issues became *the* package for the major maritime states.

In both the United States and the Soviet Union, the shift took place just prior to Caracas. Reanalyzing national interests in the light of perceived bargaining realities was not without pain. American security interests and distant-water fishing interests had been allies for many years,[69] but broke on this issue. To opt for national enclosure on the seabed, the U.S. abandoned external allies, the landlocked, and other geographically disadvantaged states at UNCLOS III.

Two inducements might have cemented an alliance of landlocked and major maritime states. First, the major maritime states might have succumbed to the moral appeal of the landlocked that they deserved access to the ocean and its wealth. Second, the major ocean users might have realized the potential value of the votes of the landlocked states and their friends to stop ocean enclosure. Unfortunately for the landlocked states, the moral appeal was not sufficiently strong to gain them the support of the developed states for rights much beyond what they had received in UNCLOS I. And, while the votes of the landlocked states added to those of the major ocean users and some of the shelf-locked states would have been sufficient to form a blocking one-third or more on both security and economic enclosure issues early in UNCLOS III,[70] clearly that would have been a spoiler strategy, not a strategy for an overall treaty acceptable to most coastal and major maritime states. A package was called for, and a conference process that avoided votes on individual issues was needed.

There was a contest between the United States and the Soviet Union at Caracas to see who could get the most out of announcing first in favor of the 200-mile EEZ. The forecasted outcome shifted quickly and dramatically, as figure 4.9 makes clear.

By the end of T-2 (or 1975), the median (rank 8) showed that no other position could have defeated the 200-mile EEZ if it had been put to the vote. More important, the swing of support made it clear to conference leaders that they had a winner in the exclusive economic zone idea. The chairman of the Second Committee correctly assumed, based on the work of the Group of Juridical Experts, headed by Norwegian Ambassador Jens Evenson, that consensus had been achieved on the exclusive economic zone and the provision was worthy of including in the Single Negotiating Text.[71] While our data do not show consensus by 1975, the pronounced shift in positions from T-1 did indicate that consensus would soon be reached. The 200-nautical-mile EEZ provision was placed unchanged in the successor negotiating texts and became Article 57 in the final convention.

In T-1, almost all states not members of the Group of 77 clustered in rank 1 on the EEZ issue. But many Group of 77 states also were found at rank 1 as well. In T-2, most of the Group of 77 moved to support the 200-mile EEZ,

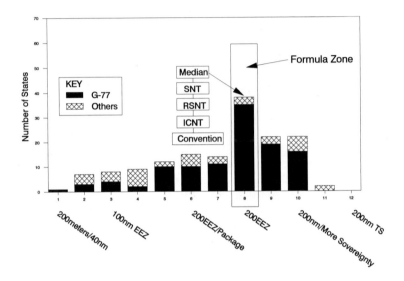

Figure 4.9:   National Enclosure of the Oceans (T-2)

as did many states from other groups. Should the 200-mile EEZ be characterized as a North-South issue? If we measure the rhetoric of the conference, it clearly was; there were many representative statements that it was in the interest of developing states to push the developed states further from their coasts.[72] But our time-series analysis indicates that the 200-mile EEZ was really a regional issue, initially a Latin American, later an African, as well as a functional group, issue (margineers, broad-shelf states). Together, they convinced their landlocked, narrow-shelf, and shelf-locked colleagues that they had to concede to coastal states rights over economic activities in order to have a treaty.

The poor landlocked and shelf-locked states fought hard against enclosure; however, by the end of the third session of UNCLOS III, some of them broke for the 200-mile EEZ. Perhaps they hoped to work out a deal whereby they would be rewarded with preferential rights in the EEZs of their coastal neighbors as the price for their agreement. This was partly realized in Articles 69–70, which gave the landlocked and geographically disadvantaged states a preferential right to the stocks of living resources coastal states declared to be surplus.[73] But this fallback was the best they could do in conceding the inevitable.[74]

Other opportunities for mischief by states and groups discontent with the new ocean regime were shaping up by 1975. Would the EEZ remain a sui generis zone, or could the sovereignty of the coastal state be further enhanced or undermined? Would the waters of the EEZ remain high seas and navigation rights be protected, or would they be attacked obliquely? Was 200 nautical miles a firm distance for coastal state resource jurisdiction, or could it be manipulated to the advantage of the coastal state? These are the next three issues to be examined.

The EEZ—A Limited or Unlimited Zone?

The Exclusive Economic Zone was the key component of the central package negotiated at UNCLOS III. But in addition to agreeing to the basic concept, and deciding that 200 miles was an appropriate distance for coastal state control (even though there was little theoretical justification in terms of ocean attributes),[75] the negotiators also had to flesh out the details of this general extension of national jurisdiction. Would outsiders lose their historical user rights after coastal state jurisdiction was extended out to 200 nautical miles? For example, would they lose the right to fish? Or to lay or use submarine cables? Would they lose the right even to navigate through the zone, as the United States feared.[76] Would the landlocked and shelf-locked states be "locked out" of benefits of the resources of the area, and be made worse off relative to their open-coast neighbors?[77]

In short, was the claim by the coastal state under the 200-mile EEZ to be exclusive and total, or in some way shared and limited? Was the EEZ to be sui generis, a mixed and balanced set of sovereign-like and freedom-permitting attributes, or was it to be a set of attributes indistinguishable from sovereignty or drafted in such a way as to easily "creep" to sovereignty? This would be determined in the UNCLOS III negotiations at two levels—first in the treaty language that defined the EEZ as a concept, and second, in the language that enumerated specific rights such as fishing. We will deal with the former here and the latter in chapter 5. The EEZ was part of an overall package, but its own components were also a delicate package of features that represented a series of trade-offs between coastal states and other stakeholders who had or desired rights in what became, after UNCLOS III, the Exclusive Economic Zone.

The need to find a balance between the coastal state and other stakeholders can be seen in the conflict issue in figure 4.10 below.

Clustered at the low end of the scale were the positions of states wishing to circumscribe the EEZ with formal limitations. At rank 1 were statements

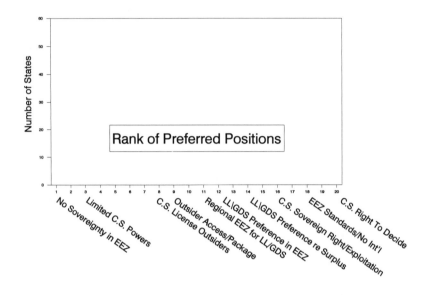

Figure 4.10:   Limited or Unlimited EEZ?

prohibiting the use of sovereignty in defining the EEZ; at rank 3, statements demanding the coastal-state control in the EEZ be limited and circumscribed by obligations to the international community; at rank 8, statements requiring the coastal state to license outside exploitation of some resources of the EEZ; and, at rank 9, statements approving the idea of an EEZ only as a trade-off for other rights.

Among the most insistent potential stakeholders were the landlocked and shelf-locked states—the so-called Landlocked and Geographically Disadvantaged States (LL/GDS). Instead of granting the coastal state exclusive rights in the EEZ, the LL/GDS favored a regional zone with all states in the region having a preferential right to the exploitation of zone resources (rank 11). More flexible members of the LL/GDS group were willing to accept a trade-off (which resulted in Article 69): in return for the coastal state's "exclusive" right to authorize most exploitation in the EEZ, the LL/GDS were to have a guaranteed preferential right to exploit the zone's surplus living resources (rank 14). At rank 16 were statements granting a full set of sovereign-like rights to the coastal state in the EEZ, limited only by the coastal state's promise to consider the rights of others; farther to the right on the scale were statements supporting an EEZ with no reference to rights for outside stakeholders. At the most extreme position, supporters insisted that the coastal state alone be authorized to exercise exclusive rights (rank 20).

On the basic question of whether there should be an EEZ, the distribution of preferences at the time of the promulgation of the Single Negotiating Text (SNT) was essentially unimodal, but the distribution of preferences on the extent of coastal-state powers in an EEZ was more complex. By 1975, the 200-mile EEZ was a fait accompli. Supporters of a coastal state's "sovereign rights" to explore and exploit the natural resources of the zone held the line, but it required a considerable effort to find appropriate trade-offs and side payments on related issues.

The struggle to create an EEZ in which a coastal state would virtually monopolize economic rights and yet still assuage the concerns of those who feared losses of existing rights can be seen in figure 4.11.

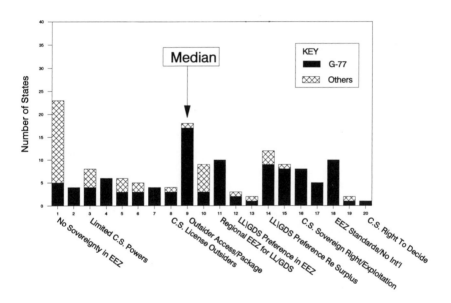

Figure 4.11: A Limited EEZ? (T-1)

Distribution of state preferences in 1973 was trimodal. There were three camps: (1) those who wanted to limit sharply the powers of the coastal state in the EEZ (ranks 1–5); (2) those who would approve an EEZ only if some specified rights for outsiders were guaranteed in the treaty (ranks 6–12); and (3) those who wanted an EEZ in which the coastal state was completely or almost completely unencumbered by obligations to outside rightsholders (ranks 13–20). The distribution indicates that, as of the Caracas session, states were still struggling with what the general idea really meant in terms of the extent of jurisdiction. Certainly no consensus had yet emerged.[78]

The question of the scope of coastal-state powers did not begin as a North-South problem. Figure 4.11 shows a relatively united North at the end of the scale supporting no or a very limited EEZ, but there are also a substantial number of Group of 77 states at that end of the spectrum. As on the basic delimitation issue, the lineup appears to be North and part of the South versus the remainder of the South.

After the United States and the Soviet Union joined the Latin Americans and Africans in support of the EEZ, they were no longer interested in restricting the framework of the EEZ and, with it, their own newly acquired rights. Yet they still were concerned with "creeping jurisdiction" and with whatever rights their citizens had acquired in what was to become other states' EEZs. They made do with language requiring the coastal state to demonstrate "due regard to the rights and duties of other States" (Article 56 (2)) in the exercise of its "sovereign rights" within the EEZ. When disputes arose over rights or jurisdiction in the EEZ between the coastal state and another state, it was to be resolved "on the basis of equity" (Article 59).

Those states rejecting the EEZ, or accepting it only with strong limitations on the coastal state's ability to terminate existing rights, were left with no major states in their camp to lead the fight. They wanted specific rights for outsiders written into the treaty, especially ones providing strong protection for residual fishing rights or creating a new right of guaranteed access by the Geographically Disadvantaged States to living and nonliving resources of their coastal neighbors' EEZs.

Supporters of the EEZ concept were willing to moderate their demands to make the idea of the EEZ acceptable—to back off from a coastal state's total sovereignty, and lack of any international standards, in the EEZ. Still, they insisted that the coastal state have "sovereign rights for the purpose of exploring and exploiting, conserving and managing the natural resources" (Article 56 (1a)). They were also willing to grant a rather weak right of access to the landlocked and geographically disadvantaged states to surplus living resources, but not to nonliving resources (Articles 69–70).

Figure 4.12 shows the situation as of 1975: neither consensus nor even near-consensus had been reached. But the shift of the median from 9 to 15 indicates that the EEZ forces were pulling in support and that consensus seemed possible in the next round of negotiations. However, the three camps of T-1 are still visible in T-2 in the distribution of states across the spectrum

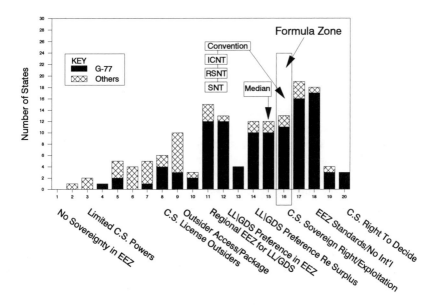

Figure 4.12: A Limited EEZ? (T-2)

of possible positions. The abandonment by the superpowers of opposition to the enclosure (ranks 1–9) shows up in a substantial weakening of the anti-EEZ forces. By 1975, the question was no longer *whether* the EEZ, but *what type* of EEZ, would find its way into the negotiating text; that is, would the power of the coastal state in the EEZ be relatively restricted (as preferred by those states in ranks 8–13) or relatively unrestricted (as preferred by states in ranks 14–18)?

Bargaining on this issue was essentially complete by 1975. The language of the Single Negotiating Text (Article 45) remained unchanged through the RSNT, the ICNT (Article 56), and the UNCLOS III Convention. While consensus had not been reached on this issue, sufficient movement had occurred to convince the conference leadership that they could safely turn their attention to other parts of the package.

Navigation Rights in the Exclusive Economic Zone
In addition to being concerned with the general conceptual framework of the Exclusive Economic Zone, some states wanted to ensure that they did not

lose on critical details, whatever the general enabling language said. One detail especially important to the major maritime states was the right to navigate in the soon-to-be Exclusive Economic Zone in the same way they had traditionally navigated the high seas. There, freedom of navigation and overflight prevailed, subject only to the proviso that activities of one high-seas user not interfere with the rights of other users.[79] Related to whether such a general right would be proclaimed in the treaty was what activities would be permitted under that general right. Presumably, transit outside the territorial sea by surface vessels going on a steady course from point A to point B would be covered. But what of overflight, or hovering, by military aircraft? Or holding military maneuvers? Or laying of submarine cables, some of which might be used for military purposes?

The basic pattern of trade-offs in Committee II was for ocean users to concede to the coastal states the right to control exploitation of living and nonliving resources within a 200-mile EEZ in return for coastal-state support for a 12-mile territorial sea and right of transit passage through straits used for international navigation. But there was an additional feature that was integral to the package—freedom of navigation in the EEZ. Major ocean-using states wanted written assurance of freedom of navigation, overflight, and laying of submarine cables in the EEZ; indeed, they (especially the United States and the Soviet Union) wanted language in the convention that would declare that the waters of the EEZ would remain high seas.[80] Proponents of the EEZ, either as a sovereign zone or as a sui generis arrangement, felt that such a declaration would give a Grotian thrust to the new jurisdictional zone, making it easier for opponents to deny the coastal state the desired degree of general control. At most, the supporters of coastal rights were willing to negotiate an exemption of specific activities from coastal-state control, including navigation, overflight, and the laying of submarine cables. Declaring the EEZ high seas was not negotiable. As it turned out, assurances on specific high-seas rights were sufficient to convince those reluctant to concede the EEZ that the new economic zone would not ''creep'' into other functional areas and eventually become a de facto enlarged territorial sea.

Was there a serious threat to the right of navigation in the EEZ? To judge from specific proposals introduced by important states—yes. Ambassador Galindo Pohl of Ecuador, chairman of the Second Committee, modified the already negotiated Evansen contribution to the SNT, and added an extra article to the high-seas chapter, restricting high-seas rights only to those waters outside the internal waters, territorial seas, or EEZs of coastal states.[81] Mexico introduced a proposal allowing the coastal state to restrict placement of military installations on the seabed within the EEZ.[82] Even as late as 1979–

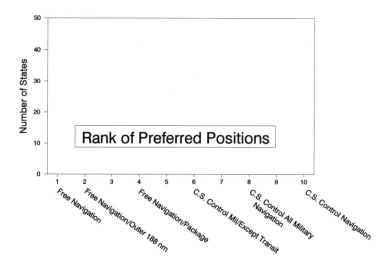

Figure 4.13:   Navigation Rights in the EEZ

80, some delegations tried to amend the negotiated text on transit rights through the territorial sea, making prior notification by warships a condition of innocent passage.[83] These were indicators to developed, especially super-power, delegations that navigation issues had to be monitored carefully. And they did pay careful attention. In figure 4.13, we examine how a successful trade-off was arranged on an issue that, if handled carelessly, might have become a serious legal liability for developed-states ocean users.

The range of possible provisions on navigation proposed for the EEZ was quite broad: from a restatement of a specific set of navigation rights within the EEZ (rank 1) to a requirement that the coastal state's permission be required for any foreign vessel or aircraft to enter the 200-mile EEZ (rank 10).

Since many of the states demanding a continuation of high-seas rights supported the package approach, and a 12-mile territorial sea was part of the package, it was not much of a fallback to accede to a clause restricting freedom of navigation in the EEZ to the outer 188 nautical miles (rank 2). Others were willing to soften some of the language on freedom of transit as long as it was part of the package (rank 4).

On the other side, all but the most ardent coastal-state-rights supporters were willing to concede freedom of navigation for foreign civilian vessels, but not for foreign military vessels, aircraft, or activities within the 200-mile zone (rank 8). The deepest fallback for proponents of strong coastal rights in the EEZ, at rank 6, would allow military transit under conditions similar to innocent passage in the territorial sea, but claimed for the coastal state the right to ban any other military-related activity, possibly including submerged transit, overflight, hovering, maneuvers, or the laying of military-related cables or intelligence devices. Military transit in the EEZ would be subject to prior authorization by the coastal state.

Figure 4.14 shows where states stood on navigation in the EEZ before the Caracas meeting.

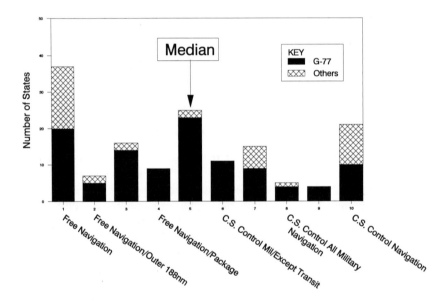

Figure 4.14:   Navigation Rights in the EEZ (T-1)

There were three camps among the delegations on this question: (1) those who supported a bundle of specific navigation rights for outsiders in the EEZ; (2) those willing to compromise between claims of coastal states and outsiders; and (3) those who supported closing off navigation in the EEZ without permission from the coastal state. At this stage, the delegates were searching for a general formula upon which to hang the details of settlement on this issue; by 1973, they had not found it.[84]

If this issue had been fought on its own merits, it could have torn the conference apart. Pairs analysis indicates that if the two extremes had stuck to their guns and pushed this issue to a hypothetical short-run decision, those supporting a freedom of navigation in the EEZ (ranks 1 or 2) would have had a 2–1 advantage over those who wanted to restrict navigation (rank 8 or 10). This was not sufficient for the issue to be brought easily to consensus or near-consensus. Fortunately, freedom of navigation in the EEZ was included in the straits-territorial sea-EEZ package. Given the shape of the distribution, the median at rank 5 tells us that the issue was not ripe for decision.

One other important observation can be drawn from figure 4.14. Although a few southern states, primarily from the Latin American and Arab groups, held that granting foreigners a right of navigation in the EEZ was betraying the interests of the South by permitting "gunboat diplomacy," the question of navigation in the EEZ did not shape up as a North-South issue. There were members of the Group of 77 in all three camps, and there were western and northern states who wanted to restrict navigation.

After the superpowers opted for the EEZ as part of a grand package in 1974 at Caracas, the distribution of preferences on this issue shifted swiftly. There would be a near-consensus outcome after all. The issue of navigation rights—whatever its substantive merits—was introduced primarily to get the major ocean users to accept the idea of an EEZ, circumscribed by limits ocean users could live with.

Protection of navigation, overflight, and cable-laying rights for outsiders was included in the Single Negotiating Text and all of its successors, including the convention (Article 58). None of the negotiating texts contained a ringing declaration of EEZ waters as high seas, but high-seas rights were included by indirection; that is, by references to freedom of the high seas elsewhere in the negotiating text (Articles 74, 76–97, 100–102 in the SNT; Article 87 of the later texts). The median at rank 2 in 1975 indicates that the negotiators were almost at consensus on the question of what rights outsiders would have in the EEZ. The U.S. delegation reported "general agreement" on this subject by the Caracas session,[85] a conclusion confirmed by pairs analysis for T-2 on this issue. Even if the strong coastal-state-rights supporters had limited their claim to the right to control military transit (rank 8), they would have had only about 15 states supporting them. Near-consensus had been achieved.

The Continental Shelf

With states around the world accepting the idea of the Exclusive Economic Zone, either as signatories of the UNCLOS III Convention or through

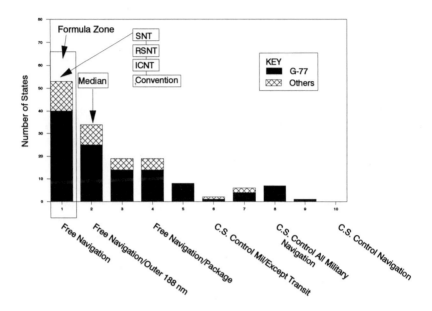

Figure 4.15: Navigation Rights in the EEZ (T-2)

unilateral acts, a turning point had been reached in the history of the enclosure of ocean space. There was little left unclaimed of relatively shallow areas
of sea bottom. Virtually all seabed areas that geologists have identified as on
the true continental shelf had come under the national control of coastal
states.[86]

Yet the idea of a legal continental shelf did not die with acceptance of the
200-mile EEZ concept at UNCLOS III. Indeed, the delegates salvaged the
idea of the legal continental shelf and filled it with new meaning. No discussion of the bargaining concerning trade-offs between security rights and economic rights would be complete without examining the continental-shelf
issue. It was the final issue of the group of enclosure and security issues
wrapped up together to make up the grand package, the core of the ''agreement in the large,'' that was almost achieved. Its negotiation demonstrates
how states that supposedly traded off economic rights for security rights
grabbed even more economic rights without relinquishing the gains they
made on security issues. They learned how to have their cake and eat it too.

Many observers of ocean law and policy cite the Truman Proclamation on
the Continental Shelf as the beginning of the modern history of ''creeping
jurisdiction.'' That 1945 unilateral act claimed jurisdiction (but not sovereignty) for the United States over the natural resources of the seabed and sub-

soil out to 200 meters depth of water.[87] The best geological advice of the time indicated that the continental shelf, or "the shallow part of the sea floor immediately adjacent to and surrounding the land,"[88] reached, on average, a break point at 200 meters and then began to curve down more sharply toward the abyssal plain. This seemed to provide a useful criterion for determining where national jurisdiction over resources (including living resources immobile at the harvestable stage) should end, and *res nullius* or *res communis* should begin.[89] The 200-meter depth was a mean that masked a substantial variance in distance from shore. The near-shore seabeds of the world's oceans vary significantly in their shape, which led to difficulties in using 200 meters (or any fixed depth, for that matter) as a criterion for boundary-making.

In the ensuing years, many states imitated the United States in claiming a continental shelf. Some, notably the west-coast Latin American states, whose true geological shelf slopes off sharply to reach the abyssal plain sometimes within 12 miles of shore, felt cheated by use of a geological criterion for extending national jurisdiction. Some scholars thought that these states developed claims to a 200-mile territorial sea to compensate for such a geologically limited continental shelf.[90]

Negotiated to guide states in their continental-shelf claims, the Continental Shelf Convention of 1958[91] only made matters worse. Article 1 of the convention provided three criteria under which a coastal state could establish a legal continental shelf: (1) a coastal state could claim the continental shelf out to 200 meters depth of water; (2) a coastal state could claim sovereignty and not merely jurisdiction[92] to a seabed area beyond 200 meters depth if the area permitted exploitation; (3) a coastal state's claim to the continental shelf was to be limited by the standard of "adjacency"—under the most common interpretation, its claimed seabed areas had to be continuous and not broken up by a trench or deep. In any case, it was not long before these three criteria were considered part of customary international law.[93]

Delimiting the continental shelf before the advent of the 200-mile EEZ raised many of the same jurisdiction issues that the EEZ was later created to resolve, especially those relating to nonwandering resources. These issues were not trivial. The principal issue was about jurisdiction over oil and gas exploitation of the seabed. Many observers thought it necessary to create rightsholders with a legally certain right to exploit seabed resources.[94] Since oil and gas are geographically fixed resources, the law of capture, which humankind had for centuries used to manage wandering resources, was never an appropriate rule for managing oil and gas operations. There was no successful oil and gas exploitation of a seabed find in waters deeper than 600 feet until the later years of the UNCLOS III negotiation, but technology was improving rapidly and specialists were already raising questions about the legality of oil and gas operations in the geological margin during the late 1960s. So the UN-CLOS III negotiation also had to deal with problems of the margin, which included all of the submerged lands adjacent to continents (beaches of the coastal region, continental slope, and continental rise or borderland).[95]

The continental-shelf issue was difficult to track during the early phases of the negotiation. At first, it appeared that proposals dealing with the continental shelf were rivals to the 200-mile Exclusive Economic Zone proposal. It seemed that if one concept were adopted, the other had to be automatically rejected. Later, when the concept of the "legal" continental shelf was transformed into the geological continental margin, the continental shelf emerged as a supplemental notion to the 200-mile EEZ for purposes of delimiting near-shore areas.

In 1970, the United States introduced a draft Presidential seabed treaty (the Nixon Proposal).[96] One of its major features was a provision to end national jurisdiction at 200 meters depth of water or 40 nautical miles. In those portions of the ocean beyond the geological shelf to the deep-ocean floor, the U.S. proposed a "priority zone." Here, the coastal state would exercise management responsibilities, but would have to share any revenues derived from exploitation there with the international community.

There was an initial flurry of interest from many delegations and indications of support from some of the groups favorable to controlling creeping jurisdiction, but the Nixon Proposal faded when it became obvious that there was strong support for a 200-mile EEZ. As it turned out, preventing creeping economic jurisdiction was less salient to major maritime states than preventing coastal-state control of movement rights. The major maritime states accepted the 200-mile EEZ as part of an explicit package.

The continental shelf concept was revived by states with extensive (beyond 200 nautical miles), relatively shallow seabeds off their coasts. Ironically, some were major maritime states as well. Until they conceded the 200-mile EEZ, they were caught on the horns of a dilemma. Ideally, they desired keeping coastal-state (meaning *other* coastal-state) claims modest, while protecting the right to control access to seabed areas off their own coasts.

The cross-cutting pressures, from wanting to control the appetite of other states without curbing their own, created dissonance within many states and groups early in the negotiations.[97] These pressures were released when the major states broke for the 200-mile EEZ. Now they were free to opt for the idea of coastal-state control of seabed areas beyond 200 nautical miles. Many became members of a negotiating group called the "margineers."[98] They caucused frequently and set the direction of the negotiation on the continental shelf issue.

The margineers' concern was no longer with the geological continental shelf, but with the entire geological continental margin. Rather than introduce a new geological concept that would have to be transformed into a legal one, they recycled an old concept—the continental shelf. Never mind that, in doing so, they would distort the scientific and technical meaning of the term almost beyond recognition.[99]

Proposals on the continental shelf are shown below, in figure 4.16.

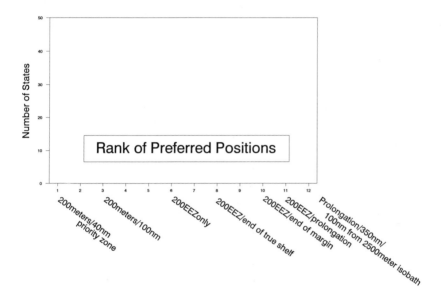

Figure 4.16:   Continental-Shelf Delimitation

The early attempt by the United States to set a conservative limit (200 meters depth or 40 nautical miles, with a priority zone beyond) to national jurisdiction on the seabed we placed at rank 1. The opposite proposal, "natural prolongation" of the continental shelf to 350 nautical miles, or 100 miles beyond the 2,500-meter isobath, that emerged later from the demands of the margineers, was placed at rank 12. After the introduction of the so-called "Irish" formula in the Sixth Session in 1977 (also placed at rank 12 since it provided more detailed criteria for the prolongation formula idea), proposals to define the end of the margin also had to carry further intellectual baggage (such as trying to define the margin as the foot of the continental slope as evidenced by a line from the outermost fixed points where the thickness of the sedimentary rocks is at least 1 percent of the shortest distance, or the line is at fixed points not more than 60 miles from the foot of the continental slope).

The margineers borrowed "natural prolongation" from the Continental Shelf Convention of 1958. In that convention, this was one of two general principles for delimiting the then-legal continental shelf (the other was equidistance). In waters less than 400 miles wide, opposite states under an exclusive natural prolongation standard would still have difficulties in separating their national seabed territories, especially if one had a true geological formation that extended beyond 200 miles, and the other did not. That is why states with limited margins insisted upon equidistance as an alternate standard. [100]

The problem of the continental shelf was not only where to end national jurisdiction on the seabed but how to write a formula that would be understandable and acceptable politically and technically. We placed a general proposal that would establish an end to national jurisdiction beyond 200 miles at the terminal point of natural prolongation at rank 11. General statements of support for establishing a limit on national seabed at the end of the margin were placed at rank 10.

The next major position was two spaces down at rank 8. Here were placed national statements allowing the limited number of states with a true geological continental shelf beyond 200 nautical miles to claim the seabed to its outer edge. All versions of this approach required a definitive depth somewhere between 200 and 600 meters.

The 200-mile EEZ, by itself, became an alternative to other attempts at defining the legal continental shelf. Some states wanted 200 miles to suffice in lieu of all other geographic or geologic criteria; we placed this concept at rank 6, in the middle. At three ranks further up the scale (rank 3), we placed the final fallback position of the narrow-jurisdiction forces—200 meters depth of water or 100 nautical miles, whichever was closer to the coast.

In the early discussions, before the major maritime states switched on the 200-mile EEZ question, the picture of where states stood on the parallel continental shelf issue looked rather favorable to the anti-enclosure forces, as shown in figure 4.17.

The distribution is unimodal with a long tail. The distribution suggests that one group—the anti-enclosure coalition—knew what it wanted. The group was mobilized to support something like the American proposal to end national jurisdiction at 200 meters depth of water or 40 nautical miles. It also seemed to approve the idea of revenue-sharing if not a full "priority zone" from the end of the continental shelf to the end of the margin. The coalition had more than 60 states, not a majority, but seemingly a powerful force.

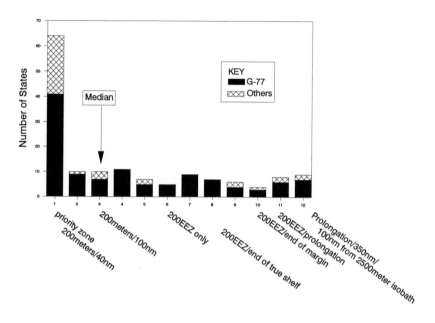

Figure 4.17: Continental-Shelf Delimitation (T-1)

On the other side, about 70 states, or approximately half of the states represented at UNCLOS III, wanted to expand jurisdiction, but in the Ad Hoc and Permanent Seabed Committees they had not focused on a specific proposal. Pairs analysis confirmed this judgment.[101]

If a decision had been forced early on the continental-shelf issue alone, with jurisdiction expanded to 100 nautical miles, the anti-enclosure forces probably would have won. But from the length and strength of the tail, the issue did not seem ripe for resolution. When the major powers switched on the 200-mile EEZ, the anti-enclosure coalition collapsed.

Neither in T-1 nor later in T-2 could the issue be characterized as a North-South issue. In T-1, the Group of 77 was split, with the Latin American and Caribbean states strongly supporting a broader continental shelf. The African and Arab states were still mostly supporting a narrower shelf, and possibly not convinced that a special provision for a continental shelf need be made. Many western groups were equally split; for example, the Scandinavians were edging toward support for a broader shelf (rank 8) while the EEC stood for a narrower shelf (rank 4).

Support for a narrow delimitation of the coastal-state seabed came from a coalition of ideological, geographic, and ocean-using groups—the Eastern

European group, Western European and Others, the landlocked and shelf-locked, and distant-fishing states.

After the superpowers announced their support for a 200-mile EEZ at the 1974 Caracas session, the continental-shelf situation was transformed radically, as shown in figure 4.18.

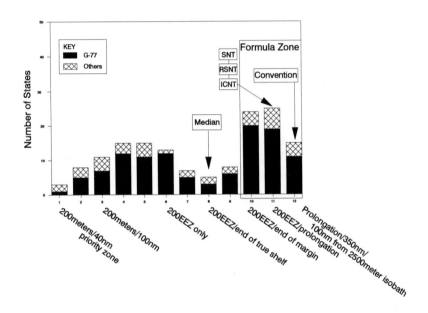

Figure 4.18:   Continental-Shelf Delimitation (T-2)

T-2 shows a bimodal distribution. The forces supporting a narrow band of national jurisdiction on the seabed slowly moved away from their maximum preferred positions at ranks 1–2 to a fallback position (ranks 3–6), somewhere between a continental shelf to 200 meters depth of water or 100 nautical miles, whichever is farther from the coast, and a maximum of a 200-mile EEZ only. Opponents supported putting the entire continental margin under national jurisdiction.

Judging by the median of 8, no decision had been reached by 1975. Neither consensus nor near-consensus had been achieved, even though the change in the distribution of national positions had been dramatic. Our results indicated that this would remain a contentious issue. It proved to be so.

Although the median of 8 suggests a region of compromise, the margineers would have none of it. All serious bargaining after 1975 took place in a formula zone from rank 10 to rank 12. In other words, all serious interactions were attempts to work out specific language—loose or tight—conceding that the coastal state would gain control of the geological margin. The SNT language of 1975 had already conceded coastal-state control out to 200 nautical miles, or if the margin extended beyond, to the end of the margin.[102] The key "buy in" needed to convince opponents to soften or drop their opposition was on the related issue of revenue sharing.[103] Article 68 of the SNT proposed that coastal states be required to share an as yet undetermined percentage of their revenues from areas beyond 200 miles. These revenues were supposed to be equitably distributed to members of the world community, considering the needs of developing countries, especially the least developed and the landlocked.[104]

The language on the continental margin as continental shelf was virtually unchanged in the 1976 RSNT,[105] and in the 1977 first version of the ICNT.[106] However, the revenue-sharing proposal was refined to exempt the first five years of production; revenue sharing would begin after the fifth year of production, and the rate paid would increase in later years.[107] In the ICNT, it was further refined to provide revenue sharing of 1 percent of value or volume after the fifth year, with a rise to 5 percent after ten years of production. Under the 1977 ICNT, developing states would be exempt from the requirement to share revenues for production beyond 200 nautical miles.[108]

The Irish Formula, which got into the UNCLOS III Convention as Article 76, transformed the geological margin into the legal continental shelf, comprising "the seabed and subsoil of the submarine area extending beyond the territorial sea throughout the natural prolongation of its land territory to the outer edge of the continental margin out to a distance of 200 nautical miles . . . where the outer edge of the continental margin does not extend up to that distance" (Article 76 (1)).

To define the outer edge of the continental margin when it extended beyond 200 nautical miles, the Convention employed several alternate and potentially contradictory provisions derived from the Irish formula. The first criterion was "a line delineated . . . to the outermost fixed points at each of which the thickness of the sedimentary rocks is at least 1 per cent of the shortest distance from such point to the foot of the continental slope . . ." A second criterion specified "a line delineated to fixed points not more than 60 nautical miles from the foot of the continental slope" (Article 76 (4) (a) (ii)). Neither of these specifications could lead to a border more than 350 nautical miles from the baseline from which the territorial sea was measured or more than 100 nautical miles from the foot of the continental slope (Article 76 (5)).[109]

How did such a complex and convoluted formula come about?[110] The data again capture the trend, if not the full final result. There was some overlap in support for a 200-mile EEZ and for extending the continental shelf to the continental margin, but mostly the two coalitions differed.

The core of support for putting the geological margin under national jurisdiction came from the major states that formerly led the narrow-national-jurisdiction forces. Once they switched their positions on the 200-mile EEZ, they did so with a vengeance! They became the heart of the margineer group determined to have its cake and eat it too; that is, they wanted both transit rights and coastal control of resources. For all practical purposes, as Arvid Pardo claimed,[111] they forced the extension of national jurisdiction out to a minimum of 350 nautical miles. We can see this development by examining, in table 4.1, the preferred positions of the broad-shelf states, most of whom were leaders in the margineer caucusing group.

As of 1975, most states with broad physical continental shelves were already tending toward supporting national jurisdiction over the entire margin. Among the broad-shelf states *not* advocating control of the margin was the Soviet Union, though by 1975 Soviet negotiators had conceded the 200-mile EEZ. This is consistent with the observations of Bernard Oxman, who noted that "the Soviet Union had been strangely quiet on the issue of the outer limit of the continental shelf for many years while the Conference worked toward an accommodation of the broad-margin states."[112] It was not until the 1978–80 period that the Soviets made it clear they preferred to define a limit to the margin by a precise maximum distance.

There was no strong pattern of support within the Group of 77 as a whole for converting the geological continental margin into the legal continental shelf. However, one of its subgroups—the Asian Group—was a consistent supporter of expanding national jurisdiction over the seabed. Many Asian states are broad-shelf states with a long record of disputes among themselves over islets or drying rocks whose possession would allow them to make the broadest claim vis-à-vis their neighbors.[113]

In sum, the margineers and Asian states won. Article 76 created a seabed under national jurisdiction, probably out to a minimum of 350 nautical miles. It may prove to be a hollow victory. The delimitation standard is complex and troublesome. As a result we probably have not heard the last of boundary-making on the seabed in the international community. It could be that seabed delimitation may be the issue that helps unravel what was achieved in UNCLOS III. Wisely, the United States has been ambiguous on whether, as a nonsigner of the treaty, it would unilaterally apply the Irish formula in its delimitation efforts. As Ambassador Thomas Clingan noted, "to date, [the United States] has announced that there is no change in the policy with regard to the shelf."[114]

STATE	DATA	ESTIMATE	POSITION
Ukrainian SSR	1.0	4.2	1.8
USSR	3.7	5.6	3.8
Byelorussian SSR	0.0	4.2	4.2
Tunisia	6.0	5.9	5.8
France	0.0	7.8	7.8
Ireland	0.0	9.2	9.2
Bahamas	0.0	9.5	9.5
Pakistan	9.0	10.7	9.6
Fiji	0.0	10.0	10.0
Australia	10.3	10.3	10.3
United Kingdom	12.0	8.9	10.4
Guinea	0.0	10.5	10.5
Guinea-Bissau	0.0	10.6	10.6
Nicaragua	11.0	10.4	10.7
Honduras	11.0	10.4	10.7
Philippines	0.0	11.0	11.0
United States	11.3	10.6	11.2
Burma	11.5	10.7	11.2
South Africa	12.0	10.5	11.2
Bangladesh	11.5	10.8	11.4
China	0.0	11.4	11.4
Mauritius	12.0	9.8	11.4
Argentina	11.2	13.9	11.5
Norway	11.7	10.8	11.6
South Vietnam	11.5	11.9	11.6
New Zealand	12.0	10.5	11.6
Indonesia	11.8	11.2	11.6
India	12.0	10.7	11.7
Mexico	11.8	11.6	11.8
Guyana	0.0	11.8	11.8
Brazil	0.0	11.8	11.8
Uruguay	11.8	12.3	11.9
South Korea	11.5	13.4	11.9
Canada	12.0	11.5	11.9
Iceland	12.0	15.0	12.6
GROUP MEAN			10.2

Table 4.1: Continental-Shelf Delimitation: Broad-Shelf Group Scores (T-2)

5

Terminating the Common
Wealth in Ocean Fisheries

Fishing is one of the traditional means of extracting wealth from the oceans. The management of this activity presents one of the oldest and most typical of ocean management problems. But until our own age, because of the primitive technological means available to catch, preserve, transport, and sell the products of ocean fishing, the scope of the problem of management was very limited.

During the long period from the dawn of recorded history to the age of the internal combustion engine, access to the ocean was either directly from the beach or from boats driven by sail or paddle. While fishing captains with superior skill or experience were more successful in locating schools of fish than others predicting when and where schools of fish would appear was largely beyond the ken of earlier fishermen. Moreover, it did little good to find large schools of fish, since fishermen had only primitive nets of natural materials subject to breakage and little in the way of deck machinery to supplement their muscles in bringing large amounts of fish aboard their vessels. They also had very little incentive to do so, since they had no means of preventing spoilage at sea and virtually no means, beyond salting, of preventing spoilage after they had landed their catch. What they caught had to be consumed quickly by the fishermen and families or sold in coastal villages.

Despite these limitations, access to known fishing grounds was highly prized and, on occasion, fought over. Answers to questions such as who owned which fish and who had right of access to a fishery were not arid exercises in legal reasoning, but often important questions of policy. For example, Elizabeth I's government ordered John Seldon in 1618 to write a refutation (*Mare Clausum*) of Hugo Grotius's doctrine of *mare liberum* or "freedom of the seas" to protect the British claim of control over the herring fisheries of the North Sea. It was a sufficiently important task to keep Seldon working on the manuscript for nine years. Despite his archaic language, Seldon's arguments sound remarkably contemporary. [1]

Until the advent of powered vessels, powered deck winches, available ice or onboard mechanical refrigeration, nets of virtually indestructible manmade materials, and a "cold chain" (a network of refrigerated storage and transfer facilities that allowed fresh fish to be kept fresh for longer periods of time and sold inland), as well as electronic location and navigation equipment, there was little that human exploiters could do to damage the major stocks of high-seas fish. Of course, the overexploitation of near-shore stocks by artisan fishermen should have long since warned us of the probable consequences of making new technologies available to fishermen of developed states.

Fishing is marine "hunting." Ocean fishermen depend upon nature to supply next year's stock, since they do not control, except negatively, the reproductive cycle of the creatures upon which they prey.[2] As a food-producing activity, fishing has social utility principally because the resource is renewable, and therefore available as long as the stock is large enough to withstand human predation. This is not to imply that even with limited exploitation fish stocks always remain in a steady state. Recent research has demonstrated a natural variability in many populations of living creatures in the ocean.[3]

While earlier political systems had little control of fish or even of fishing grounds beyond very local sites, little control was needed. Nevertheless, there was a regime or set of rules and norms which helped to regularize the behavior of ocean users.[4] While these rules have not always been consistently enforced by the dominant maritime powers since the time Grotius published his *Mare Liberum* (1608), international lawyers, for the most part, have claimed that they were an accepted part of international law. But it was not until the 1950s that economists and biologists were able to describe the economic and biological underpinnings of the formal rules. And it was these and other insights into the practice of ocean exploitation that convinced many governments in the late 1960s that the rules had to be changed.

According to the notion of freedom of the seas, ocean users could use the ocean as they pleased so long as they did not interfere with the rights of others, which meant only that they could not fish in a coastal state's internal waters, nor without permission in the relatively narrow band near the coast, called the territorial sea, in which the coastal state was sovereign.[5] But with all potential users having the same use rights, to whom did the fish of the open ocean belong? Theoretically, they could belong to no one (*res nullius*) or to everyone (*res communis*). For many centuries, the practical solution was to rely upon the law of capture.[6] While the fish in the ocean were owned by all or no one, the fish a fisherman caught and brought to the deck of his ship were his. That is, legal title vested in the fisherman, and he, in turn, could legally transfer title to the fish to the consumer.

Although the question of which was the appropriate theory—*res nullius* or *res communis*—was debated for centuries, the debate had little practical effect since neither theory could be consistently enforced on ocean users. Except when quite near the coasts of states, enforcement of rules denying access to wandering human predators preying upon wandering resources could, at best, be termed sporadic. Therefore, most coastal states that attempted to deny access except with their permission were judged not to effectively occupy the area, and their writ was null and void.[7] However, with the explosion of technology in the twentieth century, the situation has been fundamentally altered for both human predator and manager. As a result, there is a greater possibility of creating and enforcing a new regime—and also a greater need to do so.

With the rapid improvement in technology, humankind has begun to press very heavily upon the major stocks of fish of commercial value in the oceans.[8] Now fishermen from developed and, increasingly, from developing states have powered vessels, powered winches, nylon nets, and refrigeration equipment. Some states have entire industrial fleets that can stay at sea for many months, catch fish thousands of miles from home ports, process, and store them on board. Fisherman also have radar, sonar, and other powerful location and navigation gear, as well as access to much more accurate information about fish behavior and location.

Historically, reliance was placed upon the inefficiency of fishermen to allow the fish to renew themselves. Conservation took care of itself even if the fisherman was motivated to catch every fish he could. As fishermen became more efficient, it was clear that a major problem, inconceivable in the past, was emerging—that it might be possible to so prey on stocks of ocean fish as to exhaust them altogether for commercial purposes or, worse, drive them into biological extinction. The regime clearly no longer provided an effective structure for managing the interest of the stakeholders.

The underlying problem of the traditional ocean regime, identified as the "tragedy of the commons,"[9] is one in which all exploiters have a right to exploit (open access), but because the resource is "indivisible" (physically difficult or too costly to divide), none has an incentive to conserve.[10] Any exploiter that leaves a catchable stock behind should assume that it might not be there to exploit next year or season, since it is common to all and will be available for exploitation rivals. The result is a positive incentive to take as much as possible.

If the exploiters are few in number or the stocks very large, it matters little that there is no incentive to conserve. There is plenty for all who choose to fish since there are sufficient uncaught fish left to breed and renew the stock. But the historical pattern has been that when one or a small group of ocean exploiters are successful and gain wealth, others will be attracted to exploit the same stocks. Some of these will be "free riders," that is, exploiters whose expenses are lower because they have been able to "piggyback" on the first exploiters, who have paid for the costs of exploring and developing the fishery.

The result is that competition among the exploiters becomes intense and the catch becomes larger than can be replaced by natural reproduction. Two types of overfishing occur. The more destructive is "growth overfishing"— the larger individuals are harvested and only smaller individuals are left. Consequently, in succeeding seasons when smaller fish must be targeted, the count of individual fish caught is high but total tonnage declines. Less destructive, but still important when a fishery is already in decline, is "recruitment overfishing." As each year's "class" gets smaller (and even younger year classes are often exploited by reducing the size requirement), it reproduces proportionally less, is subject to variations in the natural system in a way that is not predictable from data about the larger biomass, and may be replaced altogether in the food chain by another species.[11] Ultimately the stock becomes too small to support the number of fishermen who prey upon it. The stock disappears as a commercial species until by accident or design the fishermen substantially reduce or cease fishing and the stock recovers. Alternatively, the stock might be permanently reduced to below a commercial recovery threshold but continue to exist. The third possibility is that the exploited fish actually become biologically extinct. We have examples of all three consequences of overexploitation of fish stocks.[12]

The traditional fishing literature of the 1950s and early 1960s indicated that fishermen would go broke before the fish. That is, as stocks of fish declined to suboptimal levels, the number of fisherman would also decline; and, in turn, as the fishing pressure on stocks was reduced, the stocks would probably recover to their former size.[13] Unfortunately, this did not prove true: as the size of the catch declined, demand and therefore real prices increased, "making it economically feasible for the fishermen to continue fishing even though they [were] taking smaller quantities."[14]

Fishermen can stretch out a bad situation through manipulation of the political system. Laws can be passed that slow down the rape of the ocean without addressing the fundamental problem of *who* can catch *how much*. The catch can be reduced by restricting fishing to specific seasons, and by banning certain types of efficient or least-cost gear. These efforts improve the welfare of the remaining fishermen, but not of the fish. Moreover, regulating the catch without allocating the right to fish fosters deliberate inefficiency. Under such restrictions, fisheries tend to overutilize capital and labor. Visitors to a contemporary commercial fishing port can see a large number of vessels sitting idle at dockside except during a short fishing season. Most of the vessels lying there are not equipped with the most efficient gear; efficiency usually means that the fish have no chance to survive.[15]

As fishing became economically more marginal off the coasts of a number of developed states in 1950s and 1960s, another phenomenon put increasing pressure on the remaining stocks—the appearance of distant-water fleets. These included the so-called industrial fleets from Eastern Europe and Japan, as well as the U.S.-based fishery for tuna.[16] These fleets, with catching vessels, large processing and storage vessels, research vessels, and resupply and replenishment vessels, operated as integrated units and could roam far from their home ports.

Since the operators of industrial fleets could treat the ocean beyond a narrow band of the territorial sea as an open access area, they could fish where they pleased. Knowing that what they left behind might be caught by others, they had no incentive to conserve. And since they had no hope of managing the stocks they exploited near the coasts of other states, they had little incentive even to slow down the destruction of these stocks through the use of inefficient gear. But they were aware that if they fished in the same area season after season, there would be no fish left, so they moved on. Research could be used to show them a new promising stock elsewhere. This was called "pulse fishing."[17]

Pulse fishing proved destructive not only to the stocks of exploited fish, but also to the local fishermen. Usually, they could not compete effectively with distant-water, and especially with industrial, fleets. Moreover, when the stocks had been reduced to suboptimal levels and the industrial fleets had moved on, the local fishermen could not move on with them. They were left with much reduced stocks that might or might not recover, and with no guarantee that, if stocks did recover, the industrial fleets might not return. Many local fishing industries near known good fishing grounds went into sharp decline, which led to considerable political pressures by coastal fishermen to restrict or eliminate foreign fishing near their coasts.[18] This was a consequence of industrial fishing not only near the coasts of the northern hemisphere (Iceland, Canada, United States, and Western Europe) but also off the coasts of southern hemisphere developing states, when the pickings got slimmer in the north.

Another source of tension was the fishing by U.S. and Japanese vessels for such highly migratory species such as tuna relatively near the coasts of Latin American and African states. These species usually swim thousands of miles in a yearly cycle, often approaching the coasts of a number of states. But, for the most part, they are deep-water fish and usually cannot be caught within a few miles of the beach. It requires expensive, sophisticated vessels and equipment to track and capture them, usually the kind of vessels and equipment not accessible to most poor, developing states. As a result of developing-state leaders' concern that developed-state fishermen were taking "their" resources, control of fishing became a potent North-South issue in the 1960s and thereafter. Not only did most developing coastal states not have the resources to compete with distant-water fleets, many of them did not even have the surveillance and policing resources necessary to effectively deny these interlopers access to offshore resources. At best, they could try to generate revenue from these resources through licensing fees. Most owners of tuna and other industrial vessels, backed by their national authorities in the case of privately owned U.S. and Japanese vessels, refused to pay, citing the doctrine of the freedom of the seas.[19] As a result, there ensued almost thirty years of bad relations between the United States and Latin American coastal states over the question of permission and payment of licensing fees for the right to fish.[20] During the same period, industrial fleet practices caused smoldering resentment virtually everywhere among coastal populations dependent upon local fisheries.

As long as the fishing areas in question were not firmly under the jurisdiction of the coastal states and were treated as an international commons with open access to all, it was questionable whether distant-water fishermen had a legal obligation to obey. From the viewpoint of the coastal states, the obvious answer was to change the regime and eliminate the international commons by enclosure.

Management Alternatives

Decentralized enclosure is only one of the three historical alternatives designed to solve the problem of management of exploited ocean fisheries. The first potential solution was to perfect the commons through improved cooperation. From this point of view, the problem was not the structure of the regime, but the way in which it was being abused. The ocean was being treated as a legal commons because it was a physical commons, virtually indivisible and therefore very difficult to divide. In other words, the ocean's waters flowed, and fish moved in patterns controlled only by Mother Nature; ocean fences were likely to be porous. Therefore, it made sense to try to get people to see that it was in their common interest to act for the common good.

According to proponents of voluntary restraint, the ocean could continue to be treated as a single unit (except for the narrow sovereign band directly off the coast). Moral suasion should be used to convince the exploiters of its living resources not to overstress the ecosystem by taking more than could be renewed naturally. Staying within the carrying capacity of the ecosystem is in the interest of all. Therefore, all exploiters should be persuaded to scale back their depredations so that the regime could remain both equitable and efficient. This was the premise upon which the work of the species-specific international regulatory commissions is based.

But what if an exploiter could gain more in the short run by not cooperating? Or, in the language of game theory, by defecting in a situation akin to a prisoner's dilemma?[21] We have had far too many examples from the real world of the ocean fisheries to place much faith in voluntary cooperation. More often than not the key question—allocation—was not even tackled by the many international fisheries commissions that depended upon voluntary cooperation for success. As a result they often failed to prevent the decline of important stocks.[22]

While there is considerable evidence that major world fisheries have been overfished and that stocks are stressed, this does not constitute convincing proof that the world faces a "tragedy of the commons" in the oceans. It may well be that the threat of imminent disaster is the stimulus necessary to convince states to cooperate and to grant the international commissions created to regulate separate species the powers they need to resolve the real fisheries questions. There is some indication that, thanks to stronger action on the part of some, most notably the International Whaling Commission, the commissions might have some life left.[23] The states of the world have a considerable investment in the commissions, with their infrastructures, developed and understood decision systems, scientific staffs, and expertise in the species concerned.[24] Some states might think it tragic if we turned away from our existing species-based management system.

A second alternative was to allow a central institution to enclose the world ocean. In its recent guise, this approach was called the "common heritage of mankind." Under this notion, the people of the world would claim title to the oceans of the world and their resources beyond a narrow band of national jurisdiction. In earlier centuries, the lack of appropriate technology made it impossible to operationalize *res communis*. The supporters of the common-heritage approach claimed that, using current technology, the oceans could be effectively occupied under the administration of an international organization, acting as trustee on behalf of the people of the world in the allocation of ocean resources. Being responsible for all of the world's oceans beyond traditional limits of national jurisdiction, such an organization would therefore have no difficulty in managing wandering resources wherever they wandered. It could allocate the right to fish, deciding *who* got *what* and *how much*. Its use of ocean resources would be rational. It could limit entry to the world fishery and therefore help prevent the boom-and-bust cycles of an over-exploited common-property resource. It could charge fees to fish and use part of the fees to compensate rightsholders—peoples or governments—that chose not to fish and therefore had to be compensated for forgoing a right.[25] In a dramatic speech in 1967 before the First Committee of the U.N. General Assembly, Dr. Arvid Pardo, the Ambassador from Malta, espoused just such an approach.[26] Many claim that his speech marked the informal beginning of the entire fifteen-year UNCLOS III enterprise.

The third alternative was decentralized enclosure—that is, allowing the coastal states of the world to thrust their control out into the oceans far enough to put most of the world's major fishing grounds under their domestic jurisdictions. Although these would stop short of meeting at an ocean's midpoint and leaving the ocean nothing but a series of "national lakes,"[27] they would effectively terminate the common wealth in ocean fisheries by claiming jurisdiction over most of the major fishing grounds of world importance.

Although there is no natural or scientifically determined distance from shore that can be justifiably enclosed, many states—particularly those from Latin America—chose to claim out to 200 nautical miles.[28] As we shall see, while there are important legal differences between claiming some form of limited jurisdiction and claiming general jurisdiction under the notion of sovereignty, all of the decentralized enclosure claims demanded that the coastal states control the right to regulate access to, and use of, the fishery. Decentralized enclosure did not per se solve the problem of the commons; it merely clarified the question of jurisdiction. It answered the question of *who* had the right to decide on how the area or its resources were used. It is quite possible that decentralized enclosure will merely lead to the creation of national commons.[29]

Natural resource economists claim that the key to successful management of the world fishery is control of entry. If the level of exploitation can be kept below a level that will stress the fishery and reduce the reproduction of the stocks below a sustainable yield, then the system can remain stable (within the limits of natural variability). Although all potential fishermen can appreciate the importance of avoiding boom-and-bust cycles, they do not appreciate decisions that might prevent them from fishing. If some other party gains the right to fish, that party gains the right to acquire wealth. Why should not that *other* party forgo the right to fish, particularly if the first party is an artisan fisherman, who stands to lose not only an investment in his fishing equipment, but also his way of life, even if he were to receive compensation payments as an inducement to go out of business.[30] In sum, controlling entry is exceedingly controversial—whether the oceans are managed as one, undifferentiated whole or broken up into national entities. It is easier to use the political system to shift the costs of one's behavior to other parties (e.g., kick out the foreigners and take over their share) than it is to make the difficult allocation and conservation decisions.

Decentralized enclosure as a solution to the problems of fishery management became increasingly popular after the Second World War, even though many of the real problems of managing stocks were brushed aside in the hope that reducing or eliminating competition from foreigners would allow local fishermen to thrive. As a superpower whose primary focus was preserving the security arrangements it guaranteed after 1945, the United States increasingly backed itself into a rigid defense of freedom of the seas, which allowed its navy to roam the world at will. In truth, over much of its history the United States had been of two minds on questions of freedom of the seas.[31] Indeed, during the same period when it proclaimed its navy's right to freedom of maneuver in the world's oceans, and the right of its distant-water fishing fleets to catch fish near the coasts of other states, the United States "subject[ed] to its jurisdiction and control . . . the natural resources of the subsoil and sea bed beneath the high seas but contiguous to the coasts of the United States"[32] and it claimed the right to establish fishing "conservation zones in those areas of the high seas continuous to [its] coasts . . . wherein fishing activities have been or in the future may be developed or maintained on a substantial scale."[33] Although U.S. policy-makers tried to view the Truman Proclamations as exceptions to its general rule of support for freedom of the seas, foreign decision-makers viewed them as part of the United States wanting to have its cake and eat it too. Nevertheless, the proclamation gave them—especially the Latin Americans—the wedge they needed to justify their attempts to enclose ocean space.[34] Hispanic jurists since Alexander VI's 1493 Papal Bull attempted to divide the Atlantic between Spain and Portugal 100 leagues west of the Azores have never been supporters of freedom of the seas.[35] The United States had given them even more cause to oppose it.

The new circumstances of our age, combined with the basic biological and geographic attributes of the world's fisheries, create greater hope that enclosure could be made to work effectively in the latter part of the twentieth century. Ninety percent of the world's great fisheries are concentrated within 200 miles of the coasts of states.[36] The food chain at its base required nutrients and sunlight for photosynthesis. The phytoplankton—microscopic sea plants—are converted into food for microscopic animals on a 10:1 conversion ratio that remains constant up the food chain to the higher life-forms utilized by mankind. The appropriate mixture of radiation, temperature, dissolved organic chemicals, mineral salts, and other nutrients are found mostly in waters above the continental shelves, over upwellings or in the world's major currents. As a consequence, if coastal states could control these areas within reasonable proximity to their coasts, they could control most of the world's fisheries. Even if enclosure did not, by itself, resolve the problems arising from the physical commons of the oceans, claimed enclosure proponents, the clarification of who had the jurisdiction to make critical allocation decisions was an important step forward. In any case, they asserted, a fundamental change in the regime of freedom of the seas, a reversal of direction, was necessary if humankind was to develop the tools necessary to manage the fisheries of the world.

The Exceptions That Complicate the Rule

Alas, there is no simple answer to the complex problem of managing the world's fisheries. Decentralized enclosure of near-shore areas create a different conceptual framework for ocean-resource decisions, but the basic change in framework does not, of itself, provide an appropriate direction for either efficient or equitable solution to many existing specific problems of fisheries management, and it complicates the solution of others. UNCLOS III had to cope not only with whether to change the general approach to the management of fisheries, but also with how the new approach could be used to resolve some major anomalies.

Not every coast has a major fishery. Those states that do have a major fishery off their coast obviously will gain wealth if they take advantage of decentralized enclosure, often at the expense of others who have fished there. Many fishermen from states not possessing a major coastal fishery have fished off the coasts of other states, as the phrase goes, "since time immemorial." Sometimes they have fished there virtually without competition from local fishermen. Why should these traditional users be displaced? Would their displacement be either efficient (particularly if their catch remained within a sustainable yield) or equitable?

A change in general management concepts does not alter the basic physical commonness of the world's oceans nor the shape of the oceans in relationship to the land. Not every coast is open, long, and symmetrical. Many of the world's seas are less than 400 miles wide. Some are semi-enclosed. Others are "shelf-locked," that is, to reach the open ocean, vessels from their ports must pass over the legal continental shelf of other states. Even if every state entitled to enclose the ocean space out to 200 miles from its coast was content to create an exclusive fisheries or economic zone only to the midpoint or median line in a sea less than 400 miles wide, many of the world's narrow seas would become a patchwork quilt of small national zones. Many of these would be too small to manage any but a very local, sedentary fishery. For the fishermen who exploit fisheries in narrow seas, enclosure could become an allocative and regulatory nightmare as they try to obey a wide variety of potentially conflicting rules as to who can catch how much, and by what methods.

Another problem in managing the world's fisheries arises from the inability of fish and marine mammals to read the enclosure decrees and have the decency to stay put within one zone. Alas, the creatures to be managed choose to wander where they please. This complicates management whether they choose to wander between EEZs in narrow seas or (like pelagic species such as whales and tunas) between EEZs many thousands of miles apart. If one state attempted to manage a wandering species without regard to the action of other states, chaos could ensue. Indeed, an incentive might be created to overfish a species in "your" zone before it escapes into some other state's zone or to what is left of the high seas.

A special problem arises with anadromous stocks (like salmon, which spawn in fresh water and migrate to the oceans, where they spend their adulthood, before migrating back to fresh water to spawn) and catadromous fishes (like eels which spawn in salt water and migrate to fresh water, where they spend their adulthood). These fishes live a significant part of their lives in the *internal waters* of coastal states fortunate to have them. Because these states have significant expenses maintaining the habitat of these creatures, or because they must forgo conflicting development of salmon or eel rivers and streams, they claim they are entitled to a proprietary interest in these creatures wherever they roam. Unfortunately for such states, anadromous and catadromous fishes often spend a good part of their life in salt water, either in the waters of adjacent states or in the deep ocean more than 200 miles from land.

In short, whatever basic premise for a regime is chosen by world decision-makers, there will be anomalies and exceptions that make its uniform application difficult and that exacerbate the real problems of management of the world's fisheries. In the real world it will be difficult to impose a pure form of any of the three alternatives we have examined. To resolve specialized problems, exceptions must be developed, and mixed models followed. Moreover, whatever framework is chosen, there is still a very important role for cooperation.

The Fisheries Task of UNCLOS III

It was clear even before the first substantive session of UNCLOS III in Caracas in the summer of 1974, that the main task of the conference in dealing with fisheries issues was to terminate the species approach to fisheries management. Any hope of continuing with a species approach was doomed by two fundamental factors. First, the species approach had not stopped the overexploitation of the living resources of the ocean. Second, a number of states with no faith in the 1958 species framework negotiated at UNCLOS I,[37] especially newer states of Africa and Asia, were now to join its Latin American opponents at UNCLOS III. From their point of view, the species approach merely provided a cover for the depredations of developed states off their coasts.

But it was not certain in the preparatory phases of UNCLOS III that major developed states would turn away from the species approach. Fishing interests were well entrenched in the fabric of the political systems of developed states, the United States, Japan[38] and Western and Eastern European states among them. With the muleheaded approach of many stakeholders who, when faced with strong opposition, merely dug in harder, the traditional fishing interests hoped to place a species approach in the new convention. Even the more astute representatives of distant-water interests thought that, if their states stood fast for the species approach, they could threaten deadlock for the entire negotiation and, at worst, retain their privileges should the conference fail. On the other hand, many developed states had to contend with cross-cutting pressures in their domestic politics: they had not only distant-water local fisheries interests but also security and nonrenewable-resource interests in near-shore areas to protect.[39]

Another critical factor in changing the political environment was a new manner of expressing the "territorialist" position that helped make enclosure more acceptable to skeptics. A number of new Latin American jurists and statesmen had redefined the basic goals of enclosure, which was now being described in more moderate terms as "patrimonial sea" or "exclusive economic zone," and no longer as the 200-mile territorial sea the major maritime states had fought off in 1958. Enclosure forces now claimed sovereignty over offshore resources, rather than a complete sovereignty over ocean areas that threatened the navigation, cable-laying, and other rights of outsiders.[40] This refinement in the 200-mile position, plus the depredations of industrial fleets, made the case for enclosure more cogent in a number of developed states with major near-shore fisheries that were in trouble. The handwriting was on the wall.

By 1971–72, it was obvious to all observers not blindly wedded to maintaining freedom of the seas that the political climate of the upcoming UNCLOS III would be hostile to the freedom of the seas and to a species approach as conceptual cores for the new fisheries regime. Although the decision rule of the upcoming UNCLOS III had not been decided upon before the opening meeting in Caracas of the formal conference, it was obvious in the preparatory meetings of the U.N. Seabed Committee that neither position could command a majority of delegations likely to attend UNCLOS III. Moreover, the states that previously supported the old regime barely had the votes[41] to block only the most extreme form of 200-mile territorial sea proposal.[42] While optimistic negotiators might believe they could turn matters around if the decision were to be made by consensus, they would be swimming against the tide.

By 1973, the tuna industry advisor to the U.S. delegation was informing representatives of his industry ''to expect a change in the U.S.A. position on fisheries from the 'species approach' to that of a zonal approach.''[43] The ''zonal approach'' was the price to be paid in a trade-off for a 12-mile territorial sea and a right of transit passage through straits. But even though the superpowers announced before the Caracas session that they had switched their support to a 200-mile EEZ as part of what was to be the conference's central package, establishing a 200-mile EEZ was far from a trivial bargaining problem. The fisheries component of that decision can be broken out for examination to see how much fishing issues contributed to the overall package solution.

Changing the framework appeared to be easy. Working out the details of how enclosure would work was very difficult. In some respects, especially in narrow seas and in areas where claims overlapped, many observers complained that the language negotiated was maddeningly vague and therefore unsatisfactory. But three tasks had to be undertaken in the negotiations to implement a 200-mile EEZ. How well they were managed will be shown in the following analysis. First, the question of the termination of the rights of stakeholders who would be displaced by a territorially-based regime had to be tackled. In particular, did a general conveyance of jurisdiction give the coastal state the right to displace foreign fishermen? Second, the question of highly migratory species and anadromous stocks had to be addressed. Were there to be genuine exceptions to the rule of enclosure? Third, those potentially disaccommodated by a change in regime and who could prevent agreement under a consensus or near-consensus decision rule had to be provided some quid pro quo for their willingness to agree. That included geographically disadvantaged states, as well as opposite and adjacent states in narrow seas.

The EEZ—A 200-Mile Fisheries Zone

Despite the pressures upon world leaders to resolve fishing jurisdiction disputes, there was no change in direction for the fisheries regime until a number of parallel, more comprehensive changes had occurred. These included the desire of some states to resolve jurisdictional questions relating to the ownership and management of offshore nonliving resources. In addition, the heads of delegations of the major powers made it clear that protecting the movement rights of both their civil and military vessels would be an objective of the highest priority at the forthcoming conference.[44]

Although some developed maritime states put up a spirited defense of the rights of their citizens to take advantage of freedom of the seas, once it was obvious that UNCLOS III would be convened formally in 1973 and would get down to substantive business in 1974, vocal supporters of freedom of the seas (and therefore freedom of fishing) had to decide on the salience of the various interests they had to protect and how they were to protect them. It was obvious that, in terms of a negotiating strategy for a conference whose decision-making mode would be consensus (or as it turned out, near-consensus), the only solution was a grand package composed of favorable outcomes on items of high salience, traded off for less than optimal outcomes on issues of lesser salience. The rights of distant-water fishermen became a matter of lesser salience, however difficult it was to explain the switch to them, especially to those who accompanied the delegations as advisers.

The key ingredient that made the switch possible was the development of the concept of the Exclusive Economic Zone (EEZ). It was a set of ideas that had to be fleshed out by legal theorists and negotiators in the Ad Hoc and Permanent Seabed Committees so that it could be turned into a formula during the detail phase of the negotiations. Its proponents called it sui generis. We will leave to the legal theorists what they had in mind in so describing it. From a bargaining point of view, the concept of an exclusive economic zone had the merit of being a halfway house between allowing the coastal state to sustain a singe-purpose or limited claim to control of an offshore resource and allowing the coastal state to sustain a comprehensive claim over the area, including sovereignty over both resources and area per se. The EEZ idea evolved into a zone in which there was a balance between "the rights and jurisdiction of the coastal state and the rights and freedoms of Other States."[45] It allowed the coastal state, in an area up to 200 miles "from the baseline from which the breadth of the territorial sea is measured,"[46] to exercise sovereign rights over the natural resources, living and nonliving, and jurisdiction over marine scientific research done there, as well as authority to enact provisions to protect the marine environment.[47] It specifically exempted from coastal state control navigation and overflight as well as the laying of submarine cables.[48]

While none of the rights conveyed to the coastal state pleased the true believers in freedom of the seas, the exemptions to these rights looked like a form of damage control to major developed states with multiple interests. Moreover, as observers of the bargaining process subsequently discovered when they looked at the area, quantity, and quality of resources put under national jurisdictions, the major developed states with open coasts turned out to be the big resource winners at the conference.[49] At the same time, although they sustained losses on marine science, for example, and some were not particularly enthusiastic about conceding a 12-mile territorial sea, supporters of freedom of movement lost little in the bargaining from the trade-off engineered. It was a masterstroke, as we can see if we look at the shift in the distribution of states' preferences between the first and second time periods plotted below in figure 5.1.

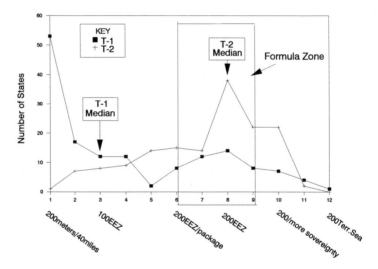

Figure 5.1:   Ocean Enclosure: The 200-mile EEZ

The switch from freedom of the seas to enclosure of waters out to 200 miles took place with remarkable rapidity. During the early debates on the general question of freedom versus enclosure (T-1), we saw a unimodal distribution with a long tail that favored the retention of freedom of the seas as a core concept. The long tail composed of those not favoring freedom of the seas meant that, while there was a good deal of opposition to freedom of the seas, there was no coherent concept around which the opposition was prepared to rally during the preliminary negotiations. Further education and bargaining was necessary before states could be convinced that the EEZ would work for them.

By the second time period (T-2), the distribution of preferences had swung the other way; there was a unimodal distribution with a peak at the 200-mile EEZ, and a long tail straggling back to the basic freedom of the seas position on resource jurisdiction questions. Although the data show that the 200-mile EEZ proposal had a substantial majority by T-2 (1974–75), it did not enjoy near-consensus support. Nevertheless, the formula zone remained between ranks 6 and 9, and very few further concessions were necessary to bring it to consensus by the time the Revised Single Negotiating Text (RSNT) was promulgated.

Why did the opposition to enclosure melt away so quickly? One reason is that, even in the first time period, the forces supporting narrow-resource jurisdiction were not all that firm on propping up a key traditional component of freedom of the seas—the freedom to fish. If we look again at the general enclosure debate and use as data only those remarks that relate directly to fishing, we see a very different picture.

Figure 5.2 uses essentially the same conflict variable and range of options as figure 4.10, but with remarks and proposals that relate to the fishing problems alone.

The possible positions range from proposals that would restrict national sovereign jurisdiction over fisheries to a 12-mile territorial sea, or a combined territorial sea and fisheries contiguous zone, at rank 1, to proposals favoring the classic 200-mile territorial sea at rank 12. Scaled close to the 200-mile territorial sea (rank 11) were suggestions to create a fishing zone that would give coastal states sovereign rights over fisheries in the waters over the continental margin. Only because the continental margin is usually less broad than 200 miles was this judged less extreme than a 200-mile territorial sea. At rank 8, we placed remarks that identified an EEZ as primarily a zone useful for conveying fisheries jurisdiction to the coastal state. At rank 7, we placed the statements of supporters of a fishing zone to the end of the continental shelf. These remarks often appeared to concede more general-purpose rights to coastal states. The only fallback for the narrow-jurisdiction forces seemed to be conceding a fishing zone out to 50–70 miles from the coast.

As we noted, the results are quite different when we look at the fisheries aspect of the debate alone. Figure 5.3 makes clear that, from the beginning of the preliminary negotiations, there was very little support for the fishing status quo.

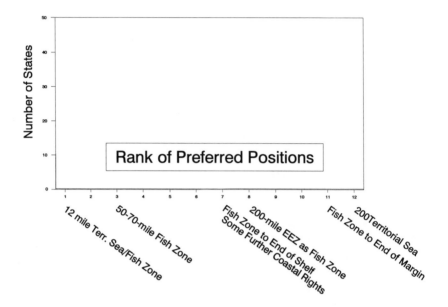

Figure 5.2:   Fishing-Zone Delimitation

Most of the states that participated in the Ad Hoc and Permanent Seabed Committee debates expressed preferences on fishing jurisdiction that clustered in the middle of the figure. In other words, it appears as if we caught them in the middle of making up their minds. They had moved away from support of narrow fishing jurisdiction, but most were not yet ready to fully support a 200-mile economic zone. Since proposals that would have created a fishing zone of less than 200 miles never got beyond the preliminary talking stage and were therefore not realistic bargaining positions, it seems reasonable to believe that the median of 5.6 was not an indication of states seeking a compromise position short of a 200-mile EEZ.

At the same time, as shown by the distribution and the median of T-1 in figure 5.1, there appears to be a significant support for a conservative outcome to the general question of enclosure or a continuation of freedom. This masks a shift that was already underway. In any case, from the beginning of the conference, it was obvious to all but stakeholders in distant-water fisheries that the world's states were ready for a change of regime. The exemptions from sovereign control that the patrimonialists were willing to accept to distinguish the EEZ from a territorial sea went far to assure those who clust-

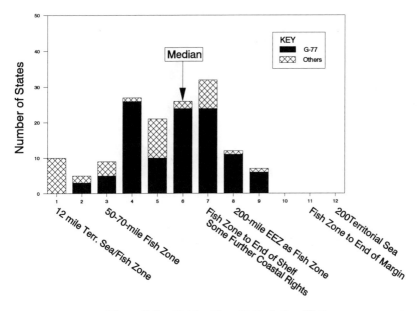

Figure 5.3:   Fishing Zone Delimitation (T-1)

ered in the first time period at rank 1. It indicated that their concern about the possibility of coastal-state interference with movement rights was understood and addressed in a 200-mile EEZ that did not threaten movement rights. As a result, in T-2, on both the general question of enclosure and the particular questions of fisheries, there was near-consensus over a 200-mile EEZ. It seems as if the fishing component of the overall problem provided a forcing function for decision. In T-1, as our pairs comparisons show, the supporters of narrow fisheries jurisdiction might, at best, have stalemated the conference if their opponents had been willing to support only a 200-mile territorial sea with no rights and no freedom for other states. Figure 5.4 shows that, by T-2, there was no hope of stopping the 200-mile EEZ. The distribution in T-2 is single-peaked with a small tail. Only some 11–19 states remain in support of fishing zones narrower than 200 miles. There was no question that the 200-mile EEZ was a winner and would find itself in the negotiating texts and the convention itself. In fact, the degree of single-peakedness tells us that the EEZ formula zone was narrow and would not allow for attempts at watering it down, however strenuous. Except for true drafting changes, the world community had opted for an enclosure regime for near-shore waters. As we

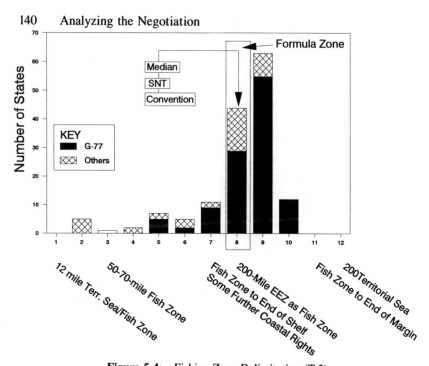

Figure 5.4:   Fishing-Zone Delimitation (T-2)

can see below, what remained to be bargained was whether direct concessions on fisheries access and management could be added to the other rights and freedoms that outside users might enjoy within 200 miles of the coasts of other states.

Before we turn to the bargaining on attempts to soften the impact of enclosure on fishing, we should ask which groups of states moved to strengthen enclosure? Since the west coast Latin American states had long advocated enclosure—thought by opponents to be the most extreme form of territorial sea—were they able to drive the rest of the Group of 77 (G77) into making enclosure a G77 position? As figure 5.5 demonstrates, enclosure in order to control fisheries certainly did become a position of the South, even if defense of fishing freedom was *not* the position of a solid North.

As we can see in figure 5.5 (a), the states of the developing world did not begin the negotiations behind enclosure, averaging in 1967–70 between ranks 2.5 and 3.5. But they moved up consistently in the remaining three time periods to support treatment of the 200-mile EEZ as an area in which the coastal state would have sovereign jurisdiction over fisheries. Their shift in position

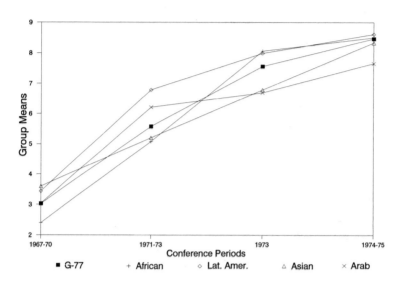

Figure 5.5(a):   Fishing-Zone Delimitation: G-77 Positions (P1–P4)

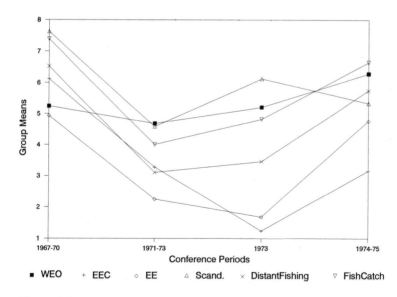

Figure 5.5(b):   Fishing-Zone Delimitation: Other Group Positions (P1–P4)

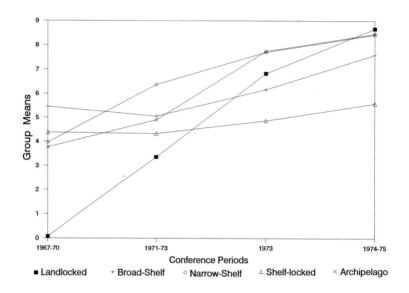

Figure 5.5(c):   Fishing-Zone Delimitation: Geographic Group Positions (P1–P4)

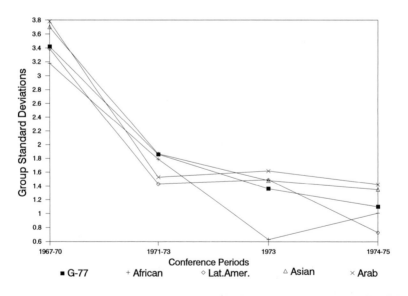

Figure 5.5(d):   Fishing-Zone Delimitation: G-77 Standard Deviations (P1–P4)

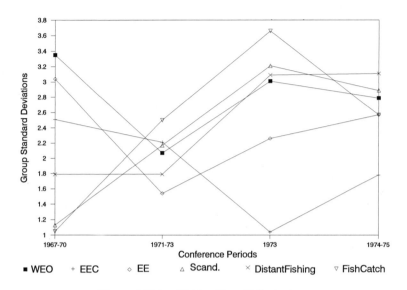

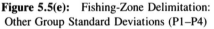

Figure 5.5(e):   Fishing-Zone Delimitation:
Other Group Standard Deviations (P1–P4)

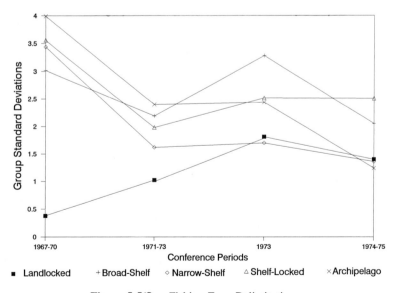

Figure 5.5(f):   Fishing-Zone Delimitation:
Geographic Group Standard Deviations (P1–P4)

was matched in figure 5.5 (d) by increasing solidarity over time. The Latin Americans were most united in favor of enclosure, followed by the Africans, with the Asian and Arab groups lagging slightly—but only slightly—behind. No group in the last time period had a standard deviation of more than 1.5 on a scale of 12. The South was solid.

Other groups showed much less unity. The Western European and Others (WEO), European Community (EEC), Eastern European (EE), and Scandinavians (Scand) groups all had members who espoused positions ranging from support of the status quo (rank 1) to support of a considerable degree of enclosure, making them average between ranks 5 and 8 in the first time period (P-1), as shown in figure 5.5 (b). In other words, there was no united North position in support of the status quo on fishing rights from the beginning of the UNCLOS III process. In figure 5.5 (e), we can see that the WEO, and even the EE, groups were poorly disciplined and had high standard deviations early on. Although they seemed to dip down to near rank 1 in the third time period (P-3), many of the developed states groups broke back toward support of moderate enclosure in P-4, albeit with some reluctance on the part of the EEC and Eastern Europeans. What drove the WEO position was the split among EEC members, as well as significant support for enclosure by the Scandinavian states.

Figure 5.5 (b) also shows the positions of two noncaucusing common-interest groups—distant-water fishing states (DistantFishing) and the largest fish-catching states (FishCatch). Many of the states that fit into the distant-water grouping were active members of different caucusing groups, among them WEO, EEC, and EE. The major fish-catching states by tonnage include not only the distant-water states but also those states that have major near-shore fisheries such as Canada, Iceland, Spain, China, India, Norway, Peru, and Chile. An obvious hypothesis concerning the behavior of the largest fish-catching states would be that, because of the presence of coastal fishing states among them, this artificial group would break strong toward a 200-mile EEZ. This hypothesis turned out to be validated by the data. But, even if it was necessary for the superpowers to announce their support of a 200-mile EEZ in 1973 for the opposition to enclosure to fall apart, it was also necessary that most of the other distant-waters states move toward support of fishing enclosure as well.

What completed the rout and assured victory for those who wished to put fishing under coastal state jurisdiction was that the landlocked states marched steadily toward support for the 200-mile EEZ as shown in figure 5.5 (c). The landlocked states began the negotiations as the most ardent advocates of the status quo, a position consistent with their oft-expressed fear about being "locked" into their continental fastnesses. By P-4, they were fully in the camp of the enclosure advocates. Throughout the negotiations, at each shift in their position, they maintained substantial solidarity as a caucusing group. Obviously, they thought they had a deal with a promised trade-off of special fishing privileges for themselves in the new EEZ's of their coastal neighbors.

The shelf-locked states were less impressed with what they might get from the broader-shelved states that held the outside geographic position. Many shelf-locked states have developed fisheries near the coasts of neighboring states. They had a great deal to lose in the rush toward coastal-state control of the fisheries directly offshore. As a common-interest group they split badly. Only Finland, Yugoslavia, Sudan, and Yemen strongly, and Sweden and Ethiopia more tepidly, supported enclosure. The rest opposed it. Accordingly, as figure 5.5 (f) shows, the group had a high standard deviation.

In summary, we have learned a number of things by looking at the fisheries aspects of enclosure. First, a fisheries consideration was the driving force in successfully shifting the general regime toward enclosure. Second, by 1975, the EEZ was a settled issue; details had to be worked out, but for all practical purposes the thrust of the remaining negotiations was set. Enclosure would be the prevailing rule, and all the discontented could do was bargain to create exceptions to the general rule. Third, enclosure was a South issue, but not a North issue. Fourth, opposition broke not only because the United States and the Soviet Union announced for the 200-mile EEZ, but also because the land-locked states decided to support enclosure, while the fishing states did not put up a unified opposition. Finally, only the shelf-locked states remained opposed to enclosure, but they too split badly.

Controlling Foreign Fishermen

Much of the time of delegates to UNCLOS III was taken up with working out detailed provisions for fisheries management within the framework of the enclosure regime that was decided upon early in UNCLOS III's sessions. While many states were willing to concede a shift in the general regime, they stubbornly attempted to protect the specific rights of their fishermen. For a number of states, this meant protecting the right of their fishermen to continue to fish in areas that would come under another state's jurisdiction when 200-mile EEZs were implemented. Often, the first line of defense was to concede the exclusive right of the coastal state to *manage* the stocks relevant to the coastal-state fishermen, but *not* the exclusive right to *allocate* the catch to whomever the coastal state pleased. At times, states disaccommodated by the new regime interpreted enclosure to mean that the coastal state had a right only to a preferential portion of the catch, but not a right to monopolize the entire catch.

One gambit in the attempt to tame enclosure was to insert specific language in the Convention that would protect the existing rights of foreign fishermen (grandfathering), thereby giving the coastal state only the right to exclude new entrants to a fishery,[50] or least requiring compensation if existing rights were phased out. If a general grandfather clause proved to be unacceptable to coastal states, a fallback was to insert language that protected the rights of specific groups or categories of states (e.g., all developing states that had historically fished in the areas which would not become the EEZs of other states, or states that were highly dependent on fisheries for a significant proportion of their animal-protein needs, or states that were geographically dependent). A variant of this approach was a proposal to create a regional zone in which the states of the region would have a preferential right to fish.

Variants or modifications of enclosure were proposed not only because total enclosure could potentially eliminate existing stakeholders, but also because, even as the core concept of the new regime, enclosure could not, by itself, resolve all problems relating to wandering resources. Highly migratory species that wander great distances throughout their life cycle are especially difficult to manage on the basis of a strict territorial approach. In the past, a number of species had been managed on the basis of their species characteristics, especially highly migratory species such as tuna. Representatives of states with interests in these species fought hard to have special arrangements made for them. But with the advent of enclosure, other species or stocks would be crossing new national boundaries. These "transboundary" stocks also needed to have their management and allocation arrangements clarified.[51]

In the remainder of this chapter, we will concentrate on the attempt to impose duties and obligations on the coastal state limiting its right to allocate arbitrarily within the new EEZ.[52] In particular, we will examine the effort to force the coastal state to justify its allocation decisions in terms of conservation principles or an "objective" standard of utilization. The process of allocating living resources has two steps: first, establishing the "allowable catch," that is, the total biomass that is to be caught; and, second, determining who will have the right to catch what part of the biomass. We will deal with the questions of how much and who in a single conflict issue. We are particularly concerned here with the right of the coastal state to limit or eliminate access of foreign fishermen to the coastal state's 200-mile EEZ. In the effort either to limit or to expand coastal-state duties and obligations, many ideas or proposals were introduced. These were scaled as indicated. At the

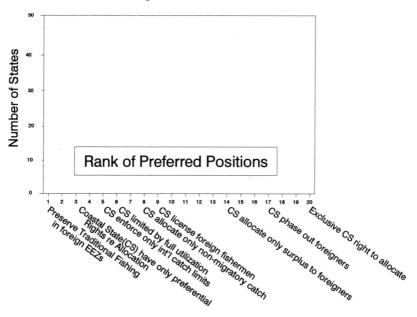

Figure 5.6:   Foreign-Fishing Access to 200-mile EEZ

low end (toward rank 1), are concepts and proposals that would restrict the coastal state's right to limit access of foreigners. The most restrictive would create a grandfather clause to freeze the existing rights of fishermen to fish. Under some proposals, foreign fishermen would be guaranteed a portion or percentage of the catch, and the coastal state could determine and allocate the catch only of those species that were not fully exploited. A fallback from the full protection of existing rights of foreign fishermen was placed at rank 3. Under this notion, the coastal state would be permitted the right to establish the size of the catch, but its own fishermen would be given, at best, only a preferential right to participate in the fishery.

If distant-fishing states could not guarantee the rights of their stakeholders to continue to fish at previous catch levels in the new EEZs of other states, they might at least provide some second-best protection for their interests. Proposals forcing the coastal state to make and enforce allocation rules that were internationally determined, and therefore presumably not arbitrary, were placed at rank 5.

The United States, with its schizophrenic attitudes on fisheries, wanted to protect both its conservation work associated with the species approach and its distant-fishing interests, especially tuna. At rank 6, it introduced conservation and full utilization as requirements that the coastal state would have to meet in its allocation decisions (what survived and was incorporated into the convention was called "optimum" utilization). Again, the idea was to force the coastal state to justify its actions on rational grounds, and thereby to limit arbitrariness. Full utilization meant that the coastal state could close off a fishery to foreigners if the catchable portion of the stock was fully utilized by domestic fishermen. First, the coastal state must justify its decision on the basis of scientific evidence in establishing the catch limit. If local fishermen were not taking or were not capable of taking, all of the allowable catch, the coastal state had to permit foreign fisherman to catch the surplus.

At rank 8 were placed proposals that would allow the coastal state to determine and allocate the allowable catch, even with a conservation and full-utilization requirement, but only of nonmigratory species. Migratory species would be governed by a separate set of rules. More freedom for the coastal states would be allowed under the proposal at rank 9. Here, the coastal state would be allowed to determine the catch and allocate it, if it guaranteed that it would license distant-water fishermen to fish in its EEZ.

Even more favorable to the coastal state were proposals, placed at rank 14, that made it clear that it was the right of the coastal state to set the catch limit, but that foreign fishermen could, at least, be given access to the surplus. At rank 17, proposals gave coastal states the right to establish the allowable catch and allocate it if the coastal state would guarantee the continuation of traditional distant-water fishing for a known transitional period. After the transitional period expired, the coastal state would be fully entitled to make conservation and allocation decisions as it pleased. The proposal at rank 20 would allow the coastal state complete discretion in making quota and allocation decisions, granting the coastal state full sovereign powers over the living resources found in the 200-mile EEZ.

Until 1973, the contest raged between the pro- and anti-coastal-state forces, as we can see in figure 5.7. Distribution is weakly bimodal. Clearly there were two camps, albeit of different strengths and intensities. At this stage the anti-coastal-state forces seemed better organized. They favored giving the coastal state only a preferential right to allocate surplus fish in the EEZ to its own citizens. Those who wanted to give coastal states stronger powers to control foreign fishing in their new EEZs had not rallied about any specific language. Even this early in the UNCLOS III negotiation, the forces that wanted to accelerate creeping jurisdiction into a gallop were rather substantial. They included a number of states that had already unilaterally tried

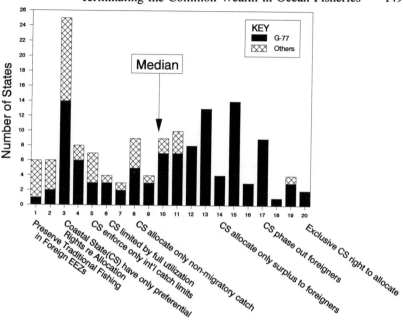

Figure 5.7:   Foreign-Fishing Access to 200-mile EEZ (T-1)

to restrict foreign fishing in waters near their coasts. While there were many states that wanted to strengthen considerably the hand of the coastal state under the notion of a 200-mile EEZ, few were advocating totally unrestricted rights of the coastal state to act without regard to previous stakeholders' rights. Only seven states clustered at ranks 18–20 in T-1.

The median of 9.9 on a scale of 20 could be interpreted as showing the need for compromise. Compromise was indeed needed, since there was still strong resistance to consenting to the termination of existing fishing rights. But it was evident that, with the substantial support the patrimonialists were receiving during the early negotiations, all the anti-coastal-state forces could do was dig in their heels to try to prevent the conference from going too far in granting new powers to the coastal states under a new regime. Hence, the emphasis was not on preventing a change in jurisdiction, but rather on preventing arbitrariness in a new regime. The losers wanted to make their loss minimally acceptable, and the winners did not want careless negotiation on details to undermine their victory. Neither had near-consensus support on this issue early on, or even relatively late in the negotiation.

By T-2, the positions of states had shifted considerably, although there was still no consensus or near-consensus in 1975.

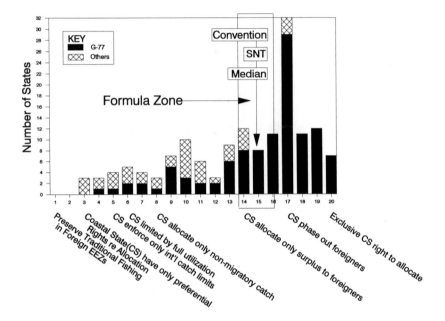

Figure 5.8:   Foreign-Fishing Access to 200-mile EEZ (T-2)

Some 30–40 states were still unhappy with allowing strong coastal-state control over foreign fishing in the EEZ. Despite this long tail, figure 5.8 shows that the tide had turned, and there was now a substantial majority for strong controls over foreign fishing. Distribution is essentially unimodal. Notice that much of the opposition to strong coastal state rights to determine the catch and allocate it is from states outside the Group of 77. The Group of 77 was by no means unanimous on this issue, and in 1975 there was still a minority that had to be persuaded in the next phase to go along with stronger coastal state controls over traditional fishing. They were not willing, like other opponents, to cave into the maximum preferred position of the pro-coastal state forces. Like the rest of the opposition to strong coastal-state controls, their positions were scattered across the spectrum, and they had no strong counterposition to rally around. This pattern of digging in heels dominates the detailed phase of the negotiation. It was to force the proponents of unequivocal coastal-state sovereignty and fisheries management to include language providing some degree of protection for distant-fishing interests in the negotiating documents, and ultimately in the convention.

The forecast was a good predictor of the outcome, and it also showed essentially why the coastal states could not sweep all before them in designing one of the key operational provisions of the 200-mile EEZ. The language of the Single Negotiating Text (SNT) was quite close to the surplus-only position where the median fell. Article 50 (1) of the SNT stated that the coastal-state could determine the allowable catch.[53] The purpose of granting such powers was supposedly the maintenance or restoration of populations of harvestable species, addressed in Article 50 (3). Article 51 went on to require the coastal state to determine its catch capacity, and where this was less than the entire allowable catch, to give access to the surplus, by agreement, to fishermen of other states.

Although the language in Articles 61 and 62 was improved through the further stages of negotiation of the RSNT and the ICNT, the core concepts that made their way into the agreement were essentially the same as in the SNT. The problem in the next seven years of the negotiation was to convince the majority to accept what had been obvious in 1975—that there would have to be some limits on the coastal state written into the treaty to prevent it from arbitrarily eliminating all distant-water fishing rights.

The provision permitting the coastal state to establish the allowable catch and giving foreign fisherman access only to a surplus it would declare is one of the most important provisions of the UNCLOS III Convention in terms of its impact upon ocean management. There were very distinctive positions on the issue assumed by caucusing and common-interest groups, which showed who wanted what, who would be disaccommodated by various degrees of enclosure, and therefore who would force the compromises necessary for agreement.

The general question of the shape and nature of the 200-mile EEZ, along with the problems of delimitation of the territorial sea and the right of transit through straits used for international navigation, were discussed in the preliminary negotiations in the General Assembly and its Ad Hoc and permanent Seabed Committees, but the details of fisheries management were not discussed seriously until after 1971. As a result, we tracked group preferences only over three time periods. The patterns are revealing. As a whole, the Group of 77 began supporting relatively strong coastal-state powers in 1971–72. Figure 5.9 (a) shows how it, and its constituent groups, moved toward support for even stronger coastal powers to set catch limits and allocate fish in 1973, and still stronger powers by 1975. The Group of 77 ended 1975 united, but there was a considerable spread of preferences among its

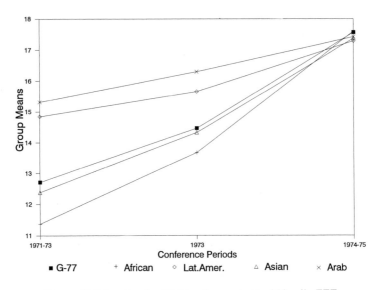

Figure 5.9(a):   Foreign-Fishing Access to the 200-mile EEZ:
G-77 Positions (P1–P3)

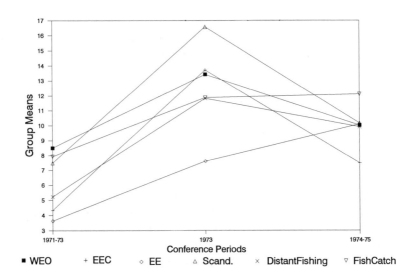

Figure 5.9(b):   Foreign-Fishing Access to the 200-mile EEZ:
Other Group Positions (P1–P3)

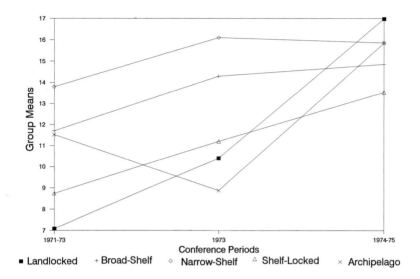

Figure 5.9(c):   Foreign-Fishing Access to the 200-mile EEZ:
Geographic Group Positions (P1–P3)

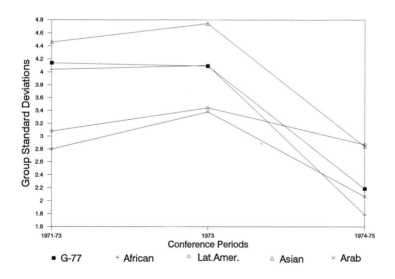

Figure 5.9(d):   Foreign-Fishing Access to the 200-mile EEZ:
G-77 Standard Deviations (P1–P3)

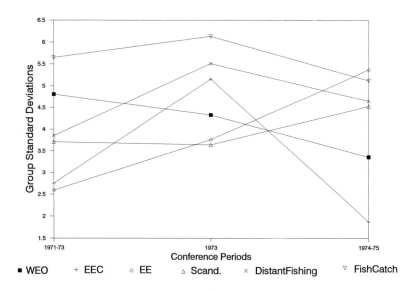

Figure 5.9(e):   Foreign-Fishing Access to the 200-mile EEZ:
Other Group Standard Deviations (P1–P3)

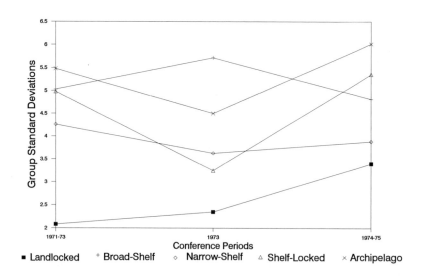

Figure 5.9(f):   Foreign-Fishing Access to the 200-mile EEZ:
Geographic Group Standard Deviations (P1–P3)

constituent groups when the serious discussions began. The least enthusiastic were the Africans, probably because it took them some time to work out an accommodation among themselves to resolve problems between coastal states and their landlocked neighbors. The Asian group also started with average support for a relatively weak coastal-state position, and later moved toward the Group of 77 consensus for strong coastal-state rights over foreign fishing. They too had to resolve internal problems between coastal-rights advocates and the substantial numbers of shelf-locked and semi-enclosed sea-state members, whose fishermen had historically fished in waters off the coasts of their neighbors.

As we can see in figure 5.9 (d), the Group of 77 and its constituent groups were the most disciplined of all groups measured, whether caucusing or common interest. By 1975, with an average standard deviation of less than 2.4 on a scale of 20, its members knew what they wanted. But they did not get all they wanted. In the SNT and later conference negotiating documents, they clearly were willing to go along with a compromise. Figure 5.9 (d) shows how far they had to go in scaling back their preferences in order to gain an arrangement that would meet the hurdle of a consensus-based decision.

Figure 5.9 (c) confirms our assessment of both why the Group of 77 was united by 1975, and why it had to compromise. The landlocked states, mostly developing states, started out as strong opponents of a coastal-state monopoly over the right to fish. But they moved smoothly in the next two time periods to become enthusiastic supporters of strong coastal rights. Since, as seen in figure 5.9 (f), they moved over time in very disciplined fashion, it is reasonable to infer that they had worked out a deal with their coastal neighbors, and expected to be compensated for their support (we will confirm this later). On the other hand, the shelf-locked states, also reluctant early on in supporting strong coastal-state control of fishing, seemed to move reluctantly toward stronger coastal-state powers, but not to the point of excluding foreign fishermen. By 1975, their average position (at rank 13) was slightly below the final outcome—requiring the coastal state to make any surplus available to foreign fishermen. However, the shelf-locked states were not united, as their high standard deviation at P-3 demonstrates.

Other geographic groups behaved according to their known or assumed interests. As shown in figure 5.9 (c), narrow-shelf open-ocean states (the so-called C-E-P states among them) and broad-shelf states started in 1971 supporting relatively strong coastal-state controls and moved over the next two time periods to stronger coastal-state control of foreign fishing. Archipelago states whose interest was in controlling fishing between their islands also moved (although with an unexplained dip in the middle period) from a relatively to quite strong coastal-state power position in 1975. However, with the exception of the landlocked and narrow-shelf states, the geographic groups were not notably disciplined on this issue, as we can see in figure 5.9 (f).

Opposition to the coastal-state right to exclude foreign fishermen from the new EEZs was concentrated in the European-based caucusing and common-interest groups. The pattern in figure 5-9 (b) shows a move from allowing the coastal state to enforce only internationally sanctioned rules to allowing it to license foreign fishermen, but not to exclude them from the newly created EEZs (rank 9). Even though the Soviet Union announced support for the 200-mile EEZ in 1973–74, the Eastern European group as a whole fought a stubborn rearguard action. Members with distant fisheries tried to protect their investment, but landlocked or shelf-locked members were concerned that enclosure would lock them further into a geographically disadvantaged position, with less access than ever to the world's oceans. Their reluctance eventually forced the majority to accommodate them.

A number of lessons can be drawn from the bargaining over coastal-state controls of foreign fishing under the new enclosure regime. The most cogent lesson is the importance of the language implementing the conceptual framework of a new regime. The conceptual core idea of a new regime (the formula) can establish a sweeping new principle, but if its supporters are careless or compromise too readily in drafting its language, the core idea can be undermined substantially. On the other hand, if a new regime's supporters are too rigid and unwilling to accommodate the losers to some degree, they can drive the losers out of the negotiation.

How much can be conceded and still keep the fundamental thrust of a new regime is a matter of considerable delicacy. The losers must be willing to come over in a consensus process. But did the winners in UNCLOS III give away too much? This is a question that must always haunt winning negotiators. Only future events will prove whether their judgment was correct. The losing negotiators have an even more difficult task—convincing stakeholders who are going to suffer a loss that everything possible was done to minimize the loss and that therefore they should accept the outcome.

The question of the right of coastal states to establish catch limits and to allocate the catch ended in agreement. Duties and obligations were added to make it appear that the coastal state could not act arbitrarily. However, it was clear that the big winners were the coastal states. Enclosure would provide them powerful rights to manage and allocate the living resources of the 200-mile EEZ. The EEZ was not going to be a hollow shell, but coastal states did have to concede that, after establishing the allowable catch and determining that their own fishermen were not capable of taking it all, they had to grant foreign fishermen access to the surplus. Theoretically, this might reintroduce common-pool problems.[54] While the obligation to open the EEZ to foreign states may be seen by some as a insult to the sovereign rights of the coastal state, the coastal state still had the power to decide. Foreign fishermen were at the mercy of the coastal state to "act fairly."[55]

The patterns of group support and movement closely followed those on the more general question of establishing the 200-mile EEZ, but revealed what arrangements between groups had to be made in order to reach closure on the issue. The Group of 77 supported increased coastal-state powers and its support got substantially stronger, with dissent within the group diminishing. Geographic groups behaved as expected, with one important exception. Open-ocean states—the broad-shelf states and narrow-shelf states—were strong supporters of coastal-state rights to control foreign fishing. The shelf-locked were considerably more reluctant. Initially, the landlocked states were the most opposed, but a trade-off was arranged and their opposition turned to support. (This will be examined in the next issue variable.) Although support for limiting coastal-state control came most from Northern groups, both East and West sectors of the North were too split on this issue to characterize it as principally a North-South issue. Ironically, though the patrimonialists and the territorialists held firm on the question of who should decide on fishing in the EEZ, some of their opponents, such as the United States, took advantage of the coastal state's right to exclude distant-water fishing in their EEZs.[56]

Landlocked/Geographically Disadvantaged-State Fishing Rights in the 200-mile EEZ

To establish a new international regime means more than promulgating an idea that can be turned into a formula and inducing or forcing states to take it or leave it. Even if most states accept its advantages, there will be enough dissenters to require at least cosmetic, and perhaps significant, adjustments to achieve agreement. Often, the judgment as to whether the adjustments are cosmetic or actually meaningful can be made from examining the process of the negotiation itself. At other times, an adequate judgment cannot be made from examining either the language or the process of agreement, but rather must wait until there is an attempt to implement the language of agreement.

We stand somewhere between these two points on the question of whether landlocked and geographically disadvantaged states (LL/GDS) got significant or cosmetic adjustments as the price for their acquiescence in the establishment of the exclusive economic zone. We can examine both the process of trying to agree on meaningful rights for landlocked and geographically disadvantaged states in the 200-mile EEZ and the history of EEZ implementation (since many states began implementing the EEZ soon after the United States and the Soviet Union announced for them in 1973–74). In both respects, although it is too early for a final judgment, the effort of the landlocked and geographically disadvantaged to wrest ironclad guarantees of access for their citizens to the resources of the 200-mile EEZ seems to have failed. They pushed the coastal-state forces hard, but all they got was a set of cosmetic changes. The decision as to who would have any real access to the EEZ was left in the hands of the coastal state.

The history of landlocked states (LL) in twentieth-century ocean politics has been characteristic of states operating with serious disadvantages. They were have-not states burdened by lack of access to the sea. They tended to be poor and nonindustrial, in part because their distance from the oceans of the world increased their transportation costs and made participation in the world economy difficult. Although the landlocked states comprised only 8.5 percent of the world's land area and only 4 percent of its population, the group included approximately one-fifth of the world's states, mostly small and weak.[57]

Politically, their numbers meant that, where decision was by majority or consensus, it would have been difficult to ignore them if they chose to make demands. But they could not go it alone in a parliamentary diplomatic setting. Even if the old rule of two-thirds present and voting prevailed (as it did in UNCLOS I and UNCLOS II and formally, if consensus failed, in UNCLOS III), the landlocked states needed allies to form a blocking one-third. They had a number of potential allies—the shelf-locked states and the semienclosed sea states. If we remove overlapping sets of characteristics, the combined group—the LL/GDS—did not form an automatic majority. To form a majority position on rules favoring their interests, they needed to develop alliances with other interest and caucusing groups. Or they could act as spoilers and try to force concessions to the general rule of a regime that was going in a direction antithetical to their general interests. Both tactics were explored at UNCLOS I, II, and III, but mostly the LL/GDS group, after failing to forge an alliance with developed ocean-using states publicly opposed to enclosure, was forced to try for special concessions in a regime that was galloping toward enclosure.

A number of ocean states questioned why landlocked states were even invited to the United Nations Conferences of the Law of the Sea, since they had no coasts, no ports, and usually no ocean-using capability. They came because they insisted upon not being left out, and because they had vital interests to protect. They came to UNCLOS I in 1958 to try to gain a guaranteed right of access to the sea. Unfortunately for landlocked states, their coastal neighbors often insisted upon total control of landlocked movement across their territory on the way to the sea, or upon taxing goods meant for the land-locked if the goods moved across their territory, or in some cases, upon pro-hibiting outright the movement of certain types of goods (e.g., military equipment, nuclear or toxic materials).[58]

Because no formal work had been done by the U.N. bureaucracy or the International Law Commission to include in the draft conventions provisions that would address their interests, the landlocked states had severe bargaining handicaps at UNCLOS I. However, they held their own preparatory session in Geneva in February 1958, and drafted seven principles in preparation for the full conference. They forced the conference to create a special committee— the Fifth Committee—to deal with landlocked problems.[59] By strenuous ef-forts, they managed to get UNCLOS I to approve general statements on the rights of landlocked countries in the conventions negotiated. Among these were the right of access to the sea, subject, however, to consent of the coastal state, and requiring reciprocity on the part of the landlocked state,[60] the right to fly their own maritime flag,[61] and the right to transit the territorial seas of coastal states in innocent passage.[62] While they won the mention of rights, these rights were carefully circumscribed.

By UNCLOS III, landlocked states still were frustrated over their inability to implement rights they thought they had won at UNCLOS I. While they were able to get UNCLOS III to discuss their access to the sea, and to remove some restrictions on their rights (e.g., most-favored-nation requirements and taxes and duties assessed for other than services rendered were prohibited),[63] they still found that they could exercise their right of access to the sea across the territory of their coastal neighbors only through "bilateral, subregional, or regional agreements."[64] Despite their numbers, they were still the poorest of the poor. Despite the leadership role assumed by several European land-locked states (notably Austria at UNCLOS III), they were still mostly mem-bers of the Group of 77 and subject to strong cross-pressures from coastal neighbors determined to bring offshore areas under their control.

The push toward the 200-mile EEZ gave the landlocked and other states making up the LL/GDS coalition a new set of worries. If their coastal neigh-bors succeeded in enclosing more ocean, the coalition members believed they would be made comparatively worse off. They saw the gap of wealth between themselves and their coastal neighbors increasing as coastal states gave them-selves sovereign rights to explore and exploit the living and nonliving natural resources out to 200 miles. The LL/GDS would have to transit through broader zones over which the coastal states had sovereign rights, if not complete sovereignty, to get to the open ocean. Moreover, the LL/GDS were as enamored of the fabled riches of the deep ocean as other states, and feared that the EEZ would be another barrier hampering their access to that pot of gold.

The strategic choice open to the landlocked states early in the negotiation was to try to work out a grand coalition with the developed states of East and West to stop enclosure, or acquiesce in enclosure and try to squeeze out guarantees for their interests in the 200-mile EEZ and the deep seabed regime, based on "Common Heritage." While there were some exploratory moves to determine whether a grand alliance to stop enclosure could have been formed, these efforts were quickly aborted when it became clear that the superpowers were going to support a 200-mile EEZ. Perhaps the price the LL/GDS asked for forming a coalition was too high. Perhaps it was a price that the major ocean-using states could not pay—a promise to guarantee enforcement of LL/GDS ocean rights against recalcitrant coastal states. Ultimately, the LL/GDS had to come to terms with their neighbors if they were to improve their access to the ocean or its resources. Pressure in a multilateral forum might get them better terms, but if the coastal states refused to cooperate with the LL/GDS, they might be much worse off. The name of the game was to use the multilateral forum to get better terms, not to try to pass international legislation which dramatically reversed their geographic disadvantages on paper.

In addition to bargaining for marginal improvements in their right of access to the sea, the landlocked group demanded a share in both the living and nonliving resources of the 200-mile EEZ as the price for agreeing to creation of the zones. They argued that the minerals of the near-shore and continental shelf, as well as the biological riches of offshore areas were a result of the runoff of sediments and nutrients that had their origin at the highest point of the continents. The end product of what flowed down to the sea should be shared.

The landlocked states met a stone wall of resistance on their demand to share in the nonliving or mineral resources of the 200-mile EEZ. They failed to convince any coastal state of their "right of access" to these resources. The idea died completely and no aspect of the demand got into the negotiating texts or the final convention. However, when nonliving resources are exploited in areas where an International Seabed Authority is sanctioned, the landlocked are guaranteed participation, and indeed, representation.[65]

One reason forcing coastal states to share the mineral wealth of the EEZ failed is that the landlocked states had no natural allies on the issue. On the issue of sharing the living resources, they had allies aplenty. If the 200-mile

EEZ's borders were used to exclude foreign fishermen, fishermen from shelf-locked states, and semi-enclosed sea states that had fished near the coasts of other states, or on the other side of a semi-enclosed sea, would be among those most hurt. In many areas of the world, fishing patterns are extremely complex. Being locked into exploiting only one's own EEZ would work many hardships. In any case, the 26 landlocked states could make common cause with the more than 25 shelf-locked and the more than 40 semi-enclosed sea states.[66] This group's demands could not be ignored if they asked for an adjustment in the general thrust of the new regime. The geographically disadvantaged group wanted a continuation of existing fishing rights for its members; in return, they were willing to support new but similar rights in the EEZ for the landlocked.

The rights of those who felt they were disaccommodated by the 200-mile EEZ were not achieved without a fight. As can be seen in figure 5.10, a wide range of ideas and proposals was introduced.

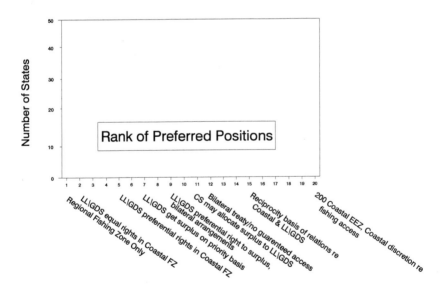

Figure 5.10:   LL/GDS Fishing Rights in the 200-mile EEZ

The concept that most favored the combined needs of the landlocked, shelf-locked, and semi-enclosed sea states was the creation of a regional EEZ (rank

1), in which all states of the region, whether they had a seacoast or not, had an equal right to fish anywhere in the zone. Slightly less favorable to the interests of the landlocked and GDS was a proposal to create exclusive economic zones for coastal states, but only if the GDS and landlocked states of the region were guaranteed an equal right to fish there (rank 2).

For less optimistic landlocked and GDS supporters, there was a fallback position, at rank 5, giving the landlocked and GDS some preferential rights to fish in the EEZs of their better endowed coastal neighbors. If forced to compromise further, some proponents of landlocked and GDS rights were willing to discuss giving their fishermen a preferential right only to the surplus fish that their coastal neighbor could not or chose not to catch (rank 7). The furthest GDS and the landlocked seemed to be willing to compromise was to have preferential access to the surplus only after formal arrangements with their coastal neighbors (rank 9).

At rank 11 was a proposal in which the landlocked and GDS would have a right to fish in the EEZ, but one circumscribed by the coastal state's right to allocate stocks, specify catch regulations, and grant others permission to participate. At rank 12, only if a formal arrangement were worked out between landlocked states or GDS and the coastal state would the coastal state be obliged to give them access. At rank 15, reciprocity would be required. And finally, at rank 20, coastal states were entitled to exercise discretion in the way they managed their own EEZs. If, in the exercise of their discretion, they allowed access to their EEZs to other states within the region, it was an indication of magnanimity, and perhaps, good sense. But the power to make such decisions was in their hands.

From the beginning, the question of whether the GDS and their landlocked allies could be brought into a consensus on the 200-mile EEZ and what price they would be able to extract from coastal states for their consent was in doubt.

The bimodal distribution in figure 5.11 shows two strong camps on the question of whether the fishing rights of the GDS would be acknowledged, and those of the landlocked created. Neither strong camp hovered at the extreme of the modal positions in T-1. While there were a few vehement coastal-state advocates willing to go on record favoring rights for the geographically disadvantaged and landlocked states in the 200-mile EEZ only at the discretion of the coastal state (say, ranks 15–19), the landlocked and GDS had already moved toward recognizing that it was probably better tactically to demand less than their optimal preferred position. They had no serious hope of forcing the creation of regional zones.

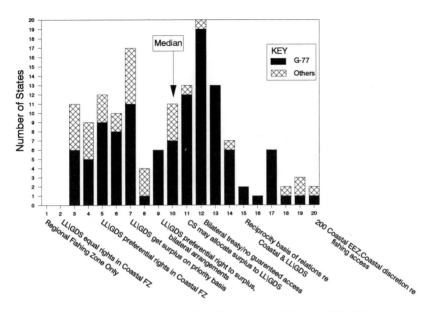

Figure 5.11:   LL/GDS Fishing Rights in the 200-mile EEZ (T-1)

The group favoring stronger coastal rights was about equal in size to its opponents, even in T-1, since the median falls at rank 10 of 20. Compromise seemed to be called for, but the rough balance of forces between pro- and anti-LL/GDS-rights camps meant that compromise would be difficult (as it often is between multilateral bargaining opponents of approximately equal strength). As a result, the issue remained contentious until fairly late in the conference. As late as 1976, the U.S. delegation reported, "significant disagreement on the issue remains."[67]

The general direction in which the negotiation had to go to succeed is shown in the T-1 median, and the actual outcome is shown in the T-2 median of figure 5.12. Distribution is now unimodal, although with a long, strong tail to the right showing the stubborn position of coastal states toward granting rights to the LL/GDS in their newly acquired EEZs. What occurred was a strong push by the LL/GDS in the 1975 sessions to get the conference to endorse provisions giving them "equal fishing rights with the coastal state's own nationals within the economic zone."[68] The landlocked and GDS did manage to induce the Second Committee Chair to include a provision in the Single Negotiating Text that would have given their members the right to

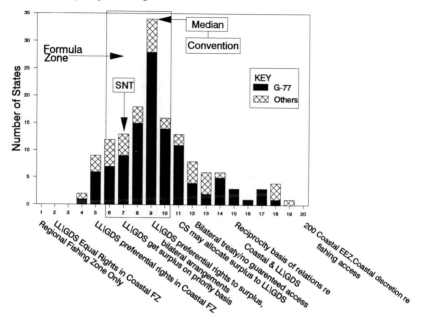

Figure 5.12:   LL/GDS Fishing Rights in the 200-mile EEZ (T-2)

participate in fishing in the 200-mile EEZ on a equitable basis with the coastal state. In addition, the fishing rights of the geographically disadvantaged were not limited to the surplus. Finally, the draft made no distinction between the rights of developed and the rights of developing landlocked states in the 200-mile EEZ.[69] As can be seen in figure 5.12, such a proposal was judged to be at rank 7. It was evident that, although there was agreement to give landlocked and GDS rights in the EEZ, there was not yet agreement on the nature and scope of those rights. In other words, the formula zone was quite wide. The general thrust was accepted, but little else.

Could we predict whether the strenuous attempt of the landlocked and GDS to push equitable access to fish in the EEZ would collapse? Did we know what would be a winning position? I believe that our data showed where the conference was going. Our median demonstrated that the substance of the SNT's provision on landlocked and GDS fishing rights did not have sufficient support to survive, but that the position at rank 9—giving the geographically disadvantaged preferential rights to the surplus after bilateral or other arrangements had been made—would command the greatest respect. It reflects the language of Articles 69 and 70 of the Convention, where the landlocked and geographically disadvantaged states gained the right to participate in fishing for part of the surplus of newly created EEZs after appropriate bilateral, subregional, or regional arrangements had been made. While the word "appropriate" was not defined and the modalities of access were carefully circumscribed, the landlocked and geographically disadvantaged did manage to limit the scope of enclosure.[70]

Were the provisions in the Convention that the landlocked and geographically disadvantaged obtained favoring their interests of sufficient worth to justify the strenuous effort they made to force coastal states to recognize their needs? They did not succeed in putting themselves in a position where they could participate in the exploitation of the EEZ in the face of a hostile coastal state. They did not gain a right to use the EEZ on the basis of equality with the coastal state. The Convention gave them rights, but only to an "appropriate" portion of the surplus, and only after formal arrangements were made. If equality, or even some ironclad guarantee to a portion of the wealth of the EEZ was their goal, one could judge that they failed. Here again, we face the dilemma of the weak. If they strenuously challenge the strong, they are likely to lose handily on measures with real teeth, but they might come away with a palliative, or better. If they do not make the effort, they are likely to be ignored, and that is a worse outcome.

Here the weak fought, and got something. If coastal states are reasonable with their landlocked neighbors in the EEZ, the landlocked will have gained a useful but minor set of privileges.[71] The problems of the geographically disadvantaged in the EEZ are a different dimension from those of their coalition partners, the landlocked. How to resolve the problems in managing transboundary stocks is a problem that must be tackled in the next generation under enclosure.

This conflict issue is a good illustration, at a secondary level, of a successful defense of the core idea of a new natural-resource regime. By 1973, there was a near-consensus that ocean management of most living resources would operate under enclosure, at least out to 200 nautical miles. Some who were disaccommodated by the shift in the core idea of the new formula tried to gain or retain their privileges by carving out a special status for themselves in the new regime. If they had succeeded, especially by creation of a regional zone, or even by right of equal access for their citizens to the living resources, they might have effectively undermined the guiding principle of the new regime. It did not happen, but the affected states successfully lobbied the chair of the Second Committee to include language favorable to themselves. Even as they succeeded in influencing the SNT, they did not have the broad support to carry it off. We were able to forecast the outcome in 1975—that the coastal states would provide access to the landlocked states and GDS—but only on their own terms.

Highly Migratory Species

Exceptions or special arrangements for certain activities or stakeholders took more time to work out than the general principle of the new regime of enclosure. This might have been anticipated both from a bargaining and from a substantive point of view. On the previous issue, a relatively large coalition of weak states—the landlocked and geographical disadvantaged—tried to gain exceptions to the thrust of the new regime. We turn now to the attempt of a much smaller, but much more powerful, group of states—the United States, Japan, the Soviet Union, and a few others who had a strong interest in one or more lucrative distant-water fisheries—to convince the delegates to exempt highly migratory species from exclusive coastal-state control in the EEZ. The outcome of their effort seems little different than what the landlocked and GDS achieved—more cosmetic than real. The integrity of the enclosure regime was preserved on this issue as well.

Substantively, there are many reasons that rigid adherence to enclosure is probably poor policy.[72] Enclosure provides the coastal state the authority to regulate and allocate most stocks that reach harvestable stage within the 200-mile EEZ, and therefore solves the first-order problems of fishery management—providing unified authority to manage and allocate. But enclosure cannot fully address the problems of managing those species that spend a significant portion of the life cycle outside the 200-mile EEZ. These include highly migratory species such as tuna, and anadromous stocks such as salmon. It is difficult under a pure enclosure regime to manage transboundary stocks, especially where, as in semi-enclosed seas, 400 miles of open ocean are not available. Fish do not pay attention to manmade borders.

If the 200-mile EEZ is used as an exclusionary device, foreign fishing states have an incentive to station their fleets 201 miles from shore, beyond the conservation or management decisions of the coastal state. Some types of arrangements must be made to induce cooperation in the management of stocks that can't be managed on a purely national basis. But if responsibility is to be divided, is it to be divided equally? Will all major stakeholders have veto power over each other on questions of conservation and allocation? Or will one retain authority, but perhaps with some limits on its authority?

The problem of anadromous stock management is equally interesting from substantive and bargaining points of view. It is treated only in passing because we were not able to assemble adequate data.

The problem of managing anadromous stocks was essentially a North-North problem. Since the problem was not salient to them, too few South states put themselves on record to try to analyze and forecast what the conference as a whole would do in devising the management system.[73] The situation was that most states were prepared to put into the convention what the principal parties—the United States, the Soviet Union, Canada, Norway and Japan—agreed was appropriate. Since the major states with salmon streams had an incentive to extend enclosure even further out to gain control of all salmon exploitation, the forces generally supporting enclosure could only watch, applaud, and snicker over the contradictions the major salmon states, who were also distant-water states, got into.

The UNCLOS III Convention provided that "states in whose rivers anadromous stocks originate shall have the primary interest in and responsibility for such stocks."[74] The convention gave the state of origin responsibility for regulating the stocks, and with negotiated exceptions, restricted fishing for anadromous stocks to within the 200-mile EEZ. In cases where this would mean economic dislocations for other states' fishermen, fishing beyond the 200-mile EEZ might continue, but only "after achieving agreement on terms and conditions of such fishing"[75] between the state of origin and the fishing state. These are relatively strong rights for the fortunate few.[76] However, enforcement is only by agreement between the state of origin and other concerned states. The states of origin might have wished for unilateral enforcement rights in international waters. In recent years, there has been concern over salmon taken as "incidental catch" in the huge drift nets set in the open ocean ostensibly to catch squid, an underutilized species.

Some called the treatment accorded anadromous stocks an extension of the rule of enclosure, but what some of the same states wanted in relation to highly migratory species was an exception to that rule. They did not want to allow the coastal state sole authority over how much would be caught and who would do the catching within, much less without, the 200-mile EEZ. They argued that, since fish like tuna migrate thousands of miles annually, often moving through a number of EEZs as well as the high seas, migratory species should be managed as a unit throughout their range, and should be exempt from the management of the coastal state, even inside the EEZ. While this approach to managing tuna has much merit in conservation or scientific circles, the conservation or scientific merits were not the principal reasons both sides of the quarrel pressed their conflict. Rather, it was wealth. American tunamen were generating it, and west-coast Latin American states wanted to capture it.

The problem was that distant-water industrial fleets from the United States, the Soviet Union, Japan, and others were antagonizing the states off of whose shores they fished. The quintessential distant-water fight was between the United States and its Latin American neighbors. It had been a bitter struggle since the Truman Proclamations were promulgated in 1945, and the Latin American states used that occasion to make more extravagant claims of their own.[77] Most of the U.S. tuna catch was taken off the coasts of the three west-coast Latin American states—Chile, Ecuador, and Peru. Although there was an attempt to develop conservation rules through the Inter-American Tropical Tuna Commission, and though the Commission had a good reputation for research, it could not allocate the resource.[78] The coastal states tried to do that through 200-mile sovereignty claims.

Most unilateral laws of the west-coast Latin American states allowed American tunamen access to the resource only under license. U.S. tunamen resisted strenuously. The fishery was highly profitable, and most of the catch was consumed in the United States. As a result, heavy pressure was exerted upon U.S. fishery officials by a well-financed and organized lobby—the American Tuna Boat Association. For some 20 years or more, the U.S. government followed the Tuna Boat Association line because the Association influenced senior administration officials and Congress. Its position was sanctioned by U.S. domestic law. U.S. vessels had good reason to refuse to purchase licenses: their fines were paid and they were compensated for seized catches by the U.S. Government. In addition, U.S. legislation imposed sanctions upon Latin American states that seized or fined American tuna vessels.[79] The struggle was pursued with fervor by both sides. It became a matter of wealth and pride, and sovereignty became more important than cash.

After the United States announced its support for the 200-mile EEZ, some pride had to be swallowed, but U.S. officials were yet not ready to jettison their tuna fishermen, though industry representatives were aware of the insecurity of their position. From that point on, the United States' delegation could only try, as the senior industry representative put it, "to make evident the fact that the coastal state's sovereign rights and jurisdiction over highly migratory species was not plenary and exclusive."[80] Below, in figure 5.13, we have scaled the ideas introduced to manage highly migratory species. The proposal most favorable to distant-water fishermen was, at rank 1, to continue species-specific management for all highly migratory creatures wherever they are found. After the superpowers abandoned this position in 1973–74, their best fallback position was to accept the 200-mile EEZ, but to make evident that coastal jurisdiction was not plenary and exclusive—in other

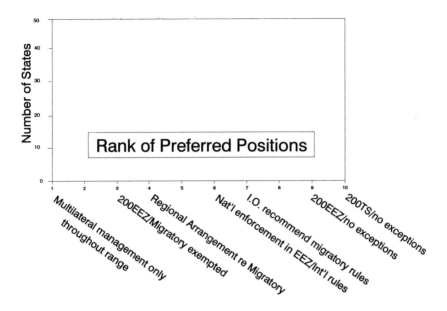

Figure 5.13:   Highly Migratory Species

words, to exempt highly migratory species from the jurisdiction of coastal states within 200 miles of shore (rank 3). Slightly less acceptable was to recognize more powers of the coastal state, but to insist that a regional body must make rules related to tuna in the EEZ (rank 4).

Looking at the problem from the other end of the spectrum, the defense of the exclusive decision rights of the coastal state regarding tuna in the EEZ was essential. Since a number of C-E-P, other Latin American, and African states would not bend in the UNCLOS III negotiations on this issue, we placed the 200-mile territorial sea position at rank 10. The 200-mile EEZ with no derogation of the exclusive nature of the coastal state's control over living resources is found at rank 9. Some relatively strong coastal-states-rights advocates were willing to discuss a compromise (rank 7) in which, although the coastal state would retain its sovereign rights to manage and allocate migratory species in the EEZ, it might be required to heed recommendations from a regional fisheries organization before it made its decisions official. Finally, we placed at rank 6 proposals that would give the coastal state an exclusive right to enforce rules in the EEZ, but would require that the rules be agreed to in a regional fisheries organization.

During the preliminary negotiations, the state of the play was reflected in figure 5.14 below.

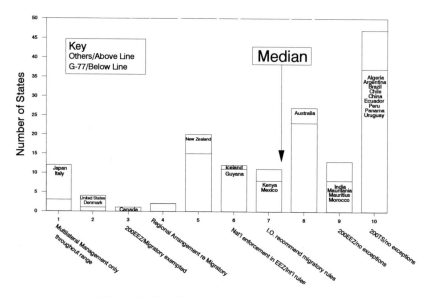

Figure 5.14:   Highly Migratory Species (T-1)

Distribution is rather lumpy, but is most favorable to the forces opposing exceptions for highly migratory species in the 200-mile EEZ. The median tells us that the forces opposing exceptions had not yet consolidated their position, either substantively or in terms of consensus. Indeed, the distribution suggests that some compromise might be called for in order to achieve consensus or near-consensus, and it points to the idea of urging the fishing and coastal states to cooperate in a regional organization. But it does not give the regional organization decision power within the 200-mile EEZ.

Since this was an issue that was strongly felt in some important states, we have shown the positions of those states in figure 5.15. The United States went on record early and often. By the end of T-1, its position averaged out to support the exemption of highly migratory species in the exclusive economic zone and the need for multilateral management (rank 3). Other distant-water states also adopted conservative positions, especially Japan and Italy.

On the other side were the forces supporting a 200-mile territorial sea or exclusive economic zone who would brook no, or extremely limited, constraints on the sovereign right of the coastal state to manage and allocate highly migratory species within their coastal zones. Only Mexico, of the Latin American group, and Guyana and Kenya, of the African group, showed any propensity to find a compromise solution. This is interesting in the light of U.S. quarrels with Mexico on distant-fishing issues and Kenyan leadership among the Africans on the concept of patrimonial sea. Also vocal were Iceland and Australia. Although not members of the original patrimonialists, they clearly advocated positions that protect their decision rights in their own EEZs vis-à-vis distant-water fishermen.

The frequency of mention indicating the salience of the issue rose substantially in T-2. Distribution, in figure 5.15, is now unimodal with a tail, seemingly hinting at a probable outcome. Again, we feature those states for whom

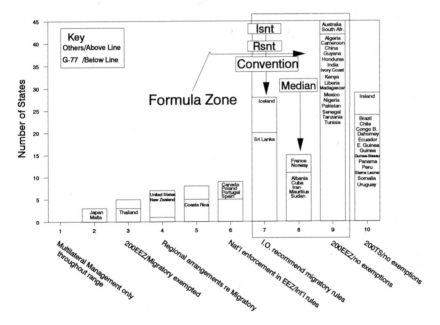

Figure 5.15: Highly Migratory Species (T-2)

this issue is salient. The forces facing each other had remained essentially the same, although a number of states, for example Mexico and Canada, that favored compromise in T-1 moved further toward the coastal-state position of few concessions in T-2. Japan remained the most conservative and out of step with majority sentiment until the Sixth Session in 1977.[81] It might appear strange that Malta would appear so conservative. But Dr. Arvid Pardo set Malta on a course of protecting the "Common Heritage of Mankind" in the widest ocean space available. Opposition to carving up the oceans into strict national zones showed in the remarks of Maltese delegates. The United States in T-2 moved slightly toward a fallback position, at rank 4, but remained a strong advocate of a special status for highly migratory species in a regional agreement. Although less adamant, Poland, Portugal, and Spain also spoke up for protection of distant-water fishermen.

A number of important northern fishing states were more concerned with protecting their coastal fisheries, and were willing to give an international organization the power only to recommend rules for exploiting migratory species. Among the vocal were Iceland, France, Norway, Australia, South Africa, and Ireland. In both T-1 and T-2, we have a very poor data sample for most of the Eastern European group on this issue, and virtually none for the Soviet Union, although the Soviets had a major interest in generally limiting the powers of the coastal state to control foreign fishing in the EEZ. However, they also had important coastal fisheries to protect, and therefore, might have felt cross-pressured to be silent and to avoid a quarrel where they could. The only Eastern European state which spoke frequently on this subject was Poland, whose interests are almost entirely distant-water. The usual enclosure supporters are found at ranks 8–10. The Group of 77 was solidly opposed to restrictions on the sovereign right of the coastal state to act in its own EEZ.

If a decision had been forced in 1975, according to our model, the outcome at median 8.4 would be close to the coastal-state position with no or very few concessions. If the decision had been taken on a purely parliamentary basis, the extreme coastal forces would have won. Opponents to concession commanded the support of about 130 of 150 states we tracked. Our pairs analysis revealed that only if the distant-fishing forces had taken a very deep fallback (say rank 6 or 7 versus rank 9), might they have commanded enough votes to stalemate the conference. Of course, avoidance of votes was a principal procedural objective of the conference. Consensus was the preferred mode of decision.

The tail indicates that consensus or near-consensus had not been achieved and the issue was not near closure by 1975. To achieve sufficient support needed to reach at least near-consensus by 1982, the supporters of the no-concession position had to soften at least the language that guaranteed their exclusive rights over highly migratory species within the 200-mile EEZ. This meant that the formula zone, or space within which states bargained, between 1975 and 1982 was relatively wide.

We judged the outcome of the Single Negotiating Text, the Revised Text, and the convention to fall at rank 7. Article 64 of the convention (and its predecessors, Article 53 of the ICNT and the RSNT) specified that "the coastal State and other States whose nationals fish in [a] region for highly migratory species . . . shall co-operate directly or through appropriate international organizations with a view to ensuring conservation and promoting the objective of optimum utilization of such species throughout the region, both within and beyond the exclusive economic zone."[82] The species concerned were listed in an appendix. While this was an outcome more moderate than we had forecast if the decision had to be made in 1975, it was a solution with no teeth. It was an exhortation and an invitation to future cooperation if the interested states were so inclined. It did not explicitly exempt highly migratory species from the decision authority of the coastal state. It did not make international fishing organization decisions binding within the 200-mile EEZ.

Our forecast was not far from the mark, but we ceased collecting data before the coastal forces made their gesture toward distant-water fishing states. It was clear that the compromise outcome was principally cosmetic on this and all other issues concerning the implementation of coastal-state powers within 200 miles. In deference to a limited number of important distant-water states that fished for highly migratory species, the winners on this issue were moderately generous to the losers. But not very generous. On all of the detailed negotiations concerning real control of the 200-mile EEZ, the coastal states at UNCLOS III conceded nothing that would diminish their virtually complete decision power within their new functional zones. They protected their victory by successfully controlling the negotiations on details.

6

Committee III:

Making the EEZ Work and Scientists Pay

UNCLOS III's Third Committee was created chiefly to solve two problems: (1) how to make the new Exclusive Economic Zone (EEZ) work (also
a chief concern of the Second Committee); and (2) how to satisfy the First
and Second Worlds in distributing positions of conference authority and control (a problem in conference management).

Although the Third Committee attempted to deal with some of the larger
problems of ocean pollution by creating general state obligations, and also
with broader problems of managing ocean science, these efforts did not occupy much of its bargaining time. The subject that was most contentious and
that occupied much of the committee's time was defining the coastal state's
relationship with shippers and with scientists, two classes of occasional or
wandering users of the EEZ that seemed especially threatening. The first
group were the shippers of goods in tramp ships, container ships, or bulk carriers, who might accidentally or deliberately pollute the waters of the EEZ,
the most productive region of the ocean in terms of known valuable living
resources. The second group were ocean scientists, who were sometimes accused of harming local wildlife with their experiments, but actually were more
dangerous to coastal-state sovereignty because they might learn too much.

These problems had to be dealt with in some preliminary proceedings before they got to a plenary session. But why a separate committee? One par-
amount reason was the need to find posts of honor for delegates from the
developed states. A distinctive attribute of parliamentary diplomacy is the
careful distribution of positions of honor as chair, vice chair, or rapporteur
among the caucusing groups. This is done for various reasons: to satisfy the
need for representation per se, to boost the prestige of a caucusing group, to
advance the career of the person honored, to provide an edge so that dominating the substantive issue will be made easier for individual, state, or
group. The First Committee (responsible for the deep seabed issues) was
chaired by Paul Bamela Engo of the United Republic of the Cameroons, and
the Second Committee (responsible for straits, territorial sea, exclusive economic zone, and continental shelf issues) was chaired by Andres Aguilar

(for the First, Second, and Fourth through Eleventh Sessions). This was not accidental, but posts of honor were also needed for Europeans or North Americans.

Cynics might prefer that suitable posts be created in a relatively harmless body. Since the key issues in Committee III were dependent upon solutions arrived at in the other two main committees, particularly Committee II, Committee III leadership could be turned over to a northerner with impunity. A third committee might be created for a First or Second Worlder to chair, but under one of the informal rules of parliamentary diplomacy, it could not be a diplomat from a superpower. The superpowers had to be content with automatic seats on the Conference Drafting Committee. The chair of the Third Committee had to be a delegate from a smaller states of the Eastern or Western alliance.

The Conference turned to Alexander Yankov of Bulgaria to chair Committee III. It was a good appointment. Yankov proved an effective chairman and was respected by the many diverging interests fighting over the issues in the Third Committee. Some states complained about the result of the committee's work, but there were no complaints that the outcome was arrived at by unfair procedures or discriminatory actions. Another northerner, a West German, was elected one of the three vice-chairs of the Committee.

While the need for posts of honor partially explains establishment of a third main committee, it tells us little about why that committee was empowered to address the seemingly odd assortment of issues put under its jurisdiction. Was the Third Committee merely a sop to developed state sensibilities? I think not. There were real needs being addressed in Committee III.

First, in the late 1960s the world experienced a number of major ship-related ocean pollution incidents.[1] Newspaper stories and pictures describing and showing oil tankers and freighters polluting beaches made at least one of the issues to be dealt with by Committee III salient to the general public. Preventing, mitigating, and cleaning up oil spills, and compensating for damages became important issues of domestic policy in many states.

But the problem was inherently international. In the 1960s, it was not primarily domestic ships engaged in cabotage (the movement of goods by sea between two or more ports of the same state)[2] that were causing damage to the interest of coastal states, but rather ships registered elsewhere, often in states providing a haven for runaway-flag or flag-of-convenience vessels.[3] The problem of ship-related pollution had to be placed on the agenda of an international meeting. UNCLOS III provided an appropriate venue.

Ship-related pollution was a difficult problem to negotiate, especially because it had to be reconciled with a change in the general regime. Under enclosure, the coastal state would have the authority to prevent or mitigate near-shore pollution caused by ships. But if the international community accepted coastal-state jurisdiction over all surface and perhaps subsurface movement, then movement through the EEZ would be allowed only with coastal-state permission. Freedom of movement, an aspect of the more general freedom of the seas, would be terminated. It would hardly be worth creating an EEZ. It would be more honest if the world community openly accepted the idea of a 200-mile territorial sea. Though the Second Committee dealt with the broad principles of the EEZ, the Third Committee was created in good part to address whether there would be limitations on its jurisdiction of coastal states to deal with certain classes of external users of the 200 miles of waters offshore.

How else could the issues relating to enclosure be divided? It would have been difficult to divide the responsibilities of Committee II any other way and still have it achieve the basic trade-offs at the core of the new regime. Committee II's agenda was very crowded, with the basic nature of the territorial sea, the right to transit straits (and related archipelago questions), fisheries, and the nature of the exclusive economic zone under its aegis. It also had to deal with rights of the landlocked and geographically disadvantaged states in the new EEZs. The question of what rights remained to users of a drastically reduced high seas (minus deep-seabed minerals, of course) might have been relegated to another committee, but it was hardly worth the effort. As long as the fate of deep-seabed minerals was excluded, there was little controversy over the user rights on the shrunken high seas. Part VII of the convention, which deals with these rights, was created mostly by assembling materials from previous efforts at codification.

What was left was to define the rights of ocean users—shippers and scientists. Both groups wanted to be able to use the waters of the EEZ but claimed no territorial rights there. But coastal states were afraid that granting others use rights would threaten their own territorial claims. Some more vocal states felt these two classes of users could also do significant harm to their resource interests in the EEZ. Doubtless both classes of users, at their worst, could seriously harm coastal states' interests in the EEZ. But the issues in Committee III seem almost as important for their symbolic as their real world impact. Ocean science, and to a lesser extent ocean pollution, were safe issues that could act as surrogates for larger concerns.

The Third Committee provided a forum for a dialogue between the ocean haves and have-nots.[4] The haves, like most colonialists, came mostly from afar and wanted rights near the coasts of the have-nots. They brought with them their powerful and expensive instruments of exploitation—advanced vessels to transport goods or extract information. The have-nots, mostly but not all developing states, saw the visitors as a danger to their newly acquired sovereign rights. Some ships' visits are periodic, such as liner conference or other vessels on a regular route; some are aperiodic, such as research ships that appear only once in a while. The temperature rose because of a supplemental problem: a few less powerful states used Committee III to take on a more powerful neighbor about behavior that concerned them. It was an arena where the less powerful could turn to allies to counterbalance the real-world advantages of the stronger. The most obvious example that affected the work of Committee III was the quarrel between the United States and Canada over their general ocean relationship, and in particular, over ocean-use rights in the Arctic.

Despite considerable heat in Committee III's deliberations, and the feeling that the noise might be disproportional to the overall salience of the issues, the question of transitors' use rights in the Exclusive Economic Zone had to be solved if there were to be a consensus outcome to the overall negotiation. Mere ratification of previous use rights would undercut the new regime of enclosure of near-shore waters. Eliminating all use rights for outsiders without coastal-state consent—especially if there were no limitations on coastal-state ability to withhold consent—would come close to creating 200-mile territorial seas. Such an outcome would have been fundamentally unacceptable to many major ocean-using states, and they might well have defected from such an outcome. Solutions providing some mix of rights and duties for both sides had to be worked out. That was the real agenda of the Third Committee.

Pollution Issues at UNCLOS III

The late 1960s and early 1970s was an era of ocean environmental disasters. Numerous incidents took place that did measurable harm to the ocean's ecosystem, and many observers questioned how robust that ecosystem was. How much could humankind abuse it without doing irreparable harm? Traditional belief was that the ocean system was so vast, and had such remarkable recuperative powers, that it was safe to use the oceans as a sink for the disposal of humankind's wastes. Indeed, one of the best arguments raised in defense of the Grotian freedom of the seas was that it was *impossible* to do the oceans fundamental harm. As a consequence, the ocean was often the preferred area for waste disposal. According to a jingle popular among environmental managers of that era, "the solution to pollution is dilution."

But what if that view were incorrect? What would the consequences be if it turned out that humankind could pollute the ocean in a manner that was essentially irreversible? By the late 1980s we became concerned that human activities had already done serious harm to the earth's atmosphere through the use of chloroflurocarbons (CFC's). The use of CFC's was associated with reducing the ozone layer which filters out ultraviolet radiation. We now worry about global warming, as a consequence of the burning of fossil fuels, which might be causing global climate change and a rise in the sea level.[5]

When preparations were being made for UNCLOS III in the late 1960s, we had less knowledge of the potential harm industrial societies might do to the entire worldwide ecosystem.[6] However, we did have a large body of evidence about the direct assault on the oceans.[7] For much of the nineteenth and twentieth centuries, industrial civilization has been polluting and poisoning the oceans via many pathways—air pollution, polluted runoffs from streams, rivers, and sewers, deliberate dumping of wastes, offshore oil and gas production, near-shore (and potentially deep-ocean) mining, using the oceans as a heat sink (e.g., power plants), and ship-generated pollution. Ships can abuse the seas they sail on by deballasting oily wastes, bilge pumping, washing cargo tanks, tossing garbage over the side, and of course, spilling oil into the ocean as a result of human error (e.g., forgetting to close a valve on a oil pump, or on a larger scale, sinking, grounding, or collision of a large tanker).

One can mitigate the impact of a major pollution incident, clean up afterward, and pay for the damage done, but what can be done to prevent future incidents? In particular, what can be done to discourage treating the ocean as a legitimate dump? As long as the ocean is treated as a commons, users have little incentive to accept resonsibility for their acts of pollution, or at best, will accept only a small part of the costs they cause us all. In fact, the costs are spread among all users of the system. The cost of pollution is treated by the polluter as external to the cost of producing the good or service.[8]

Theoretically, the answer to how states can discourage further ocean pollution is straightforward and elementary: internalize the external costs to the polluter. Make the polluter include the cost of pollution in the cost of the product. If a polluter has to pay for a unit of pollution for every unit of goods, he will have an incentive to reduce pollution so that he can reduce his cost of production.[9] Unfortunately, this is not always easy to arrange. The full, true social costs of pollution—even short-run, much less long-run costs—are often very difficult to calculate. It's not always easy to tell the polluter what his unit of pollution is worth.

Most polluters find themselves in a competitive world akin to a prisoner's dilemma, and we have difficulty solving the dilemma. Even if polluters are willing to consider internalizing the externalities they cause, they fear that others are not, that others will defect and, by not reducing or eliminating their pollution, will keep costs low while the costs of the "good citizens" will rise, making them uncompetitive. Therefore, all defect. Breaking out of this dilemma requires trust. It's not impossible to engender trust, but it can be difficult.[10]

Developing trust moves the problem to the world of international politics. In that arena, states must promise to restrain their citizens and industries, expecting that other states will faithfully carry out their promise to do likewise. But will they have the political will to undertake the task at all, or to do the job properly? Will states induce others to reduce pollution, while trying to avoid reciprocal obligations to restrain their own citizens?[11] Or, more likely, in the political arena, will negotiators succumb to domestic stakeholders' pleas and avoid fundamental changes? Will they just back down a bit and create least-common-denominator solutions that only reduce the *rate* the world ecosystem is being despoiled?

Are least-common-denominator solutions appropriate for curing assaults on the world ecosystem? Many defenders of the natural world look at that world holistically.[12] Any interruption in one part has ripple effects on other parts of the system, and eventually the whole system. Therefore, no insult to the system can be tolerated long, without engendering dangerous systemic effects.[13] Many environmental activists call for a fundamental rethinking of attitudes, and doubt that efforts under the present system can prevent pollution from reaching intolerable levels.[14]

All these attitudes were manifest in the Third Committee, among both delegates and official observers from qualified nongovernmental organizations. Many participants worked toward environmental goals, and many others hoped that, under the guise of environmental concerns, they could legitimize their demands for more complete control of their EEZs, for sovereignty as Bodin defined it in the seventeenth century: "supreme power over citizens and subjects unrestrained by the laws."[15] The environment had the odor of sanctity about it. It contained a series of "motherhood" issues. Who could oppose improvement in the ocean's health at the price of giving a party willing to protect the ocean the necessary authority to act?

Committee III did not operate on a clean environmental slate. Its work had to be put in the context of international decision-making on the world ecosystem since World War II. A series of regimes was negotiated to deal with environmental problems relating to fisheries, ocean science, and marine transportation. Often responsibility for working out these arrangements had been placed in the hands of intergovernmental and nongovernmental international organizations, particularly the International Maritime Organization (IMO, formerly the Intergovernmental Maritime Consultative Organization or IMCO), and the International Oceanographic Commission (IOC), along with its partner the Ocean Division of the United Nations Educational, Scientific, and Cultural Organization (UNESCO), and the Fisheries Division of the Food and Agricultural Organization (FAO), and more than 20 regional fisheries organizations.[16] Unfortunately, during much of the 1960s and early 1970s, the work of these organizations came under attack as providing either inadequate or inappropriate solutions to the problem of world ecosystem degradation.

For years IMCO (now IMO) had been the target of complaints about its work in assisting world shipping and reducing ship-caused ocean pollution. IMCO's pollution conventions were criticized for being too favorable to shipping states. IMCO claimed a fairly narrow mandate and concentrated on problems of safety at sea, of assigning liability for an accident, and of finding ways to pay for cleanups. These efforts were sometimes characterized as too little or too late: too little liability, and too late to prevent environmental problems. In fact, the world would have to look elsewhere for action on prevention, since it seemed a change in jurisdiction over the ships responsible was necessary.

In the 1960s, complaints arose that some functional international organizations were neglecting the interests of developing states. Third World countries attacked liner conferences (oligopolistic nongovernmental shipping organizations that restricted entry and set rates among members) on the grounds that they were often excluded from conferences dominating marine transportation routes vital to their trade. Their exclusion, they claimed, resulted in shipping costs for their goods that were much too high.[17] Despite their attempt to get UNCTAD (United Nations Conference on Trade, Aid, and Development) to establish a new liner code,[18] there were echoes of this debate in UNCLOS III.

IOC was another organization Third World states claimed was in need of reform.[19] According to the developing states, IOC was a mere plaything of the developed states, which it helped to pursue their interests in pure ocean science, and the work it sponsored had little social utility, especially for states that were struggling with ocean development and pollution problems.[20]

The agenda of the Third Committee was also affected by changing patterns in the world political economy. The 1960s and 1970s were an era of increasing demand for fossil fuels and declining domestic production among the developed countries, especially the United States. With finds being made in other areas of the world—the Middle East, Southeast Asia, and the North Sea, particularly—and with the development of VLCCs (Very Large Crude Carriers, over 150,000 tons) and ULCCs (Ultra Large Crude Carriers, over

500,000 tons), huge amounts of oil were being moved in international trade.[21] There were important strategic and environmental consequences.[22] In addition to the Arab oil embargo of 1973, states were concerned by a rash of tanker accidents that did significant damage to coastlines around the world. A convenient starting point for awareness of this transnational problem is the spill of the 60,000 tons of crude oil along the British coast in 1967 by the *Torrey Canyon*. It was followed by the grounding of the *Tokyo Maru* in the same year, a collision of two supertankers near Singapore in 1971, and a large spill from the *Metula* two miles north of Tierra del Fuego in 1974. 1976–77 was a particularly bad period, with the grounding of the *Argo Merchant* off Nantucket, followed by seven other marine disasters. It was topped quickly the next year when the *Amoco Cadiz* spilled 240,000 tons of crude oil on the beaches of Brittany.

If the delegates to UNCLOS III intended to deal comprehensively with managing the oceans, they couldn't ignore the increasing serious and highly visible problem of ocean pollution. But as a gathering of political generalists with a very comprehensive agenda to work through, the Conference had too little expertise and too little time—even presuming the political will existed—to deal comprehensively with ocean pollution.

In order not to be overwhelmed by an unmanageable pollution agenda, UNCLOS III chose to restrict its pollution tasks to two: (1) try to get signatories to control their own domestic sources of pollution; (2) attempt to control ship-related pollution. We will analyze the latter in some detail, but will touch only briefly on the former. While we collected considerable data on the perceptions of many delegations of problems of ocean pollution and their preferences for solutions,[23] most were too broadly philosophical for the purposes of our analysis. In the end, the UNCLOS III Convention included only hortatory articles obligating states not to pollute. And even this outcome was achieved only after a debate on the comparative burden of pollution control.

Third World states claimed that if state obligations were created without great care in specification, there was a chance that developing states would be burdened more than developed states, even though all states had an equal obligation not to pollute. They argued that the existing environmental degradation of the world's oceans resulted from the rush to industrialization by the developed states during the eighteenth to twentieth centuries. If the developing states took on the obligation not to pollute, they wondered if they weren't being asked to forgo industrialization via the backdoor. And, even if they were allowed to industrialize, by accepting environmental controls, wouldn't they also be accepting higher costs for achieving industrialization than the present industrial states paid? Indeed, some saw environmental concerns at UNCLOS III as a threat to transferring smokestack industries to Third World states, where cheap labor provided a comparative advantage. Since Third World states had not, by and large, created the problem of environmental degradation, some Third World delegates felt the burden of cleaning up the damage should fall exclusively on the developed.[24] It was a financial as well as moral obligation they wished to establish. Others recognized that all states had to participate in the effort to manage ocean pollution, or all would suffer. One major reason the developing states were so vociferous was that they wanted to convince the developed states to provide them with more development aid and technical assistance so that they could be good environmental citizens without adding an extra burden to their own development efforts.

The developing states wanted the Convention to record that development needs be taken into account in any scheme of international ocean environmental management. For example, Brazil and India wanted an environmental double standard, higher for developed, lower for developing states.[25] They wanted coastal states to control all activities in their EEZs yet not be obliged by a universal standard to prevent dumping in their own EEZs. The articles containing the obligation of states not to pollute, to cooperate globally and regionally on pollution problems, to render technical assistance, to monitor, and to assess environmental problems were not agreed upon until the Fourth Session (March–May 1976), and then only after an effort to reopen them was rejected.[26]

The regime created in Part XII of the UNCLOS III Convention establishing obligations for states to protect and preserve the marine environment is lofty in tone and weak on specifics. In Article 192, the state signatories solemnly took on "the obligation to protect and preserve the marine environment."[27] States were obliged to pass domestic laws preventing and controlling pollution from land-based sources,[28] as well as from sea-based sources under their jurisdiction.[29] They promised to adopt laws and regulations to prevent, reduce, or control air pollution impacting the marine environment,[30] and to "take . . . all measures that are necessary to ensure that activities under their jurisdiction or control are so conducted as to not cause damage by pollution to other States and their environment."[31] Signatories also promised to "cooperate . . . in formulating and elaborating international rules . . . for the protection and preservation of the marine environment,"[32] and to "observe, measure, evaluate, and analyze . . . the risks or effects of pollution of the marine environment."[33]

The developing states insisted that none of the obligations undertaken interfere with the sovereign right of the coastal state to exploit its natural resources,[34] and that developing states receive preferential treatment from international organizations in special services, technical assistance, and funds for the prevention, reduction, and control of pollution.[35] The developed states were to obligate themselves directly, or through competent international organizations, to provide technical assistance to developing states, including training, and equipment to prevent, clean up, and perform environmental assessments.[36]

There is an ongoing debate within the international law and environmental communities over whether it was worthwhile to negotiate a regime broadly obligating states not to pollute, without real sanctions if they violated or ignored the obligations. Those who support the general pollution provisions of the UNCLOS III Convention claim that it is quite useful, especially from a legal point of view, to get states to accept the idea of an obligation not to pollute and to cooperate in preventing and controlling marine pollution. Such provisions clarify states' responsibilities. The convention establishes a standard of conduct against which to measure their real conduct. If they do not carry out their obligations, other states can remind them of their default. If a specific dispute concerning marine pollution arises between two states, and both states are signatories to the Convention, the fact that one state is in compliance with its nonpolluting principles and the other is not can be used in any legal proceeding.

The opposing argument usually begins with the sweeping statement that the pollution provisions are so weak as to be virtually useless. It does harm to appear to have dealt adequately with an important problem when, in reality, the language of the Convention merely papers over the problem. The Convention gives the impression that the problem is solved when, in fact, it is not. It is all very well to have states promise not to pollute, say the critics, but the convention's pollution articles lack two essential features: (1) substantive content, and (2) a usable enforcement mechanism.

The antipollution language of the Convention is in fact hortatory, rather than substantive, in creating specific obligations for states. States already have the power under their existing domestic jurisdictions to prevent or manage pollution problems that emanate from their land, their territorial seas, and perhaps even from their pollution, sanitation, and other contiguous zones. The convention's pollution articles created no new jurisdictional rights useful for the management of marine-related pollution, nor did they specify *what actions* states should take to control practices causing pollution. In other words, the convention invites states to be good citizens, but does not define what good citizenship means, beyond not polluting. Critics are especially scornful of the Convention's lack of enforcement mechanisms. By creating obligations that states cannot keep, the UNCLOS III delegates have devised an ocean-pollution regime that is likely to be treated, at best, with indifference, and at worst, with disobedience and scorn.

Proponents and critics of the Convention agree that the matter of ship-generated pollution is a different type of issue. Here the debate concerned expansion of coastal-state jurisdiction over a non-resource-related use of the EEZ and the right to punish. That's a different kettle of pollutants!

Vessel Pollution Standards

UNCLOS III was not equipped to deal with the problems caused by ships polluting the seas, much less with the full range of ocean pollution problems. It did not have the technical staff, the appropriate preparation, nor the pollution specialists. But these were not needed for Committee III's task at hand—to make clear the question of *jurisdiction,* or who was responsible for what in relation to vessel-source pollution. In terms of regime creation, the distribution of power and authority is a first-order requirement.[37] Committee III's negotiation was supposed to clarify *who had the right to make the rules* and *who had the right to enforce them.* The Committee's task was political, and the delegates who specialized in its work had no doubt they were competent to handle this type of problem. To better coordinate the search for appropriate solutions, much of the work on vessel-source pollution was handled by a contact group—the Evensen Group.

Pollution problems at UNCLOS III were difficult to manage because they were a mixture of concerns about the management of vessel-source pollution and other objectives which, to a number of delegations, were primary rather than secondary objectives. Supporters of territorialist or patrimonialist positions wanted to complete the set of powers the coastal states were about to gain over the EEZ. The territorialists hoped to make the EEZ a de facto territorial sea. The patrimonialists did not want a de facto territorial sea, but wanted assurance that, in giving up a 200-mile territorial sea, they did not forfeit certain rights. They still wanted to be able to prevent passing ships from leaving a trail of pollution that would spoil their exclusive right to exploit the EEZ's natural resources.

Opponents, especially among the major maritime states, wanted to prevent the conversion of the exclusive economic zone they conceded (by 1973–74) as a sui generis concept into a fully sovereign zone, an enlarged territorial sea. Their justification was economic. Different perceptions of who should make environmental rules in near-shore waters, and who should enforce them, made the pollution work of Committee III a spillover from Committee II.

While the underlying political currents had a great deal to do with the way states perceived vessel-source pollution questions in Committee III, their related concerns had to do with vessel-source pollution per se. The late 1960s and 1970s was a period of increased oil movement by sea and of several very dramatic oil spill incidents. Some states that claimed to be especially vulnerable to oil spills had essentially unidimensional interests in controlling oil pollution. Straits states were among this group, since many tankers passed through their narrow waters with what they claimed were insufficient precautions.

Other states had multidimensional interests. They had mixed motives about trying to control vessel-source pollution. On the one hand, they wanted the authority to prevent the fouling of their land and water. On the other, they feared giving other states authority which might be used to interfere with their trade, or with their access to energy resources. This group included many ocean-using states with long exposed coasts, such as the United States. But it also included a number of developing oil exporters.

Delegates had to contend with the classic problem of reciprocity in an international system based on the legal equality of states. They wanted the power and authority to act, but feared giving others the same power and authority. Naturally, *they* would not abuse their authority, but they were disquieted by the possibility that *others* would not be so forebearing. As a result, many delegates were willing to accept constraints on the new authority they sought, and therefore helped shape more moderate solutions to the authority problem.

There are no surprises in the spectrum of ideas introduced by states in the Third Committee on establishing vessel pollution standards. They were scaled as shown in figure 6.1.

Under traditional law of the sea, responsibility for the conduct of vessels at sea rests with the state whose flag flies on the vessel. Early in Committee III's deliberations, some states proposed retaining this practice. If new pollution management regulations were needed, the flag state should have the exclusive right to write and enforce them with respect to their own vessels (rank 1).

At the opposite end of the spectrum were proposals to shift the exclusive right to make regulations concerning vessels to the coastal state through whose EEZ the vessel was transiting (rank 12). In particular, proponents sought to give coastal states the right to prohibit transit by vessels not meeting their requirements for design, construction, stowage, cargo handling, and manning, or by vessels violating their routing instructions. If a problem arose, advocates of coastal jurisdiction contended, the coastal state through whose EEZ a polluting vessel was moving was the party suffering harm: therefore the transiting ship should be obliged to obey the coastal state's laws. The new regime should shift general jurisdiction over pollution regulations to

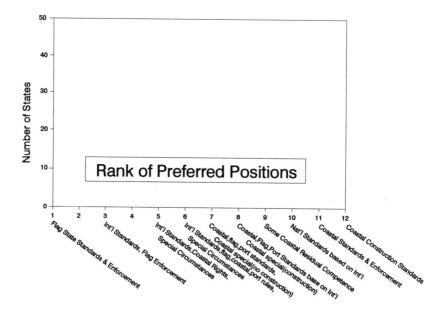

Figure 6.1:   Vessel-Source Pollution Standards

the coastal state (rank 11). This would have gone a long way toward replacing a law of person with a law of place. Some coastal-state supporters were aware that their modal position seemed threatening to marine transportation interests, and were willing to soften it. They conceded that coastal states must consider internationally agreed measures in their domestic regulations. However, they made it clear that the coastal state should have primary responsibility for regulating movement in the EEZ (rank 10).

Some supporters of pollution management by flag states would also concede a role for international organizations in creating pollution rules. They would allow pollution regulations to be established by competent international organizations, as long as enforcement was reserved for flag states (rank 3). Some went further and were willing to allow the empowering parties to participate in rule-making, as long as the primary rules were made by competent international organizations. The package approach was placed at rank 5. It gave international organizations the lead, but allowed flag states and coastal states to write rules in "special circumstances" as long as the coastal states were "implementing . . . rules and standards . . . as have been made applicable by the competent international organization for special areas."[38]

While balancing authority to act between interested parties was generally acceptable to some maritime states, it left out one key stakeholder group—port states. The British and American delegations were under pressure from domestic environmental interests in and out of government to include port states among those with authority to act. We placed the similar British and American preferred positions at rank 7. From the point of view of these traditional allies, the position they espoused was a masterstroke. It allowed them simultaneously to strengthen environmental authority useful to their domestic decision-makers, while posing a minimal potential threat to international navigation.

Other states thought this did not go far enough. Such rights would help the United States, for example, to solve its pollution control problems. Given its three open coasts, virtually all vessels within 200 miles of United States shores are heading for U.S. ports anyway. But such a provision would not help states in more congested marine regions. In semi-enclosed seas like the Mediterranean a vessel might transit through the EEZs of several states without entering their ports.

The port-state provision would not help states like Canada concerned about potential pollution problems resulting from other states' vessels transiting the so-called Northwest Passage between Canadian Arctic islands. The principal vessels concerning Canada were American, and they did not usually stop in a Canadian port before transit, so port-state rights would have done Canada little good in establishing the vessel-construction and manning standards thought necessary for the special circumstances of polar marine transportation. At rank 9, we placed proposals which included the previously stated division of authority, but without limits on what a state might regulate under "special circumstances," or with specific authority to regulate vessel construction, design, manning, and routing. Rank 8 shows a similar proposal, but one which gave coastal states only the right to regulate navigation or discharges and which specifically excluded design, construction, etc. from the regulatory reach of the coastal state. The difference seemed narrow, but it was the distance between U.S. and Canadian approaches, and it proved to be important.

Given the many countercurrents in the early debates, the results for T-1 are not surprising.

Distribution in figure 6.2 is bimodal. Two strong camps existed. One favored putting responsibility for regulating vessel-source pollution essentially with flag and port states, the other preferred empowering coastal states to take on that function. Even in the early days of UNCLOS III (up to 1973), there was no groundswell for relying exclusively upon either modal position.

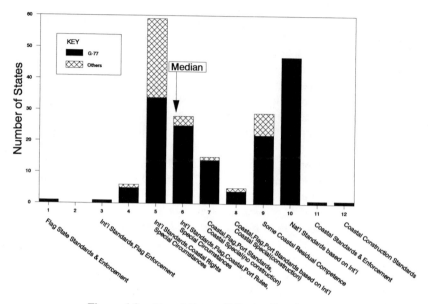

Figure 6.2: Vessel-Source Pollution Standards (T-1)

Figure 6.2 shows the extremes; ranks 1–3 and 11–12 are largely unpopulated. Serious negotiations began when both camps realized that they would not get their modal approach into international law in a pure form. They would have to compromise, share authority, and mix elements from the opposing proposed formula into the final treaty language. The key questions were how much, in which proportion, and, in cases of conflicting rival authorities, which would have priority?

In this early picture of the negotiation, it seemed forces supporting a flag-state approach had a numerical advantage over those supporting a coastal-state approach. The median of 5.9 could be interpreted as showing that flag-state supporters had about a two-to-one advantage before the Single Negotiating Text was prepared. This was not consensus, but presumably under a consensus-decision rule, the coastal forces had to assume twice the burden of their opponents if their general approach was to prevail. If preferences did not change, it did not appear as if the coastal forces could have had their way. This is confirmed by our pairs analysis for T-1. However, there was a sufficient shift in T-2 to turn the situation around, and to force an accommodation between the two camps.

Committee III was also the venue for a long, noisy quarrel between two developed neighbors—the United States and Canada. At one level, the quarrel was about vessel pollution standards, but at another, it was about the relationship between a superpower and its less powerful neighbor. It involved differences not only over the nature of the regulations needed, but more importantly over power and authority.[39]

Although the larger problem of coexisting on the same continent with the United States has been around for as long as Canada has been an independent state (or earlier), the specific problem arose only during the late 1960s, with the question of how to bring the oil discovered on the North Slope of Alaska to market. Three basic options were available: (1) bringing the oil to market on the U.S. West Coast by tanker west across the Beaufort and Chuckchi Seas, then south out the Bering Strait; (2) bringing the oil by pipeline from the North Slope across Alaska and Canada to either a Canadian, a U.S. continental terminus or to an ice-free southern Alaskan port, and by tanker to U.S. West Coast and Gulf ports; or (3) bringing the oil by tanker east across the Beaufort Sea through the Northwest Passage (in reality one of several potential routes) to East Coast markets.

An experiment was conducted in 1969 to test the third option. A tanker, the *S.S. Manhattan*, specially outfitted to be ice-resistant, loaded with ballast water instead of crude oil, and escorted by a Canadian ice breaker, was sent on a voyage eastward through the Northwest Passage. The Canadian Government was fully aware of the planning, but when information about the voyage was reported in the Canadian press, a great brouhaha broke out. The United States did not ask for Canadian permission to make the transit. Since the United States recognized Canadian sovereignty over the islands but not the water areas between them beyond a three-mile territorial sea (or six miles between the islands), the U.S. Government claimed that it did not need to request permission to have an American company stage the experiment.

While the U.S. position was legally sound according to its own interpretation, it was insensitive. Canada never officially followed a "sector theory" for defining jurisdiction in the Arctic, but Canadians have always looked North to define their nationhood, much as Americans looked westward. However, the U.S. had to protect its role as superpower—its position was predicated upon the need to resist idiosyncratic claims to jurisdiction over straits used for international navigation. Both sides had difficulty in compromising.

Since U.S.–Canada relations were generally good and there was a great deal of interdependence between the two nations, Canadian decision-makers did not want the fight to be over fundamentals, that is, over who had general jurisdiction over the water areas between the Arctic islands. Rather, they cast the problem in environmental terms (which, indeed, was a factor), the need for specific, nationally determined regulations on manning, and vessel-construction standards. These were stated in domestic Canadian regulations, the Arctic Waters Pollution Prevention Act, to be enforced in a 100-mile-pollution-prevention zone drawn around the Arctic archipelago.[40] This quarrel lasted well beyond UNCLOS III's termination date of 1982, even though the pipeline alternative was chosen, and the Northwest Passage has not been used for oil movement, but only for the transit of ice breakers and tourist liners (and, perhaps, submarines). A modus vivendi was worked out in 1988, but the problem is not yet fully resolved.[41]

Canada was determined to use the UNCLOS III negotiations to validate its right to make and enforce pollution-control regulations for Arctic waters. Multilateral negotiations can provide a useful forum for a less powerful participant facing a more powerful one. If the less powerful can gain allies to help it promote its case, circumstances might be created to force a superpower to accept what it claims is unacceptable. Since the poorer and smaller outnumber the rich, large, and powerful, it is almost always advantageous to bring problems between states in an asymmetrical dyad to a multilateral forum.

The Canadian position was forcefully advanced in Committee III negotiations over authority to make and enforce pollution-control regulations in the EEZ, and also in essentially bilateral negotiations at UNCLOS III between Canadian and United States representatives. The purpose of the latter was to find a way of resolving the specific U.S.–Canada quarrel so that it would not dominate the entire general negotiation.

An accommodation was worked out between the United States and Canada at UNCLOS III that got into the treaty as Article 234.[42] Delegates accepted the idea that coastal states have the right to adopt and enforce pollution-control regulations in ice-covered areas, as long as the regulations are not discriminatory. Canada got the right to make and enforce regulations in a specific area. The United States got the unilateral right of a coastal state to make and enforce regulations restricted to a specific area with very distinctive characteristics. In other words, in the U.S. view, Article 234 cannot be used to claim general jurisdiction over vessels in the EEZ. It would not serve as precedent for other areas that were not ice-covered. Nevertheless, the impact of the bilateral quarrel can be seen throughout Committee III's work. The frequency of remarks and proposals on pollution of Canada and the average of all states provides some measure of comparative salience on pollution issues. In T-1 alone, Canada had a frequency of mention of 50; all other states averaged .75.

The United States correctly perceived the thrust of the negotiation on pollution standards before 1973–74. It is shown in figure 6.2 as favoring an outcome acceptable to major maritime states.[43] According to the report of the U.S. delegation, by the Second Session in 1974, the "trend against coastal state standard setting is already evident. . . ."[44] By the end of the Third Session in 1975, the U.S. delegation reported that "only general applicable international regulations . . . would apply . . . in the economic zone."[45] This air of self-satisfaction was soon to be shattered. When measured in the next time period (T-2), the trend of preferences had moved in the other direction, requiring further adjustments, so that the states supporting coastal authority could be brought into a consensus decision.

The trend that would result in the language of the Single Negotiating Text and the final convention was set early in T-2.

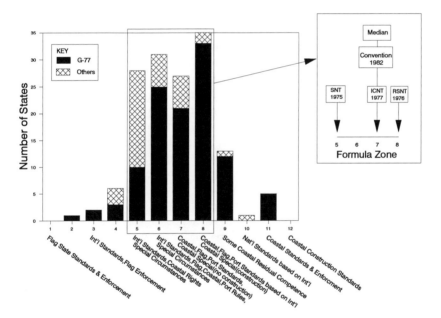

Figure 6.3:   Vessel-Source Pollution Standards (T-2)

Instead of a bimodal distribution in T-2, figure 6.3 shows a unimodal distribution with most states clustered between rank 5 and rank 9. The median was at 6.7, favoring, a bit, the forces for increasing coastal-states powers over pollution standards. Nevertheless, we appear to be seeing a move toward compromise, perhaps even an attempt at a 50-percent solution. However, it turned out to be more like a 60-percent solution, where the coastal forces got a bit more, the maritime forces a bit less, but not so much less as to make the deal unacceptable.

The Single Negotiating Text and the final convention pollution articles attempted to provide something for all positions. The U.S. reported correctly that there was little sentiment for conceding coastal states exclusive jurisdiction over vessel-source pollution in the EEZ, but there was some willingness to give coastal states a role in pollution management in the EEZ, without denying flag or port states the right to manage their own ships, or ships bound for their ports.

The Single Negotiating Text vessel-source pollution articles, their successors in the Revised and Combined Texts, and the final convention were typical of a certain type of compromise solution. Take all major approaches submitted as exclusive solutions, remove the claim to having an exclusive right, and allow all claims to jurisdiction. The bargaining moved to another level of detail and intensity. Within a broad formula zone, some of the parties maneuvered to circumscribe and limit the authority to act, and their opponents maneuvered to have the authority to act less circumscribed and limited.

Article 20 of the SNT proclaimed that states "acting through competent international organizations . . . shall establish as soon as possible . . . international rules and standards."[46] Flag states also may establish regulations for the prevention of vessel-source pollution. Indeed, their laws "shall be no less effective" than international rules and standards. Naturally, in the territorial sea, the coastal state may enact its own exclusive laws, but (to the disappointment of coastal state advocates) these laws must not hamper innocent passage of foreign ships. The coastal state also may enact rules for the EEZ, but these must conform to international rules and standards.

Article 20 in the Revised Text had a somewhat more coastal-state cast. We scaled this at rank 8 since there were no restrictions on the coastal state's ability to control vessel design, construction, and manning, and there was no port-state provision. Matters shifted back (to rank 7) in the Consolidated Text, published in 1977, which had an elaborate set of coastal-state rights to "establish requirements . . . as a condition for the entry of foreign vessels into their ports."[47] It also specifically exempted from coastal-state authority, under "special circumstances" in the EEZ, "design, construction, manning or equipment standards," leaving the coastal state only the right to regulate discharges or navigational practices.[48] This is essentially the language which entered the Convention as Article 211.

Under the new law of the sea, vessels will be subject to standards set by competent international organizations, or by their own flag states. Port states may set higher standards for vessels entering their ports. Vessels will also be subject to coastal-state controls, especially in relation to discharge and navigational practices in the EEZ under "special circumstances." Nevertheless, although coastal states gained new pollution-control authority, it was more circumscribed than many enclosure proponents might have wished. The authority the coastal state might exercise was neither exclusive, nor at times even predominant in the mix the conference created. For example, Canada was disappointed that while "the Conference recognized an enhanced role for the coastal state in pollution prevention off its coasts, the provisions of the Convention are not as favorable to the coastal state as was hoped."[49]

Consensus had not been reached when we did our last measurements. In the remaining seven years of UNCLOS III, most of the bargaining was "micronegotiation" around a series of narrow, but to participants highly salient, differences on where authority over vessel-source pollution would reside. But since there were no large shifts in the positions of states in the seven years until the Convention was signed, we were right on the mark. By 1975, the delegates were on course toward a laboriously crafted 50- to 60-percent solution on vessel-source pollution standards.

Vessel-Pollution Enforcement

The question of who has the authority to *enforce* rules controlling vessel pollution in the EEZ was even more controversial than the question of who has the right to *make* the rules. Rules setting standards are statements of preference on a piece of paper; if rules enforcing those standards are absent or weak, the standards will remain on paper. Both proponents and opponents of freedom of movement knew how the specification of enforcement rights would determine the effectiveness of the standards.

Just under the surface was the underlying bargaining problem—what type of zone was the 200-mile EEZ to be? Was the new economic zone essentially complete enclosure, whose framework was best defined by the notion of sovereignty, with the coastal state having exclusive rights over the area and not just an exclusive right to exploit its resources? Or was the EEZ to be, as the patrimonialists described it, sui generis—a special-purpose zone in which the coastal state could exploit the resources, but had to allow noncompeting activities to continue under rules it did not control completely or could not enforce unilaterally?

Delegates who worried about whether a unique or sui generis set of rules could remain stable feared the possibility of jurisdictional "creep." Delegates from other states worried about the coastal state's right to exploit the natural resources of the EEZ. It was impossible to isolate the rights about to be acquired from the activities of others in the same area. Activities such as pollution from passing ships interfered with coastal-state rights under the EEZ notion. Coastal states could not enjoy their economic rights unless they had the authority to prevent interference with those economic rights.

Was the world community going to find a solution to the problem of pollution from ships in the new regime? Traditional rules of the sea specified that beyond internal waters, and to some extent in the territorial sea (where a passing ship may be exercising its right of innocent passage),[50] the captain of a vessel in transit was responsible exclusively to the government of his flag state. Since much marine traffic would move through the areas that were to become EEZs, the relationship between the transiting vessel and the coastal government had to be clarified.

Some maritime states simply wanted to retain the status quo and ignore the coastal state on enforcement of movement rights. That was unrealistic (though such ideas became their opening bargaining position). Because of the pollution incidents of the 1960s and early 1970s, and stepped-up offshore oil exploration and exploitation, something had to be done. Flag states had simply not done an adequate job in protecting the oceans from pollution. It was difficult to justify their continuation as the only source of authority over the movement of ships.

Nevertheless, enforcement rights demanded by some coastal states in the EEZ raised the specter of "national lakes," where no activity could occur without the permission of the coastal state, and threatened to overturn completely the existing system of marine transportation. Some feared that such a jurisdictional change could effectively terminate world maritime commerce, especially if the coastal states of the world enforced widely different sets of rules, or demanded some form of compensation or rent to move through their zones. Notions such as the right to enforce national construction standards, and the right to prevent vessels that did not meet design, construction, or manning standards from entering the EEZ struck fear in the hearts of many a ship operator. The right to arrest on criminal charges any violator of coastal-state rules was also a matter of grave concern. It was only a step worse than the right to institute civil proceedings in the courts of coastal states that might result in levying of fines, seizure of a vessel, or preventing it from sailing until it had completed mandatory repairs.

Some of these enforcement mechanisms might have enabled coastal states to make sea movement safer, but they also created internal dissension within the delegations of several major maritime states. Maritime states that had long coastlines or were situated on important straits were especially vulnerable to oil spills, and had to consider their own environmental needs. Some of their delegations were pushed by domestic environmental and resource-management agencies to opt for stronger pollution-control measures. These pressures had to be reconciled with the expressed interests of oil importers, shipping companies, and navies, who feared creeping or galloping jurisdiction, and who considered the demand for more enforcement power as an attack on their rights and on the entire Grotian system. Representatives from such groups and, at times, Grotians from foreign affairs or legal agencies urged their states to resist. In sum, several delegations had cross-cutting cleavage problems on pollution issues.

Many ideas entered into the debate on vessel-source pollution enforcement. Our research group attempted to view the problem with one conflict variable, even though we knew from the beginning that many ideas introduced as separate, and sometimes described as mutually exclusive, would be combined in the final treaty language. Sometimes these separate concepts were packaged in omnibus proposals, at other times they were presented as separate articles. We still thought we could capture the underlying thrust of the solution being negotiated, since those who will interpret user rights and regulators of movement rights must read the articles together. As shown in figure 6.4, it was not difficult to identify the range of the debate and pin down the ideas on the outer edges of the issue. In the early debate some on the Grotian side extolled the idea of giving the flag state the exclusive right to enforce standards for its vessels wherever they sailed (rank 1). At the other end of the spectrum was a proposal to give coastal states the right to enforce design, construction, or manning standards (rank 20). Vessels not meeting those standards could be excluded from entering the EEZ. If they foolishly or brazenly entered it, they were subject to arrest.

Some states supporting strong measures bruited about the notion that the 200-mile EEZ should be formally recognized as a pollution-control zone. Since the actual enforcement mechanisms being proposed were sometimes vague, we placed this theme at rank 18. Much more explicit was a demand, often associated with the Canadian delegation, giving a coastal state with reasonable grounds for believing a ship might pollute the right to prevent it from entering its EEZ (rank 17). A number of states argued that creating the EEZ gave the coastal state certain "residual rights," even if there was no specific right to arrest, or to prevent a polluting vessel from entering its EEZ (rank 16).

Whose rules were to be enforced? Some states insisted that the coastal state should be entitled to enforce pollution rules adopted by competent international organizations and also rules made under its domestic decision

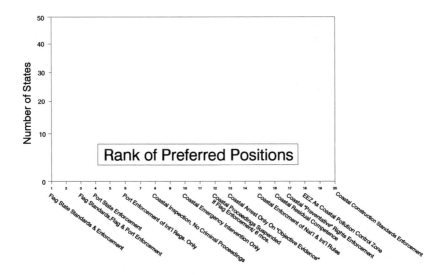

Figure 6.4:   Vessel-Source Pollution Enforcement

processes. We placed this theme at rank 15. Regardless of whose rules were being enforced, were the coastal states obligated to have adequate justification for enforcement actions? Could they enforce on mere suspicion? Did they need evidence? The proposal we placed at rank 13 would require that coastal states display "objective evidence" before ordering enforcement. Further down the line, we placed an attempt to mesh the enforcement actions of coastal, port, or flag states. Those who proposed this measure conceded to the coastal or port state the right to act and request information from passing vessels, inspect them, and impose penalties on flagrant violators of the rules. However, if the flag state acted within six months, the proceeding of the coastal or port state would be suspended (rank 12).

The most conservative approach was to rely exclusively on flag states (rank 1), but states protective of transportation rights could fall back upon various other positions. Maritime or flag-of-convenience states fell back on either the British or American versions of flag- and port-state enforcement, as long as the rules being enforced were made by the flag state (rank 3). But if port states were to take action, it would be against vessels causing problems in their internal waters or at their offshore terminals. These vessels would be violating domestic law. Therefore port states should be entitled to enforce their own domestic laws (rank 4). But the laws port states should invoke were to be agreed upon internationally (rank 6).

Many supporters of freedom of movement realized they would have to concede some rights to the coastal state in the EEZ. The easiest enforcement right they could concede was for coastal authorities to inspect passing ships (rank 9). This would not give the coastal states authority to arrest the ship or to impede its passage. In an age of ocean oil spills, some would concede to coastal states the right to intervene, but only in an emergency, where a spill had occurred or where a spill was probable (rank 10).

As figure 6.5 shows, it was difficult to argue that the problem of oil spillage from vessels was under control in 1967–73:

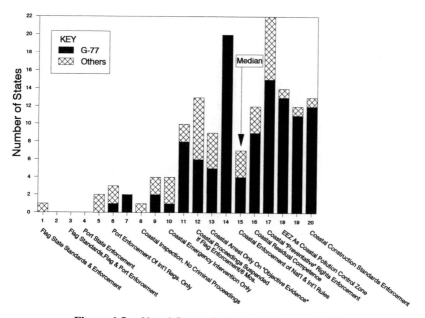

Figure 6.5: Vessel-Source Pollution Enforcement (T-1)

Distribution, while uneven, is largely unimodal with a small tail. There was little sentiment for leaving enforcement of pollution regulations exclusively in the hands of flag states. Support for a flag-state or even a flag- and port-state approach (ranks 1–10) was remarkably sparse. Only Greece stood four-square for a flag-state approach, with the United States, the United Kingdom, and Japan indicating they would be a bit more reasonable.

There was no clear trend toward giving coastal states more power over enforcing pollution regulations off their own coasts. Although it was early in the negotiation, the median of 15.3 seemed to point to an outcome favorable to coastal demands for more authority over passing ships. But, reading as much as possible into early data (often a mistake), one might see two camps among the coastal state supporters: moderates at ranks 11–15 and radicals at ranks 16–20. In any case, it was reasonable to forecast that the next bargaining period, leading toward development of a Single Negotiating Text, would show a formula zone somewhere in the middle of the coastal portion of the figure, perhaps between the two "wings" of the coastal enforcement camp. If that turned out to be true, it would be a forgone conclusion that coastal states would gain new rights to enforce pollution regulations in the EEZ. In the next period (T-2), bargaining would concentrate on two matters: (1) whether the moderates and radicals of the coastal-rights camp could resolve their differences and support a common proposal; and (2) whether the maritime and flag-of-convenience states could persuade the coastal forces to accept some limitations on coastal state powers, or at least rules of accountability for enforcement decisions.

Another attribute of the situation stands out in the distribution in T-1. Developed states spread from one end of the spectrum to the other, with substantial numbers in the coastal camp. These include old Commonwealth states (Australia, Canada, and New Zealand), Scandinavian states (Iceland, Norway, and Sweden), European straits states (Spain and Italy), as well as Eastern European states (including Bulgaria, the home state of the Committee chair).

Our prediction of where bargaining would begin in 1974–75 was essentially correct, as we can see in figure 6.6. The median had moved one rank, from 15 to 16. We judged the provisions of the Single Negotiating Text concerning vessel pollution enforcement to be quite favorable to the strong coastal-rights position, and placed it at ranks 16–17. The SNT specifies flag-state obligations almost perfunctorily: the flag state is responsible for violations wherever they occur.[51] However, a port state may make an immediate investigation of a violation and even prevent a vessel from sailing "if it presents an excessive danger to the marine environment."[52] Coastal states also have extensive powers. If a vessel violates internationally agreed rules, a coastal state may arrest the ship.[53] The coastal state can conduct inspections only when there "are reasonable grounds," although it may not have to produce objective evidence of a violation.[54] In other words, it has extensive powers to prevent potential disasters. By implication (from later documents which take this power away from coastal states), the coastal state could in-

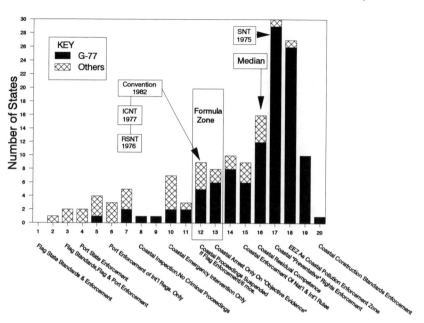

Figure 6.6:   Vessel-Source Pollution Enforcement (T-2)

stitute criminal proceedings against ships and seamen. They certainly could levy fines, and could detain a ship with a court order until a fine was paid.[55]

In 1975, it appeared that negotiations had gone badly for the maritime forces, and that a strong new coastal pollution regime was in the offing. Yet one year later, the situation was quite different. It appeared that the Revised Single Negotiating Text and successor documents had moved away from a strong coastal approach to pollution enforcement. Indeed, subsequent negotiation demonstrated that the formula zone was rather narrow after the RSNT. A much more moderate formula was refined in the negotiations that produced the Informal Composite Negotiating Text and the final Convention text.

The RSNT, ICNT, and final convention all granted new powers to coastal states, but they were much more circumscribed than those in the SNT. In all three successor documents, extensive responsibilities were given the flag state in the conduct of its vessels.[56] The most important shift, begun in the RSNT and sustained in the ICNT and the Convention, was that if the coastal state instituted proceedings against a ship, they had to be suspended if the flag state acted within six months.[57] The negotiators gave with one hand, and took away with the other. In the RSNT, the suspension referred only to criminal proceedings. In the ICNT, this was further modified to "proceedings to impose penalties in respect of any violation." Even port-state powers were cut back to the right to institute proceedings only on violations of internationally agreed rules.[58] The difference between "reasonable grounds for believing" and the necessity of presenting "objective evidence" before instituting proceedings[59] was the difference between what maritime states would not accept, and what they would. The EEZ had been made safe for marine transportation, although strong proponents of the coastal-state position, such as Canada, doubted that the Convention had made their coasts safe from the ravages of mariners, especially those carrying oil.

We successfully forecast the Single Negotiating Text approach to vessel-source pollution enforcement. As of 1975, even though the median showed substantial support for strong coastal rights, we pointed out that the issue was not ripe for solution. The tail in T-2 was much longer and stronger than in T-1. The maritime forces were putting up a much stronger fight than it appeared they might in T-1. Fewer developed states seemed willing to support coastal enforcement powers that might lead to arbitrary behavior.

A substantial shift took place in 1975–76. While the strength of the shift and its rapidity were somewhat uncharacteristic of most other UNCLOS III issues, our model would have been sufficiently robust to pick up the shift if the data had been available.

The model does not give us a definitive answer to why a majority acceded to the wishes of a minority on this issue, and not on other prominent issues such as deep-ocean mining (Part XI). Maritime states were in a position stubbornly to resist deep concessions. Supporters of strong coastal enforcement powers had a 2–1 advantage over opponents. The issue was quite salient to states that had suffered oil-pollution incidents. The model does not provide an answer to the comparative question, but if the leadership of the Third Committee was as astute as we thought, why didn't they develop coastal enforcement provisions maritime powers would accept? As of 1975, opponents of increased coastal powers might have stalemated the Third Committee. Coastal forces had at least 100 supporters, whichever formula they chose to support. If flag-state forces refused to accept any increase in coastal powers (proposals at ranks 1, 4, or 6), they would be reduced to less than 30 states. If they remained obdurate and the coastal forces conceded, as they did, accepting acting only on objective evidence (rank 13), the flag-state forces would be reduced to less than 20. This number was small enough that it might be possible to isolate the remaining obdurate states, and to achieve at least a near-consensus outcome. On the other hand, if coastal forces insisted upon the powers to arrest that seemed threatening to maritime states, and if the maritime states were willing to concede to the coastal state only the power to intervene in a clear emergency (rank 10), the conference might have been stalemated. The maritime forces had a blocking one-third. As it happened, the maritime states were willing to concede coastal states the power to arrest, so long as the proceedings would be suspended if they acted within six months.

Scientific Research at UNCLOS III

The accumulation of human knowledge might seem ipso facto to be a social good. It was not universally acclaimed at UNCLOS III. When research vessels from developed states conducted research in what was to become the 200-mile EEZs of developing states, their activities were sometimes looked upon with grave suspicion. Even if they did not commit any offense against the coastal state's laws, they were often viewed as an affront to the coastal state's dignity and sovereignty.

Many Third World states viewed ocean science with suspicion, as likely to enhance the political power of others, in particular, the researcher's state. The last thing Third World leaders wanted to foster were scientists from developed states who knew more about their near-shore areas than they did. Researchers often explained that they were searching for fundamental knowledge of ocean processes, including temperature, currents, weather, and climate data important for unraveling scientific puzzles and key environmental problems such as changing climate and global warming. Third World governments feared they were looking for knowledge about resources that could be passed on to intelligence agencies or multinational corporations, and that would give those developed state agencies and corporations an advantage in any negotiation or interaction. They looked upon knowledge as something to be controlled, not extolled.

The developing states also had strong opinions about the role of ocean science in helping developed states "grab" the minerals of the deep-ocean floor. Were that to occur, some Third World states would lose valuable raw-materials markets in developed states, and most felt they would lose leverage generally in many ongoing North-South economic negotiations. The solution was to create a new, "common heritage of mankind" regime for deep-ocean minerals that would prevent the developed states from from exploiting ocean minerals under a free-access regime. This was the task of the First Committee. But the International Seabed Authority or Enterprise, to be created by the First Committee, might be put at a disadvantage in future negotiations if scientists from developed states provided their governments with data about the International Area that was not available to the Authority or Enterprise.

To prevent this, proposals were introduced to ensure that science conducted over, in, and on the deep-ocean-seabed was to be controlled by the Authority. This would prevent abuses, and also might be converted into an indirect tax on the developed. In return for permission to conduct research, researchers would be required to provide all of their data to the Authority at no cost.

The oceanographers of the developed world were shocked. Knowledge was, by definition, a social good. Scientists should not be held responsible for how knowledge was used—or abused. Spokesmen for ocean science in the literature of the period were aware that they were also defending their self-interest, but their sense of outrage at what developing state leaders thought and proposed to do comes through strongly in their writings.[60]

UNCLOS III was not the first threat to the freedom of ocean science. That honor was reserved for UNCLOS I. In the Continental Shelf Convention signed in 1958, coastal-state consent was required for all research concerning the legal continental shelf. However, it was expected that the coastal state would not normally withhold its consent if a research request was submitted by a qualified institution.[61] This provision was included despite concern expressed by ocean scientists in general and the International Council of Scientific Unions (ICSU) in particular.[62]

The consent requirement, in addition to being a blow to the self-image of marine scientists, was also costly in money, time, effort, and effectiveness. Additional steps in preparing for research meant spending more time on bureaucratic rather than scientific matters. Expeditions had to be planned much longer in advance if a permit was needed. If the coastal state placed conditions on its consent—such as including its own scientists on the expedition, training its scientists, sharing data and specimens, restricting the area in which research could be conducted, or not allowing research at a time of the year in which an interesting phenomenon was occurring—the cost of research could sometimes increase prohibitively. Even if the cost increase was primarily monetary, that too could be a serious problem, since funding agencies normally did not provide funds for such contingencies. Most important, if a state refused permission for an expedition to enter its waters to collect data, an experiment to understand a large-scale phenomenon might be ruined because of a gap in the data.

The rhetoric being used in the earliest stage of UNCLOS III suggested that, if the rights of ocean scientists to conduct research were treated as an identifiable item on the negotiating work list, they would be roughly handled.[63] But the right to conduct science in the exclusive economic zone was more roughly handled than the right to conduct science relating to the deep-ocean seabed.

Understanding why the outcomes were different on these related issues is important to our understanding of parliamentary diplomacy. In one case, the ocean science issue was a relatively minor aspect of a larger issue and could be treated as a trade-off to help foster agreement on the larger issue. This occurred on the question of ocean science in the international area. On the conduct of ocean science in the EEZ, a comparable trade-off was not available. At the beginning of the formal conference in 1973–74, both superpowers had already conceded the 200-mile EEZ. It was a forgone conclusion. As a result, coastal states did not have to make many concessions to negotiators trying to protect the rights of ocean scientists trying to conduct science in near-shore areas.

Scientific Research in the International Area

The question of who was to control ocean scientific activities in the "International Area" was introduced early in the Ad Hoc Committee proceedings. It remained a thorny problem until the United States insisted upon putting the question to the assembled delegates and forced the final vote. At the first substantive session of UNCLOS III, Colombia tabled a proposal in an informal working group of Committee III stating that "all research in the economic zone . . . requires the explicit consent of the coastal state and that all research in the International Area . . . be conducted directly by the International Authority or under its regulation or control."[64] The portion of this proposal demanding that all research relating to the International Area be a monopoly of the International Seabed Authority (ISA) was placed at rank 10 on the scale of figure 6.7. To capture the underlying bargaining problem, we extracted the portion of the Colombia proposal that would require ISA's consent for national research relating to the Area, and treated it as a separate proposal. It was hotly debated. Since it was only slightly less restrictive than an outright monopoly, we placed it at rank 9.

In the early debate, it was not quite clear what constituted the Area. Proposals were introduced making it unambiguous: ISA's consent was required only for research relating to the resources of the deep seabed, and that research relating to the superjacent waters or airspace would *not* require ISA consent. Such a proposal was placed at rank 8. These themes would find their way into two articles on ocean science in the International Area—one by the First Committee, the other by the Third.

The fallback from ISA consent for supporters of control of ocean science was "notification." Under a proposal at rank 7, all researchers proposing research in the International Area would be required to notify ISA in advance of their expeditions. If that was too stringent for some research-capable

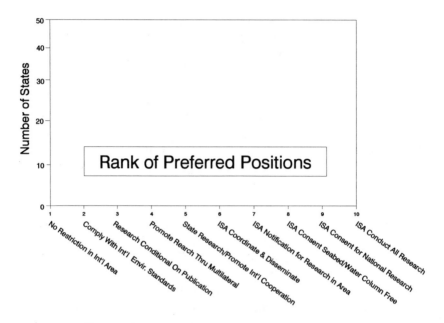

Figure 6.7:   Scientific Research in the International Area

states, a proposal was introduced to have ISA become the central coordinating unit for research relating to the area (rank 6). In that way, ISA would perform such a valuable function that, it was hoped, many reluctant ocean-research-capable states would support the international agency concept, and not so incidentally provide ISA valuable data at little cost.

The opening position of the several states with large ocean-science establishments was that no restrictions should be placed upon ocean scientists doing work in, on, or above the International Area (rank 1). Many statements on the floor of the bargaining halls in Caracas, New York, and Geneva concerned the social utility of science to the world community, and the potential cost to the world community if restrictions were placed on ocean science investigations. But states defending ocean scientists' rights to work in and on the deep-ocean seafloor, could fall back to a requirement that researchers comply with international environmental standards while conducting their work (rank 2). Many university-based ocean science programs could recommend that their governments support a publication requirement as a condition for access to the Area for their work. However, this had to be phrased carefully, since university-based scientists did not want a deadline for publication imposed, making the conduct of research less convenient (rank 3). At rank 4, we placed proposals requiring coordination of national ocean-science activities through relevant international organizations. Finally, at rank 5, we placed a proposal similar to that at rank 6 (ISA coordination and dissemination of national science data relating to the area), but somewhat vaguer about whether ISA was the sole coordinating international organization.

In preliminary negotiations leading up to Caracas, the Colombia proposal had its impact, but the situation did not look bad for forces defending the right of ocean scientists to do their work in the Area. Distribution in figure 6.8 is trimodal. Overinterpretation of the emergent pattern based on early

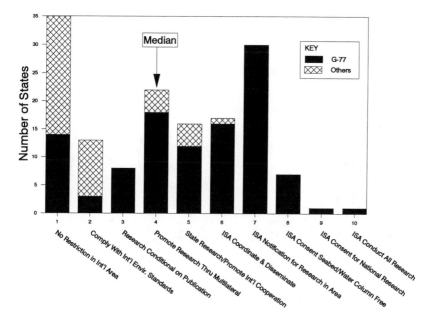

Figure 6.8:   Scientific Research in the International Area (T-1)

data should be avoided, but there seem to be three camps. One group strongly supported freedom of research (ranks 1–2); another was willing to have states obligate their researchers to publish and cooperate with the relevant international organizations (ranks 3–5); and a third insisted that researchers notify ISA and allow it to store and disseminate their data to users, and might even prefer that researchers get ISA consent for deep-seabed research (ranks 6–8).

The median (4.3) indicated that, at this stage, states would at most obligate themselves collectively to promote research through international organizations and allow those organizations to coordinate ocean research, and require researchers to obey international environmental rules, or promise to publish their data when appropriate. The figure shows a relatively united North facing a split South. A large number of the Group of 77 supported restrictions on research in the International Area; a smaller, but still important, number seemed to be willing to support relatively free research. An ISA monopoly over research, or even ISA's consent for nationally sponsored research were factors in the debate, but did not pick up major support in T-1.

The situation is much changed in T-2, after the delegates to the formal conference had a chance to meet and discuss the issue in 1973–75.

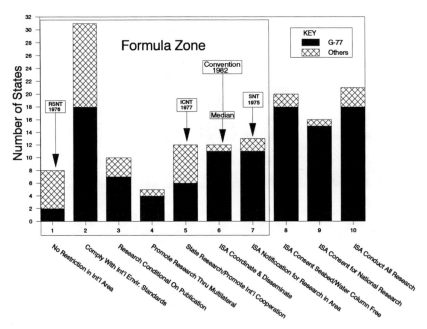

Figure 6.9:   Scientific Research in the International Area (T-2)

As shown in figure 6.9, the pattern is now more bimodal. The United States Delegation reported substantial support for ISA control of science in the International Area at least up to the Third Session in 1975.[65] Our data confirmed that assessment. There was now substantial support for an ISA monopoly, or for ISA consent to nationally sponsored research in the International Area. The median of 6.4 indicated that the balance of forces had shifted two ranks toward the control forces. Nevertheless, the states supporting open research rights for ocean science rallied around a position allowing almost no controls by ISA.

When we measured the situation in 1975, we could see only stasis on this issue. It was not ripe for resolution. Although there was movement away from freedom of science, the control forces did not have anything near a substantial majority, much less near-consensus. It was not clear where the solution might lie, but neither side was in a position to force the issue.

It was the chairman's responsibility to break the logjam. Ambassador Yankov, probably aware of the strengthening of sentiment for ISA control of science, thought consensus might emerge around a requirement that researchers notify ISA before beginning research.[66] Yankov's move to impose a notification requirement was not the wave of the future, but merely a useful starting point for further negotiations. Forces supporting freer science would not budge far from their core position. Our pairs analysis showed notification would only garner about 50 percent of the votes against most formulations of a free science regime. Notification would not be the core of the formula.

The leadership removed the notification requirement from the Revised Single Negotiating Text in 1976. The RSNT gave both states and competent international organizations the right to conduct marine scientific research in the international seabed area.[67] Obviously, this flip-flop (seemingly to a position best reflected by rank 1) meant that the conference was having trouble identifying the core idea of the formula. As we can see in figure 6.9, unlike many issues where there are incremental changes between versions of the negotiation documents on key issues, the issue of ocean science shows a jump shift. Hence, the formula zone appears quite wide. The issue was resolved by having two articles deal with ocean science in the International Area. The First Committee's article was more generous to researchers than the Third Committee's: research should be conducted for peaceful purposes. ISA was to disseminate research results, conduct its own science, and help foster cooperation.[68]

If the two articles are read together, they seem to be the proverbial 50-percent solution. In fact, the 50-percent solution was a victory for the free-science forces. In the first version of the Informal Composite Negotiating Text, the article on research in the International Area no longer referred to the right of ISA to conduct or promote research. The direct reference to the right of states to conduct research in the International Area was removed. Instead, the article presumes a national right to perform research and to "encourag[e] co-operation in marine scientific by personnel of different countries and of the Authority.''[69] And, "when appropriate, ISA is to disseminate . . . the results of research and analysis.''

By 1982, the pendulum swung back slightly. Article 257 of the UNCLOS III Convention merely gives states and competent international organizations a right to conduct research in the International Area. ISA is not named as one of the competent international organizations. However, ISA's and states' rights to conduct research in the Area was restored elsewhere in the Convention.[70] The Convention seemed to hover so close to the midpoint on our variable that it can be called a 50-percent solution.

However, while the outcome hovered around the 50-percent mark, the forces trying to preserve free ocean science essentially won on the issue. They prevented the International Seabed Authority from assuming an exclusive, dominant, or even important role in marine science in the International Area. In fact, the outcome was so satisfactory to the United States, which led the fight over ocean science issues, that when the Reagan-appointed U.S. Delegation issued its "Green Book" (which showed how it would rewrite virtually all of Part XI dealing with the creation of an International Seabed Authority and Enterprise), it left Article 143 on deep-ocean science alone.[71]

Did national preferences shift so much by 1982 that the states assembled reached consensus on the issue because the vast majority wanted a conservative outcome? Since our data extend only to 1975, we can only speculate. It seems unlikely that a substantial majority preferred essentially to endorse the status quo on ocean science in the deep ocean. The core of supporters of a strong International Seabed Authority gave way before the determined opposition of the ocean-using states. The appearance of a 50-percent solution was a useful cosmetic covering the fallback of the majority in the face of the intransigence of the minority.

Why did the majority concede? Ocean science relating to the deep ocean, while quite salient to most developed-state supporters of free science, was not particularly salient to most developing-state supporters of a strong International Seabed Authority. Control of ocean science was a useful but not essential tool for developing a strong ISA and Enterprise. What *was* important to supporters of a strong ISA and Enterprise was that major ocean-using states accept the *economic* provisions of Part XI. To demonstrate that they were reasonable on some aspects of a strong new international agency, supporters of ISA as the economic rightsholder to ocean minerals and of an Enterprise as exclusive or dominant exploiter of the minerals were willing to concede a national right to conduct ocean science in the International Area. There were other science-related issues that captured more of the attention of

ISA supporters, for example control of ocean science in the EEZ and the role of science in technology transfer.

Scientific Research in the Exclusive Economic Zone

The negotiation on the conduct of ocean science in the Exclusive Economic Zone did not result in a 50-percent solution, as it had in the International Area. Here, there were clear winners and, to the great consternation of the oceanographers from developing states, clear losers. The general theme of the negotiation was essentially the same—to determine who would exercise authority or jurisdiction over collecting information from a section of the world ocean. Secondarily, it would specify what requirements validated whether the information was a social good or a social bad.

The major difference between the two negotiations was the particular section of the world ocean in which information was to be gathered. In our current case, delegates had to grapple with determining the nature of jurisdiction out to 200 miles from the coasts of states. The problem of ocean science and the conditions under which researchers worked became part of the debate about implementing enclosure.

Why was the furthering of knowledge of the ocean, usually considered a social good, so quickly transformed into a social bad (at least as it relates to gathering data in the EEZ)? As figures 6.11 and 6.12 show, the transformation was very rapid. The principal reason was that information and data quickly became perceived as a potential threat to sovereignty, especially among developing states. The prevailing image was of the developed states' fully equipped research vessels hovering off the coasts of developing countries struggling to become new nation-states under severe handicaps, including lack of essential knowledge about their own patrimony. Developing states were particularly concerned about being placed at a competitive disadvantage in negotiations concerning offshore oil and gas fields or fisheries, if a distant state or a multinational or state corporation pursuing a concession or license, knew more about their EEZ than they did. Their perceptions were based on more than strategic calculation. There was a large element of emotion. It was humiliating to be at such a disadvantage—an insult to their dignity and sovereignty.

For oceanographers of developed states, the perception that their work might be a social bad, had both psychological and practical consequences. Many who worked in science took it as an article of faith that knowledge was by definition good. Most ocean scientists who followed the negotiations relating to ocean science within UNCLOS III hoped to protect their self-interest as well as the common good. If restrictions were imposed on re-search within the 200-mile EEZs of the world, the impact upon them could range from mere inconvenience to catastrophe.

Because the ocean is a physical common, natural oceanic phenomena can-not be contained within the borders of a single state. Currents move, tem-perature gradients cannot be controlled within the borders of a single EEZ, fish and pollutants migrate. Access to the 200-mile EEZ is essential for many types of ocean research. While some ocean research does have purely local application, much of it is generic. To understand the global weather system, one needs access to the world ocean. For many types of research, access to many 200-mile EEZs may be essential. To understand how pollutants mi-grate, fish stocks decline, or the weather might change is a benefit to all. However, this argument largely fell on deaf ears at UNCLOS III, at least as a reason for granting ocean scientists free access to the exclusive economic zone, the area with the greatest prospect of finding exploitable resources. One could predict in the early 1970s that ocean science was going to be savaged in the U.N. political arena.[72]

Why had perceptions changed? Why was it obvious that ocean science would be forced to pay a price at UNCLOS III for the right to continue to do research? First, oceanographers who were politically active wanted to roll back the clock. They complained about the cost of complying with the 1958 Continental Shelf Convention requirement (Article 5(8)) to obtain coastal-state consent for research on the continental shelf. They wanted to terminate an existing national jurisdictional right. They set themselves an impossi-ble task.

Second, it took a while for observers to recognize that those wanting to restrict ocean science, particularly developing states, were acting rationally in their self-interest, albeit in their short-run self-interest. Whatever a foreign researcher's intent, knowledge once gained is difficult to control. The genie cannot be put back in the bottle. If knowledge is an adjunct to political and economic power, if you cannot gain it, use it, or use it well, and your rival might, you are better off not allowing one of you to know. Giulio Pontecorvo and Maurice Wilkerson put it a slightly different way. While knowledge is useful to both sides, "the marginal value of scientific inquiry increases di-rectly with the degree of industrialization of a state. Therefore, in the short run, the effect of science is to increase the disparity between rich and poor, and in these circumstances science must be 'controlled' to emphasize partic-ular local needs."[73]

And third, most states of the developing world were aware of the relative political weakness of ocean scientists in developed states. By the opening session at Caracas, the developed states had effectively traded away the rights of ocean scientists by not including ocean science among issues on which they demanded a satisfactory outcome as the price for supporting enclosure. The issue simply was not as salient to major developed states as agreement on a modest increase in the territorial sea or on a right of transit through straits used for international navigation.

The right to pursue ocean science freely in the EEZ became a surrogate for myriad problems between the developed and developing states. On ocean science in the EEZ, the developing knew they were in control. Research could not take place without their permission. The heat of the debate seemed to be out of proportion to the overall importance of the issue.

While developed states espoused the cause of free ocean science, they did not offer to give up anything to get freer conditions for science—a clear lack of salience. Despite their few votes, little private economic power, and small campaign donations, oceanographers were still represented on the advisory groups and delegations of some developed states, notably the United States. They put up a valiant fight, but were never in a position to win. Some important gestures were made on their behalf. When President Reagan issued his proclamation creating a 200-mile Exclusive Economic Zone, he made a point of explaining that, although the United States recognized the right of other coastal states to require consent for research in their EEZs, the United States was not claiming a reciprocal right "because of the United States interest in encouraging marine scientific research and avoiding any unnecessary burdens."[74]

Other states were not so modest in making proposals to manage the conduct of ocean science research in the EEZ. The range of proposals included the modal positions already discussed, and ingenious attempts to find a compromise solution, as shown in figure 6.10.

The pure freedom of ocean science position was placed at rank 1 since it was the starting point for delegations supporting the general concept. The idea that scientists operating in the EEZ should be good citizens and carefully carry out international pollution-control obligations was part of the ethos of science, so this was a good fallback from complete freedom (rank 2). Developing coastal states felt they often did not benefit from scientific work in their EEZs because their own scientists had not participated. Therefore another concession, placed at rank 3, was to agree that external researchers were obliged to invite coastal-state scientists to participate in their work. Developed-state scientists grumbled because this implied delays and more costs, but it was widely conceded that such participation was a good thing. Some developed-state supporters of free ocean science, if pressed, also

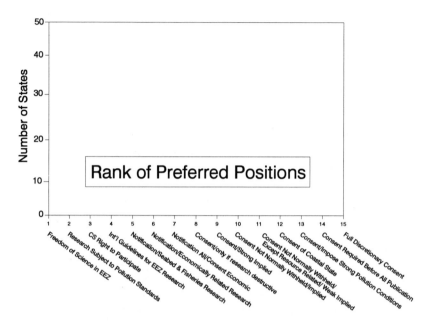

Figure 6.10:   Scientific Research in the EEZ

conceded that it might be acceptable to have freedom of research subject to an objective set of international guidelines for researchers operating in the EEZ (rank 4).

The research community wanted to avoid being required officially to notify the coastal state of intended research in advance. The weakest form of notification was limited to a specific type of research of special concern to the coastal state, such as seabed or fisheries research (rank 5), or more generally, to economically related research (rank 6).

At the other end of the spectrum, we placed statements defending a coastal-state right to exercise unlimited discretion in granting, or denying, permission to do research in the EEZ (rank 15). As part of its consent right, the coastal state would not be obligated to respond officially or to explain why it turned down a research request. At rank 14, we placed proposals that the coastal state, if it granted permission at all, would be the owner of the data and samples for any and all research done in the EEZ. Indeed, no data or interpretations of data could be published without its explicit permission, even if it had given permission to a researcher to gather the data.[75] Some proposals even gave coastal states the right to impose on researchers strong national environmental requirements, over and above those agreed upon by the international community, as a condition for granting their consent (rank

13). This was only one step more stringent than statements of general support for coastal-state consent as the basic mode of managing science in the EEZ (rank 12).

Since the consent formula in the 1958 Continental Shelf Convention was softened by the understanding that coastal states would normally be expected not to withhold consent for arbitrary reasons, we placed various "not normally withheld" candidates for the UNCLOS III consent formula at or below rank 11. Proposals that would allow coastal states to avoid the "not normally withheld" limitation if the research dealt with exploitable natural resources of the EEZ were placed at rank 11. Most of these proposals also contained a weak "implied consent" clause. That is, if a researcher applied and his request received no response within a certain time, the consent of the coastal state was implied. Straightforward proposals combining a consent requirement with a "not normally withheld" clause and an implied consent guarantee were placed at rank 10. Similar proposals with language slightly more favorable to researchers were placed at rank 9.

The middle was occupied by two proposals. At rank 8 was a consent formulation, but only for research that would be physically destructive, e.g., that used explosives, or that would emplace instrumentation or installations which might interfere with the coastal state's right to exploit natural resources. Notification and consent were combined in a proposal at rank 7. All research in the EEZ would require notification of the coastal state; research that was economically related would additionally require the coastal state's consent. This would have been even more palatable to supporters of free ocean science if the "reasonable distinction" approach was subject to impartial compulsory dispute settlement.[76]

Before 1973, the situation does not look too bad for supporters of ocean scientists' right to work under what they considered reasonable conditions in the EEZ. Distribution in figure 6.11 is unimodal, but not strongly so. There is a wide spread of preferences. The strongest position seems to be scientific access to the EEZ with only participation by the coastal state and scientists' obedience to internationally agreed standards required. Consensus is not near. But, given the strength of the forces in the middle, a proposal that many states were satisfied was a 50-percent solution might attract all states falling in ranks 1–7. Within that range fell 101 states, enough to win under the classic voting formula of two-thirds present and voting; enough possibly under consensus conditions to convince the minority to accept the basic formula, and only try to whittle away at the edges.

Since the general region where consensus lay had not yet been confirmed by negotiations, the Chair tried to show where it might lie. Yankov proposed that all research in the EEZ be subject to a notification requirement.[77]

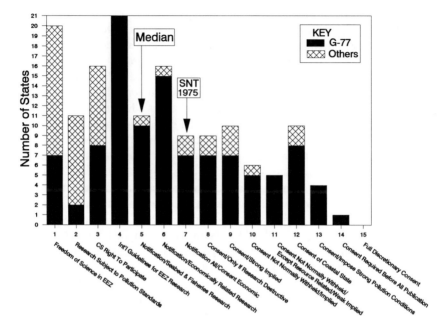

Figure 6.11:   Scientific Research in the EEZ (T-1)

Researchers were obligated to state whether the proposed work was fundamental or resource-related.[78] If any proposed research related to the living or nonliving resources of the EEZ or continental shelf, it could "be conducted only with the explicit consent of the coastal state."[79] A neat solution. Something for both sides. If scientists were pursuing pure knowledge, they would not be inhibited; if they were pursuing information about exploitable resources, they had to inform the state which exercised jurisdiction over those resources.

Unfortunately, it didn't work. The positions of most of the states changed very rapidly on this issue. Yankov underestimated the opposition to free access to the EEZ for research purposes, just as he had overestimated the opposition to free access to the International Area for research purposes. In both cases, he proposed that the core rule be notification. In both cases, the Chairman seemed to use his privilege of assembling the working text to set up a straw man—a starting point for further negotiation without regard to where consensus might lie. His proposals energized proponents of rival formulas to force the pace of negotiation. This is an important role for the chair in large-scale multilateral negotiations when bargaining on an issue does not show a clear direction for settlement. We judged that Ambassador Yankov's SNT articles were outside of the formula zone on this issue. They were swept away so quickly that they did not become part of the bargaining over the identification and refinement of the idea at the heart of the formula.

In 1973, it was first becoming evident that an EEZ for coastal states would emerge as a major accomplishment of the UNCLOS III negotiations. By 1975, states were concerned with details of their privileges and responsibilities in the zone. As a result, they took a hard look at the possibility of foreign scientists wandering around *their* EEZs gathering data.

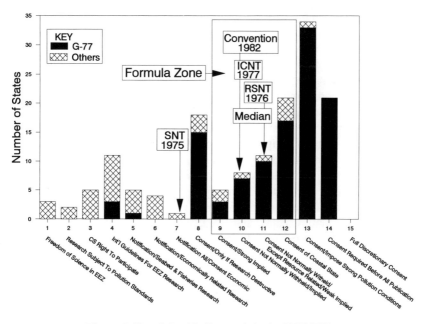

Figure 6.12:   Scientific Research in the EEZ (T-2)

As shown in figure 6.12, the distribution in T-2 is unimodal with a relatively small tail. The compromisers at rank 8 are likely to be pulled into the formula zone easily, leaving only a few states, centered on rank 4, to resist the move toward a substantial majority. There is a marked North-South split on this issue. The median of 11 indicates that if the issue were put to a vote, no other proposal could beat one requiring consent for all research, but consent "not normally withheld" unless it related to resource research, and implied if there was no response to a researcher's request. In a consensus procedure, opponents of the core concept could not hope to defeat it completely in further negotiations, but only to modify or tame it. The only alternative for opponents, if the core idea was sufficiently unpalatable, was defection.

Figure 6.12 is an illustration of where to look for a formula zone in one type of situation common to parliamentary diplomacy, namely, where there is a single peak, showing considerable support for a particular idea as the core of the formula, but also still a tail, indicating that opposition to that core idea remains. Consensus (defined as complete agreement or no further opposition) or near-consensus (defined as almost complete agreement or only relatively few remaining in opposition), does not exist. The final language of agreement will probably be found within a formula zone; under these circumstances, on the downward slope of the single peak facing the positions of the remaining opposition. If consensus or near-consensus has not been reached, the opposition will probably not accept the pure formula represented by the peak and might defect. If the majority indicates any willingness to soften the impact of the formula, more often than not a deal can be worked out.

In this case, the formula zone in which bargaining took place until 1982, extended from full consent with strong coastal-state powers to say no to researchers, to consent hedged with conditions that coastal states must act "reasonably" in considering research requests. In 1976 the pendulum swung all the way from outside the formula zone to the harshest version of the formula. In the RSNT, a notification requirement was reduced to a time limit within which the researcher had to submit information concerning the objectives, methods, areas, dates, and research institution to the coastal state.[80] On the basis of information submitted, the coastal state would make its consent decision. According to this candidate formula, the coastal state should not normally withhold consent unless the research related to resources, destructive methods such as drilling or explosives were used, or the scientific investigation interfered with other coastal-state economic activities.[81] The RSNT was judged harsher than its successors because it contained an article that could be interpreted as giving the coastal state the right to prohibit publication of research, even if it gave permission to do the work in the first place.[82]

Further negotiation produced the first version of an ICNT in 1977, and a second version in 1980. It contained a consent requirement. However, the "not normally withheld" provision was tightened. Coastal states were expected to "establish rules and procedures ensuring that . . . consent will not be delayed or denied unreasonably."[83] Implied consent was also made somewhat more favorable to researchers. These changes softened the harshness of the consent regime. The United States tried to get further concessions,[84] but the language of the convention on this issue was essentially set by 1980.[85] After 1977, the United States was virtually isolated on the issue of ocean science in the EEZ. The Soviet Union and the Eastern Europeans abandoned the other developed states in the Sixth Session.[86] European resistance to strong coastal consent weakened in the Seventh Session in 1978.[87] However, in the Ninth Session (1980), the United States and its remaining friends did succeed in beating back an effort to require consent for research on the continental shelves extending beyond 200 nautical miles.[88]

The UNCLOS III Convention repeated much of the language of the last negotiating text. Some language was toned down to make ocean researchers feel a bit better. Permission to do research should not normally be withheld, according to the Convention, if the purpose of the proposed work was "to increase scientific knowledge of the marine environment for the benefit of mankind."[89] Nevertheless, there was a clear winner—the coastal state. The right to control information about an economic zone was judged to be an important economic right and consistent with granting the coastal state sovereignty over the area.

Until the Eastern European group abandoned ship, and the Western Europeans indicated they would accept coastal-state consent, the line-up of states was strongly North-South. After the usual early search for a position that its members could support, the Group of 77 became solid supporters of a consent regime. It took several years to solidify their position, having started out supporting the value of doing unrestricted ocean research, but they were driven toward their ultimate position by the leadership of the Latin American group.[90] The consent issue became one of the key components of their view that coastal states needed consent to exercise real sovereignty over their economic zones. By the last time period we measured, the Group of 77 and all its other subgroups in addition to the Latin Americans—Africans, Asians, and Arabs—supported consent, and they were quite united in their advocacy.[91]

The developed states fell back steadily over the life of the conference, moving from outright support of freedom of research to acceptance of a consent regime, in the case of the Scandinavians. The WEO group was near acceptance by 1975. However, our data showed the Eastern European group, the EEC, and the Big 5 resisting strongly. The defections mentioned earlier did not occur until after 1975–76. The developed groups were rather disciplined in support until those groups decided to accept a consent formula.

Another indicator that the freedom-of-science effort was doomed was the steady movement toward a consent regime by *all* geographic groups. Part of the argument used by defenders of freedom of science was the nightmare that would be created if researchers had to get multiple permits to work in the narrow waters of a semi-enclosed sea or shelf-locked region, or in Southeast Asia with its overlapping archipelago claims. This argument apparently was dismissed by states of all major geographic groups; they all wanted to have control of research.

Poor ocean science! Scientists were made to pay for the state of relationships between North and South, and for the validation of a new concept in international ocean law—an exclusive economic zone. The EEZ was designed to be sui generis, and not a territory under full sovereignty, but coastal states thought it was important to their control of the zone that they control data about its attributes. Research has been made significantly more difficult, and this could be costly to all states in the future. Knowledge gained from the ocean might unlock puzzles such as climate change and global warming, pollution, or the reduction of the living resources of the ocean. But states chose to foster their perceived short-run interest.

Ocean scientists did not have a chance of pushing back the effort of states to control their work. The superpowers and others accepted the EEZ and, in return, expected proponents of the EEZ to concede to them satisfactory outcomes on certain issues. Ocean science was not among those issues, so rights of ocean scientists inevitably were bargained away (or so it seemed to ocean scientists) in the rush to enclose ocean space. Yet, as we saw on the issue of control of vessel-source pollution, major maritime states successfully fended off coastal-state control of transiting vessels. Why was one effort at control, with perhaps more short-run relevance to coastal states considering the amount of damage a major oil spill can cause, more successful than the other? We believe the comparison shows where real domestic political power lay in the developed states.

This variable also reveals much about the process of parliamentary diplomacy. On the question of science in the EEZ, we saw the development of strong support for consent by 1975, but not consensus. The outcome showed that the bargaining to achieve consensus was conducted in a fairly narrow range, a formula zone. Typically, this formula zone was not found on the peak of support for the core concept, but rather on one of its edges, the edge facing its opponents. After there was agreement on the basic approach, bargaining concerned how to make the concept palatable to the loser. This was the path toward consensus. Oceanographers felt that UNCLOS III's consent requirement made their situation measurably worse, and indeed it did,[92] But it could have been worse still if the supporters of the core formula had not been willing to compromise and try to reduce its "arbitrary" nature.

The role of a committee chair in forming consensus when none is present, by assembling a single negotiating text, was also shown on this issue. SNTs are typical of large-scale multilateral negotiations, so this responsibility of the chair is important to a successful outcome. On the two science issues, we saw the Third Committee chair overshoot on one, and undershoot on the other. He appeared to miss where consensus eventually did lie on both issues. But it didn't matter. He kept the negotiation moving and the delegates ultimately worked out formulas acceptable to the conference.

7

Committee I:

Seabed Mineral Exploitation and "Disagreement in the Large"

From the moment Arvid Pardo stepped onto the floor of the General Assembly in 1967 to give his now-famous speech, it was clear that there were substantial forces present in the United Nations of that period who wished to create a new regime for the oceans. The newness was not merely a change in the particular or specific rules describing permissible activities or the means to manage them, but, rather, a new set of rules for an entirely different political, economic, and moral framework for managing human affairs. The oceans were to be a specific area of human conduct in which this framework would be tested. As it related to the oceans, the new conceptual framework promised to terminate the first-come, first-served ocean rules of the past which favored those powerful enough to have been there first. It was going to be an equitable regime emphasizing the "common heritage of mankind" in managing ocean resources.

Unfortunately, there never has been general agreement on a definition of the "common heritage of mankind." The Convention merely states that "the Area and its resources are the common heritage of mankind."[1] Despite Pardo's desire to leave as much of the ocean and its resources beyond national jurisdiction so that a new ocean agency representing the people of the world could treat the oceans as a physical commons and deal with ocean management problems on a universal scale,[2] the delegates in 1974 quickly consented to carving up the ocean into 200-mile Exclusive Economic Zones.[3] No notion of common heritage would apply in the 36 percent of ocean space that would come under national jurisdiction. After the 1974 Caracas decision to create Exclusive Economic Zones, only the deep ocean was left as an area in which some new notion of international equity could be applied.

While there was no general agreement as to what the common heritage concept meant, many delegates spoke to the question of what the common heritage meant to them. They assumed that the general conceptual framework was understood. They were mostly developing states with some allies from among the sympathetic developed states, such as Canada and the Scandinavian states. It became evident that a common heritage approach was an integral part of the New International Economic Order (NIEO).

The NIEO, whether viewed as revolutionary or reformist, was an attempt to restructure the world economy on a basis more favorable to the states of the Third and Fourth Worlds.[4] For supporters of the common heritage idea as it was debated in U.N. Law of the Sea fora from 1967 to 1975, common heritage came to be the specific features of deep-seabed management that embodied what they said were NIEO principles. These included (1) termination of first-come, first-served access to deep-seabed mineral resources; (2) establishment of an "Enterprise"—an international minerals exploitation organization that would represent the interests of those who did not have the capability to compete with private enterprises and the state corporations of powerful states; (3) an International Seabed Agency to manage and regulate ocean mining through institutions controlled by a majority of states, and not by a limited number of powerful states; (4) production controls and mandatory technology transfer (a particularly favorite set of themes in NIEO rhetoric); and (5) the possibility, within 20 years of the treaty going into force, that new private and national rights to exploit deep ocean resources could be terminated, even over the objections of states whose consent normally would be required if they were to be bound under the conventional rules of international law.

The maximum preferred positions on deep-ocean minerals issues of NIEO supporters became clear early in the negotiation. It was not clear how they would induce nonsupporters, especially from both major developed blocs—capitalist and socialist alike—to a accept a framework that was anathema to them, under a bargaining arrangement that favored a consensus outcome. It was evident early in UNCLOS III that there was to be a North–South clash on a number of issues, foremost among them issues relating to the deep seabed, negotiated under the aegis of the First Committee. But how could a filibuster or defection, always possible under a consensus-decision rule, be avoided?

The deep-seabed minerals issue at UNCLOS III became, in many ways, the quintessential North–South clash of the 1970s and early 1980s. However, those who broke up consensus represented 63 percent of the world's gross national product.[5] It was a perfect set of issues on which to argue the questions of international equity and the widening economic gap between North and South.

The quarrel over new conceptual principles seemed an important, precedent-setting opportunity, and the application of those principles to the deep seabed was the safest issue on which to argue the problem. Ocean minerals were chosen because they were per se relatively unimportant or lacking in salience. If major contending forces defected and dropped out of the negotiation, or this portion of the UNCLOS III negotiation ended in general failure, no major party would be badly hurt. Although research and development funds had been spent preparing for the development of an ocean-minerals industry, an ocean-minerals industry did not exist in the developed states. There were thought to be no deeply entrenched stakeholders to force their governments to defect and apply sanctions that would hurt developing states for their temerity in trying to change the general structure of the world economic system.[6] On the other side, though a limited number of developing states were heavily dependent on exports of nickel, copper, cobalt, and manganese, most were not, and failure would not worsen the competitive disadvantage of developing states as a whole. It was a perfect issue on which to try to establish a new regime embodying a new conceptual framework, a new way of managing economic relations among the states of the modern world.

But how was it to be done? It was obvious from the beginning of the negotiation that, despite a number of model management schemes proposed by the developed states,[7] if the Group of 77 could agree upon a general framework and remain reasonably disciplined in supporting it, *their* framework would dominate the proceedings. The core of the Convention's general formula would be derived largely from Group of 77 preferred positions. There was a limited range of grand strategic and tactical moves available to the leadership of the Group of 77 to induce opponents to accept a document which included a majority-supported, NIEO-based conceptual framework for areas beyond national jurisdiction. The major approach upon which the negotiation depended for success was the construction of a package of provisions which balanced out the gains and losses for all major states and groups. It would require one side to make concessions or trade-offs on issues of lesser salience to itself in return for concessions or trade-offs by opponents on issues of higher salience to itself. The parts were integral segments of an integrated whole. State participants had to take all or nothing, they could not choose only those provisions of which they approved to implement.

But the package as a whole had to be accepted by all major parties if this approach was to bring about success. Moreover, it had to be negotiated in a bargaining environment which, although the formal outcome was determined by a requisite majority of voters, the actual decision rule was consensus. Consensus is useful to those in the minority position, since it allows them to filibuster if they feel overwhelmed.

The package approach also depends heavily on proper timing for success. The order in which items are resolved can have an impact upon the final outcome of a grand package. In the case of UNCLOS III, the navigation and EEZ issues were resolved early (although there were attempts to reopen them), leading many participants—developed and developing coastal states— to act as if they had achieved what they wanted on issues of immediate interest to themselves. The question of deep-seabed resources, which involved a challenge to the distribution of power in world politics and economics, was more difficult, and was bound to take longer to achieve what seemed to many states an important but not essential outcome. The early resolution of bread-and-butter issues made it easier to defect.

The United States did defect, and claimed that even so it would enjoy most of the benefits of the convention. We will not examine the merits of the U.S. legal case. It has been done by others.[8] The case for the United States being bound by a package outcome to the deep-seabed regime adopted by the overwhelming majority is not based on as strong evidence as the proponents of the case might have hoped. The argument that Conference and Group of 77 leaders have made (and are still making) is as follows: the United States knew from the beginning that the general bargaining arrangement under the consensus rule was that the outcome had to be a package. In particular, the United States knew that it could not enjoy the navigation rules negotiated without accepting the Conference outcomes on resource issues. The U.S. made statements, early in the negotiation, acknowledging both the general idea of a package outcome and the trade-off of a 12-mile territorial sea and right of transit-passage through straits used for international navigation for a resolution of resources questions. The resources issues explicitly mentioned in those statements—most often in the Second Committee—were those associated with the exclusive economic zone and the continental shelf.[9]

Not a single official statement from a U.S. delegation member or U.S. Government official has been produced to demonstrate that the United States Government put itself on record as accepting the idea of trading navigation rights for, as one analyst put it, "nodules."[10] As it happened, Group of 77 and Conference leaders assumed that the United States had bound itself to a package outcome that included nodules because it remained in the negotiation after what it judged to be an unfavorable outcome on the First Committee's portion of the Single Negotiating Text in 1975, up through the supposed breakthroughs achieved in the summer of 1980.[11] The very presence of the United States in the Part XI negotiation created a reasonable presumption of a U.S. commitment, based more on trust of the personal reputation and deeds of some of the senior U.S. negotiators than on a formal commitment.

It was the assumption that all important states would trade nodules for navigation in an overall package that formed the core of the grand strategy of the

Conference leadership after 1975. It was a fragile implied promise upon which to depend since, especially after the Reagan election in 1980, major forces in the United States already thought that they had achieved what they wanted at UNCLOS III through the earlier trade-offs they did explicitly accept. Nevertheless, the Conference leadership had little choice but to press on, assuming that with patience and good will, a sufficient mix of desirable and undesirable features would be produced in a package to attract votes, signatures, and ratifications from all important states and groups.

What tactics were available to the Group of 77 to achieve the package outcome? Three stand out. The first tactic was rational persuasion. Group of 77 members could patiently explain that the scheme was equitable and that, if their opponents accepted it in good faith, it could be made to work. All would be better off in the foreseeable future, and therefore the outcome would be "rational."

A second tactic was to stand fast on all major features of their proposals. They could stick to their opening position or close to it and make only technical adjustments, knowing that they had a substantial majority, and could not be defeated under the formal decision rules of the bargaining arena. They could force the opponents to accept *their* formula by attrition, or if that failed, at least achieve a moral victory where the onus of failure would be on the heads of their opponents.

Finally, a third tactic was to accept compromises that did not challenge the core of their preferred outcomes. They could accept the fact that the core of the formula would certainly be theirs, and make genuine concessions to provide positive inducements to their opponents to come aboard. A participant-observer put it as follows: "If one carefully examines the texts—and this is not limited to the mining texts—one can detect a consistent pattern. First there is concession to a rhetorical principle which is then circumscribed with precise language."[12] If representatives of a majority chose this approach, they had to exercise care that they conceded nothing that fundamentally undermined the heart of their formula.

In the parliamentary diplomatic setting of UNCLOS III, the minority, including some of the most important states, had available a comparable range of grand tactical moves. First, it could try to demonstrate that the position of the majority makes little sense and would not work; that its own conceptual framework—in this case, the market system—would make all states better off in the future and therefore it would be "rational" for opponents to adopt its candidate for a bargaining formula. Second, it could try to stonewall the preferences of the majority by insisting upon its own formula notion and forcing the majority to defer to it. To turn the majority around, the minority had to present a credible threat that its ability to defect would have the impact of leaving the majority worse off. Third, it could generally accede to the general framework of the majority and work on matters of detail to make its opponents' formula palatable. Within this tactic, depending upon its skill, it would have a range of opportunities from making its opponents' notions minimally acceptable, and indeed workable, all the way up to gutting its opponents' conceptual notions on details, leaving them a hollow shell.

All the grand tactics outlined above were used by developed and developing states during UNCLOS III's consideration of the deep-seabed minerals issues. At times, all three sets of tactics were pursued simultaneously; at other times, the sides alternated between general approaches. In several instances, having gone down one path, one of the sides repudiated the progress apparently made, and reverted to an alternate approach. These variances and shifts in approach guaranteed that the seabed negotiations in Committee I would be long and hard.

The least effective tactic was rational persuasion. It was obvious to any observer of UNCLOS III that trying to convince opponents of the substantive errors of their ways through rational persuasion was more window dressing that an effective bargaining tactic. On occasion, some delegations were persuaded to alter their position because they became convinced that they had misperceived the issues or had not seen correctly where their true interest lay. Mostly, states had a firm grasp on where they thought their interests lay. Where their objective interests lay was irrelevant. For states with strong affiliations to caucusing or common-interest groups, pressures were very strong to keep them in line with the group position. Nevertheless, at least one member of the United States delegation went to Caracas with appropriate models and data calculated to persuade developing states that they would be better off economically if they would only follow a capitalist model in their approach to ocean mining. Obviously, he failed. [13]

Stonewalling or making very few concessions to force your opponent to accept not only your general framework but also its details was a tactic tried by both developing and developed states. It was used by the chairman of Committee I, Paul Engo of the Cameroons, in the spring of 1975, to repudiate a working-group text assembled by Ambassador Christopher Pinto of Sri Lanka after laborious negotiations between some important developed and developing states. Instead, he submitted a draft text that was a near-replica of the Group of 77's opening position. Naturally, this caused deep disappointment among developed states, and led to a number of statements threatening defection. [14] The chairman had the numbers to win a majority decision, if it was put to a vote, but not a consensus or near-consensus decision. In 1976,

Engo was obliged to negotiate, and, as we shall see, the Revised Single Negotiating Text was more a negotiated than a negotiating document.

The United States, too, tried to stonewall at times in order to force the majority to drop its formula notion and replace it with a market-oriented approach that would only allow international regulation of seabed mining. When the Reagan Administration came into office early in January 1981, it insisted on a review of U.S. positions at UNCLOS III. That review took eighteen months, during which period, for all practical purposes, the United States dropped out of the negotiations. When the United States returned, it provided delegates, as promised, a document—the "Green Book," after the color of its cover—which was supposed to reflect what changes the United States wanted to make to Part XI (the seabed issues). It demanded that the delegates turn the result of eight years of formal negotiations completely on its head. It required that the majority surrender to the United States.

For much of the seabed negotiation, both sides—although not always simultaneously—followed the third set of grand tactical choices, accepting that the formula notion—the general framework—would be the majority's, and spending most of their time negotiating the details. The majority negotiated to retain the integrity and workability of its formula notion, and the minority tried to get the majority to accept modifications that made the outcome livable for them. In the process, they had to get either real, direct concessions on issues of high salience or language that fuzzed up the issue or provided them an escape hatch.

Did the majority, in negotiating details, successfully protect the integrity of the formula idea? Did the minority really make it possible to participate in the new regime without prohibitive costs to themselves? These measures of success can be determined only when the formula negotiated in a treaty or convention is implemented in the real world. As of this writing, it is virtually impossible to say who won on Part XI. The convention was approved by an overwhelming vote of 130 for, 4 against, and 17 abstaining. This set in train a successor negotiation by a Preparatory Commission (PrepCom) to establish the new International Seabed Agency and the Enterprise, and to license "pioneer" investors. The negotiation began in 1983 and by July 1987, in a "midnight agreement," France, India, Japan, and the Soviet Union had been accepted as pioneer investors.[15] Nevertheless, it is not clear whether the Convention's arrangements will work, or whether the new organization can come into existence without the active cooperation, financial support, and technical backing of the United States. The jury is still out.[16]

This chapter is largely about the contest to protect or attack the integrity of the core concepts introduced by the dominant group in the Committee I of the

Third United Nations Law of the Sea Conference concerning deep-seabed mineral exploitation. We will examine four issues, tracked by the Law of the Sea Study Group until 1975, that had a major impact upon the outcome of the negotiations on Part XI, and upon the hope that a viable overall treaty could be produced: (1) whether the "common heritage of mankind" would be the core concept undergirding the seabed-mining negotiation; (2) whether private or state entities, an "International Enterprise," or some mix of them would have access to the minerals of the deep seabed; (3) whether production controls would be imposed upon seabed mining in the International Area and, if so, what type; and (4) how decisions would be made in the Seabed Council, and by whom.

Two other issues, the contractual terms of access to mining nodules by private enterprises and state corporations and the financing of the International Enterprise became key parts of the Part XI after 1977. We lacked data for analysis of these issues. An observer-participant, James Sebenius, has elsewhere described and analyzed the role of these issues in the final outcome.[17]

Manganese-Nodule Exploitation: The Nature of the Problem

Why were the nations of the world concerned about manganese nodules and their possible exploitation during this period? Manganese nodules (ferromanganese or iron-manganese deposits) have been known since the first modern oceanographic expeditions, those of the *Challenger* in 1872–76. They are potato-sized lumps (approximately four inches in diameter) usually formed around a nucleus (a shell, a rock, a shark's tooth, etc.) lying on the seafloor. The principle components of the nodules are manganese (17–22 percent, depending upon where found), iron (8–11 percent), nickel (.75–1 percent), copper (.5–1 percent), and cobalt (.25–.28 percent). They are found everywhere on the ocean floor, but are more highly concentrated in certain areas, especially abyssal plains, where the rates of sedimentation are low. This means that the heaviest concentrations are under deep oceans.[18]

Until the publication in 1965 of a book by John Mero proposing recovery of the nodules,[19] there was little interest in the nodules beyond the scientific community. They were not a "reserve base," as economic geologists would define that term,[20] since, for all practical purposes, they were not recoverable in commercial quantities at marketable prices. No technology existed for removing the nodules from the deep-ocean floor, and no technology existed for processing the nodules. It appeared that the development of necessary recovery and processing technologies would be very expensive. Finally, alternate sources of manganese, nickel, copper, and cobalt existed (it was never thought worthwhile to try to extract iron). Even if the nodules were recoverable, they would have to compete on the world market with metals from these alternate sources.[21]

However, in the 1950s and early 1960s oceanographic research improved our knowledge of the nodules, pinpointing areas of the ocean floor that were potentially richer than others. This was followed by technological research to determine if cost-effective methods could be developed to recover the nodules from the deep seabed—performed or sponsored largely by Western high-technology companies, such as Lockheed, Deep Sea Ventures (then affiliated with Tenneco), Kennecott, Newport News Shipyard, that were working on related technologies as a tax write-off.

As the research progressed, some of these companies realized that if their technologies worked and others learned how to do the same thing, they might have to deal with a twentieth-century version of a Gold Rush. A number of claimants might try to move in on the pioneer sites. By "piggybacking" or "free-riding," second-generation miners could substantially lower their costs. Thus, the first generation preferred to have an exclusive right to work a particular site.

Under freedom of the seas, even if ocean miners could not "alienate" particular stretches of the deep seabed and exercise an exclusive right to them and any resources found therein, under *res nullius* and the law of capture, they could mine and claim as their property all of the nodules they were capable of bringing aboard their vessels. If claim-jumping and overproduction of minerals were not real problems, perhaps this would be sufficient. However, some companies, especially in the United States, complained that even so they would have tax problems in certifying the origin of the resources as American.

Potential ocean miners tried to reduce their risk in two related ways. First, they formed consortia, all of which were transnational in membership and composed of most of the interested and capable mining companies from a number of developed states. It seemed easier to share the risks and benefits with partners who might otherwise be rivals; even if they were not able to form a single consortium—four principal consortia were established[22]—it still seemed easier to work out amicable arrangements to split the sites between a limited number of rivals.

Second, they tried to get their governments to support or recognize their unilateral claims to seabed areas or, at least, to guarantee national government protection of their activities. For example, in 1974, Deep Sea Venture, the operating arm of one of the consortia (Ocean Mining Associates), petitioned the U.S. Department of State to recognize its claim to the nodules found in 60,000 square miles of Pacific seabed. They were turned down.

If the major mineral companies and the consortia that represented them were interested in obtaining an exclusive right to the seabed as a way of promoting an orderly regime, they had to turn to the only forum which might grant them exclusive rights—the Third United Nations Law of the Sea Conference. While wary of the dangers to their interests from other stakeholders at the Conference, for much of UNCLOS III they remained willing, if hesitant and suspicious, consultants and advisers to national delegations. They wanted a guaranteed right to an area and were willing to pay a price to other stakeholders to achieve it, but there was a top price,[23] not always firm or even well understood, they were willing to pay. Ultimately, they judged that the price demanded was too high.

Their potential rivals, land-based producers of the same minerals, were also stakeholders in the seabed-mining negotiation. They had a stake in seeing that the possible delivery of minerals from the seabed did not further depress the already depressed prices on the world minerals market. Minerals, like other raw commodities, were a major component of North–North, as well as North–South trade. However, the impact of a rival source of metals, while not affecting many developing states, could heavily affect a limited number of major mineral exporters such as Brazil, Chile, Gabon, Ghana, Morocco, Peru, Zaire, and Zambia. Developed-state mineral exporters—Australia, Canada and the Soviet Union among them—were also determined to protect their domestic miners.

Land-based producers of minerals had an interest in preventing the birth of ocean mining. If this were not possible, they could hope at least to slow down the arrival of ocean-mining products onto the international minerals market. Certainly they thought they would be better off if the ocean-mining industry were carefully regulated, and some type of production controls imposed upon it, in the hope of preventing the price drops associated with a completely unregulated market when supply is ample.

Ever since Pardo's speech promised that enormous riches could be extracted from the oceans, another stakeholder had to be accounted for—the United Nations system and its liberal internationalist supporters, particularly in developed states. They were very much part of the early debates. Their stake was the potential royalties and taxes to be paid to the surrogate who represented the owners—the people of the world—for the use of their property. That surrogate was the United Nations system. It would manage the deep ocean as part of the "common heritage of mankind." One major reason the United Nations could not bring peace to the world or control unruly nation-states, these stakeholders reasoned, was that it did not have its own resources, and therefore could not break its dependence upon the largess of its members, who were often penurious and, at times, bad actors. If it had its own resources, the United Nations could act with more courage. The resources to execute this grand design of fundamentally altering world political patterns could come from the huge surpluses that would be generated by ocean mining.[24]

Almost as soon as Pardo stated his version of the "common heritage of mankind," representatives of states other than Malta took to the floor to praise the idea—and to reinterpret it. The "common heritage of mankind" was viewed by many developing states as the ocean manifestation of a New International Economic Order (NIEO).[25] It was to be the ocean experiment which demonstrated how a new conceptual framework could be applied to North–South economic relations. Ocean resources could be used to help subsidize developing states left on a short leash by their former colonial masters, who still controlled the world economy. Moreover, control of ocean minerals could prevent the depression of world mineral prices from wrecking more Third World economies. Equity for them was equated with an equitable international system. In sum, New International Economic Order advocates had their own grand design to establish, their own ideology to espouse. It was the perfect issue on which to argue a new conceptual framework. It was important but not critical to either developed or developing states in general. Each side could afford a loss if defection occurred.

Ocean mining was equally symbolic for some major capitalist states. They viewed an NIEO-based minerals regime as unworkable under any set of conceivable circumstances, and insulting as well. It had to be defeated, and states brought to their senses, so that they would support a conceptual framework that provided a proper guide to operating the world economy. The larger issue of avoiding a bad precedent was more important than establishing an ocean-mining industry. Ideologues of the West, therefore, were also significant stakeholders in the seabed-minerals negotiation.

Would it be possible to satisfy all eight identified groups of stakeholders in a negotiated outcome on the question of a regime for ocean mining? For potential ocean-mineral producers in capitalist states, the first order of business was to arrange viable conditions for themselves for ocean mining, if not under the capitalist framework, then as an exception to the "common heritage of mankind" rule, or with a special modification of the New International Economic Order framework. Similarly, the hopes of liberal internationalist ideologues might be dashed if an NIEO-based regime discouraged development of an ocean-mining industry, and therefore choked off all new revenues to the United Nations system. They might be almost as unhappy if an industry did develop, and all of the revenues generated were devoted to direct compensation of Third World states, with nothing left over for the United Nations system.

As it turned out, it was impossible to satisfy all stakeholders at the same time. A core idea was necessary to provide framework for negotiations on this complex problem. In the case of the seabed portion of UNCLOS III, the core idea of the "common heritage of mankind," as interpreted principally by developing states, provided the framework that guided the negotiation. Little wonder that when an American president came into office fully committed to capitalism, even if it were possible to work out a seabed-mining regime acceptable to ocean miners, that would not be good enough.

The approach we will take will allow us to deal only with selected issues in a treaty that included many detailed provisions on ocean mining (60 articles in Part XI of the Convention, 21 articles in Annex III, 13 articles in Annex IV, and 6 articles relating to a Seabed Disputes Chamber in Annex VI). However, the issues analyzed below deal with most of the key provisions of the Convention that were important to a successful outcome since the beginning of the negotiation. How the "common heritage of mankind" came to dominate the general thrust of the seabed regime is the first of the four issues we will examine to illuminate aspects of multilateral negotiations in establishing a new regime.

The Common Heritage of Mankind— The Core Idea of the Formula

When delegates took the floor during the 1967–73 debates in the General Assembly and the Ad Hoc and Permanent Seabed Committees, most lacked detailed knowledge of the real problems of ocean mining and what would be necessary to create and to manage a new, high-technology industry on the deep seabed. The record of the debates is not especially revealing as to what institutions they would create, or what specific measures they would take. In some respects, they were thinking out loud, learning as they were talking on the floor and in the corridors. The record was revealing, however, on the question of the general thrust, or the core idea, of the regime. Most already knew what general direction they wanted the negotiations to take. This general thrust can be seen in how states lined up on the question of what was meant by the "common heritage of mankind," as shown in figure 7.1. At the low end of the scale (rank 1), speakers simply denied the legitimacy of the common heritage notion or its applicability to the problem of creating a seabed regime. At rank 2, we find common heritage rejected on juridical grounds as a basis for the seabed negotiations, but at least recognized as an

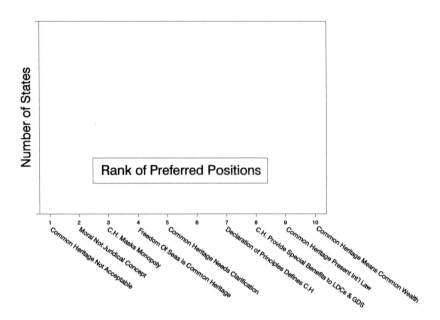

Figure 7.1:   Common Heritage of Mankind

idea having some moral content. Common heritage was also seen by some—notably Soviet-bloc states—as a Trojan Horse, since it purported to mix socialist and capitalist ideas, a manifest impossibility, they claimed, to help mask monopoly.

Common heritage was seen by the speakers at rank 4 as merely a manifestation of the existing ocean regime. Under the freedom of the seas, all states were entitled to access to, and a right to exploit, ocean resources beyond national jurisdiction, therefore the common heritage was merely an aspect of freedom of the seas. While not avidly supporting the common heritage notion, speakers at rank 5 were willing to explore its meaning. If clarified, common heritage might be helpful.

Supporters knew what common heritage meant. It meant a sharing of wealth among the peoples of the world, regardless of economic condition. At rank 10, it represented equity. At rank 9, it represented present international law, an already binding obligation on states to treat the resources of the deep ocean as belonging to all. At rank 8, to make up for the disadvantages suffered by developing states, most of whom had recently thrust off the yoke of colonialism and were struggling against neocolonialism, common heritage meant providing special compensatory benefits from deep-seabed mining to developing countries. Finally, at rank 7, we placed references to the Declaration of Principles, passed by the General Assembly in 1969, which demanded a moratorium on seabed mining until arrangements had been made for a common-heritage-based system to be put in place. The Declaration, these negotiators averred, adequately defined the common-heritage concept.[26]

The distribution of speakers for and against the common heritage notion followed a pattern evident in many other more detailed issues that had a substantial North–South component. In figure 7.2, we can see a classic weakly

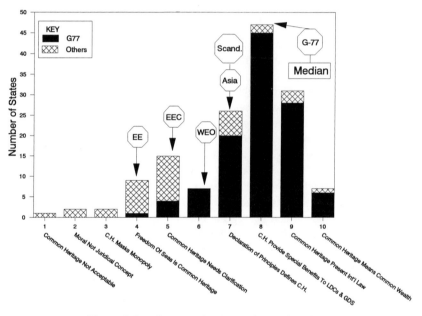

Figure 7.2:   Common Heritage of Mankind (T-1)

bimodal distribution. At one end of the scale, although not at the extreme end, a majority, the core of which was the Group of 77, stood solidly behind the interpretation of the common-heritage idea as settled international law and not subject to modification (rank 8). Common heritage, to them, meant common ownership of the resources of the deep seabed with the benefits distributed primarily to developing and geographically disadvantaged states. A substantial group of states, albeit a minority, still resisted the preference of the majority (rank 5).

To dominate the thrust of a discussion does not require consensus. For all practical purposes, the tone of the negotiations over Part XI was set by 1973, because there was a substantial majority pushing the common-heritage line, even if it could not define the concept with precision.[27] The deep seabed was to be the common heritage of mankind and exploitative practices used upon it would have to be consistent therewith. It was very sensible of the leadership of the Group of 77 and the Conference not to attempt a detailed definition of the concept, settling for the simple assertion of Article 136: "The Area and its resources are the common heritage of mankind." They might have failed technically as well as kept the assembled delegates tied up with an arid theoretical debate.

The pattern of support and opposition that developed early on this issue is also typical of many other issues in the UNCLOS III negotiation. Figure 7.2 shows a solid South versus a fractured North. The Group of 77's average position was at rank 8. Except for its Asian subgroup, all subgroups of the Group of 77 also averaged rank 8: African, Latin American, Arab. Moreover, on this issue, there was no dissonance within the Group of 77 among coastal, landlocked, and geographically disadvantaged groups. The standard deviations for these groups were also very low, demonstrating solidarity.

On the other side, clustered at ranks 4–5, were those who opposed, however weakly, common heritage as the operative framework or formula notion for the deep seabed. At most, they were expressing reluctance, rather than complete unwillingness to bargain on the basis of common heritage. The reluctance was concentrated among the developed states. Early in the negotiations, the group most strongly resisting common heritage as the framework for negotiations on the deep seabed was the Eastern European group. Following closely behind were the states of the European Economic Community. The Scandinavian group was the only group, among the developed states, willing to begin exploring the common-heritage notion as the core of the formula for seabed management.[28] This was similar to the pattern on a number of other issues where Scandinavian and some of the smaller developed states, especially those outside of the EEC, were more sympathetic to the South on North–South issues, or at least willing to mediate and bridge the gap between North and South.

UNCLOS III shows that early attempts to develop a bargaining framework in a multilateral negotiation, however general, can be revealing. First, if a majority wants to move the negotiation in a certain direction, it will be *its* framework or formula that will guide the succeeding detailed negotiations. Second, that majority will be able to maintain its domination as long as it suffers no internal dissonance. And third, minority interests will have to negotiate on the basis of the majority framework, or defect. They cannot expect, in a parliamentary diplomatic setting, to force the majority to accept their preferred framework.

Functions of the Authority

The title, "Functions of the Authority," does not convey the centrality of this issue to an overall successful outcome of the seabed portion of the UNCLOS III negotiations, indeed, of the negotiations as a whole. What was being decided under this bland title was the key question of *who* would have *what type* of access to the mineral resources of the deep seabed. What was at stake was whether there really would be a common-heritage solution at UNCLOS III or whether the formula idea would be eroded or swept aside by the outcome on this key detail.

Proponents of a pure common-heritage idea proposed an international monopoly excluding national mining organizations from access to the nodules. Opponents of that interpretation of common heritage fought to provide access to their miners under some type of guaranteed status. This was a quintessential test of whether a minority in parliamentary diplomacy could hope to tame an obnoxious formula by altering key details while leaving the formula idea largely intact. Conversely, it was also a test of whether a majority could negotiate to successfully operationalize its preferred outcome without forcing its opponents to defect. Years of hard bargaining took place on this thorny issue, and in the minds of many participants on both sides, real progress was made toward accommodation. As a result, when the United States defected, there was a sense of bitterness and disappointment not only from common-heritage supporters, but from delegates who labored to work out an acceptable set of operating principles for governing access to manganese nodules.

From the beginning, it was obvious that the seabed-mining arrangements would be subject to intense North–South pressures. We have already noted the reasons: different conceptual frameworks, different interests of consumers (mostly North states) and producers (both North and South states), an arena that gave important bargaining power to states who had a numerical majority but were economically weak, and finally, the understanding that, however salient to both sides, the issue was not so salient they could afford to have the negotiations on this matter break down.

The underlying bargaining problem was equally obvious from the beginning of negotiations in the Ad Hoc Seabed Committee. Presuming the Group of 77 saw the seabed-minerals negotiations as a perfect arena to push the developed hard, how hard could they push? The ideal goal for the developing states was clear—creation of an international economic organization that operated under NIEO principles. But how much of the ideal goal could they extract from the developed states? Leaders of the Group of 77 knew that, if the group maintained discipline, no other conceptual framework could be considered as a serious candidate for the core of the winning formula. If they could not achieve all of the ideal plan, then they must compromise. But how much? And how were they to measure their "success"? There are two measures that must be considered. The first is whether closure is achieved and all sign an accord. This is a bargaining success. The second is whether the substance of the accord works, whether it solves the problem it was intended to solve. This is substantive success. Negotiators can usually only usefully judge the first. Ratifying institutions and historians must judge the second.

The tasks of negotiators from developed states were exactly opposite those of the developing states. Developed-state negotiators had important tactical reasons to push hard for their own conceptual framework, as the basis of negotiation, however unlikely, would be acceptance. It defined where they were coming from and how far their opponents would have to move them from their opening position in order to achieve closure.

The key task of developed-state negotiators was to force the majority to accept modifications, alterations, and obfuscations in the detailed provisions intended to carry out its formula idea. If they could not get acceptable modifications to an important provision, they always could defect. Threats of defection were tactically useful, especially in a decision system where a consensus outcome was preferred. Filibuster was also possible, and patience was needed by a minority operating in a parliamentary diplomatic environment. However, if the final outcome was to be a package of outcomes on a large number of issues, the other side had an important counter to a threat of defection over an unhappy outcome on one particular issue. Presumably, if one side was not willing to accept the negative features on one issue of reasonably low salience to itself, it could not enjoy the positive features of another issue in the package of higher salience to it.

The number of candidate plans to govern ocean mining that were introduced early in the negotiations was substantial. Between 1969 and 1974, the United States, the United Kingdom, Japan, France, the Netherlands, Canada, and Poland all introduced seabed-mining proposals. They had to face proposals from the Afro-Asian Group in 1970, Tanzanian and Latin American proposals concerning an "Enterprise" in 1971, and a Group of 77 proposal in 1974.[29] The ideas embedded in these proposals are shown in figure 7.3. At one end of the spectrum (rank 1) were placed proposals to create a mere reg-

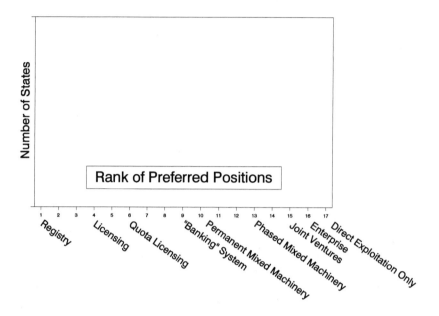

Figure 7.3:   Functions of the Authority

istry to record claims to an exclusive right to mine a section of the seabed made by nation-states on behalf of their miners, whether private enterprises or state corporations. This would be a first-come, first-served system.[30]

A registry was so minimal a position that there was a gap of three ranks between it and the next major position on the policy spectrum. At rank 4, we placed a licensing system, proposed initially by the United States as part of the so-called President's Draft Seabed Treaty of 1970.[31] In this proposal, a new United Nations agency would be created—a Seabed Authority— which would license potential miners, collect royalties and fees from them, resolve disputes between them, and regulate their activities, especially to maintain the ecological health of the ocean. For the moneys collected, the Authority would assure miners an exclusive right to mine within a specified sector of seabed.

In its original U.S. formulation, the proposal was a remarkably liberal approach to the problem of managing the seabed area beyond national juris-diction (especially considering that it carried the name of a Republican pres-ident—Richard M. Nixon). Among other features, it proposed terminating national jurisdiction at 200 meters depth of water, leaving many potentially oil-rich continental slopes and rises under international jurisdiction. All exploitation for natural resources beyond that limit, whether for minerals or oil, would require a license from an international agency. The Draft Seabed Treaty indicated willingness on the part of the United States to pay substantial royalties, and to differentially compensate the owners of the nodules or oil—the people of the world—with a disproportionately larger share to go to developing States. The liberality of the U.S. proposal stunned the domestic oil industry.

The Draft Seabed Treaty was greeted with some skepticism by developing states, as well as a number of smaller developed states. They pointed out that if the cost of the license was high, only rich states or enterprises would be able to purchase a license. This would widen the gap between rich and poor, and disproportionate royalties being paid to developing states would not make up for the growth in the gap. The developing states would also fall further behind technologically. Some participating states, however, were willing to take a licensing system as the starting base point for a formula, as long as modifications they proposed were adopted. An important modification was to limit the number of licenses, or the areas granted to a claimant, under a quota system (rank 6). This would prevent any one state or small group of states from turning the Authority into an agency that administered a monopoly or oligopoly.

At the other end of the spectrum, we find a proposal to have the Authority provide supervision to a single exploiter—an "International Enterprise" (rank 17). The Enterprise would have a monopoly right to exploit the riches of the seabed beyond national jurisdiction. Other parties would be explicitly excluded in the treaty language except as contractors to the Enterprise. At rank 16, we placed proposals that commended an Enterprise approach but didn't link it to exclusion of all other potential miners.

Since it would prove difficult to acquire mining technology without paying for it outright (where the cash would come from was dealt with later in the financial negotiations), some delegations thought it necessary to give private or state mining entities some standing in the system, so that they would be willing to "assist" the Enterprise coming into being. From a NIEO point of view, the least threatening fallback supporters would consider on seabed mining would allow private and state exploiters to participate, but only on a joint-venture basis (rank 15). The private and state joint-venture partners would be restricted to specific contractual arrangements, be required to share profits, and provide technology. If private or state mining entities were allowed to mine at all, it would not be as a matter of right. The Enterprise would still retain its monopoly right to exploit the nodules of the deep seabed.

In 1976, U.S. Secretary of State Henry Kissinger made a proposal to re-solve the impasse between developed and developing states.[32] Acting as a "rule manipulator" (someone who has the authority to alter or constrain the process of negotiation),[33] Kissinger proposed a "banking" system in which the private or state corporation interested in mining the seabed would nom-inate two areas of equal value in terms of the quantity and quality of nodules found during exploration. One would be granted under license to the propos-ing private or state entity, the other would be banked away for future exploi-tation by the Enterprise (rank 9). With some further concessions on related matters such as capital availability, technology transfer, and the like, the banking system would be a permanent, irrevocable feature of a new system, with both Enterprise and national entities having a fundamental right of ac-cess to the deep seabed (rank 10).

While a mixed system had little appeal to those who wanted to establish a new economic order without exploitation of the poor by the rich, some thought that, with appropriate safeguards, they could convince the rich to ap-prove of a NIEO-based system, and tame them over time. Since a new Sea-bed Authority and Enterprise would probably never be established without the cooperation of rich and technologically sophisticated states, exploiters would be granted licenses for a specified period, say 20 years, and then the licenses would be phased out (rank 13). By that time, the Enterprise would have been established, acquired capital, technology, and mining experience, and there would be a reduced need to have the cooperation of the rich and technologically powerful.

Over the nine years of formal negotiation (fifteen years total), the central issue—whether, and under what circumstances, private and state corporations would have access to the deep seabed along with an International Enterprise as a matter of right—was extremely contentious. It involved innumerable working-group, contact-group, and leadership-group meetings. It involved early attempts by the Group of 77, and later by the United States, to stone-wall. It resulted in agreements and compromises worked out by various del-egates and bargaining groups not being backed by their caucusing groups or the committee leadership. It was marked by bitterness and resentment, and frequent charges of extremism. Reputations were made and broken over the issue. At the time of each session, there appeared to be many occasions where backsliding took place, and the progress of the negotiation appeared to be anything but linear. Nevertheless, over the nine years there was a definite pro-gression, even though it took a very long time to emerge.

Before the opening of the Caracas session in 1973 the situation resembled the distribution shown in figure 7.4. Most states are bunched across the

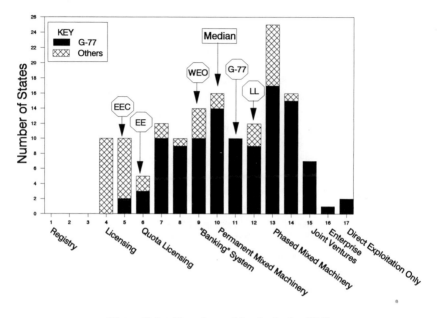

Figure 7.4:   Functions of the Authority (T-1)

center of the figure, with little or no support for the extremes. Many states had a great deal to say, but there was no definite trend. However, at this stage, the registry proposals that were floated during General Assembly and Ad Hoc Committee discussions sank quickly. Enterprise monopoly proposals had some support, but not yet the firm backing of the Group of 77.

Even though the distribution is not exclusively North–South, there is an underlying North–South current present already. The strongest support for a licensing approach could be found among members of the European Economic Community, or the Eastern European caucusing group, with the more eclectic WEO (including EEC as well as Scandinavian and other smaller European states) favoring a split-the-difference approach at rank 9. The Group of 77 didn't know what it wanted, but the distribution showed a concentration in the range of ranks 7–15, indicating its members knew what they did *not* want—a system where strong states could get a lead in ocean mining with an international agency guaranteeing their right of access to the resource. With G-77 states averaging rank 11 and landlocked states (most of whom were developing states) not being cross-pressured on this issue, it was clear that a strong Authority would likely emerge in further negotiations.

The median on this issue is revealing. It tells us that there was no clear direction for an outcome at this stage, and that the forces supporting each basic tendency, while not in balance, were each sufficiently large to block each other under most decision rules. Our pairs analysis confirmed that judgment. It revealed that if the issue could have been reduced to a contest between supporters of a licensing scheme and a joint-venture notion, the licensing forces would have the support of 61 states, and the joint venture forces, 88. On the other hand, if the licensing forces would retreat to a mixed-machinery position while the Enterprise supporters hung tough, the mixed-machinery supporters would have an approximate 2–1 advantage in potential votes. However, we could also see a hard core of 50 states pushing for an Enterprise approach. If they refused to retreat, it was going to be a long, hard negotiation.

Indeed, they refused to retreat and were able to get the backing of the Group of 77. By 1975, just before the Single Negotiating Text was issued, the distribution is quite different, as we can see in figure 7.5. This figure displays the pattern typical of North–South confrontation: a single-peaked distribution with a tail. The peak of the distribution is the Group of 77 position, the tail

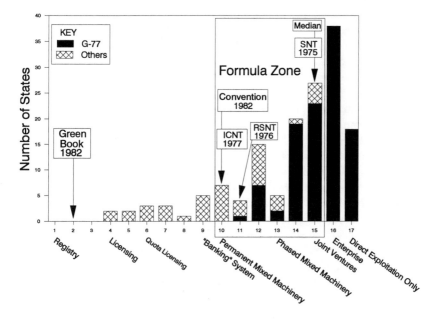

Figure 7.5: Functions of the Authority (T-2)

represents the position of the developed states. This pattern, characteristic of what we have called a North–South confrontation, really demonstrates a solid South facing a fractured North. The Group of 77 found its preferred outcome.

The United States and other Western states, in a working group headed by Christopher Pinto of Sri Lanka, had arrived at an accommodation between developed- and developing-state positions on what activities the Authority would control. They were stunned when Chairman Paul Engo submitted as the First Committee portion of the Single Negotiating Text, a text very close to the announced G-77 position. Engo merely attached the Pinto text to his report.[34] The SNT stated that "activities . . . shall be conducted *directly* by the Authority" (my emphasis). The Authority could "carry out activities . . . by entering into service contracts or joint ventures or any other such form of association which ensures the direct and effective control at all times over such activities."[35] Aside from questions of integrity and good faith, it was very clear why Engo did what he did. He knew that he could not get the Pinto text by the caucus of the Group of 77. With an internal unanimity rule, radical members of the Group of 77 were able to prevent any compromise of the group's basic NIEO position.[36] (The United States may have been shocked, but it should not have been surprised. The Law of the Sea Study Group predicted the likely outcome on this issue as early as 1974 and provided forecasts to the U.S. delegation.[37] Our median showed that if a decision was forced in 1975, the only access to seabed-mineral resources for private enterprises or state corporations that would have been permitted would have been via joint ventures.)

The degree of solidarity on this issue by groups is shown in figure 7.6. There were no developing states that preferred a licensing (much less a registry) outcome. As might be expected, support for licensing came from EEC states and allies, such as Japan and the United States. Somewhat more forthcoming and willing to look for a compromise were the members of the WEO and Eastern European groups. However, contrary to their behavior on most issues, the average standard deviation of the Eastern European group was rather high (>3) on this issue. Even more favorable to finding an accommodation with developing states were the Scandinavians at a 11.2 average rank, with a relatively low standard deviation.

The solidity of the South can also be seen in this figure. The Group of 77 was firmly behind an Enterprise approach, with access to the seabed by others only via joint ventures or contracts. It was a very disciplined group. Its standard deviation of 1.6 on a scale of 17 meant that its members, on the average, ranged in support from phased mixed machinery to an exclusive Enterprise approach. This is remarkable solidarity for a group as large and un-

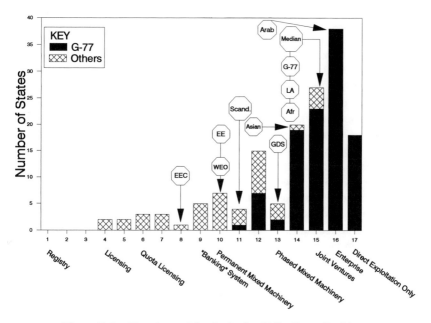

Figure 7.6: Functions of the Authority (T-2): Group Positions

wieldy as G-77 (with 110 members when we did our measurements). Finally, all of the Group of 77's subgroups clustered closely around its core position, with the Arabs a bit more radical, and Asians less so. The heart of the Group of 77 on this issue was to be the Latin American and African groups.

A single peaked distribution with a tail hints that, if a minority in the tail is stubborn in its opposition, it should be able to extract a price from the majority for agreeing to a consensus decision. Our pairs analysis showed the state of play as of 1975. If, for example, the developed states were willing to support a "banking" system and the developing states held out for a joint-venture approach, the developing states would still have to persuade 33–41 states (depending on the scenario) to accept their approach—a formidable task under consensus. No wonder the negotiation took seven years longer to resolve this issue. However, in accepting a mixed-machinery outcome in 1982, the supporters of the treaty were not able to persuade 21 states (4 against, 17 abstaining) to join the "consensus" and had to settle for near-consensus. We were not surprised at the size of the core opposition to a joint-venture approach. Hypothetically, if in 1975 the developed states had insisted upon a licensing scheme only, they could have mustered only 17 supporters compared to 132 states who would have supported a joint venture outcome. Seven years later, it was essentially the same states we identified as strongly supporting a licensing approach that voted to stay outside the treaty.

For the next seven years, the issue had to be negotiated with the SNT's basic approach as the position to accept or defeat. Progress was slow and often acrimonious. The Law of the Sea Study Group collected no further data, but the shape of the negotiation can be traced using the SNT as the base point. Figure 7.5 shows a relatively wide formula zone (between ranks 10 and 15). After the SNT was issued, only an agreed outcome within this range seemed feasible, if at all.

It was evident that Engo's maneuver to ignore the negotiated language of the Pinto draft had placed the negotiations in grave peril of breaking down. The Group of 77 was pushed by its radicals into a no-retreat position. But the group could not sustain its unwillingness to give private and state entrepreneurs a role in the Authority-supervised seabed-mining system, unless it preferred breakdown as an outcome, or thought that it could establish a seabed-mining endeavor without the cooperation of the developed states. In the effort to push the negotiations further along by revising the negotiating text, it chose to fall back.

In the Revised Single Negotiating Text, activities are conducted by the Authority "and in association with the Authority and under its control . . . by State Parties or State Enterprises or persons natural or juridical which possess the nationality of State Parties or are effectively controlled by them or their nationals, when sponsored by such States. . . ."[38] Although the language of the RSNT emphasized the tightness of control by the Authority through the use of a contract with a state party or the Enterprise, an annex guaranteed the contractor exclusive rights to explore and exploit one half of the area the contractor identified as exploitable.[39] This was a considerable step away from the idea of creating a monopoly for an International Enterprise, but it was not enough to lure developed states into acquiesence. Further changes were demanded.

The Informal Consolidated Negotiating Text the (ICNT) was issued in 1977 and revised again in 1980. The convention is essentially a somewhat revised version of the 1980 ICNT. The changes made to the RSNT version, while important, were incremental. Subtle changes of emphasis were made to attract the participation of the technically capable developed states with ocean-mining aspirations. Mostly, they dealt with language on the degree of supervision the Authority would exercise over the state-sponsored miners. For example, the ICNT states that activities are to be carried out by state entities only "on behalf of" the Authority.[40] In the Convention, activities could be "carried out as authorized by the Authority."[41] We have placed both on figure 7.5 at rank 10, since very refined changes would not show on a scale as broad as ours.

In retrospect, the fallback of the Group of 77 from SNT, through ICNT, to final convention, appears generous to its opponents. Still, the 1977 version of the ICNT was not sufficient to please the developed states. Some of them claimed the ICNT ignored proposed language prepared by Jens Evensen, the head of the Norwegian delegation, that might have bridged the differences between developed and developing states. According to Elliot Richardson, the 1977 ICNT, prepared in private and released only after the conference session terminated, did not provide an explicit assurance of access to private and state miners, and it might be read as giving the Authority the right to mandate joint ventures as a condition of access.[42] Although the Conference was again in crisis, tempers calmed and negotiations resumed. By 1980, as a result of intensive negotiations, especially in Working Group 2 on the financial conditions for contractors and the financing of the International Enterprise, Richardson was once again optimistic that a successful outcome was possible. He told the American Mining Congress only four unsettled issues remained: boundary delimitation, and the three "p's"—participation, the Preparatory Commission, and preparatory investment protection.[43] UNCLOS III, as a result of resolving the financial conditions for contractors and the International Enterprise, had achieved what James Sebenius called "agreement in the small."[44] Richardson seemed convinced that he could make further incremental improvements, and that these were all that was necessary to provide reasonable working conditions for U.S.-based entrepreneurs. Such incremental changes might be represented by placing them at, say, rank 8 or 9 on our scale.

The new Reagan Administration felt differently. It was elected on a platform extolling the private sector as the only legitimate basis of economic life. For many members of the new administration, in the White House and in the Departments of State and Defense,[45] the seabed provisions in the ICNT were not only less than what U.S. miners needed, but an insult to their value system. The entire scheme was fundamentally unacceptable. Elliot Richardson resigned as chief U.S. negotiator on October 1, 1980. He was replaced by his deputy George Aldrich who was very quickly dumped by the new administration. The Reagan administration was going to fight the ideology of the NIEO with its own free-market approach. In 1981, new U.S. representatives announced a comprehensive policy review of the entire U.S. position, and for all practical purposes the United States dropped out of the negotiations while the review was being undertaken.[46]

Richardson's successor identified six broad areas that required repair in order to bring the United States back to the bargaining table.[47] But, instead of advancing proposals to address those areas, using the ICNT as its base point, the United States proposed to rewrite all of Part XI. Essentially, in its Green Book, the U.S. proposed adoption of a registry system to manage deep-seabed-mineral exploitation. Instead of organizing, carrying out, and controlling activities, the Authority would only regulate these activities.[48] Activities would be carried out by state parties or entities, and since the Green Book eliminated the phrase "in association with the Authority," presumably state parties or entities could carry out activities without any association with the Authority.[49] The U.S. draft would allow for the existence of an Enterprise. Indeed, the Enterprise is about all the Authority would be authorized to control.[50] As far as control of national activities was concerned, a new paragraph submitted by the United States would authorize each state party to "exercise . . . control over activities in the Area carried out by that state party."[51] Under the U.S. proposal, the Authority would be stripped of the right to ensure general compliance with the convention, and would have only the right to insist upon compliance with its regulatory functions. In short, the United States demanded surrender. We placed the Green Book proposal at rank 2 on our scale. It shows how far opposing delegations would have had to go to accommodate the United States and a few (albeit important) industrial states to gain their participation. The Green Book posited a "disagreement in the large."[52]

At the time the United States dropped out of the negotiations, there was considerable consternation among delegations. They knew that a U.S. defection would significantly reduce the chances for creating a successful Authority and Enterprise. It seems that the United States could have played "chicken" and used the threat of defection to extract important and numerous, though incremental, concessions from the Group of 77. The circumstances were ripe. A group of 11 states—"good Samaritans"—tried to open up channels of communication and dialogue. The effort failed. But the United States' bargaining position was not calculated to extract the maximum price for its cooperation. It was not prepared to swerve off the highway at the last minute. It planned to speed straight ahead. The new administration simply wanted no part of an UNCLOS III Convention that did not fit its ideological notions, even if some members of the U.S. delegation claimed that they could negotiate in good faith and still achieve the President's objectives.[53] The purpose of the Green Book turned out to be justification of the Reagan Administration's planned defection. There was no realistic expectation that the

Group of 77 would surrender to it. The Reagan Administration got what it wanted. It preserved its ideological purity, and it also gained all of the benefits of the treaty without the liability of binding itself by signing and ratifying it.

There are a number of lessons to be learned concerning parliamentary diplomacy from the negotiation over access to the minerals of the deep seabed. First, if a substantial majority forms around a particular formula notion, that notion will be the position to confirm or tame in the later phases of the negotiation. Second, if the formula idea or, as Thomas Clingan, Jr., put it, the "rhetorical principle" is to be tamed rather than confirmed, its opponents must try to undercut it in incremental stages on matters of the details of its implementation. Third, even if satisfactory arrangements can be worked out on the details and the principle is tamed, the taming cannot so discredit the principle of equity embodied in the formula idea that the majority would feel it had failed to achieve an equitable outcome. As Oran Young put it ". . . there is much to be said for the proposition that satisfying major equity demands is a necessary condition for international regime formation."[54]

However, in the parliamentary diplomatic setting of UNCLOS III, it was rare that delegates were able to agree on an outcome to a seminal issue that was clear or simple. Young claims that the most successful examples of formation of new international regimes were on issues that could be comprehended by the participants because the salience was clear and simple.[55] Unfortunately, clarity and simplicity were not possible on most of the issues dealt with in UNCLOS III, particularly relating to the seabed. It was necessary to create formulas with the obscurity and complexity characteristic of legislative bargaining to bring together for closure the vast array of disparate interests and bargaining groups.

Fourth, attempts to force a substantial majority in a parliamentary diplomatic setting to surrender do not work, and only prove useful for justifying defection.

Fifth, the process of working out an acceptable outcome on a central core of a regime is long, fraught with many steps backward, and at times appears not to have a consistent direction. But with sufficient time, a direction emerges and a substantial majority of states moves toward closure on an acceptable outcome. Since near-consensus was achieved on the issue of the deep seabed, does the record of UNCLOS III on the Seabed Authority issue argue for parliamentary diplomacy as a viable means by which to create new regimes on highly divisive issues? A number of the participants who bemoaned the fact that they got close to consensus, and therefore were at the edge of success, believed that parliamentary diplomatic conferences should be tried again. Others, however, noted that "almost" does not count. Consensus was beyond reach, and the cost of getting there was prohibitive.

Pervading our analysis of the seabed issue was the problem of timing in finding acceptable solutions to all the major measures that had to be included in the overall package. Some issues in the overall package were settled early—straits transit, territorial sea, and exclusive economic zone. Therefore, a sixth conclusion must be that if a party perceives that the issues most salient to it are settled early in a negotiation, the bargaining leverage of its opponents to hold issues hostage is substantially reduced. The Reagan Administration, to this point in time, guessed correctly. It could have the benefits of the portions of the treaty which furthered its ocean interests without accepting the liabilities.[56]

Disagreement in the large was the result. That disagreement in the large was the overall outcome of UNCLOS III should not be underemphasized because agreement in the small had been achieved. However, it might well be that the United States Government, in both opting not to sign and claiming to enjoy most of the privileges of the treaty, has neglected "the shadow of the future," and too heavily discounted its future need for cooperation from those states who thought they had made all reasonable compromises to bring the United States into the agreement.[57] Moreover, the failure to reach consensus at UNCLOS III casts serious doubt on the usefulness of a consensus-based bargaining system for solving problems that require the acquiescence of 150+ states.

Production Controls

If private or state entities were to be allowed access, particularly unlimited access, to the nodules of the deep seabed, then the next major concern of those who feared the potential effect on themselves as minerals producers, or on the Third World in general, was how to limit the impact of seabed mining on the stability of the world minerals market. Land-based mineral producers, in developed as well as developing states, might wish to protect themselves from unbridled competition, which might lower already depressed world prices for minerals. Unlimited access as a general approach to the problem was unattractive to the Third World because it seemed to promise a widening of the technological and economic gaps between the rich and poor states of the world. They abhorred the uncertainty of the market system and looked to find political controls of economic activity.

The answer was to find a mechanism that would, while not denying access, limit the ability of ocean miners to depress prices by unlimited production of minerals from the deep seabed. Given the preference of the Group of 77 for political solutions, the mechanism was certain to be some form of political control. Several candidate solutions were offered, the most popular being production controls. It was a solution consistent with other known aspects of the New International Economic Order.

Most mining entities and the states that sponsored them preferred the free market in general, and because of the uncertainties of a new, untested industry, they preferred unfettered conditions for its development. This was another issue destined to result in an ideological clash. There was danger that the Conference could break down early over this issue alone if poorly managed, especially if the general ideological aspects of the problem were emphasized. Early disaster was avoided. Though the negotiation achieved an outcome that many observers felt would satisfy both producer and consumer interests, this issue became a part of the "disagreement in the large."

Disagreement in the large did not occur until after 1980. Early in the negotiation, delegates focused upon specific, detailed mechanisms that promised to offer a solution satisfying to both sides. They sought an arrangement that would give assurances to one side that the minerals market would not spin out of control as a result of seabed mining, and to the other side that a new industry would not be prevented from coming into existence because of impossible costs or conditions being imposed upon it. They found a mechanism, and it was almost good enough.

The general bargaining problem was how, using the majority's conceptual framework as a guide to work out details that were satisfactory to both sides. The details had to circumscribe the general principle to satisfy opponents, but leave the general principle viable to satisfy supporters.

If, as a potential ocean miner, you fear that political constraints upon your business might cause it to fail, you reduce your risk by insisting upon an arrangement in which there are no political constraints. If, on the other hand, you fear that uncontrolled ocean mining might have a negative effect upon world mineral prices or lead to an increase in the economic gap between rich and poor, you are safest under a system with unlimited power to regulate according to the circumstances.

The uncertainties are quite large in establishing an industry that requires new knowledge, new technology, large capital inputs, great distances to processing centers and markets. Studies and models promise to reduce the uncertainty with estimates. But that is what they are—estimates. Only after a real-world attempt will the contestants know whether the estimates that they use have served them well. Estimates used for modal positions—usually worst- or best-case analyses—are easiest to perform, therefore seemingly the least risky. On the particular issue of deep-seabed mining, one of the most notable characteristics was the need to negotiate on a problem with a very wide range of uncertainty. Both sides had to engage in risky behavior.

The range of proposals as to how much nickel, copper, cobalt, and perhaps manganese ore should be produced from the deep seabed can be seen in figure 7.7. The spectrum runs from a preference for allowing free-market interplay

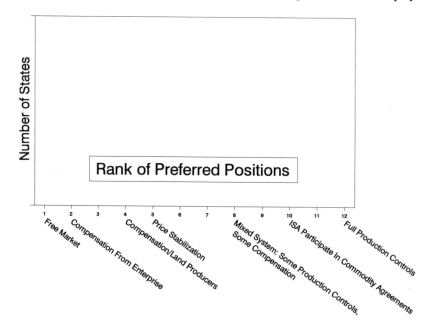

Figure 7.7:   Production Controls

between producers and consumers (rank 1) to giving the International Seabed Agency the authority to impose any form of production controls it deemed appropriate to the situation (rank 12). Some supporters of the free market, if they had to bend, and if an International Enterprise had to be created, were willing to see production controls imposed upon the Enterprise, but not upon state entities entitled to mine the international area (rank 2). A more painful fallback, hence the two-rank gap, was willingness to consider some form of compensation scheme for land producers if seabed production affected the market price of ores negatively (rank 4). But this would be after the fact of glutting the market. Moreover, it treated the problem as if it were a question of satisfying direct stakeholders only, and avoided what Third World opponents said was a systemic problem. A more fully developed price stabilization scheme that proposed to use buffer stocks and integrated commodity arrangements was placed at rank 5.

At the other end of the spectrum, few supporters of production controls proposed fallbacks that would exclude production controls per se, but rather sought to reduce the ability of the ISA to impose them arbitrarily. However, some were willing to explore the possibility that ISA be a participant in world commodity agreements as a way of stabilizing raw-materials markets (rank 10). The furthest production-control supporters said they would go was to consider a mixed system—some production controls, some compensation, and some commodity agreements—in order to prevent ocean minerals from destabilizing world mineral prices (rank 8).

As figure 7.8 shows, there was little doubt from the beginning of UNCLOS III about how the issue managing seabed minerals would be decided. Most

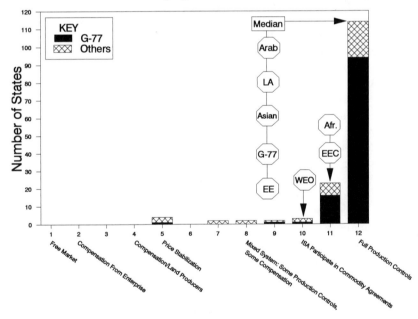

Figure 7.8:   Production Controls (T-1)

delegates to the General Assembly and the Ad Hoc and Permanent Seabed Committees had a strong preference for an approach that would create a managed system. They wanted production controls. The distribution shows a very strong peak with a very small tail. Technically, this was not pure consensus, but it was near-consensus, even before the first substantive meeting of UNCLOS III in Caracas.

This pattern goes beyond the usual North–South pattern. Virtually all states but a handful of "Northwestern" states showed a preference for production controls. With G-77 united, it would dominate the median, the position that in a voting situation could not be beaten. All subgroups of the Group of 77 were at rank 12 except the African, and it was at rank 11. The issue was highly salient to the Group of 77: 40 of its 110 members spoke to the issue and their standard deviations averaged below 1.0. From the beginning of the attempt to block out the issue, the Eastern Europeans were in favor of production controls. EEC and WEO members were not far behind.

There was very little room for maneuver. Unquestionably, there would be some form of production controls in the Convention once delegates got down to drafting negotiating texts. The only question was what form the provisions would take, and whether on matter of detail ocean-mining stakeholders and their state sponsors could induce the majority not to apply production control measures that would wreck a nascent industry.

As a result of an economic review by the U.S. Treasury Department after the 1972 oil shock, the United States and its friends put up a more spirited defense of market mechanisms when UNCLOS III met in substantive session. This changed some distributions, but the pattern of preferences remained essentially the same in 1973–75. Distribution in figure 7.9 is still essentially unimodal with a tail, albeit a somewhat longer and stronger tail. The tail was composed of the United States, the United Kingdom, France, the Federal Republic of Germany, Ireland, Israel, Japan, and even Malta.[58] The median slipped from rank 12 in T-1 to rank 11. It was clear to all delegates that some form of production controls would be in the treaty drafts the chairman of the First Committee was to prepare. If opponents had pressed the issue, it could have broken open the negotiations. But they would have been quite isolated. Joining G-77 were the states that usually tried to mediate between North and South such as the Scandinavians, as well as land-based mineral producers in both developed and developing states. One of them—Canada —spearheaded the effort to limit production according to observers.[59] The alternate strategy, used by other developed states until the Reagan Administration's participation in UNCLOS III, was to refine the details, hoping to defang production controls. Some observer-participants and outside observers thought they had succeeded, or nearly succeeded.

In figure 7.9, we have placed all serious bargaining from 1975 to 1982 at rank 12. All proposals included some form of production controls. The bar-

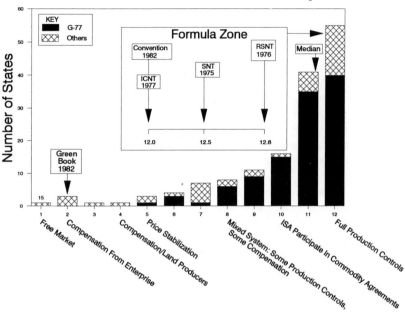

Figure 7.9: Production Controls (T-2)

gaining was vigorous, and the differences between the proposals important, but the range was narrow—too narrow to track with our conflict variable. If the Law of the Sea Study Group had continued to collect data after 1975, it would have had to create a new conflict variable, one that conceded production controls as the basic formula idea and that concentrated on the bargaining over what it meant.

The Single Negotiating Text, placed at rank 12.5, concentrated on the goal of a production-control policy, but did not specify the means of reaching that goal. In Article 9, development of the Area is to be undertaken in such a manner as to "avoid or minimize any adverse effects on the revenues and economies of the developing countries."[60] The responsibility for accomplishing this was delegated to the ISA Council.[61]

The development of a detailed production-control proposal in the Revised Single Negotiating Text (a more negotiated text than the SNT promulgated by Chairman Engo after rejecting the language produced by the Pinto Group) pushed production controls unfavorable to potential seabed-mineral producers. Hence, the RSNT language was placed at rank 12.8. In the RSNT, the Authority gained the power to limit "in an interim period [20 years] . . .

total production in the Area so as not to exceed the projected cumulative growth segment of the nickel market."[62] Production in the area was not to compete with minerals produced on land. The Authority was also authorized to participate in commodity conferences,[63] and to create "a compensatory system of economic adjustment assistance.[64]

In this period, most of the major issues had essentially been settled and bargaining was concentrated in seven working groups, three of which were concerned with unresolved seabed-minerals issues. Negotiating Group One, chaired by Francis Njenga of Kenya, and a small group of interested states led by Satya Nandan of Fiji, managed to find a technical fix on the production-control issue. As a result, matters improved for opponents of production controls in the Composite Single Negotiating Texts of 1977 and 1980.

The ICNT on production controls was placed at rank 12.0. The timing of production controls and the way the controls would be administrated were substantially refined. In earlier versions there was an expectation that the production controls would place such low limits on seabed miners that land-based producers would have little risk of adverse effects from the operations of ocean producers. In this version of the Negotiating Text, the limits were more generous, so that ocean production would not be choked in the early years of development by production limits. There was greater risk for land-based producers, but this would be made up in compensation schemes. The ICNT called for the Authority to take necessary measures to ensure "orderly and safe development and rational management of the resources of the Area."[65] These measures would include, for an interim period of seven years, a limit on total production "so as not to exceed . . . the projected cumulative growth segment of the world nickel demand." After seven years, total production should not "exceed 60 percent of the cumulative growth segment of the world nickel demand." The rate was to be calculated by the "annual constant percentage rate of increase in world demand" during a 20-year period. A least-squares method of calculation, adjusted every five years, was to be used.[66] If the limits proved so generous that there were adverse impacts upon developing-state mineral producers, the Authority was to "develop a system of compensation."[67]

Some supporters claim that the text became incrementally even more favorable to the interests of prospective miners in the negotiations leading to the Convention. In the Convention, the limit is calculated as the sum of the growth of nickel consumption over the five years prior to the first commercial mining operation plus 60 percent of the growth of nickel consumption thereafter. To protect against exaggerated restrictions during period of low market growth, the treaty imposes a 3 percent growth rate floor for the calculation.[68] The method of calculation was changed to "a linear regression of the logarithms of actual nickel consumption for the most recent 15-year period."[69] It was a formula only an economist could love. It was difficult to judge how much more favorable it was to the interest of potential ocean miners, so the treaty also was placed at rank 12.0.

However much the treaty text improved the prospects of future ocean miners, it was still not satisfactory to the United States. Production controls were another issue where the United States insisted upon complete surrender as the price of its further participation in the negotiation. The Green Book's production-control provisions were conspicuous by their absence. The United States was demanding the complete removal of production-control provisions, reneging on Secretary of State Kissinger's 1976 promise of U.S. support of production controls in a treaty with a "banking" system.[70] However, the Green Book would allow the Authority to participate in commodity arrangements "in respect of the production of the minerals derived from the Area by the Enterprise." The Authority could do what it pleased with the Enterprise, but it could not control national activity. According to the Green Book, the only assistance that mineral-producing developing states would receive would be after the fact. For the first 15 years of seabed mining, under the U.S. proposal, adjustment assistance could be provided for land-based developing mineral states that were harmed by seabed production.[71]

This issue produced a number of important lessons. First, as we have seen on other issues negotiated under parliamentary diplomacy, the majority will dominate the development of the core concept and formula. Second, when the issue is highly salient to the majority, as the issue of production controls was, the range for negotiation will be very narrow. In this case, the question was what type of production controls there would be and how it would be formulated, not whether a variation on the main idea could be worked out. Third, despite the narrow range of negotiation available, it still might be possible to circumscribe the general formula idea to the satisfaction of those who might be negatively affected by its implementation.

Since the United States defected, there is a high probability that Part XI of the UNCLOS III Convention will not be fully implemented. Therefore, it is likely that the world will never know whether the solution worked out by the conferees would have helped develop a viable ocean-mining industry. Opponents of the treaty claimed it would not.[72] Defenders of the treaty have marshaled technical arguments that the production control arrangements would have benefited developed consumer states.[73]

The Composition of the ISA Council and Its Decision Rules: The Who and How of Decision

The question of the composition and voting rules of the Council of the ISA was a critical one for those hoping, and those fearing, that a new international organization was to come into being as a result of UNCLOS III negotiations. The Council became the central decision body of the International Seabed Authority, and whoever controlled its decisions essentially controlled the effort to mine the deep seabed. This was clearly understood by the politically experienced national delegations to General Assembly, the Ad Hoc and Permanent Seabed Committees, and the Conference.

It was not a forgone conclusion that the Council was to become the real supreme organ of ISA. Some early plans for a Seabed Authority envisaged a secretariat with general management functions, and some proposed a separate executive agency for managing the Enterprise. While it is possible to design a self-motivated executive agency, most plans assumed that policy direction would be provided by an organ external to the everyday management personnel. But would policy direction come from all members of the organization, or some select subset? The classic problem for international organizations arose—should responsibility be separated from representation? That is, should important decisions be made by all participants in a committee of the whole, or should responsibility be delegated to a subset of the whole that is either responsible, representative, or both?

The Group of 77 clearly preferred to create an egalitarian ''Assembly'' in which all members would be represented, each would have one vote, and decisions on important questions would be made by simple, or at most two-thirds, majority. The Assembly would be the ''supreme organ of the ISA.''

As expected, objections arose from a small number of powerful states that had a stake in ocean mining and that were aware of the possibility of being repeatedly outvoted. There were also the usual objections that a large decision-making body would be cumbersome. An Assembly could not meet often—at best, only once a year. It would be expensive to muster all interested parties. Experience had shown that only a smaller decision-making organization could meet with the frequency necessary to keep proper control of day-to-day activities. The rights of representation would have to be restricted to approving or disapproving the actions initiated by a responsible smaller body.

There were diehards among the most egalitarian-minded members of G-77, but most negotiators conceded fairly early on that an ISA Assembly could only approve or disapprove the initiatives of a smaller body on key issues such as rules, regulations, and procedures for exploitation of deep-seabed minerals or the equitable sharing of benefits.[74] The Assembly had the honor to be formally declared the "supreme organ" of the Authority,[75] but real decision power would lie elsewhere, in a smaller "principal organ" of the Authority. Therefore, the question of *who* would sit on the smaller principal organ—a Council—and how decisions would be made was a central question of the negotiation on deep-seabed minerals. Indeed, it was a central question from the beginning right up to the day the draft convention was put to the vote in 1981.

The goal of the contending parties was to put themselves in an assured position, from which they could either force through or block decisions. This assured position could be written into the treaty by a guaranteed number of seats, a favorable decision rule, or both. The Group of 77 wanted to avoid granting either a formal or tacit veto to the developed states over proposed actions of the Authority. Being a substantial majority, the group preferred to replicate in the Council the proportion of seats it occupied in the Assembly. Presuming perfect, or even good, discipline, the Group of 77 could win any simple majority vote and most two-thirds majority votes, representing as they did at UNCLOS III, 73 percent of the votes.[76] Thus, G-77 preferred a simple-majority decision rule. As a sign of a willingness to take a slight risk, it fell back to support of a two-thirds-majority rule.

Developed states that were important stakeholders in ocean mining were aware from the beginning that if seats on the Council were distributed strictly on the basis of proportional representation, not only could they lose almost all votes, but some of them would not even be represented on the Council. The first issue, therefore, was to alter the seating scheme so that both more developed states, as well as specific developed states, were assured seats. In particular, both the United States as an individual state, and the Eastern European Group as a group, insisted on a guaranteed seat.

The second issue was to alter the numbers necessary to form a requisite majority. Major developed states recognized that they could lead a majority in the Council only if the issue were nonpolitical. If it was politicized—treated as a North–South or great state–small state issue—they would be in a permanent minority and, under the usual rules, could not block decisions adverse to their interests. As a result, they concentrated more on a decision rule that could block adverse results than on a decision rule that would foster favorable results. The best-known decision rule that fully protected their interests was unanimity or strict formal consensus, however cumbersome that might be. Other decision rules, often quite ingenious, would be proposed later, as would some compromise rules that increased the risk to the developed states of adverse decisions.

Agreeing upon a decision rule was necessary because, in rejecting the Pinto text in 1975, Chairman Engo also rejected an acceptable representation and voting plan worked out with Ambassador Pinto. Article 28 of the Pinto text provided for decision by a three-quarters majority present and voting. In addition, of 36 Council seats to be allocated, 18 were to be set aside for representing "special interests" involved in or affected by activities in the Area and, of those, 9 were to be allocated to the most industrialized countries.[77] Even under the three-quarters-majority decision rule, developed states, particularly the most developed wanting seats set aside for themselves, were on the edge of what they considered acceptable risk. The developed states would need perfect discipline among themselves (not likely given the history of smaller, especially Scandinavian states' support of South aspirations), and possibly a few defections from the developing states to block actions by the Authority they found unacceptable. One reason Engo could safely ignore this aspect of the Pinto text is that there was little support for its representation and voting provisions in 1975.

Let us turn to our scale, in which we tried to relate the various proposals to each other. At one end of the spectrum in figure 7.10 (rank 1), we placed consensus as the decision rule, and at the other (rank 10), we placed simple

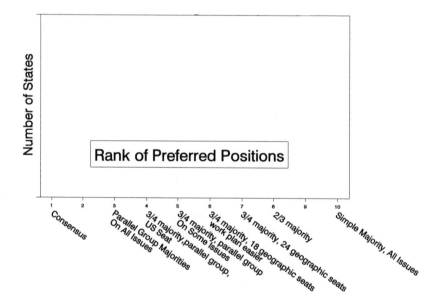

Figure 7.10:   Decision-Making in the ISA Council

majority. As noted, if consensus became the decision rule, the value of guaranteed seats would be enhanced substantially. If decisions were to be made by a simple majority of those present and voting, having a guaranteed seat on the Council would make little difference in terms of controlling outcomes.

Another plan for preventing a runaway majority is shown at rank 3. Under this scheme, members of the Council would be divided into two or more groups representing, for example, North and South or producers and consumers. Decision would require a requisite majority of each group. If any one group voted no, the measure would be vetoed. A more refined version would permit decision by a three-quarters majority on a wide range of issues, but require that majority in two or more panels, with guaranteed seats for some important states (rank 4). Slightly more accommodating was a proposal with the same arrangements, but required only for the most critical decisions.

Some states preferred a more stringent standard for decision—a two-thirds-present-and-voting rule (rank 8). A deeper fallback would peg the requisite majority at three-quarters and distribute 24 of 36 seats to geographic groups (rank 7), all but two representing developing states. Twenty-seven votes would then be needed for a three-quarters-majority decision, so this would put the Group of 77 at some risk of not being able to control Council decisions without counting on some defections from among developed Council members.

Even more risky to the Group of 77 was a proposal to keep a three-fourths majority rule, but allocate 18 seats to the investors, consumers, exporters, etc. (many of whom were from the most developed states) (rank 6). A further wrinkle was an elaborate arrangement to provide more favorable conditions for approving the work plans of private and state entities, a key question. This provision could largely bypass the voting rules.[78] Finally, we placed at rank 5 a demand that the decision rule be three-fourths majority, but that it be met within the separate panels representing groups of concerned states.

This was a bitterly fought issue which was not resolved until late in the negotiation. It required much parleying behind closed doors, since the position of the majority was manifest from the earliest days of the UNCLOS III negotiation. What the superpowers wanted—a special position—was bound to be controversial, as we can see in figure 7.11. To describe the distribution on this issue as weakly bimodal is an act of charity. The median shows near-consensus in favor of a two-thirds majority voting system with no special seats set aside for individual states or groups and no more than the usual General Assembly-based division of seats. The distribution shows that while all the serious opposition came from 11–24 developed states, depending on the scheme, the issue was not North versus South, but rather the superpowers and

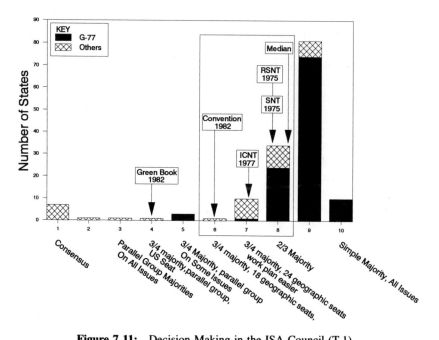

Figure 7.11: Decision-Making in the ISA Council (T-1)

their closest friends versus everyone else. Only the United States and members of the Soviet bloc spoke in favor of a three-quarters-majority voting system, particularly with parallel majorities or special seats set aside.

The North was mostly willing to accept a decision system which it could not control. A number of important large and middle developed states even spoke in favor of a two-thirds-majority system. They included Australia, New Zealand, Canada, Spain, Japan, Italy, France, Greece, Sweden, Finland, and Denmark. As a result, WEO had a group mean of 7.85 (with a standard deviation of 1.1) and even the usually more conservative EEC had a mean of 7.7 (with a very low standard deviation of .6). Group of 77 members were solidly in the two-thirds-majority camp with a mean of 8.7 (and a .6 standard deviation, remarkably low, considering the size of the group). The superpowers and the other most developed states were isolated. But they were still potent.

This issue displays a classic situation in parliamentary diplomacy. Near-consensus is achieved without participation of a handful of important states, but it is not good enough to create a stable and workable outcome. The superpowers, however, were not willing to allow themselves to be treated merely as sovereign equals. They insisted upon being given special decision privileges as the price of participation. The egalitarian forces did not give in soon or easily. Nevertheless, they realized this was an issue of high salience to the superpowers, and if superpower participation was important, they had to be accommodated even if this violated egalitarian principles. But it was, indeed, a slow and grudging accommodation and they did not concede until the bargaining came down to a make-or-break point.

We presented data from only the first time period—before 1973. The situation did not change substantively, except that it was such a controversial issue that it virtually ceased being debated in public between 1973 and 1975 (and, indeed, after), hence our sample size dropped. Since the pattern remained the same, it is safe to say that there was insufficient support for the Pinto three-quarters formula in 1975. What was supportable at that time was what Engo placed in the Informal Single Negotiating Text. In Article 27 of the SNT, he had the Council made up of 36 states, 24 elected on the principle of equitable geographic distribution; 12 granted to special interests; 6 to offshore-mining "investor" states; and 6 to developing-state land-based producers of minerals, importers, and landlocked states. Decisions on important issues were to be made by two-thirds plus one of states present and voting.[79] The formula remained the same in 1976 when the RSNT was released. According to Chairman Engo, "the Committee held several preliminary discussions on the composition of the Council but did not have time for necessary detailed discussions on the vital question of its decision making process at all."[80]

Serious negotiations on the issue occurred during preparation of the Composite Negotiating Text. Again, the Council was to be made up of 36 members, but was to make important decisions on the basis of three-fourths present and voting, as long as the total included a majority of state participating in the session. Only 18 seats were set aside for geographical distribution, while 4 seats were to be allocated to major investors, "including at least one State from the Eastern (Socialist) European region," 4 to major importers of minerals (also including an Eastern European), 4 to major exporters, including 2 developing states, and 6 to states representing special interests such as the landlocked, the geographically disadvantaged, and the least developed.[81]

The major remaining problem was gaining the cooperation of the United States, which wanted a guaranteed seat, but which, by denying that it was a member of any geographical caucusing group, could not claim a "geographical region" seat (as the Soviet Union in the 1970s probably could with an "Eastern European" seat, if it chose). Since the politics of the General

Assembly was based on recognization of regional caucusing groups but not of the special position of individual states—however powerful or important—it was difficult to guarantee the United States a seat. It was highly probable the U.S. would qualify for a set-aside under more than one category, but not for a guaranteed seat. Nevertheless, Elliot Richardson claimed that the delegates had implicitly guaranteed the United States a seat, and that "it [was] likely that the 77 would now agree to make the guarantee more explicit."[82]

Even the Reagan Administration recognized the dilemma and in the Green Book accepted the 36 total, and the 4, 4, 4, 6, 18 breakdown, but created a seat for the United States without naming itself directly. The Green Book language required that the four investors be chosen from a list of "seven State Parties specified in paragraph 7 (c ter), including at least one State Party from the Eastern (Socialist) European region."[83] Moreover, three of the four consumer states would have to be chosen from the panel of the seven named states.[84] The United States would qualify under either or both categories.

While the Reagan Administration claimed it would accept a three-fourths-majority outcome for decisions on important questions, the Green Book also required a small supplement to the rule. The United States insisted that in addition to an overall three-fourths majority, there would also have to be a simple majority in favor from each of the five named categories represented. If three of the four major investors, or three of the four major consumers voted no, even if there was an overall three-fourths majority, a proposal on a major issue would fail to meet the requisite majority. The United States was proposing a veto system. The Green Book added a new issue that required a double majority—financing of the Enterprise.[85] It also removed an issue from majority voting altogether. If the U.S. amendment had been adopted, any future amendments to Part XI of the treaty pursuant to Article 314 could only occur through a process of consensus.[86] Again, this represented surrender to the United States. The Green Book proposals were placed at rank 4 on the scale. United States intransigence on this issue was a major reason that the vast majority of states saw the gentlemen's agreement for a cooling-off period before voting as a meaningless formality. The decision-making system for the Council would not be satisfactory to the United States, no matter how many incremental concessions the Group of 77 made. Only the surrender of the Group of 77 to the United States would have proved satisfactory.

On the issue of how and by whom decisions were to be made in the ISA Council, we saw a pattern similar to the modal pattern of a single-peaked preference or weak bimodal preferences forming at the end of the first phase of negotiation. The strong peak identified the formula idea and was the beginning of subsequent negotiations whose purpose was to refine it into an agreed outcome. In the second phase—as we have seen on other issues—defenders of the formula tried to preserve its conceptual thrust in operative language, opponents tried to undermine it in practice without replacing it.

On this issue, however, there was a twist. It took a very long time for the agreed outcome to emerge. This was due, in part, to the forces facing each other. Control of the Council, along with whether entities under the control of nation-states would be permitted to exploit deep-seabed minerals under the aegis of ISA, were matters of extraordinary importance to a limited number of powerful developed states, including the superpowers. They would not subject themselves voluntarily to a situation they saw as inherently majoritarian. The second phase of this negotiation focused upon whether a substantial majority could be forced to concede that they might not control key decisions in an authoritative institution. If Stephen Krasner is correct—that "in meta-political situations, the Third World has consistently attempted to move regimes from market-oriented toward authoritative modes of allocation"[87]—it would be a bitter blow if the Third World and those states that believed in a NIEO-dominated system succeeded in creating what appeared to be an authoritative institution, and lost control of its decision-making. Therefore, they gave ground slowly.

Did the Third World concede too little or too much? Unless or until an International Seabed Authority comes into existence, it is impossible to answer the question. But the inability of nations to bridge their differences on the four issues we reviewed in this chapter constituted a disagreement in the large. There are clearly limits to how far a negotiator in a minority position in a parliamentary situation can push in trying to make the majority's formula palatable, without making the agreed result unpalatable to the majority. The Third World stopped short of making concessions on all major issues of Part XI that would have resulted in an outcome unacceptable to itself. However, the United States chose not to test how far in the end the Third World might have been pushed, opting instead for defection.

PART III

Conclusions
and Inconclusions

8

UNCLOS III—
The Regime Negotiated

The United Nations Convention on the Law of the Sea took 14–15 years of effort. The document opened for signature on December 10, 1982, was intended to be a legal regime to govern the conduct of humankind in virtually all uses of the world's oceans. It was to be a "constitution" for the oceans. The Convention attempted to state the rights, rules, and obligations of states and others using one of the largest areas of the world (70 percent of the earth's surface), the airspace over it, the water column below, and the seabed. While not every aspect of human conduct in the oceans was included, the Convention's 320 articles and 9 annexes were certainly comprehensive in scope.

What type of a regime was promulgated in Kingston, Jamaica, in 1982? Does it do what a regime should do? How well? Or how badly? Does it have significant weaknesses? Did all stakeholders win, or did some win more than others? Were there losers? Will it be a stable regime? How does it affect the international order? Was the 15-year commitment of talent, time, and money to produce the treaty worthwhile? Did its benefits to the world community, major states, and groups of states outweigh its liabilities? These are the questions this chapter will address.

Some of these questions can be tackled with methods that yield reasonably precise answers. Because no method is sufficiently comprehensive to adequately assess the whole, I will depend upon my judgments of the UNCLOS III regime and the possible alternatives. I will make my judgments as explicit as possible so that readers can examine my premises, and if they differ with them, pinpoint where. I invite readers to use the same model to test their own assessment of who won and who lost, of whether UNCLOS III's benefits outweighed its liabilities, and whether new ocean regime is likely to be stable.

International Regimes and the Oceans
The UNCLOS III Convention was intended as an explicit legal regime. When the Convention is ratified, its signatories (and perhaps others under the notion of customary international law), will be bound to obey the rules stated

and obligations[1] undertaken in the formal document. The rules negotiated are prescriptions for specific actions. The obligations are explicit applications of the norms or standards of expected behavior, as are the notions of rights imbedded in the treaty. They are based upon principles that were extensively discussed and agreed to, although at times either left fuzzy or, when understood, agreed to reluctantly by some of the participants. Likewise, decision-making procedures agreed upon to implement collective choices were, in some parts of the treaty, somewhat sketchy, while in other parts were stated with greater precision.[2]

Commitments undertaken were not ad hoc arrangements, but were intended to govern the behavior of ocean users for the indefinite future. One important function of the new ocean regime was to influence the expectations of the adhering parties about the probable obedience by others of the rules, rights, and obligations negotiated. The expectation of reciprocal obedience, so that common and therefore customary practices lead to a reasonably ordered system, is critical to the success of a legal regime. It is especially important to a regime which directly impacts the 120+ states with seacoasts. Since the ocean is a continuous physical system, jurisdictions and uses overlap. No manmade borders can completely contain natural processes. If each of the 120+ coastal states had its own rules and attempted to impose them not only on its own domestic stakeholders but on others, chaos might result. The transaction costs of interaction among 150+ states with interests on all aspects of ocean use were expected to be very high. This was the principal fear of ocean users as they viewed the trends of ocean uses and rules, and the principal reason that they believed it was necessary to create a new regime by universal conference. Some were aware of the dangers and probable limitations such a conference might entail, but they felt they had little choice, given the limited alternatives.

The new ocean regime had to be a negotiated regime, and probably one that was negotiated in a universal forum. There had already been a history of collective decisions concerning the ocean in the twentieth century. The consent of all members of the international system with standing had been sought three times before. States found they could not easily isolate themselves from decisions of other states, nor often control the consequences to themselves of the actions of others, whether intended or unintended.[3] States and issues were increasingly interconnected and exhibited issue density.[4] A collective solution was the only viable option.[5]

World leaders did not have to deal with the oceans de novo—there was an existing regime, but it was under increasingly heavy assault by the middle 1960s. It could no longer be relied upon to guide ocean users and reduce conflict. Indeed, it was the object of conflict. As Oran Young has shown, regimes could be created by at least three methods—negotiation, imposition, or spontaneity[6]—but the latter two had become increasingly unattractive for the oceans. There were staunch defenders of the idea that what was occurring spontaneously was decentralized enclosure by nation-states, and if the process was not artificially (politically) constrained, a new and quite adequate regime would eventuate.[7] However, most ocean decision-makers around the world felt that waiting for a new regime to evolve over time would not do. Some had normative or ideological objections to the principles that would underlie a regime of decentralized enclosure; some feared not the direction but the severity of the impact on other needs and values; many feared that the processes of spontaneity would work too slowly to create a viable regime in a period of rapid social and technological change, and finally, many were concerned about the possibility of chaos that might result from an uncontrolled process.

Imposed regimes were even less attractive. It was often stated in UNCLOS debates that the Grotian regime of the oceans was a regime that was imposed by the hegemons of the past—Great Britain and the United States—in order to shore up their versions of the liberal international economic order. By the mid-1960s, the hegemons of that time, the United States and the Soviet Union, were seriously cross-pressured because the old regime did not fully protect all domestic stakeholders. Some important domestic stakeholders importuned their leaders to continue to support a total Grotian-based ocean regime. The superpowers were able to salvage only the parts most critical to their state interests. And these had to be purchased by a trade-off. In that sense, the parts of the Grotian regime that survived were not imposed on others.

Lately, some analysts have viewed negotiated regimes critically. Oran Young has remarked that negotiated regimes often produce high transaction costs and intrusive restrictions on individual liberties, but that, in eras of rapid social and technological change we often turn to them, even if "we have only a limited understanding of how to manage such arrangements in a cheap and efficient way."[8] Such comments are apt and useful in evaluating the new ocean regime brought about by long years of negotiation, but other means of regime formation also impose costs, and these are even more difficult to measure. That virtually all states in the world political system chose to come to Caracas, New York, Geneva, and Kingston to negotiate suggests what they thought the price might be if they had allowed the ocean regime to evolve spontaneously, or be imposed by hegemons. Later, we will attempt a post hoc assessment of their judgments.

One important reason states chose to negotiate is that the law of the sea negotiations dealt with first-order structural questions on the nature of the modern state. Many issues related to the question of who states were. States have always attempted to define themselves, but in a world where other actors with similar characteristics exist, it becomes critically important that others accord you the status you believe you deserve. If you choose to exercise authority over certain activities within a geographic area (that is, make a claim to competence,[9] or merely define what is "yours" by erecting a border) and others deny your jurisdiction, they also question your authority, and they may be challenging your legitimacy. These concepts—jurisdiction, authority, legitimacy—are institutional myths whose acceptance is critical to the successful functioning of the modern state.[10] If first-order structural demands of one state are denied by another, conflict will likely ensue. Claims can be imposed upon others, but there are costs involved. At the most extreme, where no state recognizes the competence of another, we would have the Hobbesian war of all against all. Hence, reciprocal recognition of each other's claims to competence is an important means of lowering the cost of operating the modern state system.

The purpose of the UNCLOS III negotiation was to create an ocean regime, but its participants were not agreed about whether this was to be a new regime, based upon a new international order. Many, including the present writer, interpret the efforts of the Group of 77 and its allies in Committee I as in attempt to impose a New International Economic Order framework upon deep-seabed mining, and to use the hoped-for success in one real-world economic activity as a model for other assaults on the liberal international order.[11] The Group of 77 achieved tactical negotiating victories, but probably at the price of losing the chance of significantly altering the international order, even in one relatively insignificant economic area. I contend that failure to reach consensus, or even near-consensus, on the NIEO principles that were to influence the shape of new international institutions and practices meant that many major provisions of Part XI of the Convention were hardly worth the paper they were written upon.[12] They will not alter the present international economic system in any fundamental way. In successor negotiations, either the NIEO features of the new International Seabed Agency will be quietly shelved, or the new organization will be stillborn. The market system for minerals is safe; it will not be converted into a centralized allocation system.

Even more fundamental than the international economic order, is the international political order, also the object of negotiation in UNCLOS III. When stable, this political order creates the environment where exchange can occur without prohibitively high security costs. But the existing international political order was hardly challenged in UNCLOS III, except marginally by few states, and more frequently, by observers from nongovernmental organizations.[13] Idealists complained that the fundamental international political order of independent national states would be left intact by the provisions on which consensus was being sought. Beyond the early effort of Arvid Pardo, no serious attempt was made to ask the nation-states assembled to give up their right to separate existence or to act independently of each other.

Grotianism has two faces. One, derived from Grotius's work *Mare Liberum,* posited an open-entry regime for the oceans under the rubric of freedom of the seas.[14] But featured in his major work, *De Jure Belli Ac Pacis Libri Tres,*[15] is another related regime notion for which Grotius was an "intellectual pathfinder."[16] After Jean Bodin refined the concept of sovereignty in his *Six Books Concerning The State* (1576)[17] Grotius (and then Pufendorf) posited a world order of largely independent states, "a family of nations, or group of sovereign national states, who have no common superior, and who acknowledge no allegiance to any extraneous authority whatsoever."[18] Moreover, Grotius viewed these nation-states, whatever their size and condition, as legally equal since "the law of nature knows no distinction between great and small in the family of nations."[19] This is the world political order we have inherited and the delegates of UNCLOS III were content to leave alone.

Although the ocean is a very large region in which the frequency of human interaction is relatively low, access and use rights of claimants can conflict, and have. What emerged from the UNCLOS III negotiations was not merely a resource regime, but a multiple-use regime for all ocean users on all important ocean uses. Resource allocation and management were among the most important issues under negotiation, but delegates to UNCLOS III were constantly reminded of the need to resolve conflicts between various classes of users, even though it was rarely possible to optimize the outcome for any single class of users, whether public or private.

UNCLOS III was a negotiated regime, and therefore we should examine the purchase price. It was a legal regime, and therefore we should see what legal remedies it provides for failure to respect the rights and privileges of others. It was a comprehensive regime that attempted to deal with all aspects of human conduct within a geographic region, and therefore we should see if its arrangements are workable—both equitable and efficient. It was also a regime that dealt primarily with first-order structural questions for nation-states (borders, rights to allocate within a particular geographic area, etc.), and therefore we should question whether the structural arrangements it made between states could hold up, and whether an environment was created in which workable second-order users rights could be fostered.

The new ocean regime, after a failed challenge to the international economic order, essentially accepted and built upon the existing anarchic political order of separate, equal nation-states, each with a right of self-help. If one judges that the real purpose of UNCLOS III should have been to foster the common interests of mankind, and not the parochial or special interests of certain states, groups of states, or privileged ocean users, one might judge the work of the negotiators to have been largely useless.

Instead, we will evaluate the new ocean regime as a social institution within the context of the existing anarchic world order. We accept, with Oran Young, that international regimes as social institutions are human artifacts.[20] Therefore, we will examine the substantive core of the new ocean regime in terms of its contribution to human welfare. We will concentrate on the rules and obligations created, and ask whether these are based upon coherent principles, principles sufficiently clear to users and sufficiently accepted by them to be useful as guides to action. We will look at whether the rules created, rights specified, and obligations undertaken clarify the relationships of those who interact upon the oceans. We will look at whether the decision processes the regime establishes are clear and workable, and consider whether they are likely to reduce the possibility of conflict. And finally, we will look at the degree to which the rules, rights, and obligations are largely self-enforcing, and therefore the costs of enforcement low. Enforcement costs will be low also if expectations about appropriate behavior converge. If the expectations of most states and private rightsholders converge on most issues of ocean use and the rules are enforced easily, even if few of their interests will have been optimized, we then can say that a good regime has emerged.[21]

The Regime Negotiated

One thing is clear about the results of UNCLOS III negotiations. The delegates probably killed forever the Grotian notion of freedom of the seas or unrestricted access to the property of the ocean commons as the only legitimate paradigmatic idea to guide ocean users. While the free use of portions of the commons remains an important feature of the UNCLOS III regime, it can no longer be relied upon as a concept that provides a sense of direction for the management of scarce resources.

What replaced freedom of the seas as paradigmatic idea for the new ocean regime? Nothing. As a negotiated regime, the UNCLOS III Convention incorporated what the delegates were willing to put in it. What they consented to was a set of rules, rights, and obligations that they hoped would resolve specific ocean-use problems. We must characterize UNCLOS III—if we look at the oceans as a whole—as a mixed or differentiated regime. It is anything but coherent. It creates different sets of rules and rights in different zones of the oceans. Authority was to be exercised on either a geographic or functional basis. The treaty incorporates elements of the existing "imposed" regime of freedom of the seas. Some claim that the proposed creation of an Authority and Enterprise for managing deep-ocean mineral resources is an attempt to impose the will of the majority on a very reluctant minority—to create an antihegemonial imposed regime based on the notion of the common heritage of mankind. Finally, the treaty has strong elements of a spontaneous decentralized enclosure of ocean areas out to 200 nautical miles. Some claim that in the portions of the Convention that will be made operational, UNCLOS III is useful only for ratifying what was happening anyway, but at a higher price than had to be paid.

UNCLOS III is composed of four modules. In the first module, the 200-mile Exclusive Economic Zone supposedly blends exclusive property rights for the coastal state and free communication and transportation use rights for all potential stakeholders. This blend of territorial property rights and functional use rights within the same geographic space is supposed to be sui generis. It is also not well developed theoretically, despite the efforts of a small number of mostly Latin American legal theorists; therefore, we do not yet have a good way to estimate its consequences.[22] For example, it leaves unclear which rightsholder should prevail if there is a conflict between the coastal state's right to control fisheries and a foreign user's right to lay a submarine cable in a prime fishing area. This mixed aspect of the UNCLOS III regime was to prevail in about 36 percent of ocean space.

In the second module, governing approximately 64 percent of the ocean surface, water column, and the airspace over it, with some limitations (such as anadromous fishing), accepted specific sets of flag-state rights derived from the Grotian notion of freedom of the sea will prevail. All potential users will have a right of access, a right to exploit on a first-come, first-served basis, and a right to retain jurisdiction over the activities of their citizens. Supposedly, these Grotian freedoms are to be exercised under a general set of state obligations in Part XII not to pollute the oceans, but the treaty contains no operational language to guide states' behavior in the exercise of their freedoms.

The third module, in Part VI, relates to what was referred to in earlier debates as an "intermediate zone" between the 200-mile EEZ and the open ocean and controlled seabed.[23] Here the continental shelf has been stretched into the continental margin. No firm boundary was established, but a set of highly elastic specifications was created. This third module contains an outline of the jurisdictional rules that may be used to determine whether coastal states get more than 36 percent of the oceans, or whether there will be anything left that either noncoastal states or the International Seabed Authority may allocate or exploit in the oceanic borderlands.

Finally, the fourth module, in Part XI, concerns the deep seabed or the bottom of the 64 percent of the ocean that may be used under Grotian rules. The new regime for exploiting the deep seabed's mineral resources is guided by principles that are anything but Grotian. Access to the deep seabed for exploiting nonliving resources is supposed to be controlled by the International Seabed Authority—directed, in turn, by a democratically elected Assembly and Council. If the groups representing the majority of states at UNCLOS III, especially the Group of 77, have their way, this control would be used to exclude all state or private rights claimants and to create a monopoly of access for an International Enterprise.

The new ocean regime, as a negotiated regime, is composed of sets of specific bundles of rights, rules, and obligations. The delegates to the UNCLOS III sessions had no theoretician to guide their actions. As yet, no theoretician has emerged to show how all the parts can be fitted together into a coherent whole. As a result, it is difficult to discern where UNCLOS III is pointing us, and whether UNCLOS III parts are sufficiently well integrated to form a coherent whole. If the whole is not worthy of support, rightsholders who are favored under one but not another module will continue to attempt to undermine the implementation of rules in the other module. If this happens, the regime of the oceans will not be stable.

One important reason it might not be stable is the failure of the treaty-makers to deal adequately with the physical nature of the oceans. The ocean as a physical entity is undifferentiated. Attributes of the oceans are interconnected and interactive. Despite the attempt to create property rights based on the notion of territoriality (national territory in the case of near-shore areas, international territory in the case of the deep seabed), it will be difficult to build fences that exclude natural processes, and even some human interventions may interfere with the ability of the property rightsholder to treat the property as an exclusive domain. Pollutants move with wind, tide, and current. Some fish migrate between the territories created. Even people using the deep-ocean water column for legally permissible activities, for example, might interfere with ISA's right to treat the ocean seabed as property. Mixing movement rights and property rights in the EEZ is a prescription for jurisdictional overlap and interference.

Every conceptual regime notion has some defect. The idea that egoistic states would realize it was in their own best interest, under freedom of the seas, to voluntarily cooperate so that the commons would not be overstressed has been tried and found wanting. Central enclosure of all commons areas depends for its success on the willingness of states to suppress their individual egos and cooperate for the good of all. It presumes that participants recognize a single good, and not try to use the institutions created to foster their private goods at the expense of other participants. States are sufficiently wary about being put at a disadvantage that the unity of all peoples advocated by idealists like Dante over the centuries has never actually been tried.[24] States claiming exclusive rights that exclude others may adjust to each other's demands to enclose near-shore areas and unmanaged harmony may prevail, or they may engage in intense struggles with others over rights, or they may simply create national commons that they will protect inadequately.

Since no single principle or construct could provide a sensible guide on all aspects of prospective ocean uses, the conferees relied on aspects of all of the above theoretical frameworks for guidance in creating particular parts of the UNCLOS III Convention. Consequently, the new ocean regime is complex and ambiguous. Real-world regimes often are.[25]

We will examine the four main modules of the ocean regime—the sui generis EEZ, the free and open ocean, the intermediate zone between the coastal and deep oceans, and the centrally enclosed seabed—to see if the complexities can be understood and estimate whether the regime is manageable. We will show the influence of the three main sets of principles or schools, and whether they complement or conflict with each other in creating an ocean regime that is coherent and workable.

Mixing Enclosure and Grotianism in the Coastal Ocean

Observers of UNCLOS III proceedings have often focused on what supposedly was new in the Convention. But the skillful updating of the old Grotian rules that governed movement was also important and is sometimes overlooked. One reason the updating, and extending, of movement and communications use rights in the coastal ocean is overlooked is that movement rights were espoused by the hegemons and their allies, and few commentators from developed or developing states will admit that hegemonic power is still substantial. Another reason is that the revival of flag-state rights to use nearshore waters for moving vessels, overflight, and laying of submarine cables was easily achieved. It was part of a package deal of a 12-mile territorial sea, a right of transit passage through straits, and the creation of an exclusive economic zone that was offered and accepted at the first substantive session of the conference in 1974.

The package deal essentially eliminated the territorial sea as an object of international controversy, no mean feat, since it had been contentious through the first eight decades of the twentieth century. The territorial sea had always combined coastal-state property rights to the waters, seabed, subsoil, and air-space with a limited use rights of others to transit coastal waters (innocent passage). But the degree of coastal-state control over the use rights of others has been a matter of dispute, especially since both property and the use rights were defined under the notion of sovereignty, with its implication of total control. Therefore, transitors of the coastal waters of other states opposed rigid sovereignty claims to "traditional" distances from the coast, and also opposed the geographic extension of coastal states' claimed territorial seas.

Some coastal states claimed that Grotian rules to manage exploitation of near-shore ocean resources were increasingly ineffective under the assault of more efficient ocean technology. Consequently, they expanded their claims to sovereignty. The result was a set of claims around the world that ranged from three miles to 200 miles. The nature of the rights they claimed under the doctrine of sovereignty also varied considerably.

Most states desired a uniform distance. Ocean users wanted a "moderate" uniform distance. Most desirable of all to most states not already claiming a 200-mile territorial sea was a moderate, uniform distance with the rights of the coastal state and external users carefully specified. This was achieved at UNCLOS III, because the focus of the coastal states on property rights was shifted to the new Exclusive Economic Zone. Coastal states no longer had to treat the territorial sea or contiguous zone as the exclusive legal mechanism for controlling exploitation of the living and nonliving resources near their shores. The territorial sea retained its property-right attributes, but was reduced in importance to the coastal state.[26]

The 12-mile territorial sea agreed upon at UNCLOS III should help promote reasonably uniform claims to territorial seas around the world. It is a clear standard. It eliminates objections to that distance by those who traditionally have claimed less maritime space for their territorial seas. While it is unlikely that most states that claim greater distances for their territorial seas will roll them back, they are not likely to be successful in leading another rush to expand the territorial sea in the foreseeable future unless other allocation features of UNCLOS III, such as the 200-mile EEZ, fail. Opponents who resist the uniform standard can be treated as legal mavericks.

An equally important achievement of UNCLOS III was the clarification of the rules, rights, and obligations of coastal state and transitor concerning transit and communication use rights within 12 miles of shore. Procedures for the interaction of coastal states with those who use its coastal waters were also clarified. The coastal state retained its sovereignty, but outsiders will continue to have a right of innocent passage (Article 17). The question of what acts a coastal state may legitimately construe as noninnocent is addressed by listing such acts in Articles 19 and 20, thus reducing the fear that the coastal state may arbitrarily interpret its right to interfere with or terminate passage. The list also shows the transitor clearly what behaviors it should avoid. In sum, an elusive and important goal was achieved at UNCLOS III—a uniform territorial sea with a well-developed set of property and use rights that should help to reduce conflict.

A right of transit passage through straits used for international navigation was an integral part of the package resolving the territorial-sea problem and that of coastal-state property rights over resources. If the territorial sea was to be set at 12 nautical miles without a special provision for straits transit, straits less than 24 miles wide would come under the sovereignty of the coastal state, and could be traversed by foreign ships only under conditions of innocent passage, or by aircraft only with the consent of the coastal state. Those who supported a three-mile territorial sea presumed that, in 24-mile-wide straits, a 18-mile band of high seas existed down the center of the strait that could be traversed at will by foreign transitors exercising full high-seas rights. Many of the major straits used for international navigation are less than 24 miles wide.

Technically speaking, the conferees produced a new right of transit passage. However, transit passage was a restatement of the Grotian freedom of movement applied to straits which, without it, could have become wholly national. Without the right of transit passage, movement through straits used for international navigation might have been treated as a property right by the coastal state, and taxed or selectively restricted. Although it was the hegemons who fought hardest for the right of transit, presumably so that they could move their gunboats at will, all states with ships and aircraft benefited by retaining freedom of movement (a use right) since it was the least-cost solution. For most states, transit passage brought a substantial benefit, even if some would have preferred to restrict or exclude military passage. It was not a mere trade-off for more salient issues.

They did trade off on military transit, but in return got a well-developed set of rules that specified the rights and obligations of coastal state and transitors. While all users may transit as long as their passage is continuous and expeditious, there is a list of duties their ships and aircraft must assume if they do transit (Article 39). In return for refraining from any threat or use of force against the coastal state, transit users are assured that the coastal state may not suspend transit passage (Article 44). To ensure that appropriate regulatory action can be taken by coastal states, after appropriate consultations, they are permitted to create sea lanes or traffic separation schemes (Article 41) and to pass nondiscriminatory laws relating to navigation safety and pollution prevention (Article 42). In sum, UNCLOS III produce a well-balanced and clear set of rights and obligations for all interested parties, and clarified the processes to be used if a dispute arose.

A major accomplishment of UNCLOS III was resolving the special status of archipelago states in language acceptable to them and to other states that claimed use rights in areas between some archipelagic islands. Until UNCLOS III, archipelago states had claimed, in vain, a need for a special legal status for the waters between their islands. Because of the scattering of their population and territory over numerous islands, they had trouble binding their people together in a cohesive social and political whole, and in enforcing their fishing, sanitary, and fiscal regulations. Smuggling was a major problem. They claimed that their people were more dependent upon the ocean for their livelihoods than most other states and that, as a consequence, they should be entitled to draw baselines from the outermost points of the outermost islands of their island chains. Within these baselines, all waters would become internal waters, creating an exclusive property right for the archipelago state. For years, the demands of archipelago states had been rejected by most other states as much too extravagant.

UNCLOS III created a special category of archipelagic waters within 100-mile-long, straight baselines between the outermost points of the outermost islands (Article 47). The archipelagic state gained sovereignty over the airspace, seabed, and resources (Article 49). But the principal use right of concern to nonarchipelagic states was the right to transit through the waters between some of the major islands of archipelagos. While transitors did not retain the right to roam wherever they pleased, archipelagic states were required to create sea-lanes so that major shipping routes would not be impaired (Article 53). Within archipelagic sea-lanes, transitors would enjoy all the rights of transit passage—and all of its obligations (Article 54). While archipelagic rights are, like the EEZ, an interesting, supposedly sui generis creation of new property rights, the conferees managed to preserve the most important Grotian use rights.

What made the exclusive economic zone unique was the blend of coastal-state property rights over resources and foreign use rights to move through and over the EEZ or to lay submarine cables under it (Article 58). Ocean-using states insisted upon assurances of nonresource use rights in return for granting coastal states property rights over wealth-producing resources. They attempted, and failed, to add a provision in the Convention declaring the waters of the EEZ high seas. Nevertheless, the core of Grotian use rights for noncoastal-state users was preserved. Without the list of permitted movement and communications activities, the rights of coastal states in the EEZ would be so close to full sovereignty as to be indistinguishable.

The key question for the future will be whether the property rights of coastal states and the use rights of transitors can continue to coexist in the same geographic space. There are many pressures for the coastal state to attempt to reduce or eliminate the use rights of outsiders over time—its own resource or space needs may have changed or expanded, outsiders exercising their use rights might impinge on its resource-management rules (e.g., a sealane crosses a possible seabed oil field), or might pollute its coastal waters. In short, it is quite possible that 200 miles is still a way station on the path toward more extensive coastal enclosures of ocean space once the coastal state has absorbed its ocean property rights within 200 miles. It is premature to assess the probabilities of success or failure for the EEZ. Time will tell.

We can say with greater certainty that the EEZ represents a significant shift of wealth, since it conveys to the coastal state a property right over all natural resources found within 200 miles of the coast. Virtually all use rights to resources by outsiders were terminated. To be sure, there are formal bows to certain classes of noncoastal-state users such as states with distant-water fisheries for highly migratory species, but their right of access to a surplus stock of fish is dependent upon the coastal state declaring the stock surplus. The final arbiter is the coastal state, since it is the property rightsholder.

Within 200 miles of the coast, the law of capture, used by foreign fishermen to legitimize their efforts, was terminated.[27] A resource found within the 200-mile zone can now be taken legitimately only with the consent of the coastal state. Since the 1945 Truman Proclamation on the Continental Shelf, nonliving resources on the coastal seabed had been territorialized. UNCLOS III completed the process for living resources in the coastal ocean. In addition to terminating capture rules, the EEZ also eliminated the species approach for fisheries management. Before UNCLOS III, few international or regional fisheries organizations were empowered to allocate resources. The UNCLOS III Convention made it clear that, in the EEZ, competent organizations were merely to advise the coastal state so that, hopefully, it would not make decisions that might overstress the stocks (Article 61(2)). The decisions were up to the coastal state.

The 200-mile EEZ changed authority patterns. Jurisdiction to make allocation decisions was conveyed to the coastal state. It was now the right of the coastal state to say *who* might take a resource, and *how much* of the resource might be taken. This was a significant achievement for the UNCLOS III Convention. Under voluntary cooperation efforts of the Grotian regime, international fisheries organizations were rarely able to say who should get what. Essentially the organizations provided data and information on the *what*—the state of the stocks and the size of the sustainable yield—but had little or nothing to say abut *who* could catch it. *Where* responsibility lay for making ocean-resource allocation decisions was now known.

Allocation decisions remain painful and difficult, clarification notwith-standing. Coastal states must now establish a domestic decision process to find a mix of efficiency and equity in allocating scarce resources that is ac-ceptable to affected domestic stakeholders. Since states began to enforce the 200-mile EEZ in the mid-1970s, they have had to choose between (1) devo-lution, or transferring their resources from the public domain into private hands; (2) operation, or exercising their monopoly rights to participate di-rectly in exploiting their resources; and (3) regulation, or allowing private party access to their resources, but attempting to control its conduct.[28] The goal is to avoid turning the EEZ into a national commons where entry is still open and all the incentives to economic waste still exist.

The right to control ocean science within 200 miles of the coast also helped clarify the coastal state's exercise of property rights over its EEZ.[29] Under the UNCLOS III regime, information was treated as a property right, via the requirement that all scientific research in the EEZ be conducted only with the consent of the coastal state (Article 246(2)).

While some might insist, on philosophical grounds, that access to knowl-edge must always be the free and open right of all, the former rightsholders were still not very badly served. Access was not completely terminated. While their rights were transformed into a privilege, the privilege was supposed to be granted under reasonable conditions by the coastal state. A list of reasons, mostly relating to possible interference with coastal state economic rights by scientific expeditions, specified the circumstances under which permission to conduct research could be denied (Article 256(5)). Another list specified the types of information foreign governments representing ocean researchers must supply the coastal state before it need grant them a permit (Article 248). Specific duties that would devolve upon researchers who were granted a per-mit were also included in the Convention (Article 249). The treaty also had an implied-consent provision to prevent the coastal state from denying a re-search request by failing to answer the request in a reasonable time; the coastal state had to respond within four months of a research request, or the researchers could begin the expedition two months later (Article 252).

The Convention's detailing of the rights and obligations of researchers in the EEZ shows how, even in a negotiated regime, processes of future inter-action of interested parties can be specified with reasonable precision. Some scientists may still complain about the conversion of their right to a privilege in UNCLOS III, but the level of conflict over ocean science has not grown.[30] While it is more time-consuming and somewhat more expensive to conduct research under a consent regime, ocean science, despite predictions to the contrary, is still vigorous.

Ironically, the enclosure of coastal waters pushes ocean decision-making in the opposite direction from most international decisions of our time. If the states of the world have become more interconnected, even integrated, and the issues more dense, then the enclosure movement (which extends the physical borders of states further away from their coasts) makes coastal states more capable of going their own way, more capable of being economically independent or autarchic. While it is doubtful that ocean rights will provide sufficient resources to make many states truly autarchic or capable of independent decisions without reference to the concerns of other states, UNCLOS III gives coastal states valuable rights—a monopoly over the allocation of near-shore natural resources.

UNCLOS III clarified authority and ownership questions on near-shore natural resources, but the fact that it was a negotiated regime meant that much of the bargaining was over whether previous rightsholders could retain some vestige of their former rights in the coastal ocean. It could be said that a transfer of wealth had occurred, and therefore the previous rightsholders had failed to salvage their rights, but actually the relationship between new and old rightsholders was left fuzzy, except in relation to transportation and communications rights.

Negotiators representing those with a stake in highly migratory species (chiefly tuna) struggled mightily in the negotiation to have these species managed by joint decisions of the interested parties. What they got was a hope that coastal-state and other fishermen who fished the region for highly migratory species would "co-operate directly or through appropriate international organizations with a view to ensuring conservation and promoting the objective of optimum utilization" (Article 64). The coastal state did not have to share its property rights to any highly migratory fish that wandered into its new economic domain, the EEZ. States whose nationals who previously fished the coastal ocean lost any right to access to highly migratory species while these species remained within the 200-mile EEZ. If their nationals were to continue to fish within 200 miles of the coast, whatever the hope of cooperation, it would be only with the consent of the coastal state.

Treatment of highly migratory species is only one of many examples of imprecision in the EEZ provisions of the Convention. To be sure, it is an intellectually demanding task for even the single analyst, away from the hurly-burly of a large-scale negotiation, to specify the details of an ideal regime based on norms that should be acceptable to winners and losers alike. It is an even more demanding task for delegations of 150+ states in an environment of vigorous bargaining to go beyond positing the principle of enclosure and to create a coherent, detailed set of rules that make the new concept workable. Still, many of the treaty's rules fail to define either the physical boundaries of the EEZ or the rights and obligations of the coastal and other states. Most important, the paucity of implementing detail in the decision-making procedures provided for overlapping or conflicting claims within the EEZ makes resolving future disputes more problematic than it probably should be.

It is all very well to postulate "states shall co-operate . . . with a view to ensuring conservation" of highly migratory species. But not specifying a norm upon which that cooperation should be based is a major omission. States dealing with transboundary stocks (that migrate between or beyond EEZs) could use standards for "the measures necessary to co-ordinate and ensure the conservation and development of such stocks" (Article 63(1)). Unfortunately, none was stated. Presumably the negotiating states are free to develop their own norms and rules in the negotiations they are encouraged to conduct.

The situation on delimitation of the EEZ is equally fuzzy. The new regime is based on the principle of territoriality, but defining where a coastal state's territory ends and another coastal state's territory begins, or where the EEZ meets the international commons was difficult for the delegates to UNCLOS III to negotiate. They left boundaries of the EEZ indeterminate, subject to future negotiation, or defined by a set of principles so difficult to interpret they are bound to cause international quarrels (e.g., the continental-shelf provisions in Part VII). Not all sea coasts are long, open, and easily marked on a marine chart. Many are deeply indented, fringed with islands, or hemmed in by the coasts of opposite and adjacent states, and therefore have complex baselines for determining the shape of the EEZ. If quarrels arise between states over their rights and obligations in the EEZ, the treaty calls for their resolution "on the basis of equity" (Article 59). In the case of opposite and adjacent states, "delimitation . . . shall be effected by agreement on the basis of international law" (Article 74(1)). While delimitation of specific boundaries will clearly require detailed negotiations between interested parties, it would be helpful if the UNCLOS III Convention had stated a coherent set of principles and norms upon which the parties could base their detailed implementing negotiations.

However precisely or imprecisely the delegates were able to implement the principle of territoriality in the Convention, territoriality as the basis of resolving problems of managing wandering resources will inevitably lead to less than optimal outcomes if sustaining stocks at high levels is the goal of policy. Only an ecosystem approach could pretend to control living resources over their full range of movement and in the context of the webs of relationships that control their lives.[31] Ecosystem approaches, however, are not very helpful if existing stakeholders are quarreling over allocation of a scarce resource. To succeed, ecosystem approaches must have implementing parties that are more concerned with improving the common interest than merely their own. Thus far, ecosystem approaches have been tried only in regions such as the Antarctic, where the salience of resource access to the parties has been low. Since states have failed to limit access to resources in the Grotian commons voluntarily, perhaps territoriality was the best available principle upon which to base the next generation of near-shore ocean management. But it has its flaws.

The Wildcard—The Continental Shelf

If attempts at delimiting EEZ boundaries between opposite states in waters less than 400 miles wide, or between adjacent states, were unsatisfactory because the state parties were provided with principles no more illuminating than "equity," the treaty makers may have been wise not trying to work out precise criteria of choice. The attempt to create detailed rules of boundary-making on the continental shelf based upon an applicable principle turned out badly at UNCLOS III. Indeed, if broad-shelf states interpret the principle of "natural prolongation" so as to maximize their territorial reach, the continental-shelf provisions of the UNCLOS III Convention may start another round of enclosures. In other words, the treaty provides broad-shelf states a wild card to substantially alter the geographic consequences of the treaty, which might unglue the UNCLOS III Convention and force the calling of an UNCLOS IV. This is likely to occur only if ocean explorers in the next decade discover valuable resources on the outer margin, making further enclosures obviously worthwhile, but it is not an idle worry.

After initially opposing substantial extensions of jurisdiction, the major ocean-using states switched to support of enclosure in the package deal that combined the 200-mile EEZ, a 12-mile territorial sea, and transit passage through straits used for international navigation, and most of them switched with a vengeance. Since many, including the United States and the United Kingdom, had long coast lines, they would benefit by maximum extensions of coastal-state resource jurisdiction. As a result, they cooperated with the bargaining group—the margineers—to promote the principle of natural prolongation as the basic criterion for delimitation decisions on the outer edge of the continental margin (which was still described as the legal continental shelf).

The margineers promoted the "Irish Formula," which contained multiple alternative criteria for delimitation (Article 76). Under it, a state is permitted to extend its claim to a continental shelf out to the edge of the continental margin, or 200 nautical miles, whichever is farther. The coastal state may establish its marginal boundary by straight baselines up to 60 miles long. Or the coastal state may claim out to where the thickness of the sedimentary rocks is at least 1 percent of the distance beyond the foot of the continental slope, or not more than 60 miles beyond the foot of the continental slope. If that produces results that do not please the coastal state, it might try to delimit its outer-seabed boundary at 100 miles beyond the 2,500-meter isobath, or 350 miles from the coast. But there is also the question of which is the appropriate measure for natural components of the continental margin, such as plateaus, rises, caps, banks, or spurs.

In short, the menu approach invites a choice by the coastal state. It also invites confusion, and perhaps greed. The Convention does provide a process which might limit the arbitrariness of coastal states. Supposedly, the coastal state will submit its delimitation plan to an international expert commission, which will examine it and issue a "recommendation" (Article 6, Annex II). In addition to the Commission's recommendation not having any binding effect, the Commission itself cannot be created until the Convention is in force. Moreover, the coastal state has a grace period of 10 years after the Commission's entry into force before it must submit its delimitation data to the Commission. By that time, any delimitation plan that the coastal state has been enforcing without objection might be considered justifiable under customary international law.

Another possible limit on coastal-state ambition might be a requirement that a developed coastal state make payments and contributions to the international community for resources exploited in the area between 200 nautical miles and the end of the margin (Article 82). But if the prospects are good for valuable resources, a developed coastal state wanting to maximize its own benefits might see this provision as a major deterrent to ratifying the Convention. That debate, as well as one on the technical adequacy of Article 76, took place in the United States in the late 1970s and early 1980s with a decision not to decide.[32]

The continental shelf as continental margin was intended to be a transition zone in which the coastal state had the dominant set of rights but, since it had to share benefits derived from resource exploitation at the outer edge, it was not fully sovereign. Unfortunately, this did not ease the change from coastal jurisdiction to international commons.

The Open Ocean

UNCLOS III reaffirmed that the high-seas regime was to remain Grotian. Access and use rules for the open ocean were to remain essentially the same as those followed for centuries by states that sent their ships on and aircraft over the high seas. Users could use the open ocean with minimal limitations so long as they did not interfere with the rights of others. Many traditional use rights and obligations that were renewed in the Convention gained further clarity and predictability over the previous statements. Where the exercise of a use right degraded the commons or its resources, the Convention provided no cure.

Grotian rules on the open ocean survived at UNCLOS III essentially for two reasons: (1) most still had remaining social utility, and (2) uses of the high seas were less salient to most negotiators than uses of the coastal ocean; hence, they were less willing to expend their negotiating capital attacking problems that occurred far from land.

Though Grotian rules failed to resolve resource uses in a commons where resources were growing increasingly scarce, they were the least-cost rules for managing other human uses of the waters of the world. It would have been uneconomic to extend the notion of property rights to the deep ocean. Because of span-of-control problems, the cost of protecting a deep-ocean property right far outstripped any benefit. There was little reason to restrict entry to the open ocean, especially for movement and communications uses. The opposite theory—central enclosure—where a new public agency would control access to the ocean, also had little appeal. Most states in the anarchic political system were not prepared to acknowledge a central authority's right to make binding rules on access to the airspace over, water column below, or surface of the open ocean. Preserving access of all claimants to the coastal ocean was a difficult notion to sell at UNCLOS, but it was not difficult convincing virtually all parties to consent to preserving the use rights of all in the open ocean.

Grotian rules depend for their effectiveness on the notion of self-help. As long as the probability is low that activities will lead to conflict, that is an efficient principle on which to base use rights. Therefore, states should have a right to have ships bearing their nationality (Article 91). But states also have important but limited obligations such as maintenance of a register of ships (Article 94), a duty to require their vessels render assistance to persons and vessels in distress (Article 98), to punish the transport of slaves (Article 99), to cooperate in the suppression of piracy (Article 100), the traffic in narcotic drugs (Article 108), and unauthorized broadcasts from the high seas (Article 109). They also have a right to lay submarine cables under the high seas (Article 112), or to engage in hot pursuit on the high seas of a vessel that has violated a coastal state's laws while in its internal waters, territorial sea, contiguous zone, or archipelagic waters (Article 111).

Problems arise because the right to fish on the high seas was also preserved, without any rules that might restrain fishermen from catches that exceeded a sustainable yield (Article 116). To be sure, states are exhorted to "co-operate with other States in taking such measures for their respective nationals as may be necessary for the conservation of the living resources of the high seas" (Article 117). But cooperation is a weak principle that alone provides few incentives for states or their fishermen to comply, except good will or comity.

On the high seas, all the problems of open entry are preserved that hopefully might be eliminated under enclosure in near-shore areas. Even if competent regional or subregional fisheries organizations are created to deal with high-seas fishing, or even if they provide high-quality scientific evidence to those states that make up the organizations, it is expected that, at best, they can help in "determining the allowable catch" (Article 119). This is a conservation approach that avoids the key problem of allocation—*who* will be allowed to catch *what* percentage of the catch. Until there is agreement—based on a widely shared norm—on how allocation will be accomplished, the new law of the sea will not be able to adequately address high-seas fisheries problems.

This is not merely a hypothetical problem, but an existing real-world problem of the early 1990s. One of the predictable consequences of creating the exclusive economic zone was reduction of foreign distant-water fleets in EEZs, and in a number of cases, their elimination. Coastal states simply availed themselves of their right to set the allowable catch and to declare, or not declare, a surplus. Even if they declared a surplus, they could charge a rent for the right to fish. As a result of displacement from the EEZ, many distant-water fishing vessels were sent to explore new high-seas fishing areas and develop new fishing techniques.

Some distant-water fleets began to fish transboundary stocks just beyond the 200-mile EEZs. Others, in the North Pacific, found a "doughnut hole" between the EEZs of the United States and the Soviet Union that contained the same species that they formerly caught within the coastal states' EEZs, principally hake. Enterprising fishermen, mostly from Japan, South Korea, and Taiwan, set drift nets, some 30–40 miles in length, ostensibly to catch underutilized species such as squid. The use of drift nets came to be known as "strip-mining the sea." In 1989, the Western Pacific Fisheries Council of the United States reported that 700 vessels from the three Asian states were setting some 15,000 miles of nets each day.[33] Since the mesh size was small, and the spread of the nets very large, it was virtually impossible for any marine creature of more than miniscule size to escape the nets. Many of these were not squid, but "incidental" or "by-catch" salmon, billfish, tuna, birds, and mammals. Many fisheries specialists were convinced that the more valuable creatures of the incidental catch were the real targets of the drift-netters.[34]

The UNCLOS III provisions on high-seas fisheries provided no relief from these depredations. Ironically, the principal contribution of the UNCLOS III Convention toward corrective action came from the EEZ provisions concerning anadromous and catadromous stocks (Articles 66 and 67). States that have freshwater streams that nurture anadromous and catadromous stocks were granted a property right to them. Fisheries for these species are supposedly restricted to the 200-mile EEZ. However, a good proportion of the incidental catch has been salmon, an anadromous stock. Japan and South Korea have been brought to the bargaining table since they cannot ignore the coastal state's right to establish conservation regulations even beyond 200 miles from shore, or refuse to negotiate over the enforcement on the high seas of coastal-state regulations. As of this writing, the problem has not been resolved, but Japan and South Korea have agreed to allow U.S. observers aboard their driftnetters to determine if the incidental catch is significant, and what corrective measures might be taken.

Unfortunately, the spirit of Grotianism also pervaded the efforts of the delegates in their attempts to control human actions that might degrade the ocean environment. The principle, again, was the fundamental principle of an anarchic political system—voluntary cooperation (if they saw it in their interest) on problems originating both in areas beyond and within their territory. All promises of voluntary cooperation by states must be viewed with skepticism. But a promise of voluntary cooperation for controlling polluting activities within their territory must be looked on with the greatest skepticism. After all, states claimed final authority there. While UNCLOS III generally conveyed sovereign rights over resources to coastal states, they demanded more, including an explicit assurance that no environmental obligation could erase their sovereign right to exploit their natural resources (Article 193).

Not that the Conference didn't try. Part XII is devoted to measures to protect and preserve the marine environment. It is full of obligations for states who ratify the Convention. But these obligations are expressed as exhortations to protect and preserve the marine environment (Article 192), "to take all measures necessary to ensure that activities under their jurisdiction or control are so conducted as not to cause damage by pollution to other States and their environment" (Article 194(2)), not to transfer damage or hazards from one area to another (Article 195), or introduce damaging technologies or new and alien species (Article 196). There is no operational language or rules specifying what these obligations mean in practice. There is no mention of the types of actions forbidden or permissible. There are no norms specifying socially desirable goals. For example, nothing is said about discharge standards, percentage-reduction goals, restoration to a pristine state, mitigation, etc. While these are notoriously difficult (and possible faulty) concepts to use in managing an ecosystem, some attempt to use them or develop more appropriate concepts might have been tried by delegates to UNCLOS III had pollution problems been high on their agenda.

Instead, the Convention calls for voluntary cooperation under elaborate international rules consistent with its standards either on a global basis or through competent regional organizations (Article 197). States also promise to conduct research (Article 200), develop contingency plans (Article 199), notify each other if a pollution incident occurs (Article 198), monitor pollution (Articles 204–206), and assist developing states on pollution problems (Article 202). Again, no guidance is provided on norms that should be used to reach the goals stated.

In the context of current concerns over the impact of global warming, the ozone hole, acid rain, and other potential global problems, the pollution-control measures of the UNCLOS III Convention seem very weak. Little attention was devoted to the problem of how the entire ecosystem might be impacted by human activity. Indeed, there was no ecosystem consciousness shown in the design of the approach to pollution. Pollution control was assumed to be the business of states. It was conceded that states would take the initiative, and it was feared by some delegations that other states would go too far in controlling ocean activities. The principal bargaining effort on pollution control came on those issues where the coastal or port state demanded rights to control activities off its coast, and states with a stake in marine transportation fought to prevent the coastal or port state from exercising authority "arbitrarily."

The most controversial issues related to efforts by coastal and port states to exercise authority over foreign vessels that might have been involved in a pollution incident within their territorial seas or EEZs. The concerns stretched over the right of coastal, port, or flag states to establish standards (Article 211), as well as enforce them (Articles 217–220). An elaborate set of procedural rules was developed to force coordination between the three claimants to jurisdiction, although if the flag state promised enforcement action, the port and coastal state would have to defer to it. The Grotian rules of flag-state dominance in jurisdiction were bent and modified, but not eliminated. Port and coastal states did gain more authority, but the flag state still remained dominant in terms of controlling vessels transiting the EEZ (Article 228), much to the chagrin of coastal-state advocates, who claimed that even in the coastal ocean the Convention's output on pollution problems was too weak.[35]

The Common Heritage of Mankind as Central Enclosure

In a vote of 130 for, 4 against, and 17 abstaining, the states represented at UNCLOS III presumably terminated freedom to exploit the nonliving resources of the seabed beyond national jurisdiction. Supposedly, claimants would no longer have access on a first-come, first-served basis. The resources of the Area will "not be subject to alienation" (Article 137(2)). Although aspects of Grotianism were salvaged in other parts of the convention, the right of claimants to take what natural resources they wished on the deep seabed, as long as they did not interfere with the rights of others, was terminated. Grotianism as a conceptual framework for the management of nonliving resources of the deep seabed was supposed to be dead.[36]

The core concept that underlay the new regime for deep-seabed resources was the common heritage of mankind. No attempt was made to define the concept in the treaty (Article 136), but the common heritage of mankind looks like a twentieth-century attempt to make operational the age-old notion of *res communis,* albeit supplemented by sentiments drawn from the New International Economic Order. The resources belong to the people of the world; they are communally owned and cannot be alienated by some members of the community. They cannot be divided, but if access is allowed, any financial benefits must be distributed "taking into particular consideration the interests and needs of developing the States and peoples who have not attained full independence or other self-governing status" (Article 160(f)(i)).

Under the notion of the common heritage, access to seabed resources is to be only by permission of the rightsholder—mankind as a whole—or at least its surrogate, the International Seabed Authority. This clarifies the identity of the rightsholder. A formal set of use rules was promulgated and, though not entirely unambiguous, gives any potential user a reasonably good notion of the hoops he must jump through to gain access to seabed-mineral resources. In any case, his obligations not to pollute (Article 145), his liability for damages (Article 139), and the production policies he must operate under (Article 151), while again not entirely unambiguous, are at least specified. Finally, processes for equitable dispute settlement are specified (Part XI, Section 5, and Annex VI).

If the delegates had merely controlled access to seabed resources and forced each claimant to pay the rightsholder—the world's people—an appropriate fee for extracting "their" resources, distributed the benefits in an equitable manner, and forced claimants to act responsibly in their use of the

International Area, the seabed portion of the UNCLOS III negotiation might have been a notable success. Instead, the negotiations over management of the deep seabed seems to be a notable failure of large-scale multilateral negotiations. It was a failure of North and South to find mutually acceptable grounds. Unfortunately, UNCLOS III became the arena for the acting out of one major episode of the North–South quarrel that has shaped the outcome on many issues in multinational organizations in the late twentieth century.[37]

The states of the Third World attempted to impose on the major states of the world the idea that economic exploitation must occur under new, equitable conditions. In the case of seabed exploitation, all access by private or state corporations would be closed and an "International Enterprise" would hold a monopoly. Most of the seabed portion of the negotiation consisted of the Group of 77 stubbornly trying to impose this monopoly idea upon other members of the international system, and other states trying to modify these notions to create conditions of ocean access they could live with. A number of middle states from Scandinavia, Western Europe, and North America, sympathetic to the moral case of the Group of 77, tried to mediate between the contestants. Although the major ocean-using states conceded that the framework would be based on NIEO concepts, they just as stubbornly tried to secure access to deep-ocean mineral resources for their private and state corporations. They conceded an Enterprise, but one that would have to share its access right, perhaps through joint ventures, and operate under rules that would not be economically ruinous.

They succeeded in forcing a substantial modification of strict monopoly. Whether the compromises that made their way into the treaty will undercut the NIEO features to the point where it can be said that the Group of 77 lost tactically in the bargaining remains to be seen when the Convention goes into force. Despite some softening of the Group of 77's positions, its willingness to make some concessions was not enough for the United States, who chose to call the question, force a vote, and vote against the Convention. The United States was not alone in refusing consent to the seabed portion of the agreement. In all, 21 states voted against or abstained from approving the Convention. They represent more than half of the world's product. If they do not cooperate with the effort to bring the International Seabed Authority and its Enterprise into existence in the next decade, the entire Part XI of the UNCLOS III Convention may be stillborn.

Efforts are underway at present in the Preparatory Commission negotiations to try to persuade the dissenting states to cooperate.[38] Indeed, some already have and at least one (the Soviet Union) has been rewarded with the status of "pioneer investor." But the key states are the United States, the

United Kingdom, and the Federal Republic of Germany. They have little incentive for either ideological or practical reasons to cooperate in the short run. In each, the government in power is committed to private-sector solutions to economic problems, and with the end of the Cold War, have even less incentive to make concessions to socialistic solutions.[39]

But even if the major Western states do not demand complete surrender, what type of modifications would be required to make Part XI of the Convention minimally acceptable politically, and workable economically? First, assurances would be needed to convince dissenting states that their economic entities would have access to choice seabed-mining sites under conditions no worse than joint enterprise (Articles 151 and 153). They would have to be convinced that they and their companies, or consortia operating under their flags, would be better off under a fairly administered limited-entry system than an open-entry system, which despite the legal posturing of Convention supporters who claim it has been terminated by the Convention, probably is still open to them. Clearly a closed-entry system—an international monopoly—is not acceptable, nor is a system that ostensibly is limited-entry but is merely a disguise for future attempts to close entry.

Second, access rules are needed that do not require practices (Article 151) or payments (Article 162) that so burden the exploitative effort that it is doomed to fail economically, no matter how efficiently it operates. Assurances would also be needed by the major developed states that the organs of the Seabed Authority would not operate by "majoritarian" practices in which they would be automatically outvoted. This might be accomplished by a combination of reserved seats (Article 161) or consensus-decision rules. It would also be necessary to alter the present text so that, if technology is to be transferred from a private or state corporation to the Enterprise, it would be transferred on commercial terms (Article 144(2); Annex III, Article 5). The last formal change that might be demanded would be revocation of the treaty provision allowing a future Review Conference by a three-fourths-majority vote to impose as binding upon members new deep-ocean regime rules, even if those members voted no and refused to ratify the agreement (Article 155). Finally, supporters of the new organization would have to be trusted to create only a "lean and cost-effective" secretariat and not, as opponents fear, a bloated bureaucracy to provide jobs for unemployed intellectuals and bureaucrats of Third World countries.

Satya N. Nandan, Under Secretary-General of the United Nations and Special Representative of the Secretary-General for the Law of the Sea, optimistically portrayed these "five or six issues" as little more than trivial and claimed that "satisfactory compromise(s) can be found for all of these issues."[40] I am less certain. If further alterations are made so that the industrialized states can agree to Part XI, virtually all the NIEO character of the seabed portion of the Convention will have been removed from the Convention. To be acceptable to industrialized states, the seabed portion of the treaty would have to become a limited-access regulatory regime, not much different in its seabed-access rules for "banked" areas than the registry system proposed by the United States in 1970.

If a claimant, through a nation-state, nominates two sites and is assured of being granted one of them, then the rule of first-come, first-served is only slightly modified. For all practical purposes, such a regime would be regulatory in character, since the claimant, and not an international operating regime, would accept liability, payment, and other obligations. Clearly, if sufficient modifications are made to attract the industrialized states, they will have an effective advantage in terms of access to the resources because of their superior technology, knowledge, wealth, and capabilities, even if all states formally will have an equal right of access to the mineral resources of the seabed. If ISA must become lean and mean to come into existence, and the rents derived from seabed exploitation are sufficiently modest so as not to provide a disincentive to seabed mining, where will the millions and billions come from to compensate the developing states for their years of colonial rule and current neglect by the developed states? Finally, what will happen to the demonstration project that was to show the nations of the world how an international operating regime could be both efficient and equitable? It would be extremely hard for the developing states to swallow enough modifications to make Part XI attractive to the developed states if the issue is still sufficiently salient to the members of the Group of 77 to make them refight the old battles. Ennui might set in or, perhaps with time, a dose of realism. At the moment, if ISA comes into existence, it will be in much reduced form, and its impact on the international political and economic order is likely to be slight.

Was UNCLOS III Worth the Effort?

Was the nearly 15-year effort worthwhile? There are many ways to address this question. One common way of answering a question of this complexity is to rely upon the impressions of an expert who uses his/her brain to total up the gains and losses and to render an overall judgment. A more precise way is for a stakeholder or analyst to identify a stake that might be maximized by a policy choice, and, using an objective measure, attempt to determine how close the negotiated regime came to some ideal outcome. Both ways have problems. Experts have been known to differ—often widely—in their judgments. Finding sufficient measures for all stakes valued by stakeholders can be prohibitive. As a result, too many efforts at maximization examine only one stake, often out of the context of the complex world in which trade-offs are necessary. It is impossible to find a policy concerning an international regime that optimizes all values for all stakeholders simultaneously.

Almost all important decisions are multidimensional. In order to make an overall choice when more than one value is at stake, the decision-maker must decide not only what is preferred on each dimension, but also whether a favorable outcome on one dimension is worth the same, more, or less (and how much more, or less) than a favorable outcome on the other dimensions. To understand decisions one needs to know what is valued, and how much compared to other values. Even if we were to restrict our stakeholders to nation-states and assume they are unitary actors (and therefore presume, for the sake of analysis, that a politically strong national subactor would not, in attempting to maximize his stake, completely dominate a national decision),[41] gathering data to carry out such an assessment can still be a formidable task. And even if most nation-states represented at UNCLOS III are conducting analyses now in order to make a sensible decision whether to sign or ratify the treaty, they are not likely to share them with outsiders.[42]

To answer the question of whether the negotiation of UNCLOS III was worthwhile, we must proceed with what we have available—the opinions of an "expert," assisted by a Multiattribute Utility Technology model (MAUT).[43] In the previous section, as the "expert," I assessed the major provisions of UNCLOS III in terms of their probable contribution to the solution of the world's ocean problems, presuming they come into force. They were not evaluated in comparison with other alternative regimes. Nor was salience, or the comparative importance of the issues to the parties included as part of the analysis, making a solution to one ocean problem seem as important as another. These dimensions might be added informally, but they are best added through a formal model which forces the analyst to be systematic, even if not objective.

In order to conclude this review of UNCLOS III properly, I have attempted to assess what major stakeholders might perceive as their best option among alternative regimes. To simplify the effort, I estimated the probable payoffs for (1) the major developed states, (2) the Eastern European Group, (3) the middle developed states (Canada, some of the Scandinavian and other middle-sized European states), (4) members of the Group of 77, and (5) the geographically disadvantaged and landlocked states. Each of these stakeholders was forced to compare as policy options (1) following UNCLOS III's regime, (2) reverting to the previous regime (UNCLOS I and II), (3) relying upon a new regime to form spontaneously, (4) letting the hegemons impose a regime on the states of the world political system, (5) obeying a regime that favors the preferences of the major coastal developing states, and (6) enforcing a regime that favors appeals to equity, as interpreted by the geographically disadvantaged and landlocked states.

All scenarios were constructed assuming that the stakeholders would view how each of the six regimes might help them solve ocean problems to their satisfaction during the period 1990–2010. Each stakeholder modeled was forced, by my estimates, to evaluate how well it would be served over 25 issues (value dimensions) in the coastal ocean, open ocean, continental shelf, and deep seabed under each of the six regime types. Since trade-offs had to be made, I also had to estimate how salient each of the issue-areas (e.g., coastal ocean) and each of the issues (e.g., EEZ delimitation) were in relation to each other for each stakeholder. These saliences will be treated as cumulative weights.

To make the two categories of generated data—policy options and value dimensions—useful analytically required two measures: (1) the estimated contribution of each value dimension under each option; and (2) the calculated comparative importance of each value dimension to each decision-maker for the period 1990–2010.

To accomplish the first of these tasks, I constructed a scaling system to create measures of value for each stakeholder for each issue on each regime considered. A scale of 0–100 was used. A score of zero was assigned to the policy option that was of no benefit to the stakeholder on the particular value examined. A score of 100 was assigned to the policy option that would maximize that value. The other values were placed between these extremes, usually at 10-point (sometimes 5-point) increments. Ties were also allowed. If more than one policy option seemed to have the same high, medium, or low impact upon it from that value, the same scores were assigned.[44]

Filling in the cells created a matrix of policy options and values. The next step was constructing a scale for cumulative weights for each value, that is, a measure to replicate the comparative importance of each value to each stakeholder.[45] The scale was constructed in two distinct steps. In the first, the values were scaled ordinally. This was done in two substeps. The interest of each stakeholder in each issue-area was estimated. Then the interest of each stakeholder on each issue within each issue-area was estimated as a proportion of the stakeholders interest in the issue-area. In the second, the ordinal scale on each issue was converted to a ratio scale. The question asked was: how much more does the stakeholder value the value dimension next in order from the last value dimension considered, starting with the one least valued? The least valued dimension was assigned .5. The raw weights were normalized (summed to 1.0) so that the cumulative weight scores accounted for 100 percent of the estimated value of the stakeholder. It is understood that the set of values generated is only a subset of the total values of a stakeholder. However, it is reasonable to assume that the unstated values are trivial (for this situation), and can be assumed to be equal.

With options, value dimensions, and cumulative weights created, it is possible to calculate utilities. The formula is:

$$\sum_{j=1}^{n} \frac{\text{scale number for each value} \times \text{normalized cumulative weight for each value}}{\text{Total number of value dimensions}} = \text{utility}$$

The output is a utility score for each option. The option with the highest utility score is the option that promises the best payoff for the stakeholder. The value of each regime for each stakeholder can be viewed in rank order. In addition, the relative distance between scores for a stakeholder on each regime can provide useful clues as to how much better one regime would be for a stakeholder than another.

MAUT Analysis

Major developed or industrial states were among the most vocal participants at UNCLOS III. Not many of their spokesmen were considered among the most influential Conference leaders, but there was an awareness that if the wealthiest developed states were substantially dissatisfied a convention might not emerge, or if it did, it would not be easily enforceable. Cooperation from the developed was essential. But was the Convention in their interest?

In earlier chapters, we saw important differences in bargaining positions on several issues among the United States, the United Kingdom, Japan, the Federal Republic of Germany, France, and Italy. But there was also a substantial degree of commonality on overall goals. That commonality is shown in table 8.1. The issues dealing with problems of the coastal ocean were important to major developed states (estimated 55 percent of their total interest). These states are in the best position technically and financially to exploit the resources of the coastal zone. But they also have strong distant-water interests, therefore it seemed reasonable to believe that issues relating to the open ocean were also fairly important to them (20 percent of total interest). As free-market states, they were also under considerable pressure from

	UNCLOS I & II	UNCLOS III	UNCLOS III (Renegotiated)	Spontaneous	Imposed	Developing Coastal	LLGDS Equity	Weight
COASTAL OCEAN								0.550
1.1 EEZ Delimitation	10	80	80	50	80	60	40	0.080
1.2 Terr. Sea	30	90	90	20	90	10	80	0.080
1.3 Straits Transit	60	80	80	10	90	10	60	0.080
1.4 Arch. Rights	20	70	70	10	50	30	60	0.020
1.5 EEZ Transit	100	90	90	10	100	20	90	0.040
1.6 Fish Allocation	30	70	70	90	70	40	40	0.060
1.7 Migrat. Species	70	20	20	0	80	0	40	0.040
1.8 Anad. Species	10	70	70	60	80	0	50	0.040
1.9 LLGDS Access	60	70	70	0	40	40	70	0.010
1.10 Science Control	70	50	50	10	90	0	60	0.040
1.11 Vessel Pollution	40	60	60	10	60	20	40	0.060
OPEN OCEAN								0.200
2.1 Transport Access	100	80	80	100	100	50	70	0.060
2.2 Fishing Access	60	60	60	90	90	50	70	0.050
2.3 Environ. Manag.	10	20	20	30	40	10	50	0.030
2.4 Vessel Pollution	10	60	60	10	30	10	50	0.040
2.5 Science Access	80	80	80	100	100	20	70	0.020
CONTINENTAL SHELF								0.050
3.1 Delimitation	40	80	80	100	80	70	10	0.025
3.2 Revenue Sharing	100	0	0	100	100	0	0	0.025
DEEP SEABED								0.200
4.1 Common Heritage	10	30	30	100	100	0	60	0.030
4.2 Exploit. System	40	50	70	40	80	0	70	0.040
4.3 Production Cons.	60	50	60	60	100	0	50	0.020
4.4 Tech. Transfer	60	30	70	100	100	0	50	0.020
4.5 Financial Cond.	20	50	60	100	100	0	40	0.010
4.6 Decision-Making	100	30	70	100	100	0	50	0.040
4.7 Review Conf.	100	0	100	100	100	0	0	0.040
SCORES	50	60	68	47	79	20	54	1.000

Table 8.1: Ocean Regimes: MAUT Preference Scores of Major Developed States

domestic entrepreneurs to solve the problem of managing the deep seabed. Companies that made up the transnational mining consortia were largely headquartered in the territories of the developed (20 percent). Delimitation of the continental shelf and concerns likely to be troublesome in the latter part of our estimating period (early 21st century), took up the remaining 5 percent of their interests.

If they were in a position to choose, they would probably prefer an imposed regime,[46] not surprising since imposed regimes usually reflect the interests of dominant states. Under a great-power ocean regime, I assumed, the major industrial states could come close to their ideal situation of protecting their near-shore interests without jeopardizing their distant-water interests. Thus, they probably would impose a narrow territorial sea, protect straits transit, work out a modus vivendi with other major states on fishing, and allow as few constraints upon their behavior as possible. They would not accept an International Seabed Authority except in the form of a registry whose function was to register the claims of the few competent claimants of seabed resources. This would help avoid claim-jumping. As a result of the freedoms they would allow themselves, they might have some difficulties on some fishing and pollution issues. Nevertheless, an imposed solution over the 25 issues clearly would be their best option.

The second-best option would be the regime that was worked out at UNCLOS III. The major states would do well under the near-shore provisions of the UNCLOS III Convention. Only on the issues of migratory species and the right to conduct ocean science would they have to consent to outcomes ranging from unacceptable to merely adequate. I estimated that the deep-ocean regime, though not to their liking, would be minimally acceptable, since the developed had whittled down significant details of the NIEO features of the regime.

Two other options were not far behind. The third-best policy option for major developed states would be a regime reflecting the concerns of geographically disadvantaged and landlocked states (LL/GDS). In general, it would favor geographically conservative solutions to coastal-state claims, with special features providing equity for the geographically disadvantaged. The major states would get near-optimal outcomes only on transportation issues, but they would be asked to pay for the costs of equity through revenue sharing, access to coastal resources for the LL/GDS, and a special place for the LL/GDS in a strong International Seabed Agency.

The fourth-best option would be to continue with the traditional, mostly Grotian regime of UNCLOS I and II. Important states have a great deal of flexibility in addressing their problems. The analysis shows that they could cope a while longer under a Grotian regime, although they would not get outcomes near optimal on any issues except transportation. Nevertheless, they might work out satisfactory arrangements on deep-seabed minerals among themselves.

Major developed states would not do well under the spontaneous regime that I posited. Under a future ocean regime that formed spontaneously all states could exercise their individual will and solve their problems by their own enclosure measures. Any problems that arose between them because of overlapping claims would be resolved by one-on-one negotiations. No central coordinative mechanisms would be encouraged, and it was assumed that at some point in the indefinite future harmony would prevail and resources would be used efficiently.[47] Under a spontaneous ocean regime, the major developed states would probably experience significant conflicts on overlapping claims to territorial seas, continental shelves and margins, rights of straits transit, fishing, and deep seabed minerals. Perhaps these conflicts could be resolved by spontaneous adjustments or negotiations between the parties affected so as to create a harmonious whole, but this is unknowable.

I estimated that major developed states would perceive as least valuable for fostering their interests a regime which promoted outcomes favorable to developing coastal states combined with attributes of the New International Economic Order. Such a regime would attempt to push developed states further from the coasts of developing states, give the latter maximum control of ocean resources, pay little heed to the problems of marine transportation, be hostile to military rights in the oceans, and attempt to exclude the developed—on paper at least—from access to deep-ocean resources, or at least force them to acknowledge a new framework for equitably sharing the world's resources. If the developed states took the rhetoric of the developing states literally, it is little wonder they would oppose a regime based upon such norms.

The Eastern European group preference on regimes, in table 8.2, are in the same rank ordering as the major developed states, even though the cumulative weights show a different weighting of interests. The Eastern European group at UNCLOS III reflected the normative preferences of a single dominant or hegemonic state—the Soviet Union—combined with a sensitivity toward some geographically disadvantaged preferred norms (since several members of the group are landlocked), and, to a lesser degree, sensitivity toward the equity claims of the Third World. Given the effect of perestroika and glasnost on the positions of its state members, it was difficult to estimate whether the group would even continue to exist as a bargaining group in the United Nations system during the forecasting period, much less continue

	UNCLOS I & II	UNCLOS III	Spontaneous	Imposed	Developing Coastal	LL/GDS Equity	Weight
COASTAL OCEAN							0.650
1.1 EEZ Delimitation	40	70	10	80	50	80	0.070
1.2 Terr. Sea	20	90	20	90	20	90	0.090
1.3 Straits Transit	70	90	20	90	10	70	0.090
1.4 Arch. Rights	30	65	20	80	50	70	0.040
1.5 EEZ Transit	100	100	100	100	40	100	0.070
1.6 Fish Allocation	40	70	60	60	50	50	0.090
1.7 Migrat. Species	60	80	60	60	10	50	0.020
1.8 Anad. Species	50	70	80	80	10	60	0.070
1.9 LL/GDS Access	60	60	40	70	60	40	0.040
1.10 Science Control	80	60	10	90	40	60	0.050
1.11 Vessel Pollution	20	70	10	80	40	50	0.020
OPEN OCEAN							0.200
2.1 Transport Access	100	100	100	100	100	100	0.070
2.2 Fishing Access	100	100	100	100	100	70	0.070
2.3 Environ. Manag.	20	40	0	70	40	30	0.010
2.4 Vessel Pollution	30	40	10	70	40	30	0.010
2.5 Science Access	80	80	80	80	60	70	0.040
CONTINENTAL SHELF							0.030
3.1 Delimitation	70	60	40	100	50	70	0.010
3.2 Revenue Sharing	100	0	100	100	0	0	0.020
DEEP SEABED							0.120
4.1 Common Heritage	100	50	100	100	40	50	0.010
4.2 Exploit. System	80	60	80	80	20	40	0.030
4.3 Production Cons.	100	60	100	100	10	50	0.010
4.4 Tech. Transfer	100	60	100	100	10	50	0.020
4.5 Financial Cond.	100	70	100	100	30	40	0.010
4.6 Decision-Making	100	70	100	100	30	40	0.030
4.7 Review Conf.	100	60	100	100	30	30	0.020
SCORES	67	78	58	87	44	67	1.000

Table 8.2: Ocean Regimes: MAUT Preference Scores of Eastern European States

to be dominated by the Commonwealth of Independent States (CIS) in the future to the same degree as the USSR dominated in the past. For the sake of scenario construction, I assumed the group would continue to exist (minus the German Democratic Republic), and the Soviet Union's successor, the CIS, would still be influential, even if not able to dictate outcomes (in other words, the group would no longer be a true bloc).[48]

I estimated that coastal issues would be of considerable importance to the Eastern Europeans (65 percent), and since they have major distant-water fishing, merchant marine, and naval fleets, so would open-ocean issues (20 percent). Deep-ocean seabed issues and continental-shelf issues, requiring technologies that are too expensive or not available to group members in the early part of the scenario period, comprise 12 percent and 3 percent, respectively, of their total interests.

Since the Eastern Europeans would still reflect the interests of the Soviet Union, they did best under an imposed regime, by a substantial amount. An imposed regime would do well for them in all aspects of future ocean policy concerning near-shore, distant-water, continental-shelf, and deep-ocean minerals issues.

Like the major Western developed states, they would find the regime actually negotiated at UNCLOS III their second-best regime. They would benefit most from the negotiated outcomes concerning near-shore rights. A 12-mile territorial sea delimitation, a right of transit passage through straits, a right to traverse the EEZ, and the economic rights for the coastal state in the EEZ would be close to optimum. Although they would have to trade off some of their distant-water rights for coastal rights over fisheries, they would still judge the EEZ as a net benefit. They would also do well on most of the negotiated features which preserved movement and exploitation rights in the open ocean. They would be stuck with disproportionate burdens of the deep-seabed regime in terms of control, representation, decision-making, and technology sharing. If they ever attempted to exploit the outer margin during the forecast period, they would be burdened by revenue sharing.

The Eastern Europeans, despite different saliences from the major developed states, under my estimates would have the same rank order of preferences for the remaining regimes. In third place would be a LL/GDS regime. This is not surprising, since some of the group's members are landlocked. Inasmuch as group members did well using the freedoms of the old regime, they could still function under it if they had to. It was fourth on their list of preferred regimes. The fifth was a spontaneous regime, since it contained so many unknowns. Bringing up the rear was the coastal developing-state regime, which would restrict group members from many distant-water rights near developing states' coasts and the open ocean, and put an even greater burden on the group's members to support an NIEO solution to deep-seabed minerals exploitation.

The preference order of middle developed states (e.g., Canada, Scandinavian states, etc.) for an ocean regime is different from those of stakeholders with hegemonial aspirations or capabilities, as we can see in table 8.3. Again, the UNCLOS III regime plays second fiddle, but not by much, to the regime embodying norms comfortable to the middle developed states—the regime associated with the geographically disadvantaged states (LL/GDS). The LL/GDS appeal to equity, their willingness to regulate those who would use deep-seabed mineral resources, to share continental-shelf (margin) revenues, and to impose moderate controls over users of near-shore waters resonated with the middle developed states. In both of these regimes, I estimated that the middle developed states would *not* achieve maximum satisfaction (80–100 points) on many issues. This is consistent with their behavior at the conference. They often played the bridging role between the major developed states and G-77, and were the major architect of compromise solution. For them, even more equitable norms would have been better, but they would be very comfortable with UNCLOS III.

The scores of the third (developing coastal), fourth (imposed), and fifth (UNCLOS I and II) regimes were grouped close together. They are substantively very different regimes. Why were they grouped this way? Middle developed states are technologically capable. Perhaps because they could use the oceans effectively under most regimes, they could function effectively under imposed or status quo regimes. But they also are not as fearful of the equity claims of G-77 as are the major developed states, hence they have a more pragmatic and adaptive set of attitudes that would allow them to believe they could do moderately well under all prospective regimes except the spontaneous one. But, while they *could* function under the less favored regimes, they have clear preferences. There is a substantial drop between the two favored, and four less-favored regimes.

Many journalistic, and some scholarly, accounts of UNCLOS III have emphasized the radical nature of the Group of 77's demands. They are correct—as far as they go. Too often, however, these accounts do not mention the willingness of most members of G-77 to compromise and live with a regime that fell far short of their maximum demands. Both of these attributes show strongly in my estimate of the group's preferences among the six regimes. The case made by the Group of 77 at UNCLOS III emphasized the need for developing states to gain control over their own destinies in their near-shore waters. Thus, I estimated that 72 percent of their interest in a new regime was

	UNCLOS I&II	UNCLOS III	Spontaneous	Imposed	Developing Coastal	LL/GDS Equity	Weight
COASTAL OCEAN							0.600
1.1 EEZ Delimitation	30	90	20	80	70	60	0.080
1.2 Terr. Sea	30	100	20	60	40	90	0.080
1.3 Straits Transit	50	60	30	50	20	70	0.060
1.4 Arch. Rights	40	70	10	40	40	80	0.040
1.5 EEZ Transit	80	90	90	90	20	100	0.060
1.6 Fish Allocation	30	80	50	40	50	60	0.080
1.7 Migrat. Species	50	50	50	50	20	60	0.020
1.8 Anad. Species	40	75	30	70	10	70	0.040
1.9 LL/GDS Access	50	50	40	30	60	80	0.040
1.10 Science Control	60	70	50	50	50	60	0.030
1.11 Vessel Pollution	20	30	5	20	20	60	0.070
OPEN OCEAN							0.150
2.1 Transport Access	80	100	100	100	70	100	0.040
2.2 Fishing Access	80	80	80	80	70	100	0.040
2.3 Environ. Manag.	10	30	0	10	30	40	0.040
2.4 Vessel Pollution	10	30	0	10	30	30	0.020
2.5 Science Access	70	70	50	50	50	60	0.010
CONTINENTAL SHELF							0.050
3.1 Delimitation	60	60	30	50	50	20	0.025
3.2 Revenue Sharing	0	80	0	0	20	70	0.025
DEEP SEABED							0.200
4.1 Common Heritage	0	60	0	0	60	80	0.030
4.2 Exploit. System	40	70	50	50	50	80	0.040
4.3 Production Cons.	30	70	10	0	40	70	0.020
4.4 Tech. Transfer	30	70	20	0	50	80	0.030
4.5 Financial Cond.	30	70	40	0	50	80	0.020
4.6 Decision-Making	50	70	10	0	70	80	0.030
4.7 Review Conf.	50	70	30	0	80	80	0.030
SCORES	42	71	34	44	44	72	1.000

Table 8.3: Ocean Regimes: MAUT Preference Scores of Middle Developed States

found among coastal ocean issues. They also led the fight to get agreement on a NIEO-based regime for the deep ocean, and so I assigned 20 percent of their ocean interests to the deep seabed. That left only 5 percent for the open ocean, and 3 percent for the continental shelf (margin), figures that seemed reasonable in the light of the limited ocean reach of many developing states.

If G-77 could overcome internal dissonance with geographically disadvantaged members and could impose a regime favoring developing coastal states, tie up developed states in ocean uses near developing states' shores, limit open-ocean obligations on developing freedom of action, collect revenue from the developed on the continental margin, and impose an NIEO model regime on deep-seabed resources, they would have succeeded in grand fashion. Since their spokespersons laid out their case articulately, it is clear they saw the solution to many of their problems in an enclosure of near-shore waters, restrictions on movement, control of science, and an NIEO-based International Seabed Agency and Enterprise.

The UNCLOS III Convention would be second-best, and by a substantial margin. The Group of 77 got much of what they seemed to want at UNCLOS III—but in watered-down fashion. As the bargaining analysis makes clear, they often dominated the creation of the formula notion, but usually had to fall back on critical details. They compromised on almost every issue. They got the 200-mile EEZ, but it was carefully constrained with specific rights of outsiders to transit through. They got strong coastal controls of fisheries, although they had to allow the GDS some limited rights, and they had to tolerate vague references to "cooperation" as part of the solution to the migratory fish problem. They got coastal control of science, but had to concede implied consent. The Group of 77 also had to take a deep fallback on the control of "gunboats" through straits and, though the United States failed to sign the convention, they made a substantial number of compromises on the deep-seabed minerals issue. Indeed, the UNCLOS III minerals regime as NIEO model is close to being a hollow shell—a statement of principles concerning the "common heritage of mankind" with few instruments available for achieving it.

The Group of 77, considering its equity-based demands, would find itself more comfortable with a spontaneous regime than an equitable but weak coastal regime (LL/GDS). I pegged G-77 as rating the spontaneous regime higher than any other modeled stakeholder. If the Group of 77 could not impose its maximum preferred regime, or negotiate an acceptable regime, its next-best alternative would be one which restricts least the powers of its members individually to act under their domestic laws. Since the group was very enclosure-oriented, freedom to act, if necessary in defiance of

	UNCLOS I & II	UNCLOS III	Spontaneous	Imposed	Developing Coastal	LL/GDS Equity	Weight
COASTAL OCEAN							0.720
1.1 EEZ Delimitation	20	70	35	0	80	10	0.120
1.2 Terr. Sea	20	50	60	20	60	10	0.120
1.3 Straits Transit	20	40	0	25	60	20	0.040
1.4 Arch. Rights	10	70	50	30	70	40	0.060
1.5 EEZ Transit	40	50	30	40	80	40	0.020
1.6 Fish Allocation	40	80	90	10	90	30	0.140
1.7 Migrat. Species	10	60	80	5	100	30	0.015
1.8 Anad. Species	5	30	10	5	100	10	0.005
1.9 LL/GDS Access	70	60	70	20	90	20	0.060
1.10 Science Control	20	75	90	30	90	50	0.090
1.11 Vessel Pollution	30	60	70	30	90	60	0.060
OPEN OCEAN							0.050
2.1 Transport Access	60	60	50	60	80	60	0.020
2.2 Fishing Access	40	60	40	20	80	30	0.010
2.3 Environ. Manag.	20	60	20	20	70	30	0.005
2.4 Vessel Pollution	40	50	10	20	80	30	0.010
2.5 Science Access	40	40	20	20	90	40	0.005
CONTINENTAL SHELF							0.030
3.1 Delimitation	30	40	70	20	40	10	0.010
3.2 Revenue Sharing	0	90	0	0	90	70	0.020
DEEP SEABED							0.200
4.1 Common Heritage	0	70	0	0	100	70	0.060
4.2 Exploit. System	0	60	0	20	90	80	0.050
4.3 Production Cons.	0	50	0	10	90	70	0.040
4.4 Tech. Transfer	0	60	0	10	90	70	0.020
4.5 Financial Cond.	0	40	0	20	90	80	0.005
4.6 Decision-Making	0	70	0	30	100	70	0.020
4.7 Review Conf.	0	80	0	10	100	80	0.005
SCORES	23	64	47	18	86	38	1.000

Table 8.4: Ocean Regimes: MAUT Preference Scores of Developing States (G-77)

developed stakeholders, was important to them. The Group of 77's assessment of the remaining two modeled regimes shows them rating imposed and UNCLOS I and II regimes two orders of magnitude down the scale. Much of the group's rhetoric concerned fear of hegemonial behavior and the loathing of a Grotian solution. Hence, it is no surprise at all that they would rate hegemonial and Grotian regimes quite low.

The geographically disadvantaged–landlocked states are the last group of stakeholders for whom I role-played. Their scores are found in table 8.5.

I estimated that LL/GDS with no or only a small seacoast, had an important interest in the coastal ocean (56 percent), since their access to the sea was usually circumscribed by coastal neighbors. They also had high hopes for participation in, and wealth from, the International Seabed Agency. Therefore, I rated their interest in deep-sea minerals issues at 26 percent of their total national interests. While they did not use the open ocean as often as coastal states, they had an interest in maintaining access to it (10 percent). LL/GDS usually had no continental shelves, but through revenue-sharing they hoped to share in the bounty of the sea (8 percent).

The regime closest to demands they made at UNCLOS III represents what would please LL/GDS states most if they could have it as the operative new ocean regime. But as we have seen, the bargaining position of the group at UNCLOS III was weak, and once it was determined that the major developed states had no interest in joining the LL/GDS in a spoiler role, LL/GDS had to accept significant fallbacks, many promising paper rights to the geographically disadvantaged they are unlikely to use (e.g., the right of priority access to the "surplus" fish in their coastal neighbors' EEZ). Hence, they had to find allies among the coastal developing states and middle developed states. They found the UNCLOS III regime second-best, but not much better than the developing coastal regime, which promised them access to their coastal zone (but no mineral rights) and promised to bring riches to the LL/GDS through a strong seabed regime. Since LL/GDS did make appeals on equity grounds that the major developed states might respond to in an imposed regime, my simulated decision-makers rated an imposed regime in fourth place. UNCLOS I and II do have minimal guarantees of the rights for the landlocked (for which they fought hard at the earlier conferences), and therefore they would probably find the status quo minimally acceptable. Spontaneous regimes with the considerable liberty they would grant coastal states to enclose at will, making LL/GDS members relatively worse off, would be the least acceptable regime to the LL/GDS.

	Unclos I & II	UNCLOS III	Spontaneous	Imposed	Developing Coastal	LL/GDS Equity	Weight
COASTAL OCEAN							0.560
1.1 EEZ Delimitation	60	50	0	30	60	80	0.040
1.2 Terr. Sea	80	90	0	70	20	80	0.050
1.3 Straits Transit	60	70	20	60	40	80	0.030
1.4 Arch. Rights	30	70	50	60	40	90	0.070
1.5 EEZ Transit	70	80	10	80	20	100	0.060
1.6 Fish Allocation	60	40	20	70	10	100	0.060
1.7 Migrat. Species	60	70	0	20	10	100	0.005
1.8 Anad. Species	50	70	0	20	10	100	0.005
1.9 LL/GDS Access	30	60	1	50	60	100	0.200
1.10 Science Control	70	70	30	40	80	70	0.010
1.11 Vessel Pollution	60	70	10	30	60	70	0.010
OPEN OCEAN							0.100
2.1 Transport Access	90	90	90	90	90	90	0.050
2.2 Fishing Access	70	80	90	90	100	100	0.005
2.3 Environ. Manag.	20	30	0	20	20	90	0.030
2.4 Vessel Pollution	30	40	10	30	30	80	0.005
2.5 Science Access	60	60	70	60	80	90	0.005
CONTINENTAL SHELF							0.080
3.1 Delimitation	0	40	0	0	10	100	0.010
3.2 Revenue Sharing	0	80	0	0	100	100	0.070
DEEP SEABED							0.260
4.1 Common Heritage	0	80	0	0	100	100	0.070
4.2 Exploit. System	0	60	0	0	100	100	0.050
4.3 Production Cons.	0	70	0	0	100	100	0.010
4.4 Tech. Transfer	0	70	0	0	100	100	0.030
4.5 Financial Cond.	0	80	0	0	100	100	0.020
4.6 Decision-Making	0	90	0	0	100	100	0.030
4.7 Review Conf.	0	90	0	0	100	100	0.050
SCORES	35	69	13	39	64	74	1.000

Table 8.5: Ocean Regimes: MAUT Preference Scores of Landlocked/Geographically Disadvantaged States

Conclusion

Was the 15-year bargaining effort to produce a new ocean regime worthwhile? Did it produce a regime that accomplishes what a social institution of that type should do? Will it be stable? From my estimates of how the major stakeholders view their policy options for ocean management in the next 20 years, the answer is yes. UNCLOS III produced an agreement that, despite its flaws, solved major allocation problems and created an ordered environment in which the major stakeholders can function effectively for the next 20 years.

In all the cases examined, the UNCLOS III regime was the second-best alternative to the maximum preferred position of the major state groups with a stake in future ocean use. No stakeholder enters a negotiation believing that it can solve its order and allocation problems without the consent or cooperation of other stakeholders. Therefore, unless states were willing to pay a very substantial price for going it alone, the second-best was the best they could expect from a negotiated outcome. If my estimates are correct, no stakeholder felt comfortable going back to the pre-1973 status quo—it was, at best, the fourth, and more often, the fifth choice out of six.

All stakeholders paid a price in the process of crafting a world ocean regime. Middle developed states paid the lowest price. In many respects, given the leadership role many of their representatives played in the negotiations, UNCLOS III is their treaty. They often built bridges that helped avert fatal clashes between the developing states and the major developed states without giving up their own national objectives.

I believe members of the Group of 77 paid a higher price than is usually acknowledged. Not having a right to exclude all others from some uses of *their* coastal ocean must be painful. A 12-mile territorial sea is unsatisfactory to some. Many have reservations about allowing transit passage, especially by warships. Not being the final authority on a pollution-control measure if the flag state invokes its privilege to take over the case certainly means that they must treat the EEZ as a limited-purpose zone. They also failed to limit the great ocean powers in their use of the open ocean. Finally, it remains to be seen whether the International Seabed Authority will come into existence, and if it does, whether it will be able to run a successful economic exploitative effort under New International Economic Order principles. Even with the Authority, developing states may not be able to exclude developed-state companies or consortia from access to deep-seabed resources; production controls may be too generous to be meaningful; they may not be able to extract sufficient financial resources from the developed states to allow for priority distribution to themselves; and they may not be able to impose decisions on the developed states using an automatic majority.

The biggest substantive winners in the UNCLOS III negotiation were the major developed ocean-using states, West and East. Measured in terms of the amount of near-shore ocean real estate they put under their national jurisdictions and the Grotian movement rights they were able to retain, they did very well indeed. For example, the United States acquired in excess of 3.9 billion acres in its EEZ.[49] Its vessels can roam freely in ocean areas more than 12 miles from shore and transit through archipelagic straits or straits used for international navigations. They are winners despite the fact that, even after hard bargaining, the deep-seabed portion of the Convention (Part XI) remains of marginal value.

The reality is, the new ocean regime has proven satisfactory in ten years of use. The Convention has not come into force, but most states are already abiding by most of its major provisions. Their expectations have converged in that they are usually granting to others the same types of rights they themselves have claimed. EEZs have been proclaimed around the world with little quarrel about a state's right to proclaim one. To be sure, where waters are narrow and claims overlap, problems exist, but not problems relating to the *right* of a state to make a claim. Despite some trepidation about the costs of enforcing the fisheries provisions of the EEZ, there has been remarkably little conflict over the right of the coastal state to make allocation decisions. The right to transit straits has been exercised, and except for a few incidents (notably between the United States and Canada over transit of the so-called Northwest Passage)[50] the problem has not been the subject of headlines for some time. Ocean scientists, despite grumbling, can do their work.

Thus far, the major weakness of UNCLOS III has been in the environmental area. The Convention's general provisions on vessel-source pollution, which require that states avoid polluting the commons, have not helped prevent the recent spate of ocean-pollution incidents. Indeed, they have no operational language. But should we expect a general regime-making conference to deal adequately with a worldwide, complex, technical set of problems? In any case, it is now time to deal with ocean pollution as part of the larger agenda of reducing human degradation of the global commons.

Despite the positive benefits of other parts of the Convention, Part XI (deep seabed) stands out as intolerable to a number of major developed states. Like the United States, they either have not become signatories or are proceeding cautiously with their ratification processes, leaving them in a position to free ride on the Convention. They can choose to accept, enforce, and reciprocally recognize rights and obligations under all parts of the treaty but Part XI. In the short run, this gives them the best of all possible worlds— they gain order without paying much of the cost. Will this always be so? At some point those who are free riders may face the question of whether it is in their interest to remain outside, especially if sufficient changes are accepted in the ongoing Prepcom negotiations to make the ISA a viable organization. Despite the fact that the Convention has a no-reservation clause (Article 309) and does not allow formal amendment until after the treaty has been in force for 10 years (Article 312), there is still a possibility that the provisions of Part XI can be substantially altered.

I have tried to envisage what the changes demanded by the major developed states might do to their MAUT scores (table 8.1). "Improvements" in Part XI would make a revised UNCLOS III Convention a very satisfactory regime for the major developed states. If exploiters from developed states or transnational consortia could gain assured access to seabed resources—even regulated access—they could avoid the problem of monopoly and free riding on their efforts by the Enterprise. If they could be assured that technology transfers would occur only under commercial conditions, they could protect their investments. If the problem of a runaway majority making important ISA decisions could be solved, once exploiters gained rights, they could retain them except for malfeasance or nonperformance. The United States would also have to be provided an assured seat on the ISA Council. Finally, to the dismay of liberal internationalists and NIEO advocates, the provision making amendments binding on states that voted against them would have to be eliminated.

These are trivial tasks, but efforts should be made to accomplish them. Fortunately for the major developed states, the current status quo is not UNCLOS I and II but UNCLOS III without Part XI. The states of the world are already enforcing this regime. Hopefully, opponents of altering the treaty will recognize that those who have not come aboard the existing Convention have available, viable options.[51] If stakeholders don't insist on greater gains than usually can be achieved through negotiation, the last major barrier to a successful comprehensive new ocean regime will fall.

9

Negotiation of the Regime—
Lessons Learned

One of the most difficult results to achieve in a global political system as heterogeneous and anarchic as the one under which we have operated late in the twentieth century is agreement among the many. This modern version of "the consent of Europe" is further complicated by a large number of new stakeholders from other areas of the world with different cultures and political agendas, and by an increasing number of issues that cannot be resolved satisfactorily within a national territorial domain. Increasingly, many important issues of concern within national borders are affected by the uses of un-owned areas or resources beyond national borders. Our interconnectedness demands that we find solutions to problems that inevitably will affect the many. But, such an outcome is very difficult.

Parliamentary diplomacy is one of the processes developed by world statesmen to cope with the problem of achieving agreement among the many. It operates within a particular environment—the United Nations system. It borrows a great deal from practices in the U.N. General Assembly—particularly the means used for aggregating preferences. But because it tries to foster agreement among parties capable of defecting, and therefore not bound by the decisions made, it has its own distinctive attributes, most important of which is the need to achieve consensus.

Perhaps the major attempt in our times to foster agreement among the many using parliamentary diplomatic techniques was negotiations in the Third United Nations Conference on the Law of the Sea. In the eyes of its proponents, the UNCLOS III conference came very close to creating a major convention, acceptable to all, that would set rules for the use of 70 percent of the earth's surface. But after 12 years of negotiation, it only achieved near-consensus, with 4 states voting no, and 17 abstaining out of 151 states. However, opponents pointed out that, although the dissenters were few in number, they were important states. The conference achieved an "almost," making attempts to assess the value of its efforts difficult.

This work looks at the process of using parliamentary diplomatic techniques to resolve conflict among the many over ocean jurisdiction and management. With a sample of one, any generalizations derived from the case under investigation must be viewed only as suggestive. Nevertheless, a good deal was learned about the use of negotiation to form an international regime. Before proceeding directly to the findings, some observations will be made, and assessment criteria elucidated. Patterns of interactions typical of parliamentary diplomacy then will be reviewed, and a number of assets and liabilities of this bargaining system assessed. Finally, an attempt will be made to determine whether the long and costly effort achieved enough positive good to make it a candidate for use again in resolving future problems that require the consent of all, or nearly all.

Observations

Criteria for Judgment

After 15 years negotiation and the promulgation of a convention with 320 articles and 9 annexes, commentators are still arguing as to whether the Third United Nations Law of the Sea Conference was a success or a failure.[1] Even some of those who proclaim it a success are concerned about the cost of achieving that success and wonder whether the leaders of the world need to find a less costly process of resolving global problems.[2] Our assessment *will not* provide definitive answers to transaction-cost questions.[3] The analysis we performed is not particularly suited to directly answering such questions. At this stage in the development of social science methodology, we lack both measurement tools and appropriate data for definitively answering transaction-cost questions on problems of a global scale. Yet they are important questions to raise.

Not even its most ardent proponents can argue that the Convention is an unqualified success. Its adoption was not universal, and some of its provisions are likely not to resolve problems of the ocean commons, but instead, perhaps exacerbate them. One portion of the Convention—Part XI—remains controversial and even many of its supporters now admit it cannot be implemented without significant modification.

Nevertheless, the UNCLOS III Convention is no mean achievement—a comprehensive regime for two-thirds of the earth's surface which deals with virtually every human use, endorsed by 130 of 151 states assembled, and rejected by only 4 (with 17 abstaining, some of which later adhered). The degree of agreement attained is rare in human annals, and considering the heterogeneity of the participants and the complexity of the subject matter, the quality of many of the solutions found (substantively and in terms of the low probability of implementation increasing conflict) is relatively high.

One must view UNCLOS III like the proverbial glass, half filled with liquid. It is in the eye of the beholder as to whether it should be described as half empty or half full. The Third United Nations Law of the Sea Conference worked. It achieved an outcome. Although it is difficult to measure the cost of that outcome with precision, some portions of it can be elucidated. It took 15 years to achieve, from the time Ambassador Arvid Pardo of Malta introduced the seabed item to the General Assembly in 1967 to the signing of the Convention in 1982. UNCLOS III has been characterized as the longest continuous single negotiation ever attempted in modern times—and one of the costliest. No official figures exist, but I have estimated that the costs of sending a thousand delegates and hundreds of secretariat officials to the Conference, of providing the meeting halls, translations, documents, etc. were in the neighborhood of $210 million.[4] The Conference provided a measurable boost to the professional careers of some delegates, and ended the careers of others. These are transaction costs.

Even more difficult to calculate are the opportunity costs of the conference.[5] While the nation-states of the world were pursuing agreement on ocean problems via a United Nations conference, they were forgoing the opportunity of finding solutions to ocean problems by other means. What was the cost of that forgone opportunity? What would have been the cost of discovering an appropriate ocean regime, say, by spontaneous means, as compared to a universal conference?

Perhaps allowing each state to take what actions it thought best to protect its own interests would have worked best. Perhaps if late-coming states had acted sensibly, they might have imitated examples of successful policies or rules by early leaders in making their own ocean policies, thereby creating a pattern of consistent outcomes, but creating it spontaneously. If they had been especially sensitive, they might have adjusted their policies to those of their neighbors, either unilaterally or bilaterally, thereby avoiding conflict on ocean interests. On the other hand, states might have chosen to coordinate their policies through smaller, more specialized conferences between all states on ocean transportation, fishing, and science; on military transit, straits, deep-seabed mining, the environment, or other issues. Perhaps meetings between states within a particular region, or between like-minded states, would have produced better solutions. Limitations in measurement theory and appropriate data put the costs of creating a new ocean regime by other means beyond calculation. Any attempt at comparison is therefore based largely on speculation.

Nevertheless, we must keep these larger considerations of effectiveness and cost in mind as we assess what we learned about parliamentary diplomacy. The world community is now being faced with worldwide problems, such as global warming, that require a collective solution. Probably some of these problems will be brought to future large-scale conferences. Will these U.N.-managed or associated conferences be effective venues for solving such problems, or will they be too slow, too costly, and too apt to impose the poorer rather than better solution?

Consensus as a Decision Rule

Another key consideration in assessing the merits or demerits of UNCLOS III as precedent for the future is whether it created a viable decision system. UNCLOS III operated under a consensus-decision rule which allowed decision before unanimity was reached. We must understand what this meant as a collective-decision mechanism.

The task for UNCLOS III was gaining the consent of participants on a regime for the oceans—a modern version of Frederick the Great's "consent of Europe"—on a "constitutional" question.[6] A collective choice was needed. That collective choice of the many (who are also heterogeneous) meant that consensus had to be achieved in order to have a positive-sum outcome. Students of collective choice have debated whether consensus in constitutional rule-making is the most desirable or the most efficient decision procedure.[7] But there is little debate on the conclusion that consensus means unanimity, and that it is costly to achieve.

What does consensus mean in a collective-choice situation such as UNCLOS III? No document produced by UNCLOS III defined consensus. The best the conference could do (in its rules of procedure) was to indicate that voting would not be undertaken until "all efforts at reaching general agreement have been exhausted."[8] The phrasing of "all efforts" implies that, if necessary, the conference had to be prepared to reach decision even if it had not achieved unanimity. That is precisely what was done after strenuous efforts were made to achieve the consent of all.[9] Earlier such a decision—for want of a better term—was characterized as a near-consensus decision. The decision of a very substantial majority, but not all, is an example of a paradox of collective choice.[10]

While such a decision is paradoxical, the delegates were not concerned with the development of social theory. They had a decision-mode problem to solve if the Conference were to be brought to a successful conclusion. They were on the horns of a dilemma facing a paradox they could not solve. If they used consensus-as-unanimity as the decision rule, they provided a veto to the one or few over the many and might greatly increase the transaction costs of the Conference. On the other hand, if they attempted to force decision on a recalcitrant few—especially the powerful states—they risked defection and the undermining of the value of the outcome agreed to by the many, since it might allow the few to free ride.

This was understood by Conference leaders, especially Third World delegates. They preferred the traditional U.N. decision rule—two-thirds present and voting—and therefore viewed the near-consensus rule as a compromise with the minority of major industrial states. I believe they implemented near-consensus because it also accorded with the value systems of a number of non-Western participating states. Delegates to UNCLOS III treated consensus as a process in which a maximum effort would be made to reach unanimity. However, if that proved impossible and the will of a substantial majority was manifest, dissenters were expected to accept the decision of the overwhelming majority. The majority owed to dissenters the opportunity to exhaust every argument to attempt to persuade the majority to alter or modify its preferred outcome. In other words, maximum consultation before decision was the operative decision rule. (This is similar to what consensus means in the Japanese decision system, a system noted for its dependence upon a consensus-style of decision.)[11] Missing at the global level is the social compact that exists in societies that treat consensus as maximum consultation. In such societies, if the rules of consultation have been followed, the decision normally would be accepted by the minority.[12] Without that social compact, participants can defect, usually with impunity, as they did in the case of UNCLOS III. In short, the decision system adopted by UNCLOS III did not solve the paradox, but did result in a convention that was widely accepted, and arguably a convention where most provisions were accepted by all.

Findings

The findings summarized don't fit into any of the schools of bargaining analysis identified by I. William Zartman.[13] The model developed by myself, Dr. Joseph Kadane, and other colleagues allowed us to examine the movement of state preferences over time as delegates worked toward closure on the myriad issues.[14] While the model was developed originally to provide forecasts for the U.S. delegation to UNCLOS III, it also proved useful for understanding when issues were ripe for decision, and for evaluating the complex trade-offs in the development of a package approach. The model also allowed us to determine who among the participants were loyal supporters of caucusing and common-interest groups, who were driving forces among the contestants, who were winners, and who were losers. Consequently, the method created opportunities for insights most often associated with the incremental, tactical, and structural schools of bargaining analysis. It is related most closely to the work of analysts who pay close attention to phased change in negotiations.[15] Thus, this work has concentrated on examining the phases in the process of UNCLOS III.

Findings will be shown in eight categories: (1) the three-phase process of parliamentary diplomacy—diagnosis, formula, and detail; (2) typical patterns of phased changes in Phases II and III; (3) the construction of packages and trade-offs; (4) behavior within bargaining groups in parliamentary diplomacy; (5) the impact of parliamentary organization on outcomes; (6) tactics in parliamentary diplomacy; (7) the impact of ideology and symbolism in parliamentary diplomacy; and (8) the impact of the nature of the issues on the outcome.

Diagnosis, Formula, and Detail in Parliamentary Diplomacy

An examination of the evidence concerning the process by which accommodation was sought in UNCLOS III confirms the observations of I. William Zartman and his associates that, typically, international negotiation is composed of three phases. The UNCLOS III negotiation moved from a diagnostic phase, through a phase of finding and agreeing to a formula, and finally, to a phase in which the details were worked out.[16]

We should first be clear on *what* was being accomplished in a negotiation such as UNCLOS III. To create an outcome in which all parties are better off by agreement than disagreement, a set of ideas must be found to which all (or virtually all) can subscribe. These must be "referents" or principles of justice that provide a cognitive structure to the suggested solution to the problem, and that reflect the underlying values which give meaning to the item under discussion.[17] Finding principles upon which two can agree is difficult; finding principles upon which three or more can agree is more difficult; finding principles upon which large numbers with heterogeneous perceptions, needs, and interests can agree is most difficult of all. Yet, what is most difficult to accomplish is precisely what must be accomplished if issues are to be negotiated by the many. This must begin in the diagnostic phase.

Phase I—Diagnosis   Negotiations can proceed either inductively or deductively. That is, negotiators can begin with interactions on details, and then move toward identifying principles underlying the details worked out, or they can first identify principles and then proceed to work out details appropriate to them. Because it was a process that necessitated identifying as early as possible a set of referents with which large numbers of diverse participants could identify, the UNCLOS III negotiation proceeded deductively from the beginning.

Four factors pushed UNCLOS III into early concentration upon finding an appropriate set of referents. First, sheer numbers dictated that to avoid chaos, the participants had to have an understanding of what they and others were saying. To communicate, they had to understand the underlying principles of the items discussed. Second, UNCLOS III was a formal negotiation, therefore early in the diagnostic phase many governments went through extensive preparations. Such preparations forced a consideration of principles. Third, the subject matter of the Conference was the legal regime of the ocean. The existing legal regime was based upon well-known principles. It was well understood by most delegations that the general task of the Conference was to either reform and retain freedom of the seas as the operative principle, or replace it in whole or in part with a different principle. And fourth, formal debate took up much of the time of delegates in the Ad Hoc and Permanent Seabed Committees, as well as the First Session of the Conference. Ironically, the decision to proceed without a formal agenda but with a mere list of issues, a decision that seemed likely to lead delegates to an inductive process of fumbling their way through a mass of detail to later discover what they were getting to, produced the reverse. Delegate after delegate stood up on the floor to announce how his delegation understood the underlying principles. Although there were numerous documents with specific language introduced early, most were either ignored or not acted upon until all delegates had an opportunity to state their principles and listen to the principles or referents introduced by others.

The search for underlying principles or referents can be viewed as a cooperative process of developing common perceptions, a problem-solving search,[18] or as a competitive process of stating principles and attempting to induce, with appropriate incentives, those on the other side of the table to accept those principles, or a modified version, as the basis for settlement. UNCLOS III was, on most major issues, an open contest between two or more opposing principles, with the supporters of each hoping their principle or conceptual notion would be the guide to the outcome on an issue or issues.

The diagnostic phase of UNCLOS III was composed of two parts. In the first, the parties decided that negotiation was the appropriate mechanism for resolving certain substantive problems, that the time was ripe to initiate the resolution process, and that an acceptable venue was available. In the second part, which began with preliminary discussions in the General Assembly, Ad Hoc and Permanent U.N. Seabed Committees, and First Session of the Conference, delegates attempted to sort through the rival principles vying for the role as guide to the outcome, choose one or more to back (if they had not already introduced their own candidate principles), and search for allies and friends who supported similar principles or referents. On some issues for some delegations, affiliations were fixed by membership in U.N. caucusing groups. On others, common interests had to be identified and common-interest groups formed. The structure of the negotiation was, after all, parliamentary, and the process of aggregation had to be put into full swing.

From the middle 1960s, after the First U.N. Law of the Sea Conference failed to establish an agreed outer boundary for the territorial sea, many states, especially those which had oil operations moving further out to sea, were looking at whether they should negotiate again. But was the time ripe, or would the world's statesmen suffer another failure? And what was the appropriate venue for resolution? A parliamentary conference had failed at the beginning of the decade. Was it sensible to reconvene a U.N.-sponsored conference, especially since membership had increased greatly in that decade, mostly from developing states? The answer depended upon where a state was located in the international system. The major maritime powers wanted technically tighter rules to guide their ocean users, but they preferred to negotiate with each other, or, if in a large-scale venue, at least in "separate packets," on the issues of security, transportation, fisheries, and the seabed. Developing states wanted an opportunity to renegotiate the rules, which many of them claimed had been made without their consent. Therefore, many developing states wanted to attack the big picture. They were after the referents which structured the existing regime.

By 1967, the die was cast. The Soviet Union had approached the United States concerning the resolution of straits and territorial-sea issues. The United States canvassed its friends, and even indicated a willingness to link these issues with the question of how to accommodate the special fishing interests of coastal states beyond 12 miles. However, after Pardo's impressive speech describing the mineral riches of the deep seabed and his introduction of the idea of the seabed as the "common heritage of mankind," there was no turning back. The negotiation would concern all major issues of ocean use. The negotiation would be under U.N. auspices. The rules of the game would be parliamentary diplomatic rules. Phase I of UNCLOS III began in 1967 and ended after the first substantive session in Caracas in early 1974.

Data collected by the Law of the Sea Research Project show what occurred in the interactive latter half of Phase I or T-1 (1971–72). As we shall see below, it was rare that there was substantial support, much less unanimity, for any set of principles introduced in Phase I. Setting the formula would be a competitive process. Typically in Phase I, when plotted on a histogram, the distribution of expressed preferences was either "lumpy" or bimodal. Lumpiness indicated that there was no discernible pattern; states' preferences were recorded all over the entire spectrum of principles introduced on the issue. One could interpret this to mean that there was early confusion, and that a core of states that could be the heart of a consensus had not formed to back even one, much less two, candidate principles to form the backbone of a formula. Frequently, as a result of the early interactions, two candidates emerged visible on the histograms, in which case the distribution was bimodal, indicating two camps. These camps were not necessarily equal in size, but the very existence of two camps indicated a long, hard negotiation on the issue while one side attempted to persuade the supporters of the other to come over. On rare occasions toward the end of Phase I, a single-peaked distribution could be seen, indicating agreement on a framework of principles.

Phase II—Establishing the Formula   The function of Phase II was to establish the formula idea, that is, to convince most of the delegates that one core concept embodying a principle of justice on each issue would be the likely formula idea to be refined in the final phase into an outcome acceptable to all or virtually all. This phase established one formula as the concept to beat, undermine, or refine. At UNCLOS III, Phase II began after the primarily exploratory First Session in Caracas (1974), and culminated at the end of the Third Session (1975), when the first negotiating text was issued. Data for this period were captured in the second time period used in this study (T-2).

With no formal agenda and much of the early interactions devoted to speech-making, formation of bargaining groups, and a wide variety of essentially exploratory activities, there was no formal device forcing the delegates to move toward an outcome. The promulgation of single negotiating texts had that forcing function. The chairs of the main committees were instructed to write up draft language embodying conceptual ideas that appeared to the committee chair to have substantial support. If no trend had emerged, the chair was empowered to indicate in the draft the idea around which he thought consensus *might* emerge. In theory, the Single Negotiating Text (SNT) was to be "the starting point for further negotiations"[19] In fact, it was "regarded as the first draft of the Convention."[20] As a result, while opposing candidate formula ideas were not dead, the odds of getting a formula idea in the SNT removed and replaced by an opposing idea were poor. Opponents' options were then reduced in the final phase to: undermining the formula idea, if possible; making it minimally acceptable through modifications on the details; accepting it as part of a package or trade-off, where the losing issue was of lower salience than winning issues; or defecting.

In T-2, the median of distributions that are not strongly bimodal provided a useful measure for determining whether chairs accurately gauged the state of play. Often it showed the chairs did their jobs well. Occasionally it showed the chair acting arbitrarily by trying to impose a solution for which there was little support. When the distribution of preferences on an issue at the beginning of T-2 showed a unimodal pattern—even with a tail—or at worst a weakly bimodal pattern, that was an indicator that the process of conversion toward a negotiated outcome had begun. The process had to be completed in Phase III.

Phase III—Refining the Formula   Refining the formula might seem to imply that the remainder of the process was largely mechanical—that the delegates knew what they wanted, and now only technical expertise had to be applied to quickly put the agreed concept on paper in the most felicitous language. For most issues at UNCLOS III, that was not the case. Phase III was a long and tedious process. It began with the issuing of the Revised Negotiating Text in 1976 and was not completed until the final session in 1982. Although drafting skill was needed, technical drafting was *not* the most important task of the third phase. Bargaining on details was, and it was complex and intense.[21]

Essentially, what occurred in Phase III was an attempt on the part of the supporters of the candidate formula idea to protect the integrity of their concept while inducing opponents to accept it. To promote consensus or near-consensus, supporters had to be willing to offer positive inducements to opponents to attract them to support of their formula idea. But if support from opponents was not gained from trade-offs on other issues opponents valued more highly, then supporters of a formula had to be willing, to some degree, to accommodate opponents who demanded modifications of the formula. The winners might be asked to accept exceptions to the rule, fuzzy language which made it unclear who was supposed to do what or pay for what, escape clauses, time limits, numerical formulas for distribution of benefits that might not be as favorable as some parties had hoped, or implied application of the opposing concept if a state does not positively claim a right under the formula concept. The range of human ingenuity is great on the part of losers to mitigate or, if they are skillful and their opponents careless, negate the impact of the principle underlying a negotiated formula. What seemed to be won in Phase II could be lost in Phase III.

Typical Patterns in Parliamentary Diplomacy
All three phases of parliamentary diplomacy can be tracked visually in the histograms. There are typical patterns among the 25 major Conference issues analyzed. They are shown below. They are revealing because they capture the essence of the process of movement and accommodation in parliamentary

diplomacy. The patterns exemplify the normal process and most major variants well, but this doesn't mean that all parliamentary negotiations inevitably move smoothly from one phase to the next, with no backsliding, doubling back, or confusion among delegates or observers as to where matters stand.[22] Even where the histograms show some parties winning and others losing in relation to their maximum preferred positions, national objectives for a number of states were not as hard and fast as the term "maximum preferred position" might imply. For some states, objectives were obscure, uncertain, and contradictory at the outset. Some states negotiated to determine what their objectives should be.[23] For them, the gains or losses at the end were difficult to calculate.

The most typical or "classic" pattern, in figure 9.1, shows the formation of consensus as a move by a substantial majority of states spread over most of the spectrum of possible positions in Phase I, to a single-peaked distribution with a tail at the beginning of Phase II, and finally to a consensus decision within a narrower formula zone in Phase III.[24]

In this classic case (the functions of the International Seabed Authority), negotiations caused movement from the broad spectrum of ideas supported in T-1 to a single-peaked distribution with a tail in T-2. A trend had emerged and the Single Negotiating Text reflected it very well, both formula idea and median falling at rank 15. If the decision mode was voting, the median tells us that the formula idea at rank 15 would defeat any alternatives. But voting was postponed and used only to confirm a decision to be reached by negotiation. Version 1 of the negotiating text was the beginning point of negotiations in Phase II. It defined one edge of what has been characterized as a formula zone, which captured the range of serious negotiations in Phases II and III. Though expression of the formula idea at rank 15 may not have been the purest reflection of the core concept that was placed at rank 17, it was not too heavily amended to lose the support of those delegations enthusiastic about the underlying principle of justice found in the idea at rank 17. Therefore, the formula notion at rank 15 was the idea to be defended or amended in Phase II.

The opposing formula notions (ranks 1–9) had been defeated by Phase II. At that juncture, the scores of the key supporters of the formula notion averaged at rank 15, the median figure. A candidate formula notion that commanded wide support had been found. However, the long sloping tail indicates that even near-consensus had not been achieved by the end of Phase II. Therefore, to write the detailed language acceptable to all or virtually all in Phase III, formula-idea supporters had to be willing to negotiate incremental concessions to attract opponents to accept that idea as the conceptual core of

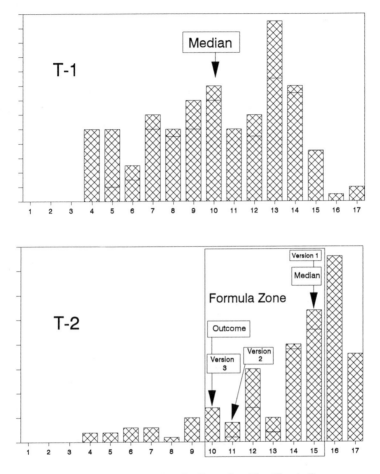

Figure 9.1: Developing the Formula—The Classic Pattern

the solution. The task of supporters was to make only the concessions necessary to create consensus without allowing opponents to gut the core idea.

Opponents had the opposite task. Their assignment was to make an obnoxious formula idea palatable, to force its proponents to accept limitations,
modifications, and obfuscations that might make the formula idea livable.
Since the remaining phases of the negotiation concerned parleying over detailed, precise language, skillful opponents might leave the formula core notion intact, but undercut it as much as possible in the description of the

detailed obligations. A skillful opponent, if not opposed by a skillful proponent, might leave a formula notion a hollow shell.

In our classic case, the opponents—favored by the rule of maximum consultation—were able to force the proponents in two more iterations of the negotiating text to back down to the formula language placed at rank 10, as shown in figure 9.2. It was found acceptable to the maximum number of participants at the Conference and became part of the Convention. It is typical that if a single-peaked preference with a tail was formed by T-2, that proponents of the idea found at the peak had to move down the slope of the peak, forcing them to accommodate opponents in order to create a consensus-based outcome.

While the development of an outcome in smooth incremental steps was the most typical or classic pattern, the process was subject to numerous variations. The illustrative issue, here, is the consent rule for the conduct of science in the Exclusive Economic Zone. We see a weak but still single-peaked distribution formed in T-1 transformed in T-2 to a strong peak at the opposite end of the scale, but not achieving single-peakedness. While our data do not allow us to say with certainty whether near-unanimity was achieved in 1982, other evidence indicates it was not. It appeared in T-1 that, although preferences spread from rank 1 to rank 14 on a 15-point scale, a majority of states would support a formula notion that represented a watered-down version of the modal notion found at rank 1. The chair attempted to find a 50-percent solution outcome that would bring both sides together. (In this particular case, he chose to promote notification of a coastal state by a researcher as a halfway point between freedom of research and a requirement that a researcher obtain the consent of the coastal state before proceeding with research.) The effort failed.

In T-2, preferences shifted sharply toward the opposing core concept (i.e., consent). The negotiating text proposal at rank 7 was never a part of any further serious bargaining. The opposing core concept was the formula idea that would be refined into an outcome—if one could be reached. What was being negotiated in the next several steps was whether consent proponents would accept any limitations on their right to apply the doctrine, making the concept livable, but far less than optimal to states with vocal domestic ocean-science stakeholders. That the consent forces understood the strength of their position is emphasized by the median falling at the same rank as version 2 of the negotiating text. If the item had been put to a vote, the consent forces would have won. But the figure also shows that there were two spikes of opposition, at ranks 4 and 8, that had to be overcome in order to reach an acceptable outcome under the rules of maximum consultation. Thus, further negotia-

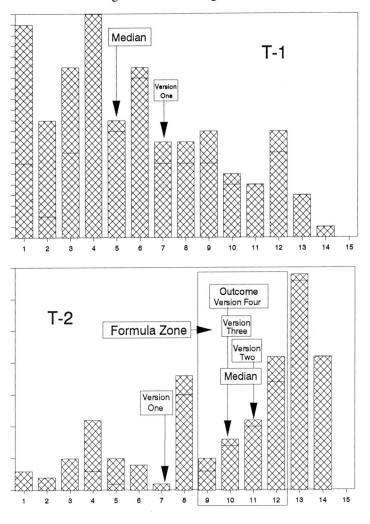

Figure 9.2:   Variations on the Classic Pattern

tions reflected in version 3 resulted in an outcome ("implied consent," at rank 10) which limited some of the circumstances under which coastal states could exercise the right to control access under the core-formula concept. To this day, this outcome remains controversial among the losers, even though the winners were willing to soften the blow by more conciliatory language in Phase III.

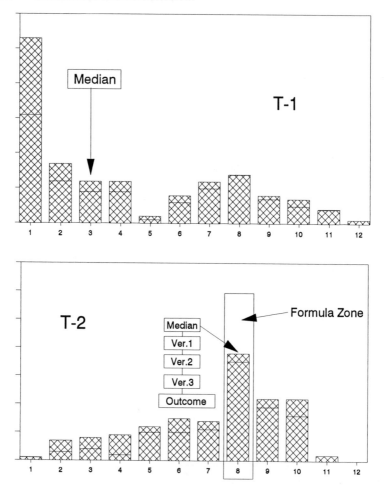

Figure 9.3:   Quick Resolution

Wide swings of preferences between T-1 and T-2 could at times be managed with much less controversy on other issues. On occasion, some issues
were resolved quickly and smoothly. An example that concerned the delimitation of the Exclusive Economic Zone is shown in figure 9.3. When
UNCLOS III began, the distribution was weakly bimodal. The forces represented at the low end of the spectrum seemed to have the situation well in
hand despite a relatively large but dispersed opposition. The median in T-1
indicated that they might hope they could lead an effort to refine the idea

represented at rank 3 into the core of the formula. However, their hopes were dashed quickly in a dramatic shift, early in T-2, to the opposing formula notion (rank 8). For all practical purposes, bargaining terminated once the core formula concept was identified. All versions of the negotiating text remained essentially the same. Refinement of language was not meaningful because the action required in this case was go/no go. The choice made here was to create a 200-mile Exclusive Economic Zone. By 1976, it was clear that a 200-mile EEZ would be part of the treaty, even though near-consensus had not been reached. Those states whose preferences fell into ranks 1–7 (the rearguard of Grotians) thought the conference had gone too far, those at ranks 9–11 complained that it had not gone far enough (the territorialists). They would have to be content with success on other issues in the package.

While quick convergence in the 200-mile EEZ effectively terminated later negotiations on the details of the issue, quick convergence can also lead to strenuous bargaining in Phase II, but over a narrow range, as can be seen below in figure 9.4. At the beginning of Phase I, distribution was already strongly unimodal with a small tail. This meant that there was no further serious negotiations on *what* the formula idea would be. However, in T-2 intense negotiations took place on *how* the formula idea would work. There were major swings over a narrow bargaining space, with version 1 of the negotiating text trying to split the difference, version 2 moving closer to the core idea, and version 3 and the Convention moving to accommodate the opposition. Compromise was necessary because, despite the median moving only from rank 12 (in T-1) to rank 11 in (T-2), opposition grew, as indicated by the thickening of the tail. Under a voting-decision system, states represented in the thickened tail would not be able to block or alter the will of the majority. But if decision could be taken only after maximum consultation, states finding themselves in the tail had to be offered an opportunity to make an idea they initially opposed palatable to themselves, or there could be no positive-sum outcome. Some observers claimed that a reasonable outcome had been negotiated by the dissenters in the detail phase on this issue (production controls on deep-seabed mining). But unanimity was never reached. The U.S. decided to defect, despite its representatives' vigorous (and perhaps successful before 1980) attempt to establish a numerical formula for production controls that was so generous to developed-state miners as to pose no financial threat to developing a successful mining venture.

For some observers of negotiation, a 50-percent solution to a bargaining problem is morally desirable. A 50-percent solution could be achieved by a convergence of both sides in incremental steps to a point where a perfect

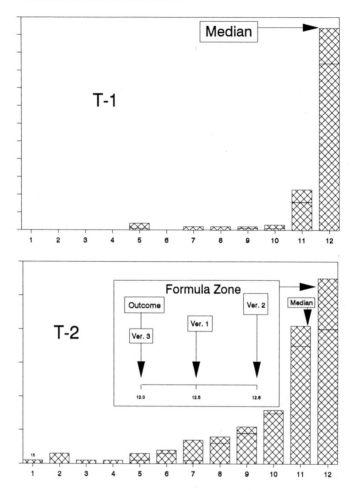

Figure 9.4:   Quick Formula/Intense Negotiations in a Narrow Range

compromise is identified which includes ideas from both sides in operation-
alizing the formula concept. That is, they discover a real new formula idea
composed of elements of both opening positions.

Did 50-percent solutions happen at UNCLOS III? Yes, but they were comparatively rare. When a seeming 50-percent solution showed up in the distributions, it often masked conflict, rather than reflecting a compromise
which combined the ideas of both sets of contestants. Even if a 50-percent
solution formula idea found its way into the Convention, it usually resulted in
an ineffective solution to the problem being negotiated. One is shown in fig-

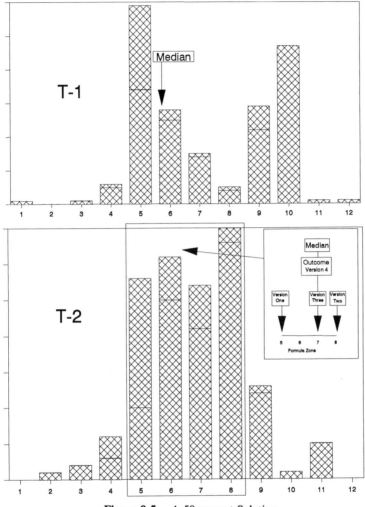

Figure 9.5: A 50-percent Solution

ure 9.5. It concerned *who* among coastal, port, or flag states would exercise jurisdiction over enforcement activities against vessel-source pollution of near-shore waters. This appears to have something for all participants. It begins (in T-1) with a bimodal distribution, or two strong camps of states with opposing candidates for the formula concept. The median indicates that one camp is stronger than the other, but the size of the weaker forces indicates a long, hard negotiation to find an acceptable outcome. At the beginning of T-2, there is convergence toward the center by supporters of both extremes, and the weight of support shifts slightly from the lower end of the spectrum to the higher end with a median shift from rank 6 to rank 7. But that shift is not reflected in the first SNT version of the provision on this issue (rank 5). It jumps to rank 8 in the second version of the negotiating document, and finally settles between the two at version 3, right on the T-2 median. The perfect compromise! However, when one looks at the substance of the issue, it was evident that there was insufficient support for a clear-cut solution empowering one or the other of the contending parties with exclusive jurisdiction. Therefore, all were empowered to exercise aspects of general jurisdiction in a formula which dissatisfied most participants—but equally. Nevertheless, it saved a number of faces and allowed the Conference to complete its work on the issue.

On most issues at UNCLOS III, negotiations began with either a lumpy or bimodal distribution in T-1 and moved to a single peaked distribution in T-2, with the anointed formula idea usually representing a compromised version of the core formula idea of one of the sides. Therefore, it was displayed in figure 9.5 on one side of the center-rank number. Convergence seemingly was accomplished in reasonably smooth increments in a narrow bargaining space.

In figure 9.6, we can see a different pattern, where there were wide swings in the candidate for the formula idea in Phase II before the Conference worked out its final language on the issue in Phase III. T-1 was trimodal, indicating that there was a possibility of a compromise outcome (the issue was rights and obligations in the conduct of ocean science in the International Area). By T-2, distribution had become more bimodal, but with two different types of opposing forces. One, centered at rank 2, were strong supporters of a particular outcome (in this case, no restrictions on the conduct of ocean science other than compliance with international environmental standards), while opponents opposed such freedom, but had not agreed upon what they considered to be appropriate restrictions. However, the first version of the SNT, prepared by the chair of the First Committee, would have required researchers to notify the International Seabed Agency (ISA) of their intention to conduct research in the International Area (rank 7). That did not last long. Version 2 swung all the way over to no restrictions (rank 1). Version 3 moved back toward the center (rank 5), where there would be some vague language concerning international cooperation on ocean science. The Convention moved one rank toward those who wanted to control ocean research, by empowering the ISA to coordinate and disseminate data concerning the Area (rank 6), but otherwise put no meaningful restrictions on the right to conduct

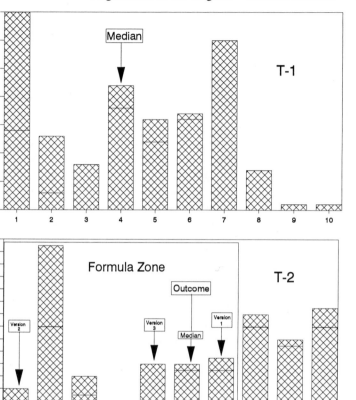

Figure 9.6: Swings in the Formula

research under the high seas. A compromise was found, probably because those who favored an outcome at ranks 1–2 in both time periods treated the issue as highly salient. A loss on the issue might have imperiled their willingness to accept the overall package. Although the forces that favored empowering the International Seabed Agency to potentially restrict the conduct of ocean science felt strongly about creating a powerful ISA, control of science was a less salient portion of their overall interest in seeing a NIEO-based ISA come into existence.

Rarely can a major issue in a multilateral negotiation be analyzed in isolation from other major issues. The very fact of multiple issues being decided in the same venue promotes trade-offs and packages.

A typical pattern in our analysis was the handling of an issue in a package that was acceptable to a large number of participants only because they gained something of greater value on other issues. Even at the time of decision, preferences of a substantial number of states did not converge much, although the issue (right of transit through straits used for international navigation) was brought to decision. The issue had been traded off. Figure 9.7 shows that distribution in T-1 was bimodal, with two strong peaks, one (ranks 11–18) somewhat stronger than the other (ranks 1–5). The median fell between them, indicating that neither side could win if the issue was forced to decision on its merits in the short run. Resolution appeared difficult. Each side was of roughly equal strength and preferred a formula that was anathema to the other side. Resolution came about only because of a trade-off—another issue was resolved in favor of the losers on this issue.

By T-2, there was a bit more convergence between sets of participants, but the gap between them remained. Other evidence indicated that a preference gap remained when the Convention was promulgated with the losers accepting their loss on this issue. From the beginning of T-2, each version of the negotiating document remains in the same place (rank 6) in a very narrow formula. The details were locked in when the basic principle of justice was enunciated. That was part of the price paid by those who preferred a favorable outcome on the other linked issues in the package.[25] Although there were attempts to reopen the issue or backslide during the later stages of the Conference, the deal held up. A successful attempt at backsliding on this issue probably would have unraveled the entire agreement.

Packages and Trade-offs

For the purpose of this study, issues on which trade-offs were arranged have been treated as components of packages. By definition, a trade-off occurs when a stakeholder accepts a less favorable outcome on one issue in return for other stakeholders conceding to it a more favorable outcome on another issue. Normally, the trade is made to gain a favorable outcome on a more salient issue. Issues that were the subject of trade-offs were often collected together as a package. Data are available to discern when a participating state was willing to accept a trade-off on a specific issue. Many of the analyses I supplied the U.S. Navy and the U.S. delegation concerned potential trade-offs by individual states, caucusing groups, and common-interest groups on specific

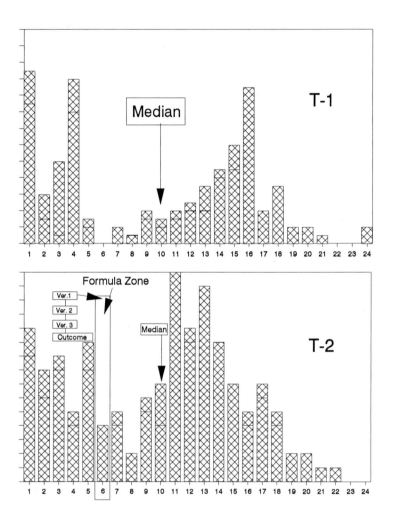

Figure 9.7: Trade-off

issues or small sets of issues. For present purposes, it would be too laborious to trace all known trade-offs. We will restrict ourselves to findings concerning the major packages. Communication among the many in a complex bargaining arena meant that eventually almost all trade-offs were collected into well-known packages. Some participants even claimed that underlying the entire negotiation was a giant package deal.

We will review findings concerning trade-offs and packages in five categories: (1) packages as a solution to the unanimity or near-unanimity requirement; (2) implicit and explicit components of packages; (3) timing, trade-offs, and packages; (4) packages and subpackages; and (5) packages and the notion of commitment in bargaining.

Packages as a Solution to the Unanimity Requirement   Figure 9.7 shows a typical issue traded-off after a number of rounds of negotiation. Although some convergence has taken place, it is not sufficient to indicate that the issue is likely to be resolved on its merits. If this issue were negotiated separately, it is unlikely that a solution would emerge. The most probable outcome would be mutual withdrawal or defection. Yet a solution was found. A trade-off was demanded by supporters of one formula concept on this issue because the issue was highly salient to them. In return, they conceded a favorable outcome on an issue of higher salience to the opponents on this issue. A package was worked out. It is not always necessary in parliamentary diplomacy to persuade others that your principle of justice is so superior that opponents must accept it. Nor is it necessary in Phase III to accept a significantly watered-down version of your formula notion. Unanimity or near-unanimity of preferences is not required, just unanimity or near-unanimity of willingness to accept a package, balancing out losses with gains.

The issue used for illustration is the question of the right of vessels to transit straits used for international navigation. It was resolved by packaging it together with delimitation of the territorial sea, and the creation of 200-mile Exclusive Economic Zones. The situation looked grim in Phase I, strongly bimodal on an emotionally charged issue. For some, transit by foreign vessels, especially military vessels, through straits near their coasts represented a violation of their sovereignty. For many, especially Third World states, approval of a *right* of transit was tantamount to approving gunboat diplomacy. Preferences changed little in Phase II. But supporters of a right to transit made acceptance of that right central to their willingness to accept the treaty as a whole. In return for acceptance of a right of transit at the beginning of Phase II, they indicated a willingness to accept the termination of Grotian rules on near-shore resources. They were willing to accept the idea of a 200-mile EEZ. In order to make the pill a bit easier for opponents of free transit to swallow, proponents were willing to make language changes. The right became known as "transit passage," but the detailed rules budged not at all in Phase III from their earliest formulation by proponents of free transit. They remained as formulated. Efforts were made late in the negotiation to reopen the transit passage issue, but they failed, and the key trade-offs in the best-known package of negotiation held up.

Explicit and Implicit Components of Packages   The value of precision or vagueness to a negotiator depends upon the tactical situation. This is also true of how precisely conflicting states have communicated with each other concerning whether an issue can be resolved at all, and whether it is to be resolved by being included in a package. Often a negotiator finds it tactically useful to be vague about a "commitment" to support all components of a package in order to keep his options open, but at some point all parties must understand what issues are in and what issues are out of a package, or a serious breakdown can ensue. This is one of the major lessons of UNCLOS III. Such a breakdown did occur.

The United States and other industrial states were explicit from the beginning about the nature of the package they were demanding. In 1973 and after, the U.S. specifically linked a favorable resolution of the straits and territorial-sea issues to its willingness to support a 200-mile EEZ. This was clearly communicated to all states and to the Conference leadership. Also from the beginning, Conference leaders, especially from Third World states, described the entire negotiation as a "package deal." However, the developed states who saw their issues accepted early as the core of the overall package never publicly acknowledged that they were committed to particular resolutions of other issues in the grand package. Whatever was said or implied in confidential negotiations between major developed-state representatives and Conference and Group of 77 leaders cannot be reconstructed. However, Conference and Group of 77 leaders thought they had an implicit commitment to their interpretation of the shape and content of the overall package. Late in the negotiations, when it seemed the United States might defect, various spokespersons for bargaining groups alleged that the U.S. was bound to an overall package deal because it did not withdraw earlier, before the overall package was arranged. That was, of course, an unenforceable claim.

Three possibilities exist as to whether there was an overall package with an agreed set of components. The first possibility is that no overall package deal existed. Its proponents invented it after the fact to justify their unwillingness to state openly what issues they expected would be traded off by opponents in their favor, because they feared it would cause opponents to defect. Proponents invoked the idea of a package deal but never really worked one out, therefore it did not exist. The second possibility is that the idea of an overall package deal was known and accepted, but that the required components existed only in the minds of the proponents of a particular interpretation of the package. Until the overall deal broke down, what each state or bargaining group expected to be in it, existed only in the mind of the beholder. The third possibility is that, because the package deal and its components were largely implicit, opponents of the most popular interpretation of what its necessary components were cynically remained silent about their unwillingness to commit themselves to such a package, and left the impression that they were committed to the deal. This created a situation of plausible deniability for themselves when they chose to defect.

I am inclined to believe the second possibility, that the components of the deal were only in the minds of the beholder. The entire negotiation depended upon a common understanding among the many delegations as to the nature of the package deal. It was not clarified until too late. As a result, not only did some major delegations defect, but those who were left holding the bag of the package they claimed had been agreed to were upset, and felt betrayed and abandoned. Implicit packages must be clarified and made explicit before a final deal can be worked out.

Timing of Trade-offs and Packages   Another important lesson relates to the timing of trade-offs and packages. Those who traded off to others early lost much of their leverage when it came time to insist that their opponents reciprocate. What they conceded was a done deal. What they wanted later in return they never got from their bargaining partners.

As we just saw, the United States and its friends announced early their willingness to trade off a 200-mile EEZ for a 12-mile territorial sea and a right of transit passage through straits. Whatever the preferred interpretation in the previous section on the nature of the components of the overall package, it was understood early on that the three issues—territorial sea, straits transit, and EEZ—were the core of the emerging package. The quarrel came about as to whether later the developed- and open-coast-state winners on the core package should concede, or even had conceded, adding the NIEO-based Part XI on arrangements for managing deep-seabed mineral resources to the existing issues in a new overall package. However, because of prolonged, intense bargaining over the formulas for the major issues in Part XI, the final shape of the concepts and language of Part XI did not emerge until the three-issue core of the package deal was so widely accepted that threats to deny states rights under these "negotiated" issues, unless they accepted Part XI, were useless as a threat to bring recalcitrant states aboard. States were already enjoying privileges on some of the core issues even before a formal treaty was signed. Many proponents of Part XI were beneficiaries under the new EEZ and territorial-sea provisions, and could not afford to cut off their nose to spite their face. In sum, early concessions on issues cannot be counted upon to create leverage to get later issues resolved.

Packages and Subpackages   Perhaps another reason for the inability of the Conference leaders to induce the United States and its industrial-state friends to accept Part XI is that there was no indication of trade-offs arranged on the seabed minerals issues *within* Part XI. Well-understood trade-offs within components of the overall package might have been useful. The creation of subpackages might have helped.

Part XI was the most contentious set of issues in UNCLOS III. Considerable convergence took place over the life of the negotiation between the contending parties on a number of these issues, and clearly recognized compromises were made by all sides. However, each of the issues was negotiated on its own merits. There is nothing in the record of the Conference to indicate that Conference leaders or representatives of the major caucusing groups viewed trading off as a viable tactic within the issues of Part XI. To be sure, after 1979, the financing of the Enterprise was linked to the financial terms of seabed-mining contracts.[26] But as important as those two issues were, they were narrow and technical, and the linkage was made late in the game. It might have been helpful to attempt early to establish a trade-off of one major issue highly desired by the major industrial states for another highly desired by the Group of 77. For example, access to seabed minerals under favorable terms by entities of the developed states might have been traded off for financial support for the International Seabed Agency (ISA) or the Enterprise, or tight production controls that would protect mineral-producing states might have been traded off for limiting the "arbitrary" power of an ISA Council.

Because of the nature of the issues, no one was willing to try trading off major issues within the seabed-minerals regime. Control of seabed minerals per se was of relatively less importance to the normative or ideological goals of the negotiators on both sides. The major aim of the Group of 77's leaders was acceptance of a formula sufficiently pure to demonstrate to the world how justly and efficiently a New International Economic Order system for exploiting the world's common resources could work. To leave open the possibility of undercutting the purity of the concept by a trade-off was anathema. They were met in kind by a new American President's representative who was just as determined to concede nothing to the NIEO and was looking for an opportunity to extol its presumed opposite—the free market.

Packages and Commitment in Bargaining   One of the most critical—and difficult—tasks of parliamentary diplomatic conference leaders is holding together willingness to continue negotiations on a package until consensus is reached, or maximum consultation exhausted. This is usually done on the presumption that the negotiators can and should hold to a commitment. However, for a number of reasons, the notion of commitment is a weak reed.

Putting together packages is notoriously time-consuming. The complexities of issues, and the large number of delegations who must interact—the very structure of the situation—means that if resolution does not come reasonably quickly, pressures build up to undo what was thought done. Even if the negotiators are persons of good will, their commitments are personal and their commitments as agents are not necessarily binding upon their principals. Over time, coalitions shift, and new coalition partners may make demands that require that their partners backslide on old commitments. New negotiators may replace trusted old friends and bring with them a new or different view of the state of the play on the components of the package. The external environment might change. What appeared to be a sensible trade-off under the old environmental conditions may not appear so sensible under new environmental conditions. Most important—at least for UNCLOS III—the governments sending delegations may change. They may have new goals and objectives. Their reservation price may differ from that of a previous administration. Time is critical to parliamentary diplomacy. Insufficient time to deal with the complexities leads to failure. But beyond a certain point, time becomes an enemy, since commitments made earlier may not hold up.

Behavior of Bargaining Groups

With more than 150 states participating in UNCLOS III, it was manifestly impossible to conduct the negotiation under a process whereby each state interacted directly with every other state on all 150 items on the List of Issues. A method was needed to help negotiators with reasonably common positions on certain issues bargain as a unit and confront other states organized into bargaining units. Aggregation was an important process in the large-scale multilateral negotiations. In this regard, parliamentary diplomacy takes on certain legislative attributes, and bargaining groups behave in a manner akin to political parties within legislatures.

The patterns of interactions among caucusing, common-interest, contact, mediation, and secret groups within UNCLOS III provide important data for understanding its outcome, and illustrate some generic attributes of the negotiating system. Below are shown findings concerning: (1) the behavior of the Group of 77; (2) the patterns, and therefore the meaning, of North–South confrontation; (3) the bargaining role of economic common-interest groups; (4) bargaining by groups representing the weak; and (5) the ability of states to protect their individual interests through their own group-bargaining efforts.

The Group of 77 at UNCLOS III   The title Group of 77 is a misnomer. It was established as the caucusing group of the then-77 developing states in the United Nations General Assembly. By 1967, when the informal preparations for UNCLOS III began, the group had more than 120 members, or well over two-thirds of the delegates participating in the Conference. It had an internal-consensus rule; no policy position could be adopted that was binding on the members of the group without all members reaching agreement. As with most consensus rules, this allowed the most intransigent to exercise disproportionate influence. To make solidarity on issues more difficult, G-77 was composed of subgroups—regional groups (Latin American, African, Asian) and common-interest groups (landlocked, geographically disadvantaged, etc.) with their own special interests on a number of the issues.

Some commentators have denied that the Group of 77 played a dominating role at UNCLOS III. For example, Ambassadors Koh and Jayakumar have noted that, though there was considerable Group of 77 solidarity on Committee I (deep-seabed) issues, the Group of 77 "was not very effective in taking a united stand on Committee II matters and was only moderately effective on Committee III matters."[27] While I believe the distinguished scholar-participants were correct about Committees I and II, I think they were wrong about Committee III. I believe they were measuring the influence of spokespersons in shaping the language of the Convention, not in measuring where most states stood on the issues.

What G-77 was able to do—given the size of its membership—was to create a presumption of dominance on issues where it took a stand. If the group's spokespersons stated a position, it had to be treated, in computer parlance, as the "default setting," the position to beat. If G-77 members supported a modal position, it was likely to be the core of the formula idea to be adopted. This often happened early in the negotiation. Later, when subgroups with particular interests that crossed caucusing-group lines began to press their interests, and compromise groups began to form, "mechanisms . . . for reconciling interests [began] to dominate . . . later stages of the negotiation."[28] At a later stage, many influential negotiators representing contact or mediation groups often had to deal with a solid South, which had to be persuaded to accept a somewhat watered-down version of their preferred formula idea. The Group of 77's standard deviations decreased from the first to the fourth time period on most issues, except those noted below, where solidarity either fractured, or group members did not consider the issues particularly salient.

The looming presence of a bargaining group as large and influential as the Group of 77 had a substantial impact on this parliamentary diplomatic negotiation. If it could maintain its solidarity on any given issue through Phase III of the Conference, there was no question that it would dominate the outcome. Getting it to move in a particular direction, inducing its members to accept a trade-off, or to accept compromise language that might vitiate its core formula idea, or driving a wedge between its subgroups so that a different formula idea might emerge victorious—these efforts took up much of the time of the Conference. The positions adopted by the Group of 77 did not always win, but they had a profound effect on framing the process of the negotiation.

UNCLOS III as a North–South Negotiation If the Group of 77 played a prominent role at the conference, was UNCLOS III a major North–South confrontation? Like a number of others, I have so characterized the negotiation, or at least a portion of it.[29] But those of us who emphasized the North–South aspects of the negotiation painted a picture of the Conference with brush strokes so broad that we can see only impressions. To refine the image, we need snapshots.

First, the bargaining alignment was North–South principally on those issues that were associated with New International Economic Order themes. Certain groups, especially the coastal Latin American and African states, were able to identify coastal issues as "South" issues, making enclosure measures attractive to South states because such measures drove developed researchers or fishermen further away from their coasts. The question of whether to require consent or allow freedom to conduct research in the new Exclusive Economic Zone was almost exclusively a North–South issue until after 1978, when a number of developed states were willing to accede to a consent regime. Most major fishing issues, especially those that conceded jurisdiction over fisheries to coastal states, garnered solid Southern support, but did not have to face solid Northern opposition.

Most issues in Committee I (Part XI) were framed as North–South issues. These included whether to characterize the deep-ocean regime as a common-heritage regime, whether to allow private and state economic institutions direct access to the minerals of the Area, whether to impose production controls upon minerals extracted from the deep seabed, and what would be the composition and decision rules of principal decision organ of the International Seabed Authority.

However, as the negotiations evolved over time, on many issues North–South confrontation came to mean a solid South versus a fractured North (the major industrial states). The Landlocked/Geographically Disadvantaged did not fragment Southern cohesion, but some North delegations (European,

Scandinavian, or Canadian) either because of sympathy to South positions or because they were attempting to play a mediating role, broke Northern solidarity. Even on the quintessential North–South issues of Part XI, the lineup was the South, its friends, sympathizers, and states trying to play a bridging role versus the major industrial states.

On one issue, the North (and East) was solid, and the South suffered internal dissension. That was the issue of the territorial sea, where a number of developed and developing states found it in their interest to support a moderate (12-mile) uniform territorial sea, while the 200-mile territorialists tried and failed to rally major Southern support for an extensive territorial sea.

The principal lineup on a number of other major issues, particular those under the jurisdiction of Committee II, was not driven strongly by North–South considerations. The question of straits used for international navigation, for example, was essentially a superpower issue. Virtually no group measured had a coherent position on straits transit. On the EEZ, the Latin Americans, Africans, and margineers were strongly united, but it was not a North–South lineup. The delimitation of the continental shelf was driven by geographic and geological interests. Nor was vessel-source pollution North–South in orientation.

Economic Common-Interest Groups   Some observers point out that many economically based common-interest groups were effective in influencing UNCLOS III outcomes on issues which united their members.[30] Our data generally confirm these observations. Economically based common-interest groups, particularly those who shared geographical characteristics, were effective in promoting changes in the existing rules of the sea. Those economically based groups which attempted to defend the existing rules mostly failed to advance their interests, for example, distant-fishing states.

Territorialists, coastal states, and archipelago states were effective on Committee II issues, often pushing the Conference toward adoption of enclosure measures (EEZ, fishing, etc.). One conspicuously successful common-interest group on the issue of the delimitation of the legal continental shelf was the margineers' group. They were able to convince a majority of states that had either no margin (because they had no seacoast), or a narrow margin, to allow broad-margin states to claim seabed jurisdiction out to 350 miles. In the rush toward enclosure, some groups not benefitting particularly by enclosure were not able to stop it, but were effective in slowing it down or mitigating its effects. For example, the shelf-locked states forced broad-coast states to concede that shelf-locked-state fishermen might have access to "surplus" stocks in EEZs. Whether this will turn out to be a cosmetic gesture or a meaningful concession will be learned only in the implementation stage. Finally, on one key issue, all major groups, caucusing as well as common-interest, splintered. A key barrier to a treaty was removed and the necessary trade-off arranged. Transit passage through straits used for international navigation was achieved because groups with an interest in restricting navigation were not effective in preventing the superpowers from having their way.

Groups Representing the Weak   Despite the egalitarian rhetoric that permeated the negotiations, especially during sessions that concerned North–South issues, groups representing the economically weak fared poorly at UNCLOS III. They had nothing to sell but their votes, and they got a very poor return for their willingness not to disrupt the process of consensus formation.

Poverty is highly correlated with geography, especially among the developing landlocked states. While their allies among the developed landlocked and the shelf-locked states often were economically more affluent, all members of the LL/GDS Group, the quintessential group representing the weak at UNCLOS III, recognized that enclosure by open-ocean coastal states of their near-shore waters would make them worse off. For the landlocked and shelf-locked, it might make access to the sea more difficult. It might isolate them further from the major oceanic trade routes. If open-ocean coastal states put wide swaths of potentially valuable oceanic territory under their national jurisdiction, those without large offshore areas that could be reduced to 200-mile EEZs would be made relatively worse off.

LL/GDS members shared a common interest in stopping or significantly slowing down enclosure, or at least in making their coastal neighbors compensate them in some way, so that the gap between them did not grow wider. Unfortunately for LL/GDS members, they had to turn to an international forum to counterbalance real-world weakness that all negotiators recognized. If their coastal neighbors chose to make a unilateral claim, LL/GDS members could not stop them. Although, under international law,[31] landlocked states had a right of access to the sea, their coastal neighbors could have sharply reduced the value of that right by harassing tactics, even if such tactics were legally dubious.

Nevertheless, in terms of numbers, LL/GDS should have been a formidable force at UNCLOS III. The group had 55 members (28 landlocked states; 27 shelf-locked states). Even without alliances with other groups, LL/GDS alone had a blocking one-third. There was also a chance of a strategic alliance with the major groups representing the developed states. Both groups had sentimental and practical reasons for favoring Grotian solutions to ocean problems. If such an alliance had been worked out and the members had proved disciplined, the combined forces would have been impressive indeed—over 75 members or half of the 150 delegations at the Conference. Such an alliance was explored by some of the developed states in Phase I, but it never emerged.[32]

There were two principal reasons why an alliance of the weak and the strong against those in the middle never emerged. First, weak and strong realized that the best result that could be expected from such an alliance was a spoiling strategy, that, by itself, the alliance could not have produced a convention that had a chance of adoption. It might have stopped enclosure, but to what purpose? Its goal would have been negative. The basic reason to negotiate in the first place was that problems were getting out of hand under the existing regime and needed to be addressed by the affected parties.

Second, states within both groups were cross-pressured by their other affiliations.[33] Cross-cutting cleavages were particularly strong for states that were LL/GDS and also members of the Group of 77 and its subgroups, especially the African group. As a result, an alliance between LL/GDS and developed groups did not emerge and LL/GDS members found it difficult even to threaten to defect from the positions espoused by the other groups with which they were affiliated. They simply did not present a credible threat.

The consequence to LL/GDS members was that, in terms of major substantive provisions of the UNCLOS III Convention, they benefited least of all the major bargaining groups. Their coastal neighbors bought off LL/GDS acquiescence in the creation of the 200-mile EEZ, with a promise of allowing them "to participate, on an equitable basis, in the exploitation of an appropriate part of the surplus of the living resources" of the EEZ (Articles 69, 70). Of course, it is the coastal state that determines whether a surplus exists. Perhaps if coastal states do not declare surpluses of living resources, LL/GDS states can make themselves wealthier through their assured participation (Articles 140, 148) in the exploitation of deep-seabed minerals. Unfortunately, the guarantees to LL/GDS will not provide many benefits unless Part XI is fully implemented, and that is uncertain.

Individual States Protecting Their Own Interests in a Group-Bargaining Environment   In a bargaining arena where states are often constrained to act through groups, or particular negotiators who claim to represent groups are obligated not to go beyond the group mandate, it is very difficult to determine how effectively a negotiator has been in representing his or her principal (state). Despite the ultimate one state–one vote formula used to confirm the bargains made, which should argue for equal potency in affecting outcome, some individuals and delegations clearly had more influence on the outcome of key issues than others. Notwithstanding its parliamentary trappings, UNCLOS III was a negotiation. The data collected for this project are not appropriate for definitively answering the question of how independent or how constrained delegates were in protecting their own national interests. Other researchers, using interviews of the delegates as a major research tool, are in a better position to illuminate the question.[34] They focus upon whether delegates succeeded in influencing the outcome on specific issues because of the political power of the state pushing a provision (a structural argument), or because of a given delegate's forceful personality or clever tactics.

Yet the data show movement over time, and often convergence on issues. Data collected included information not merely about what a state wanted, but about the salience of each issue in relation to the other. Data showed that most major states were not forced by the parliamentary diplomatic process to accept an outcome they considered anathema on an issue of high salience, unless they suffered internal cross-cutting cleavages on the issue. In sum, most states protected their interests quite effectively at UNCLOS III.

The United States was deeply suspicious of the parliamentary diplomatic process and, given a choice, would have preferred to deal with each set of major issues separately. It was obvious that, operating within a parliamentary diplomatic setting, its superpower status would be less than fully respected. Yet, though some observers rated the United States influential at UNCLOS III and others rated it less effective than it might have been, it achieved acceptable outcomes on most major issues where it made its demands clear. It did not manage to get effective measures in the treaty to eliminate or reduce coastal-state control over highly migratory species within the 200-mile EEZ, but its multiplicity of fishing interests left it with domestic cross-cutting cleavages. It failed on freedom of ocean science in the EEZ, but the issue was less salient than its articulate scientific proponents proclaimed. Finally, through much of the negotiation, the United States conveyed the impression to others that the issue of deep-seabed minerals was not as salient as those of security and near-shore economic control. Hence, the U.S. was less successful in convincing others that its preferred formula must become the core of the regime. The new Reagan Administration announced to the world that it was altering the salience of the seabed-minerals issue, making it at least as salient as security and near-shore control, and perhaps more so. But it was too late to convince others of its seriousness, and therefore the U.S. chose to defect.

While major states, especially superpowers, had to be concerned with the general shape of the Convention, smaller states were freer to concentrate upon issues that were of interest mainly, perhaps idiosyncratically, to themselves. This is consistent with findings derived from other negotiations.[35] Canada was an example of a state which claimed great success in protecting its interests at UNCLOS III. Almost all observers identified Canadian Ambassador Alan Beesley as an influential negotiator. Canada played a role in attempting to bridge differences between developed and developing states on several issues.[36] Canada also relentlessly pursued its own interests on fisheries, and especially environmental, issues. It was to placate Canada that Article 234, giving coastal states that had ice-covered areas (read Canada and a few other states) special rights to control marine pollution. But even Canada did not get all it wanted. For example, it was not successful on the question of exclusive coastal-state control of vessel-source pollution.

Leadership, Parliamentary Organization, and Bargaining

Both formal and informal organization play an important role in shaping the outcome of a parliamentary diplomatic interaction. Formal leaders are elected under the rules of procedure, and informal leaders emerge from the process of interaction. Both play leadership roles, but often of a different nature. Formal leaders are officially responsible for moving the proceedings to an outcome, and were, among other things, the traffic police at UNCLOS III, controlling the debate, appointing working-group leaders and participants, interacting with important formal groups such as the Drafting Committee, controlling many of the informal interactions, supervising the drafting of the Single Negotiating Text at several stages, and deciding when the time was ripe to declare consensus, or put the final version of the SNT to a vote.[37]

A sina qua non of successful leadership is trust; trust in the fair-mindedness, integrity, and competence of the leaders. At the same time, it cannot be expected that formal leaders in a parliamentary diplomatic negotiation will be neutral. They cannot be; they remain representatives of the governments which sent them, and must operate under their instructions. However, if they too clearly favor outcomes acceptable to their states or groups, they will encourage defection. Considerable powers of decision were granted to Conference leaders—president, main committee chairs, and specialized committee chairs. None was more important than the power granted a main committee chair to judge whether the issues under his jurisdiction had reached a point where the direction of consensus was reasonably clear, or whether he had to exercise his prerogative and show his fellow delegates where consensus might be reached.

On the whole UNCLOS III was blessed with fair-minded, competent, and continuous formal leadership from the days of the Ad Hoc Committee to the end of the Conference. The two Conference presidents—Hamilton Shirley Amerasinghe (Sri Lanka) and Tommy T. B. Koh (Singapore)—have received almost universal praise for their contributions to the outcome of the Conference. The record of the main committee chairs was more mixed. Alexander Yankov (Bulgaria) was well regarded, but as our data showed, some of his tactical moves, such as proposing "notification" to the coastal state as a requirement for researchers to do work in the 200-mile EEZ, did not succeed. But he did move negotiations along and did not lose the trust of his fellow delegates.

Another main committee chair did, however, lose the trust of some important fellow delegates. In the view of some major developed states, Ambassador Paul Engo (Cameroons), chair of the First Committee, went beyond his expected role several times. He rejected as "negotiated" some articles produced by a working group headed by Ambassador Christopher Pinto (Sri Lanka) in the Third Session (1975),[38] and at the Sixth Session (1977) altered a text negotiated in a working group chaired by Ambassador Jens Evensen (Norway) before it was incorporated into the ICNT.[39] While it is understandable that Engo might have been under pressure from his caucusing group to reject compromise texts and revert to the core Group of 77 position, his behavior legitimized some of the developed states' objections to Part XI of the Convention.

Informal leadership at UNCLOS III was often mediatory in intent. That is, an important delegate, well trusted by opposing sides on a particular issue, might have others turn to him to bridge the gap between conflicting groups. He might be asked to introduce an idea or proposal that, whatever its substantive merit, might be rejected out of hand if the originating delegation were to introduce it. He was often expected to introduce proposals or language bringing opposing sides closer together. The requirement that consensus or near-consensus be reached before action increased the importance at UNCLOS III of delegates who could play a bridging role. Some individuals played significant roles principally because of their personal attributes. They were known as talented mediators, and they could be trusted. Evensen and Pinto were among that elite group. Others were trusted to mediate not only because of their personal attributes, but also because their delegations had a history of mediating between, for example, rich and poor, large and small. Canada, for example, prided itself on playing such a role.[40] Despite the willingness of others to trust mediators, they too were representatives of their sovereign states, they too had national as well as personal goals. That they were not neutral at UNCLOS III is quite consistent with findings from other negotiations.[41]

Leadership can have an impact upon a negotiation, even if the leader is not a major inside player in the negotiation. An outsider can intervene to play the role of "rule manipulator," someone who can "modify the rules of the game."[42] This was done at least once in UNCLOS III, and resulted in a material impact on the outcome. When the negotiation over Part XI got bogged down over whether the Enterprise would be allowed a monopoly of access to the deep seabed, or whether access to deep-seabed resources would be granted to private enterprises or state corporations, a proposal was needed to break the impasse. U.S. Secretary of State Henry Kissinger personally attended the Fourth Session of the Conference and, on April 8, 1976, proposed the idea of the "banking" or parallel system. After prospecting, an ocean miner would nominate two areas of supposedly equal value for exploitation. It would be granted one, and the other would be banked away for the future exclusive use of the Enterprise. Kissinger also assured delegates that sufficient funds would be found to allow an International Seabed Agency and Authority come into existence. While the banking system found its way into the Convention, Secretary Kissinger did not convince his successors in the next Republican Administration that his scheme would work.

Tactics in Parliamentary Diplomacy
The abundant complexities of the parliamentary diplomatic process, the considerable time needed to interact, and the heterogeneity of the stakeholders and stakes created an environment rich with tactical possibilities. At best, we can only sample a small set of the available tactical moves that had an impact upon the outcome of UNCLOS III.

Many observer-participants emphasize the importance of personality and clever tactics that, in their view, helped some delegate win the day for his or her principal. This is to be expected, given their positions within the day-to-day cut and thrust of diplomatic interactions. This analysis proceeds from a different type of data, and therefore accords somewhat less importance to clever tactics in molding the overall outcome. The success of tactics depends significantly upon whether the move attempted was based upon a correct perception of the overall stategic situation and the stage of the negotiation. Under some circumstances, issues will be ripe for decision. Under others, the same tactics will fail completely.

Many of the most important decisions that set the tone for the negotiation were taken in national capitals, and were therefore exogenous to the negotiation. For example, a change in the perception of major industrial states of their national interests before the first substantive session in Caracas in 1974 paved the way for the emergence of the basic package of a 12-mile territorial sea, a right of transit through straits used for international navigation, and the creation of the exclusive economic zone. Up to that point, there was a possibility that the major industrial states would rigidly defend Grotian positions on the territorial sea (3 miles), and therefore would not need a new right of transit passage and would not consent to the creation of a zone which extended coastal-state economic rights out to 200 miles. They made the switch as much because they were cross-pressured by some increasingly strong internal stakeholders who were not well served by the traditional policies as because a switch would lead to tactical advantage.

Whatever the cause, the effect on the negotiation was profound. The basic package was assembled fairly quickly, and the core of the future treaty was set. Without such a switch, it is very likely that UNCLOS III would have been short and unproductive. No delegate had to twist the arms of industrial state delegates or outmaneuver them. If there remained important North-South clashes in portions of the future negotiation, they were relatively minor compared to what might have happened if the developed states abandoned enclosure or continued to support Grotian positions on commons problems important to the developing states.

The failure to reach consensus (viewed as the agreement of all) at the end of the negotiation was also exogenous, and no endogenous maneuvering had any impact. A new Administration came into office in the United States in 1981. Despite the efforts of "pragmatists" on the U.S. delegation, the willingness of the Group of 77 to entertain some changes, and the efforts of a compromise group (the Group of 11), the delegation's "ideologues" and their masters in the new Administration were determined to defect, and so the United States did.

On the other hand, there were important instances of endogenous efforts at resisting exogenous pressures to shape the negotiation. A number of tactical attempts were made to dictate or shape outcomes, most notably by the United States. They failed. The first was when the U.S. Congress considered domestic ocean-mining legislation, supposedly as a means of forcing G-77 to retreat or be "more reasonable." It only led to the hardening of the group's position. The second was the promulgation of the Green Book, which made it appear that the United States was no longer willing to negotiate sincerely, and was demanding surrender. In any case, the Green Book was not taken seriously as a negotiating document.

Tactics and Formula   For success, tactics in the final two phases of a multilateral negotiation must be tied to a formula. Once a formula idea has been identified as the leading candidate for inclusion in a convention, then the range of tactical devices that might be attempted is limited. Threats of defection are not usually a useful tactic, except late in a negotiation, and only on the most important issues. A delegate can push an idea in the last two phases of a negotiation that is a rival to a leading formula candidate, but this is usually not productive. By Phase II, the core idea or principal of justice that will prevail on an issue is well known. Tactics must relate to refining or modifying the leading formula idea. Depending upon which side is engaged in tactical maneuvers, the object of the tactics must be to defend the integrity of the core idea, or to modify it so that it is livable, or if the proposers are very clear, to undermine it to the point where it becomes a hollow shell that does not mean what its proponents hoped.

Concession-making is an integral part of the tactical maneuvering of parliamentary diplomacy. Bargainers in UNCLOS III usually did not expect a tit-for-tat rate of concession. Nor did they necessarily require that the other side move an equal distance (as measured on our conflict-issue scales) from their previous position to a new position. Convergence was not linear or symmetrical. But a response—a quid pro quo—was necessary from the second party, after the first party offered a concession in order to keep the negotiations moving.

The most important concessions were (1) the concession by the minority that their formula candidate was not viable and (2) the concession by the majority that their formula candidate could not get into the final agreement without modification. For those who did not favor the winning formula idea, the latter portions of the negotiation had to be approached tactically as a form of damage control. They had to peck away at the formula concept with exceptions to the rule, loopholes, time limitations, weak allocation or implementation provisions, narrowing the circumstances under which the formula concept could be invoked. The nature of the moves open to them were familiar to experienced negotiators. In addition to creativity needed to invent various potential outs, negotiators not favoring a formula idea also needed judgment—concerning whether the outs they invented would be effective in the implementation phase, and how far they could tactically push negotiators trying to preserve the formula's effectiveness in addressing the underlying problem.

On the other side, supporters of a formula had to work tactically to prevent its emasculation, but make sufficient concessions to indicate to opponents that the latter could live with it. The tactics appropriate here had to be approached with equal delicacy. How far could they push a minority to accept a formula before the minority would defect? Much of this took place in Phase III, where the details of the agreement were worked out and were often expressed as subtle changes in language. Nevertheless, they represented meaningful concessions when they worked.

Sometimes concessions worked because they were worded so fuzzily that some negotiators could make themselves believe that they had not been forced to make a meaningful concession in accepting certain language. Creative ambiguity was used frequently in UNCLOS III to avoid making decisions that would indicate clearly who were the winners, and who were the losers on a particular issue. The price in dealing with the consequences, of course, is not usually paid by the negotiator. Most often someone else in the implementation or interpretation phases must cope with the problems caused by not understanding the rights and obligations supposedly agreed to. Still, fuzzy language helped produce agreement among the many on negotiating text and draft treaty. But a new generation of interpreters will have much work to do, among others, in sorting out who was meant to have access to the resources of the deep seabed, how opposite and adjacent states will resolve overlapping claims, who among the several claimants to jurisdiction—coastal, port, or flag state—will enforce the rules on vessel-source pollution, and which of the several alternative specifications a state should use to define the outer limit of its legal continental shelf for a maximum legitimate claim.

Consensus or maximum consultation before decision made stonewalling a useful short-run tactic for important individual states and groups in UNCLOS III. With their cooperation deemed essential to a bargained outcome, and no time limit on interactions, the rule of maximum consultation gave losers considerable leverage in a parliamentary diplomatic negotiation provided the minority was weak only in numbers and not in real-world capability to undo the effect of a paper victory by the majority. It paid to be relatively obstinate at UNCLOS III if you represented a major state or a strong bargaining group. Even if you shared the desire to see a positive outcome and were willing to accept a formula notion proposed by others, it made sense to give ground slowly, waiting for maximum concessions.

On the other hand, those weak in real-world capabilities did not find intransigence a particularly useful tactic. If a state or group could be safely ignored on a particular problem in the outside world, it was dismissed as relatively insignificant within the negotiation, despite having a claimed number of votes at its command. This was the fate of the LL/GDS Group at the hands of the Group of 77 and major developed states. However, face-saving gestures were often used to mask the degree of loss by losers. In effect, LL/GDS, for example, was bought off by assuring them a place in the deep-seabed mining system and a right to fish for the surplus in the EEZs of their coastal neighbors. Unfortunately for them, the price paid to buy them off is not likely to be significant.

At times, tactics used displayed considerable creativity. For example, the idea of a 200-mile EEZ that was sui generis was a creative solution to a difficult problem. An EEZ per se implies just another zonal concept for enclosing the oceans and granting sovereignty to the coastal state. Although the title indicates that the coastal state's rights are exclusive, proponents used the tactic of splitting the idea of general jurisdiction into a set of separable rights, and granted only some of them to the coastal state, retaining others for all potential users in the international community. As negotiated, the coastal state is "sovereign" over resources, but has less than sovereign rights to control the movement of others through the EEZ or to make use of the zone for other purposes (e.g., cable laying). It was an ingenious solution to what might have been an insoluble problem if pure enclosure had been attempted.

With one major exception, the use of rational persuasion as a tactic was rarely attempted after Phase I. No doubt the informational value of various national statements during Phase I's sorting out did help persuade some delegations to alter their positions on some issues, particularly those which were unfamiliar or not highly salient. However, there were clear limits to such persuasions. It was unlikely that a state would be persuaded by a rational argument even on a relatively unfamiliar issue that forced it to adopt a position which did not accord with its known general values, or which pushed it away from the positions of states with whom it normally agreed, cooperated, or caucused. One such attempt was made—to persuade states that a market system rather than a command system for managing the resources of the deep seabed should be adopted—but it failed.

Much more successful was the use of a model—a tool of rational analysis—in bringing to a successful conclusion the negotiations on the financial arrangements relating to financial terms of deep-seabed mining contracts and the financing of the Enterprise. Detailed discussions on these subjects did not begin until 1977 in New York (Sixth Session), but earlier debate made it clear that opinions on the subject would strongly divide on North–South lines. Developing-state representatives believed ocean mining was going to be so profitable that hefty front-end payments from private miners could fund ISA and the Enterprise, while developed-state representatives feared such front-end payments would inevitably make ocean mining unprofitable.

Before the participants got locked in on expected lines, Ambassador Tommy Koh, then chair of Negotiating Group 2, discovered a cost model developed at the Massachusetts Institute of Technology. Although developed by academics from a superpower under a government grant, it had all the trappings of objectivity and certainty. Through the use of its forecasts, both sides were able to back down from a confrontational position. The model and the modelers played a mediating role. This effort was so successful that, even though the United States attempted to rewrite virtually all of Part XI, it left the financial arrangements actually negotiated intact in the Green Book. It is difficult to determine whether the delegates "learned" or used an available rational choice mechanism to get themselves out of a situation which, if maintained, would have led to failure. They got themselves off the hook: "allegedly superior information or analysis allowed relatively costless movement from entrenched positions."[43]

Ideology, Symbolism, and Incremental Bargaining

If the core of a formula is a "principle of justice," all matters that are negotiated have an ideological content. Interactions over ideology are inherent in political bargaining, UNCLOS III included, since all participants expressed their ideologies in the rules they wanted binding on all parties. This is to be expected and, of itself, should not raise a concern about the role of ideology at UNCLOS III. But many commentators have attempted to show that much of the maneuvering at the Conference was not intended to work out a solution that would meet the requirements of all parties, but rather to impose, if possible, an ideologically loaded solution upon the reluctant. If that proved not to be feasible, negotiating for effect—to keep their concepts and symbols pure but visible, and to use the opportunity to create propaganda in favor of their cherished idea without hope of a formal negotiated outcome— was the goal of those inclined to engage in what Johan Galtung called "expressive behavior."[44] Hortatory language is not congruent with bargaining language, and hortatory language was much in evidence at UNCLOS III.[45]

If we view ideology not as a specific concept but as a passionate commitment of intellect and feeling about a preferred concept, we can better understand the impact of ideology on UNCLOS III.[46] We define ideologues as those who are rigid in the defense of *their* principle, or are very reluctant to have their principle vitiated by compromise. At UNCLOS III, they demanded surrender by opponents to their unmodified formula. It made sense to them because, in their view, their conceptual framework represented a total mode of thought[47] and it had a monopoly on the truth. In sum, we view ideology as rigidity in defense of an conceptual idea, not as the idea itself.

The demand by one stakeholder or group of stakeholders that their opposite numbers accept their total framework intact or virtually intact creates a very difficult environment in which to negotiate seriously. Until late in the negotiation, that is precisely how the radicals among the Group of 77 approached the bargaining over many of the issues in Part XI. In turn, after the election of the Reagan Administration, the United States viewed its conceptual framework with passion and refused to accept anything but its maximum demands.

In both cases, this raises the question of the appropriateness and effectiveness of using the tactic of incremental concessions on details to reach a mutually acceptable outcome in the face of an all-out ideological assault. The underlying assumption of incremental concessions is that passion can be overcome by careful step-by-step work; that the commitment of the other side is merely rhetorical; and that the principle can be "circumscribed with precise language."[48] Elliot Richardson and Lee Ratiner, head and deputy head at various times of the United States delegation, believed that incrementalism was an appropriate tactic, and they pursued vigorously an attempt to get G-77 leaders to adopt more "realistic" positions on matters of detail. In their views, success was almost achieved, and indeed, they might well have succeeded if not sabotaged by their masters. On a number of Part XI issues, provisions were negotiated that could be characterized as positive sum: the parallel or "banking" system, financial terms, reasonable rates under production controls, and even representation and decision-making in the ISA Council.[49]

Unfortunately, passion begets passion. By the time there were indicators that the radicals in the Group of 77 could be persuaded to go along with incremental modifications that circumscribed the purity of a NIEO-based regime, the newly elected U.S. President ordered an 18-month hiatus in U.S. participation at UNCLOS III, while new domestic decision-makers studied the issues, and the U.S. delegation returned to the negotiation with their new demands specified in the Green Book.

As all delegates quickly understood, the Green Book was not a negotiating document in the sense that it took the last version of the negotiating text as its basis and demanded modifications of various provisions. During the period of study, and during the Tenth Session, there was an internal fight between realists and ideologues within the U.S. delegation. The ideologues won, and as a result, the United States refused to negotiate incrementally. The Green Book attempted to begin the Part XI negotiations over again. The U.S. demanded a market-based outcome on all major issues.

If the United States intended to encourage incremental concessions, it chose the wrong tactic. However, it is doubtful that such was the intent of its last head of delegation. If he could not get surrender, he preferred defection and a treaty created under conditions of near-consensus. As the U.S. discovered, it could be a free rider and accept the treaty's benefits without accepting its liabilities.

Is it always wrong to attempt to handle an ideologically based assault with an incremental response and hope that patience and balancing "emotions with reason" will be the best approach for creating positive sum outcomes?[50] Like so many aspects of the UNCLOS III negotiation that almost succeeded, the near-success of the Richardson approach leaves the matter in limbo. It would be equally plausible to characterize such an approach as risky, and probably fruitless.

Influence of the Type of Issue on the Probable Outcome

The process by which negotiators interact is influenced by the type of issues over which they interact. If issues, as understood by negotiators, allow relatively easy division of the benefits, then the process will reflect that attribute. If they require a high degree of cooperation among the participants to beat a "prisoner's dilemma" inherent in the nature of the issue, then the process is likely to be different, and much more difficult to accomplish.[51]

UNCLOS III experienced both types of issues. The first led through distributional bargaining to its greatest successes, the second led through integrative bargaining to its greatest failure, or as some would insist, its greatest near-success.[52]

Several issues—particularly those associated with enclosure, in which an open-coast state would gain substantial rights over an extensive stretch of waters and an extensive set of economic rights—could be treated in zero-sum fashion if almost all open-coast states behaved similarly, based on geographic attributes and less influenced by cross-cutting obligations of previous legal theory (e.g., Grotianism) or obligations to other groups and associations. They would gain extensive new rights at the expense of other claimants who previously exercised rights within 200 miles of coastal regions under the notion of freedom of the seas. Some bargaining moves associated with integrative negotiations were helpful in resolving issues associated with enclosure, such as packaging, compensation to losing parties, and bridging or inventing new options that satisfied all or most parties' major concerns (e.g., transit passage rather than freedom of transit). But these integrative tactical moves were the final elements necessary to allow a division of a rather fixed pie.[53]

On issues that were resolved by distributional outcomes, the participating states were their own best clients. They were acting on their own behalf more than merely as agents for internal stakeholders. Many of these issues related to the allocation of authority in the international system; they were primarily jurisdictional in nature. They resolved the question of which institution in the international system could exercise jurisdiction over a particular ocean area or function. In turn, if jurisdiction was conveyed, the conveying party had the right to allocate access to wealth or wealth-creating activities. Most issues that were resolved successfully primarily involved "power-conferring rules."[54]

At UNCLOS III, participants allowed coastal states to arrogate to themselves jurisdiction over more extensive territorial seas, legal continental shelves (physical continental margins), 200-mile exclusive economic zones, anadromous fish, and a right to permit certain activities such as the conduct of ocean science with the 200-mile EEZ only with their consent. Once the idea at the core of the enclosure formula was identified, there was little doubt *whether* the issue would be resolved. In Phase III, there was considerable bargaining to determine *how* the idea would be operationalized, but what the general rule would be was not in doubt. Enclosure was an idea whose time had come as the core of the formulas worked out at UNCLOS III on near-shore problems.[55] A distributive outcome could not be prevented because coastal states had the technology, military and policing resources to "effectively occupy." They were more capable of managing the resources under a territorially based claim than the claimants who wandered in and asserted rights under freedom of the seas. Hopefully, managing the most valuable areas of the oceans territorially will allow the winners, while reducing or excluding other claimants, most notably distant-water fishermen, landlocked, and to a lesser extent, shelf-locked states, to reduce the abuses that occurred on the formerly unowned commons. But it will not be an "equitable" solution. This is one reason the "father of the Law of the Sea Conference," Arvid Pardo, repudiated his child.[56]

For an effective as well as equitable solution to the issues associated with ownership of the resources of the deep seabed, management of their exploitation, and how as well as who will have a right of access to exploit them, an integrative outcome was necessary. The pie had to be larger before it was divided, or it wouldn't work. Unfortunately, the issue was seen, from the beginning of U.N. consideration in 1967, as a testing ground for theories of economic equity and efficiency between North and South. Consequently, the proposals put forth exemplifying market and command rules seemed to be mutually exclusive, and incapable of being blended through negotiation. Market supporters such as the United States were extremely suspicious of command-based proposals that the Third World and its friends put forth as their formula candidates. As a result, although the U.S. and other market supporters were willing to use some of the tools of integrative bargaining that led to joint benefits, they moved slowly. This exploration was principally associated with Elliot Richardson and ceased with his resignation as head of the U.S. delegation and with the election of a new President. Reagan's ideologues preferred defection.

In turn, there was firm unwillingness on the part of the Group of 77 to seriously entertain exploitation rules that would have allowed private firms and states corporations access to deep-seabed resources until they were convinced they could not realize their NIEO-based scheme without some compromise. They did not have the real-world capability to operate a seabed exploitation scheme without the cooperation of the developed states, nor did they have the assets to "effectively occupy" the deep seabed against unilateral claims. This is despite indications early in the negotiation, that if deep-seabed mineral exploitation were permitted under rules proposed in the Nixon Draft Seabed Treaty (1970), and national jurisdiction ended at 200 meters depth of water, generous royalties from manganese-nodule and oil-and-gas operations might have been forthcoming to aid the poorest states. The Group of 77 also bent, and despite the bargaining difficulties created by its internal unanimity rule and the personality of its nominee as chair of the First Committee, also used the moves of integrative bargaining. They were willing, at times, to cut their opponents' costs, to provide compensation for sacrifices, to logroll, and to listen to mediators who tried to bridge differences between themselves and the major industrial states.

Unfortunately, the pie almost got larger, but the effort failed. If sliced now, there will be very little for each participant for many years to come, as those responsible for completing the work of the Preparatory Commission recognize.[57] This is a pity for many reason, not least of which is that it puts a cloud on parliamentary diplomacy as a means of resolving complex problems among the many. Can it be trusted as the bargaining method most appropriate for resolving the world community's future problems?

Conclusion—Parliamentary Diplomacy and the Future of the International System

Ambiguity in outcome places a great burden upon judgment. Did UNCLOS III succeed, or should its partial success be counted as a failure? Can parliamentary diplomacy be the method of choice for resolving the many complex future problems in which many if not all states have a stake, and are therefore likely to insist upon playing a role in crafting an outcome?

The late twentieth century is a time of increasing interconnectedness. The old nationalist notion of autarchy as a goal might never have really been feasible, but it is now unthinkable. We are our brothers' keeper, whether we wish to be or not. There is no region so remote, nor problem so obscure, that it will not have at least an unintended consequence across a national border. It is also a world of rapid change. Problems that occur in one region too often quickly become systemic problems. The "joint supply" attribute of physical commons means that many problems with international commons can never be fully resolved by enclosure. This creates a need for more comprehensive orders and regimes, as more players recognize the stakes for themselves, and perhaps for the first time, that what might be at stake is the survival of mankind.[58]

Interconnectedness is bound to increase the transaction costs if we try to resolve problems at the universal level in universal conferences using the most complex process of interaction yet devised. Yet there are already demands to do so. For example, in 1988, Malta proposed that "the global climate be declared a common heritage of mankind."[59] Under any conceivable scenario, global climate negotiations are likely to be more difficult than the ocean regime negotiations. It is impossible for a solution to be worked out only by, or for, the developed states. If development proceeds as the developing states hope, the latter will be much larger future contributors to global warming unless remedial action is taken.

Because of the reputation of UNCLOS III for—at best—partial success, for ideological acrimony, and for glacially slow consensus procedures, "many view the LOS as precisely the *wrong* way to negotiate a convention."[60] Instead, world statesmen have mostly used a "framework-protocol" approach on global climate problems since negotiation of the Vienna Convention for the Protection of the Ozone Layer (1981–85) and the Montreal Protocol on Substances That Deplete the Ozone Layer (1986). Under these bargaining procedures, some like-minded states came together quickly, developed a set of principles, and postponed the action items until a protocol could be negotiated later. Since they divided the problems to be solved, they were able to develop in a step-by-step fashion, and with reasonable speed, action measures on some key issues. Although we have only limited experience with it, the framework-protocol seems to be a more parsimonious approach than parliamentary diplomacy.

Parsimony is clearly desirable. Resolving a problem with one's own internal means is obviously the most efficient. If one needs the cooperation of others to achieve a positive-sum outcome, one-on-one or bilateral monopoly is the easiest and cheapest to manage. If the problem is such that participation by more parties is needed to create a viable outcome, then participation by more parties must be accommodated. But if possible, for parsimony's sake, the number should be restricted even under framework-protocol procedures to the irreducible minimum without whose consent a solution would not work. Considerations of efficiency dictate that the simplest means available should be used to achieve the desired end. But circumstances are such that often in our own times, the desired end can only be achieved with the cooperation of a large number of stakeholders.

Must we always negotiate to achieve a cooperative outcome among the many? Oran Young has noted that international regimes can be formed by three means: they can be imposed by the stronger upon the weaker; they can be formed spontaneously; or they can be negotiated among the concerned stakeholders.[61] Perhaps the world's statesmen can rely upon imposed or spontaneous regimes to manage problems that spill over international borders. However, imposed regimes in our times seemed to have lost their legitimacy, however stable they are, and often how technically superior the outcomes they achieve as long as the stronger back them with their power.

Spontaneous regimes are more promising as an alternative to other means of regime formation. If customary practices emerge spontaneously that create an effective pattern of human conduct across international borders, problems can be solved at low cost. If the solutions found are technically sound, or are the least-cost alternative for those who were not among the original developers of the practices, it might make sense for newcomers to adopt similar practices and create a more general regime. Unfortunately, this usually takes time, and therefore spontaneous regimes are not always appropriate for creating patterns of cooperation in rapidly changing situations. Equity problems also may arise. It is usually the dominant players who establish customary practices which often favor their own interests. Indeed, it is not always easy to distinguish spontaneous from imposed regimes.[62]

While consent for international regimes can be created implicitly as well as explicitly, the many transformations that have led some to characterize the world as a global village point to the probability that active consent-formation processes will be employed more frequently in the future, among them parliamentary diplomacy. Can an observer feel confident that the ability of human beings using the practices developed at UNCLOS III and other U.N.-related conferences will lead to the creation of effective international regimes? Again, the "almost" results of 15 years of effort on UNCLOS III make one cautious. However, there is a short list of problem attributes that can be extracted from the UNCLOS III experience that, in a future situation, might lead to parliamentary diplomacy being the best means used to create consent.

First, the problem cannot be resolved by simpler processes—unilateral action, spontaneous behavior, bilateral or smaller-scale negotiations in, for example, users' clubs, regional groupings, etc. In sum, a universal conference can be recommended only when a solution to the problem will not be effective without widespread if not universal consent.

Second, the problem cannot be time-urgent. Years, not months, must be devoted to diagnosing the problem, discovering the necessary formulas, and working out the details through a process in which aggregation of the interests of large numbers of participants is often complex, tedious, and essential for success.

Third, participants must be willing to accept consensus as maximum consultation as the decision rule. UNCLOS III did not solve Arrow's dilemma of social choice. It did not achieve unanimity; parliamentary diplomacy is not a rational aggregation device. Given the present divisions among the world community, it is not likely that unanimity can be achieved on many important issues. Consensus as maximum consultation gives the recalcitrant a greater voice. In the world system of the foreseeable future, the recalcitrant will often include the great powers, who are being pushed by a coalition of lesser states, often developing states. Those who wish to push the great powers must recognize that voting or other decision mechanisms which promise quick results merely foster defection. The best they can hope to achieve will be achieved under the UNCLOS III consensus rule. In turn, the great powers will have to learn to live with not achieving their maximum preferred positions on all major issues.

Fourth, participants must be willing to negotiate deductively. They must put forth their candidates early for the formula ideas that will help shape the outcome. The public nature of parliamentary diplomacy demands such an approach. Utter confusion will reign if participants begin the negotiation by concentrating upon significant details, hoping that the operative concepts will eventually emerge. Parliamentary diplomacy requires communication among the many, and therefore general principles must be used as a guide. Consequently, there is always a danger that a parliamentary diplomatic encounter will turn into a clash of principles, making resolution more difficult, if not impossible.

Fifth, quality leadership must emerge if parliamentary diplomacy is to be successful. Although this study has only dealt descriptively with leadership, success depends heavily upon the quality of the people who try to pull together the complex forces and issues, and who play the bridging roles between individuals, states, or groups in deadlock.

Sixth, under parliamentary diplomacy, trade-offs assembled into packages play a central role in achieving a viable outcome. But it is critical that the assembling of the package be managed skillfully. An agreement that must be approved by numerous parties must balance out gains and losses—gains on issues of high salience and losses on issues of lesser salience. If one side insists upon achieving all or most of its demands, the encounter will fail. Although at times of intense conflict, there is tactical merit in assuming implicitly that all states are committed to approve the negotiating text as a package, the question of what issues make up the package must be clarified and made explicit, or some participants may wait until their issues are settled to their satisfaction, and then defect. Early resolution of some issues may imperil satisfactory resolution of others that are fitted into the package later.

Seventh, the losses entailed by trade-offs must be mitigated through compromises negotiated issue by issue. This mitigation or softening of the losses to the loser is essential to the negotiating success of parliamentary diplomacy. Our examination of the negotiation of all of the major issues showed that each went through a diagnostic, formula, and detail phase. While the formula phase showed that one side's candidate formula would guide the outcome and would therefore win, there was a along and intense third phase, during which the winner had to try to balance out protecting the integrity of his formula idea with concessions that limited the impact of the formula upon the losers. Usually, this was done through exceptions to the rule, vague language, or careful enumeration of the circumstances under which the rule applied. As a result, few formula ideas survived into the treaty in pure form.

Eighth, there must be cross-cutting affiliations among the participants. If UNCLOS III participants did not have affiliations, obligations, and interests other than Group of 77, Western Europe and Others, and the Latin American, African, and Asian groups, it would have broken down quickly. Future large-scale negotiations will need cross-cutting affiliation to prevent issues of future global management from being handled strictly on ideological lines.

Finally, the probability of success for a future parliamentary diplomatic conference is higher if the issues lend themselves to being resolved by distributive outcomes. Where UNCLOS III succeeded, it did so because participants were willing to divide up the coastal ocean among coastal states. The outcome needed on Part XI should have been integrative, not distributive or redistributive. But such results eluded them. Unfortunately, many of the issues of future global policy cry out for integrative solutions.

It is difficult to imagine any future set of circumstances where all of these conditions can be fulfilled. Very likely future negotiations over global issues will blend attributes of the package approach of UNCLOS III and the framework-protocol approach of Vienna and Montreal. Neither alone is capable of managing future negotiations in a manner that is least-cost, sufficiently fast-paced to keep up with changing needs, technically sound, and at the same time garners the active consent of—at least—all important states, and is sufficiently comprehensive so as to solve problems that cannot be solved without dealing with them holistically. Hopefully, this volume has provided future decision-makers with an assessment of the assets and liabilities of the parliamentary diplomacy part of the equation.

Notes

Chapter 1: The Regime of the Ocean:
Where We Were and Why We Had to Change

1. Kenneth A. Oye, "Explaining Cooperation under Anarchy: Hypotheses and Strategies," in Kenneth A. Oye, ed., *Cooperation Under Anarchy* (Princeton: Princeton University Press, 1986), p. 1.
2. See Nicholas Onuf and Frank F. Klink, "Anarchy, Authority, Rule," *International Studies Quarterly* 33, no. 2 (June 1989) 149–173. Also see Oran R. Young, *Compliance and Public Authority* (Baltimore: Johns Hopkins University Press, 1979), pp. 18–25.
3. See Oran R. Young, *International Cooperation: Building Regimes for Natural Resources and the Environment* (Ithaca: Cornell University Press, 1989), pp. 84–89.
4. "A stakeholder is simply an individual or group with a reason to care about the decision and with enough impact on the decision maker so that the reason should be taken seriously," Ward Edwards and J. Robert Newman, *Multiattribute Evaluation* (Beverly Hills, Calif.: Sage, 1982), p. 18.
5. Robert Abrams, *Foundations of Political Analysis* (New York: Columbia University Press, 1980), p. 17.
6. Karl von Clauswitz, *On War*, trans. by O. J. M. Jolles (New York: Random House, 1943, Book I, Chapter I, p. 16).
7. See Robert O. Keohane, *After Hegemony: Cooperation and Discord in the World Political Economy* (Princeton: Princeton University Press, 1984), pp. 31–41.
8. See Richard A. Falk, "Toward A World Order Respectful Of The Global Ecosystem," *Environmental Affairs* 1, no. 2 (June 1971): 251–264; Richard A. Falk, *This Endangered Planet* (New York: Random House, 1971).
9. This is not to denigrate the rather ingenious adaptation by international lawyers of the concept of customary international law, so that practices that become reasonably common, but do not have long historical standing, can be used as universal standards. See Zdenek Slouka, *International Custom and the Continental Shelf: A Study in the Dynamics of Customary Rules of International Law* (The Hague: Nijhoff, 1968). Also see Brian Flemming, "Customary International Law and the Law of the Sea," in *Law of the Sea: State Practice in Zones of Special Jurisdiction* (Honolulu: University of Hawaii Law of the Sea Institute, 1982), pp. 489–505.
10. See, for example, Jessica Tuchman Mathews, "Redefining Security," *Foreign Affairs* 68, no. 2 (Spring 1989): 176.
11. See Howard Raiffa, *The Art and Science of Negotiation* (Cambridge: Harvard University Press, 1982), pt. 2, pp. 35–132.
12. See Mancur Olson, *The Logic of Collective Action: Public Goods and the Theory of Groups* (Cambridge: Harvard University Press, 1965), pp. 53–65.
13. See Kenneth Arrow, *The Limits of Organization* (New York: Norton, 1974), pp. 68–71.

14. For a series of essays on multilateral negotiations, see Frances Mautner-Markhof, *Processes of International Negotiations* (Boulder, Colo.: Westview, 1989), pp. 7–105.

15. For an application of the "Coase Theorem" to international affairs, see John A. C. Conybeare, "International Organization and the Theory of Property Rights," *International Organization* 34, no. 3 (Summer 1980): 309–313. The original paper is R. H. Coase, "The Problem of Social Cost," *Journal of Law and Economics* 3 (1960): 1–44.

16. See Richard E. Walton and Robert B. McKersie, *A Behavioral Theory of Labor Negotiations* (New York: McGraw-Hill, 1965), pp. 126–143; Dean G. Pruitt, *Negotiation Behavior* (New York: Academic Press, 1981), pp. 137–162.

17. See James M. Buchanan and Gordon Tullock, *The Calculus of Consent* (Ann Arbor: University of Michigan Press, 1962), p. 112.

18. As we shall see in the next section, some economists and anthropologists object to the use of open access as the key feature in defining a commons, arguing that commons historically were areas in which members of a community had shared rights. What distinguished common property from private property was communal sharing of the commons to the exclusion of outsiders. Not every identifiable person was a member of the community. See S. V. Ciriacy-Wantrup and Richard C. Bishop, " 'Common Property' as a Concept in Natural Resource Policy," *Natural Resource Journal* 15, no. 4 (October 1975): 713–727.

19. World Resources Institute, *World Resources 1988–89* (New York: Basic Books, 1988), pp. 326–327.

20. Keohane, "The Demand for International Regimes," *International Organization* 36:2 (Spring 1982): 339.

21. See, for example, Ross D. Eckert, "United States Policy and the Law of the Sea Conference, 1969–82: A Case Study of Multilateral Negotiations," a paper prepared for the Conference on the Political Economy of International Organizations, Claremont Graduate School, Claremont, Calif., November 10–11, 1989.

22. Arvid Pardo, the "father" of the Law of the Sea Conference has expressed such views: "The Law of the Sea Conference—What Went Wrong," in Robert F. Friedheim, ed., *Managing Ocean Resources: A Primer* (Boulder, Colo.: Westview, 1979), pp. 137–148; "The Symbolic and Practical Import of the Negotiations," *Center Magazine* 15 (March/April 1982): 26.

23. "To achieve [a] state of universal well-being a single world-government is necessary." Dante Aligieri, *On World Government or De Monarchia* (Indianapolis: Bobbs-Merrill, 1949), p. 39.

24. Thomas Hobbes, *Leviathan,* (1651; reprint, Oxford: Clarendon Press, 1909), chap. 13, p. 97.

25. See Young, *International Cooperation,* p. 82.

26. See Arthur A. Stein, "Coordination and Collaboration: Regimes in an Anarchic World," *International Organization* 36, no. 2 (Spring 1982): 311–316.

27. See Douglas M. Johnston, "The Political Mode of Legal Development: From Stockholm to Caracas," presented at the Annual Meeting of the Western Political Science Association, San Diego, Calif., 25–27 March 1982.

28. See Donald Puchala and Raymond Hopkins, "International Regimes: Lessons From Inductive Analysis," *International Organization* 36, no. 2 (Spring 1982): 245–276; Stephan Haggard and Beth Simmons, "Theories of International Regimes," *International Organization* 41, no. 3 (Summer 1987): 493.

29. "International law, like domestic law, is not a policeman, or a prison, or a gallows, or a judge, but a set of ideas. Like domestic law it is binding. Like domestic law, it is, as it were, being played." C. A. W. Manning, *The Nature of International Society* (New York: Wiley, 1962), p. 109. Also see C. K. Allen, *Law in the Making*, 6th ed. (Oxford: Oxford University Press, 1958), pp. 444–445.

30. Among them: Stephen D. Krasner, *Structural Conflict: The Third World Against Global Liberalism* (Berkeley: University of California Press, 1985), esp. pp. 231–250; Robert O. Keohane and Joseph S. Nye, *Power and Interdependence*, 2d ed. (Glenview, Ill.: Scott, Foresman, 1989), esp. pp. 86–98; 129–162; and Young, *Resource Regimes* (Berkeley: University of California Press, 1982); and *International Cooperation*.

31. There is a danger in such an approach, as William T. Burke noted in a comment on an earlier draft of this chapter: "The 'other sources' show substantial departures from the Convention and can be left out only at considerable risk." 30 June 1990.

32. See Haggard and Simmons, "Theories of International Regimes," p. 508–509.

33. Anne-Marine Burley, "Building Bridges: International Relations Theory and American Foreign Relations Law," paper delivered at a meeting of the Center for International Studies, School of International Relations, University of Southern California, 16 March 1990 (mimeo).

34. Stephen D. Krasner, "Structural Causes and Regime Consequences: Regimes as Intervening Variables," *International Organization* 36, no. 2 (Spring 1982): 185.

35. See John Austin, *Lectures on Jurisprudence*, 4th ed. (London: John Murray, 1873); Sir Henry Sumner Maine, *Ancient Law* (London: John Murray, 1930), p. 6; H. L. A. Hart, *The Concept of Law* (Oxford: Clarendon Press, 1961), pp. 18–25; and Michael Barkun, *Law without Sanctions* (New Haven: Yale University Press, 1968), pp. 7–10.

36. See Lawrence Haworth, "The Standard View of the State: A Critique," *Ethics* 73, no. 4 (July 1963): 272.

37. I. William Zartman and Maureen R. Berman, *The Practical Negotiator* (New Haven: Yale University Press, 1982), p. 98.

38. My understanding of the notion of "spontaneous" regimes differs from Young's. Young looks to Hayek's definition of an arrangement that is "the product of the action of many men but . . . not the result of human design" as the basis of his definition of spontaneous regime. Young, *International Cooperation*, pp. 84–85. I include both the spontaneity of market behavior and human design over a long historical period, when it is difficult to separate the influence of either on a set of rules that a substantial group of decision-makers treat as a regime, especially one that is justifiable under the notion of customary international law.

39. As one commentator has pointed out, regime theory based on liberal premises might be viewed as an "apology or justification, a form of special pleading by and

for the powerful and satisfied." James F. Keeley, "Toward a Foucauldian Analysis of International Regimes," *International Organization* 44, no. 1 (Winter 1990): 84.

40. See Susan Strange, "*Cave! Hic dragones:* A Critique of Regime Analysis," *International Organization* 36, no. 2 (Spring 1982): 486–488.

41. See Keohane, *After Hegemony,* pp. 31–46.

42. On the role of leadership in international regime formation, see Young, "The Politics of International Regime Formation: Governing the Global Commons," a revised version of a paper prepared for presentation at the Annual Meeting of the International Studies Association, St. Louis, 29 March–1 April 1988.

43. This discussion is beholden to Young's writings, especially his *International Cooperation* and *Resource Regimes.*

44. See Hugo Caminos and Michael R. Molitor, "Progressive Development of International Law and the Package Deal," *American Journal of International Law* 79, no. 4 (October 1985): 871–890.

45. For the concepts of integrative and distributive bargaining, see Walton and McKersie, *A Behavioral Theory of Labor Negotiations,* chaps. 2–4, pp. 11–183.

46. Hugo Grotius, *The Freedom of the Seas* ed. by James Scott Brown (New York: Oxford University Press, 1916).

47. See Grotius, *Commentary on the Law of Prize and Booty* (Oxford: Clarendon Press, 1950). For an account of the discovery of the manuscript, see William S. M. Knight, *The Life and Works of Hugo Grotius* (London: Sweet & Maxwell, 1925), p. 79.

48. This discussion of the basic thrust of the Grotian regime is based on my earlier essay, "The Political, Economic, and Legal Ocean," in *Managing Ocean Resources,* pp. 26–44.

49. For reasons of space, the discussion of the traditional ocean regime concentrates on Grotius to the neglect of many writers who refined or enriched the basic regime, particularly, van Bynkershoek. On these writers, see Charles G. Fenwick, *International Law,* 4th ed. (New York: Appleton-Century-Crofts, 1965), pp. 60–66. Also for reasons of space, we will not deal more broadly with Grotius's nonocean writings, which are integral to a tradition of idealism and progress, and which have attracted many supporters to the ideal of world peace through world law. For Grotius's contribution here, see H. Lauterpacht, "The Grotian Tradition of International Law," and Richard Falk, "The Grotian Quest," in Richard Falk, Friedrich Kratochwil, and Saul H. Mendlovitz, eds., *International Law: A Contemporary Perspective* (Boulder, Colo.: Westview, 1985), pp. 10–36; 36–42.

50. On the types of rules found in resource regimes, see Young, *Resource Regimes,* pp. 25–29.

51. See Ciriacy-Wantrup and Bishop, " 'Common Property' as a Concept in Natural Resources Policy," p. 724.

52. See J. L. Brierly, *The Law of Nations,* 6th ed., ed. by H. Waldock (New York: Oxford University Press, 1963), pp. 163–164; Fenwick, *International Law,* pp. 404–409.

53. See Phillip C. Jessup, *The Law of Territorial Waters and Maritime Jurisdiction* (New York: G. A. Jennings, 1927); William E. Masterson, *Jurisdiction in Marginal*

Seas (New York: Macmillan, 1929); P. T. Fenn, "Origins of the Theory of Territorial Waters," *American Journal of International Law* 20 (July 1926): 465–482; and T. Baty, "Three Mile Limit," *American Journal of International Law* 22 (July 1928): 503–537.

54. See Douglas M. Johnston, *The International Law of Fisheries* (New Haven: Yale University Press, 1965), pp. 82–97.

55. The most complete exposition of Grotian principles can be found in Myres S. McDougal and William T. Burke, *The Public Order of the Oceans* (New Haven: Yale University Press, 1962). For McDougal's impassioned defense of his approach, as being in "the common interests of the peoples of the world," see "International Law and the Law of the Sea," in Lewis M. Alexander, ed., *The Law of the Sea: Offshore Zones and Boundaries* (Columbus: Ohio State University Press, 1967), pp. 3–23.

56. See J. E. Farnell, "The Navigation Act of 1651, the First Dutch War, and the London Merchant Community," *Economic History Review* 16 (April 1964): 444–445.

57. Unfortunately, maritime states clashed with some frequency, more often because they chose the easy way to gain wealth by seizing each other's ships, seamen, and cargoes than because they quarreled over scarce ocean natural resources. After all, Grotius wrote *De Jure Praedae* on a retainer from the Dutch East India Company to justify the seizure by a Dutch captain, Heemskerck, of a Portuguese vessel. Fortunately, this practice, while it has not died out completely, is no longer a persistent or major problem. See Knight, *The Life and Works of Hugo Grotius,* pp. 80–82.

58. See Andrew Dickinson White, *Seven Great Statesmen in the Warfare of Humanity with Unreason* (New York: Century, 1915), p. 60.

59. See David C. Loring, "The United States–Peruvian 'Fisheries' Dispute," *Stanford Law Review* 23, no. 3 (February 1971): 391–453.

60. Paul Kennedy, *The Rise and Fall of the Great Powers* (New York: Random House, 1987), p. 29.

61. F. J. C. Hearnshaw, "Grotius and the Reign of Law," in *Some Great Political Idealists of the Christian Era* (London: Harrap, 1937), p. 91.

62. Grotius, *De Jure Belli Ac Pacis Libri Tres* Vol. 2, Carnegie Endowment for International Peace, Classics of International Law no. 3 (Oxford: Clarendon Press, 1925), I,i,14.

63. See Albert W. Koers, *International Regulation of Marine Fisheries* (Surrey, U.K.: Fishing News, 1973), p. 17.

64. As quoted in Norman V. Breckner et al., *The Navy and the Common Sea* (Washington, D.C.: Office of Naval Research, 1972), p. v.

65. See, among others, Ciriacy-Wantrup and Bishop, " 'Common Property' as a Concept in Natural Resources Policy"; B. McCay and J. Acheson, *The Question of the Commons: the Culture and Ecology of Community Property* (Tucson: University of Arizona Press, 1987).

66. See F. Berkes, D. Feeny, B. J. McKay, and J. M. Acheson, "The Benefits of the Commons," *Nature* 340 (13 July 1989): 91–93; Fikret Berkes and David Feeny,

"Paradigms Lost," *Alternatives* 17, no. 2 (1990): 48–55; Daniel W. Bromley, "The Commons, Property, and Common Property Regimes," paper presented at the First Annual Meeting of the International Association for the Study of Common Property, Duke University, 27–30 September 1990; Susan Hanna, "The Eighteenth Century English Commons: A Model for Ocean Management," *Journal of Ocean and Shoreline Management* 14, no. 3 (1990): 155–172.

67. Per Magnus Wijkman has noted that in the early nineteenth century Ricardo did anticipate the transition from abundance to scarcity and from an inability to occupy effectively to effective occupation. "Managing the Global Commons," *International Organization* 36, no. 3 (Summer 1982): 513, n. 5.

68. Francis T. Christy, Jr., "Marine Resources and the Freedom of the Seas," *Natural Resources Journal* 8, no. 3 (July 1968), p. 425; see also Christy, "Property Rights in the World Ocean," *Natural Resources Journal* 15:4 (October 1975), p. 696.

69. See Ross D. Eckert, *The Enclosure of Ocean Resources* (Palo Alto, Calif.: Hoover Press, 1979), p. 118.

70. For a more extended discussion of the application of the theory to the fisheries, see chapter 5, "Terminating the Common Wealth In Ocean Fisheries."

71. See H. Scott Gordon, "The Economic Theory of a Common Property Resource: The Fishery," *Journal of Political Economy* 62, no. 2 (April 1954): 131.

72. See James Crutchfield and Giulio Pontecorvo, *The Pacific Salmon Fisheries: A Study in Irrational Conservation* (Baltimore: Johns Hopkins University Press, 1969). Other major works on the economics of modern fisheries include Francis T. Christy, Jr., and Anthony D. Scott, *The Common Wealth in Ocean Fisheries* (Baltimore: Johns Hopkins University Press, 1965); Anthony D. Scott, "The Fishery: The Objective of Sole Ownership," *Journal of Political Economy* 63 (1955): 116–124.

73. See Giulio Pontecorvo and Maurice Wilkerson, "From Cornucopia to Scarcity: The Current Status of Ocean Resource Use," *Ocean Development and International Law* 5, nos. 2 & 3 (1978): 383–395.

74. Kenneth Boulding, "Societal Aspects of Ocean Food and Energy," *Second International Marine Technology Assessment Conference*: Texas A. & M. University, October 5–8, 1976), p. 2.

75. Charles S. Pearson, *International Marine Environmental Policy: the Economic Dimension* (Baltimore: Johns Hopkins University Press, 1975), p. xi.

76. Allen V. Kneese, *Economics and the Environment* (Harmondsworth, U.K.: Penguin, 1977), p. 28.

77. See, for example, Garrett Hardin, "The Tragedy of the Commons," *Science* 162 (1968): 1,243–1,248.

78. See Martin Shubik, *Game Theory and Related Approaches to Social Behavior* (New York: Wiley, 1964), pp. 36–38; Anatol Rapoport and Albert M. Chammah, *Prisoner's Dilemma: A Study of Conflict and Cooperation* (Ann Arbor: University of Michigan Press, 1965).

79. See Robert Axelrod, *The Evolution of Cooperation* (New York: Basic Books, 1984), p. 13.

80. See my article, "The 'Satisfied' and 'Dissatisfied' States Negotiate International Law," *World Politics* 18, no. 1 (October 1965): 20–41.
81. Christy, "Ode To The Grotian Ocean," *ASIL Newsletter* (November/December 1978). Quoted with permission of the author.
82. See Friedheim et al., *Japan and the New Ocean Regime* (Boulder, Colo.: Westview, 1984), pp. 22–23; 354–357; Tsuneo Akaha, *Japan in Global Ocean Politics* (Honolulu: University of Hawaii Press, 1985), pp. 39–58.
83. See McDougal and Burke, *The Public Order of the Oceans.*
84. See Young, *International Cooperation,* pp. 13–14.
85. The U.S. Bureau of Oceans and International Environmental and Scientific Affairs has been monitoring coastal-state claims since 1967. The latest version of its standard publication assessing the state of national claims is Robert W. Smith, ed., *Limits in the Sea,* no. 36, *National Claims to Maritime Jurisdiction,* 6th Revision, 3 January 1990.
86. See F. V. Garcia-Amador, "The Origins of the Concept of an Exclusive Economic Zone: Latin American Practice," in *The Exclusive Economic Zone: A Latin American Perspective,* ed. by Francisco Orrego Vicuña (Boulder, Colo.: Westview, 1984), pp. 7–25.
87. Leonard Legault, a senior Canadian delegate to UNCLOS III, as quoted in Thomas A. Clingan, Jr., *Law of the Sea: State Practice in Zones of Special Jurisdiction* (Honolulu: University of Hawaii Law of the Sea Institute, 1982), p. 233.
88. See Alfonso Arias Schreiber, "The Exclusive Economic Zone" in *The Exclusive Economic Zone,* pp. 123–142.
89. See Slouka, *International Custom and the Continental Shelf;* Anthony D'Amato, *The Concept of Custom in International Law* (Ithaca: Cornell University Press, 1971).
90. Ann L. Hollick, *U.S. Foreign Policy and the Law of the Sea* (Princeton: Princeton University Press, 1981), p. 52. For an account of the struggle within the U.S. Government, after the Truman Proclamations were issued, between those who favored unilateral action ("realists") and those who favored managing U.S. ocean interests through multilateral organizations ("internationalists"), see Harry N. Scheiber, "Pacific Ocean Resources, Science, and Law of the Sea: Wilbert M. Chapman and the Pacific Fisheries, 1945–70," *Ecology Law Quarterly* 13, no. 3 (1986): 430–457.
91. "Proclamation by President Truman of 28 September 1945 on Policy of the United States with Respect to Coastal Fisheries in Certain Areas of the High Seas," *Department of State Bulletin* 13:327 (1945).
92. For a scientific description of the area concerned—the continental margin—see David A. Ross, *Introduction to Oceanography,* 4th ed. (Englewood Cliffs, N.J.: Prentice-Hall, 1988), pp. 100–110.
93. "Proclamation by President Truman of 28 September 1945 on Policy of the United States with Respect of the Natural Resources of the Subsoil and Seabed of the Continental Shelf," *Department of State Bulletin* 13:327 (1945).
94. See Breckner et al., *The Navy and the Common Sea,* p. 150.

95. Hollick, *U.S. Foreign Policy and the Law of the Sea*, p. 61.

96. For example, in 1979, the United States formalized in a "Freedom of Navigation" program practices that were begun earlier. The U.S. sent warships into the coastal waters of states it claimed were illegally attempting to restrict navigation.

97. Young, "Bargaining, Entrepreneurship, and International Politics: Escaping the Dead Hand of Nash and Zeuthen," An Essay Prepared for Delivery at the Annual Convention of the International Studies Association, London, 28 March–1 April 1989, p. 37. Also see Young's earlier essay, "The Politics of International Regime Formation: Governing the Global Commons," a paper prepared for presentation at the Annual Meeting of the International Studies Association, St. Louis, 29 March–1 April 1988.

98. See Fenwick, *International Law*, pp. 97–106.

99. Charles C. Hyde, *International Law Chiefly as Interpreted and Applied By the United States* vol. 1, 3d rev. ed. (Boston: Little, Brown, 1945). For conference documents see "Official Documents," *Supplement to the American Journal of International Law* 24 (1930): pp. 1–80; 169–258.

100. See William E. Butler, *The Law of Soviet Territorial Waters* (New York: Praeger, 1967) and *The Soviet Union and the Law of the Sea* (Baltimore: Johns Hopkins University Press, 1971); P. D. Barabolya et al., *Manual of International Maritime Law* (Washington, D.C.: U.S. Department of the Navy, 1968); G. I. Tunkin, *Theory of International Law* (Cambridge: Harvard University Press, 1974; A. A. Volkov, *Maritime Law* (Jerusalem: Israel Program for Scientific Translations, 1971); National Ocean Policy Study, Committee on Commerce, U.S. Senate, *Soviet Oceans Development*, 94th Cong., 2d Sess.

101. Harry N. Scheiber, "Pacific Ocean Resources and the Law of the Sea," p. 431.

102. Reprinted in United Nations Conference on the Law of the Sea, *Official Records* vol. 3, *First Committee* (A/Conf.13/39), pp. 209–211.

103. See chapter 3, "Methods of Analyzing the Negotiation: Parliamentary Diplomacy."

104. See Young, *Bargaining: Formal Theories of Negotiation* (Champaign: University of Illinois Press, 1975), p. 131; Raiffa, *The Art and Science of Negotiation*, pp. 33–34.

105. See Friedheim, "Factor Analysis as a Tool in Studying the Law of the Sea," in *The Law of the Sea: Offshore Boundaries and Zones*, pp. 47–70.

106. Friedheim, "The Politics of the Sea: A Study of Law-Making by Conference," (Ph.D. diss., Seattle: University of Washington, 1962), Appendix, Tables 16, 17.

107. "Convention on the Territorial Sea and the Contiguous Zone," Document A/CONF.13/L.52, in United Nations Conference on the Law of the Sea *Official Records* vol. 2 *Plenary Meetings* (A/CONF.13/38), pp. 132–135. The four UNCLOS I Conventions are reprinted in Platzoder and Vitzthum, eds., *Seerecht* (Baden-Baden: Nomos, 1984), pp. 17–68.

108. Christy, "The Distribution of the Sea's Wealth in Fisheries," in *The Law of the Sea: Offshore Boundaries and Zones*, pp. 112–115.

109. Breckner et al., *The Navy and the Common Sea*, p. 223, n. 2.

110. U.S. Aide-Mémoire (mimeo, n.d.).

Chapter 2: A Short History of UNCLOS III

1. United Nations, *Second United Nations Conference on the Law of the Sea,* 17 March–26 April 1960, Official Records (A/CONF.19/8).
2. Articles 24, 25, Convention of the High Seas (1958), reprinted in Platzoder and Vitzthum, eds., *Seerecht* (Baden-Baden: Nomos, 1984), p. 34.
3. See Platzoder and Vitzthum, eds. *Seerecht,* pp. 475–476.
4. For the most recent update of the standard catalog of state claims, see Robert W. Smith, ed., "Maritime Boundaries of the World," *Limits in the Sea,* no. 108, 1st rev. (Washington, D.C.: Office of Ocean Affairs, U.S. Department of State, November 1990).
5. See Smith, ed., "Maritime Boundaries," pp. 10–13.
6. See a number of papers evaluating the results of UNCLOS I and II in Lewis M. Alexander, ed., *The Law of the Sea: Offshore Boundaries and Zones* (Columbus: Ohio State University Press, 1967).
7. See Zartman and Berman, *Practical Negotiator,* p. 45.
8. See Pardo, "Law of the Sea Conference—What Went Wrong," and Friedheim, "Arvid Pardo, the Law of the Sea Conference, and the Future of the Oceans," in Friedheim, ed., *Managing Ocean Resources,* pp. 137–161.
9. I was part of one effort to think through the problem for the U.S. Navy that began in 1967. See, Breckner et al., *The Navy and the Common Sea,* pp. 135–225.
10. See James P. Lester, ed., *Environmental Politics and Policy* (Durham, N.C.: Duke University Press, 1989), pp. 2–5; 289–295.
11. See John L. Mero, *The Mineral Resources of the Sea* (New York: Elsevier, 1965).
12. See Hollick, *U.S. Foreign Policy and the Law of the Sea,* pp. 160–226.
13. See Friedheim et al., "Assessing the State of the Art in National Ocean Policy Studies," *Ocean Development and International Law* 7, nos. 3–4 (1979): 179–220; John King Gamble, Jr., *Marine Policy* (Lexington, Mass.: Heath, 1977); Center for Ocean Management Studies, University of Rhode Island, *Comparative Marine Policy: Perspectives from Europe, Scandinavia, Canada and the United States* (New York: Praeger, 1981; Friedheim et al., *Japan and the New Ocean Regime;* Tsuneo Akaha, *Japan in Global Ocean Politics* (Honolulu: University of Hawaii Press, 1985).
14. See Edward Wenk, Jr., *The Politics of the Ocean* (Seattle: University of Washington Press, 1972).
15. See Robert E. Osgood et al., *Toward a National Ocean Policy* (Washington, D.C.: Government Printing Office, 1975).
16. Many of the studies that became publicly available are described in my *Understanding the Debate on Ocean Resources* (Denver: Monograph Series in World Affairs, University of Denver, 1969).
17. William T. Burke, "Law and the New Technologies," in Alexander, ed., *The Law of the Sea: Offshore Boundaries and Zones,* p. 223.

18. Clyde Sanger, *Ordering the Oceans: The Making of the Law of the Sea* (Toronto: University of Toronto Press, 1987), p. 21.

19. U.S. Aide-Mémoire (mimeo), 24 October 1969.

20. Pardo claimed that he was not put up to his speech and that it was not prompted by others. In many discussions with the author, Pardo indicated that he gathered his own data, wrote his own speech, and took the initiative on the issue on his own authority. Indeed, there was an adjournment halfway through for lunch, during which he wrote the latter half of the speech. This is consistent with what he told the press at the time. Also see Wenk, *Politics of the Ocean*, p. 262.

21. See Hollick, *U.S. Foreign Policy and the Law of the Sea*, pp. 197–202.

22. United Nations General Assembly A/Res. 2340 (XXII).

23. Myron H. Nordquist and Choon-ho Park, eds., *Reports of the United States Delegation to the Third United Nations Conference on the Law of the Sea*, Occasional Paper No. 33, Law of the Sea Institute (Honolulu: University of Hawaii Law of the Sea Institute, 1983), p. 6. Hereinafter, *Reports of the U.S. Delegation.*

24. U.N. General Assembly A/Res. 2574 (XXIV).

25. U.N. General Assembly A/Res. 2749 (XXV).

26. U.N. General Assembly Doc. A/9021, suppl. 21, 1973.

27. John R. Stevenson and Bernard H. Oxman, "The Preparations for the Law of the Sea Conference," *American Journal of International Law* 68, no. 1 (1974): 4–8.

28. Hollick, *U. S. Foreign Policy and the Law of the Sea*, pp. 208–216; Eckert, *Enclosure of Ocean Resources*, p. 331.

29. Edward Miles, "The structure and effects of the decision process in the Seabed Committee and the Third United Nations Conference on the Law of the Sea," *International Organization*, 31, no. 2 (1977): 174.

30. Committee on the Peaceful Uses of the Seabed and Subsoil Beyond National Jurisdiction, *List of Issues and Subjects Relating to Law of the Sea*, (A/AC.138/66).

31. Zartman and Berman, *Practical Negotiator*, p. 102.

32. For the formal details, see "Final Act of the Third United Nations Conference on the Law of the Sea," *The Law of the Sea: Official Text* (New York, United Nations, 1983), pp. 158–174.

33. "Declaration Incorporating the 'Gentleman's Agreement' made by the President and Endorsed by the Conference at its 19th Meeting on 27 June 1974," Appendix, Rules of Procedure, A/Conf.62/36 (2 July 1974).

34. Rule 39(1), Rules of Procedure, A/Conf.62/36. As it happened, this alteration of the two-thirds rule had no effect on the Conference outcome, since there was only one vote. The Law of the Sea Study Group's consultant, Dr. Joseph Kadane, was asked by U.S. delegation leaders, just before the Caracas session, to develop a rule that could affect the outcome if there was to be decision by vote. What was adopted was not the rule he recommended, but its opposite. Under the rule adopted, there would have had to have been massive abstentions or absences before results obtained would have been different than under the usual two-thirds-present-and-voting rule. Joseph B. Kadane, "Analysis of the Voting Rule Adopted for Law of the Sea," Center for Naval Analyses, Memorandum 1223–74, 29 July 1974.

35. It also left enough time for recreational activities. This may also help account for the slow pace, as charged by some critics. Barry Newman, "The 'Law of the Sea' Is Still Unwritten, but Please Don't Fret," *Wall Street Journal* (27 August 1974), p. 1.

36. The forecasts of the Law of the Sea Study Group were consistent with the perceptions of the leadership. Law of the Sea Study Group, "The View from the Beginning of the Conference: Projected Outcomes on Seven Major Law of the Sea Issues," Center for Naval Analyses, Memorandum 01011–74, 26 June 1974.

37. "Kampala Declaration," U.N. Doc. A/Conf.62/23.

38. Revised versions of some of these papers were published later. See Eckert, "Exploitation of Deep Ocean Minerals: Regulatory Mechanisms and United States Policy," *Journal of Law and Economics* 15 (1974): 143–147; Kenneth W. Clarkson, "Economic Effects of Work Requirements in Leases to Develop Seabed Resources," *Virginia Journal of International Law* 15 (1975): 795–814; and Richard J. Sweeney, Robert D. Tollison and Thomas D. Willett, "Market Failure, the Common Pool Problem and Ocean Resource Exploitation," *Journal of Law and Economics* 17, no. 1 (1974): 179–192.

39. Nordquist and Park, eds., *Reports of the U.S. Delegation*, p. 82.

40. Sanger, *Ordering the Oceans*, pp. 169–173.

41. Treasury Department representatives objected not only to the chairman's articles, but also to the Pinto text. This was revealed in a confidential report by the House Oceanographic Committee Chairman leaked to the press. See Jack Anderson, "The Sharks of Geneva," *Washington Post*, (11 May 1975), p. C7.

42. This process of radicalization is well documented in Miles, "The structure and effect of the decision process," pp. 205–214.

43. See Zartman and Berman, *Practical Negotiator*, pp. 147–202.

44. Nordquist and Park, eds., *Reports of the U.S. Delegation*, p. 141.

45. Quoted in Bernard H. Oxman, "The Third United Nation's Conference on the Law of the Sea: The 1977 New York Session," *American Journal of International Law* 72 (1978): 59.

46. Note 8, Richardson Press Release in Oxman, "The Third United Nations Conference on the Law of the Sea: The 1977 New York Session," 59.

47. U.N. Doc. A/CONF.62/62, para. II(11).

48. Nordquist and Park, eds., *Reports of the U.S. Delegation*, p. 252.

49. Oxman, "The Third United Nations Conference on the Law of the Sea: The Eighth Session," *American Journal of International Law* 74 (1980): 2–3.

50. Elliot L. Richardson, "Seabed Mining and the Law of the Sea," *Department of State Bulletin* 80 (1980): 60–64.

51. Oxman, "The Third United Nations Conference on the Law of the Sea: The Ninth Session (1980)," *American Journal of International Law* 75, no. 2 (1981): 235.

52. See Daniel Druckman, "Stages, Turning Points, and Crises," *Journal of Conflict Resolution* 30, no. 2 (1986): 327–360.

53. Nordquist and Park, eds., *Reports of the U.S. Delegation*, p. 457.

54. Nordquist and Park, eds., *Reports of the U.S. Delegation*, p. 533.

55. Leigh H. Ratiner, "The Law of the Sea: A Crossroads for American Foreign Policy," *Foreign Affairs* 60, no. 5 (Summer 1982): 1,006–1,021. For other contemporary accounts, see Tom Alexander, "The Reaganites' Misadventure at Sea," *Fortune* (23 August 1982); William Wertenbaker, "The Law of the Sea—II," *New Yorker* (8 August 1983), p. 57; and Sanger, *Ordering the Oceans*, p. 187.

56. "Statement by the President," White House Press Release (July 9, 1982).

57. *Ocean Policy News* (July 1990), p. 1.

58. See Satya N. Nandan, "The 1982 United Nations Convention on the Law of the Sea: At a Cross-Road," *International Challenges* 9, no. 3 (1989): 4–7; Jose Luis Jesus, "Statement on the Issue of the Universality of the Convention," *Special Report* (Washington: Council on Ocean Law, July 1990).

59. Remarks by U.S. Ambassador Thomas Pickering, as reprinted in *Ocean Policy News* (December 1990/January 1991), p. 2.

Chapter 3: Methods of Analyzing the Negotiation: Modeling Parliamentary Diplomacy

1. Young, *International Cooperation*, pp. 107–144.

2. Alexander George, "Policy-Oriented Forecasting," *Research Notes* (n.p., n.d.), pp. 1–5.

3. Harry Eckstein, "Case Study and Theory in Political Science," in *Handbook of Political Science: Strategies of Inquiry*, vol. 7, ed. by Fred I. Greenstein and Nelson W. Polsby (Reading, Mass.: Addison-Wesley, 1975), p. 104.

4. George, "Case Studies and Theory Development: The Method of Structured, Focused Comparison," in *Diplomacy: New Approaches in History, Theory, and Policy*, ed. by Paul Gordon Lauren (New York: Free Press, 1979), pp. 43–68.

5. Eckstein, "Case Study and Theory," p. 131.

6. P. Terrence Hopmann and Charles Wolcott, "The Impact of External Stresses and Tensions on Negotiations," in *Negotiations: Social-Psychological Perspectives*, ed. by Daniel Druckman (Beverly Hills, Calif.: Sage, 1977), p. 321.

7. Friedheim, "The Politics of the Sea," Ph.D. Diss.

8. See Breckner, et al., *The Navy and the Common Sea*.

9. For a complete description of the model, its functions, and uses, see Robert L. Friedheim, Karen W. Goudreau, William Durch, Joseph B. Kadane, *Forecasting Outcomes of Multilateral Negotiations: Methodology* [CRC 291], vols. 1–2, *Techniques and Models* (Arlington, Va.: Center for Naval Analyses, 1977); Karen W. Goudreau, *Forecasting Outcomes of Multilateral Negotiations: Computer Programs* [CRC 290], vol. 1, *Guide for Users* (Arlington, Va.: Center for Naval Analyses, 1977); and Karen W. Goudreau, *Forecasting Outcomes of Multilateral Negotiations: Computer Programs* [CRC 290], vol. 2, *Guide for Programmers* (Arlington, Va.: Center for Naval Analyses, 1977).

10. Friedheim, "Research Utilization Problems in Forecasting the U.N. Law of the Sea Conference; Or, the Perils of the Persian Messenger," in *Formulating Marine Policy: Limitations to Rational Decision-Making* (Kingston, R.I.: University of Rhode Island Center for Ocean Management Studies, 1978), pp. 144–167.

11. I must acknowledge my intellectual debts to Joseph Kadane, Carnegie-Mellon University, who put the project on a sound statistical basis; to Karen W. G. Sherif, U.S. Government, and William Durch, MIT, who also made major contributions to the project; and to the many analysts and coders who, because of their numbers, must remain anonymous.

12. Earlier published examples of how these methods were used can be found in R. L. Friedheim, J. B. Kadane and J. K. Gamble, Jr., "Quantitative Content Analysis of the United Nations Seabed Debate: Methodology and a Continental Shelf Case Study," *International Organization* 24, no. 3 (1970): 479–502; Robert L. Friedheim and Joseph B. Kadane, "Ocean Science in the U.N. Political Arena," *Journal of Maritime Law and Commerce* 3, no. 3 (April 1972): 473–502; Robert L. Friedheim and William J. Durch, "The International Seabed Resources Agency Negotiations and the New International Economic Order," *International Organization* 31, no. 2 (1977): 343–384.

13. Zartman, "Many Are Called but Few Choose: Managing Complexity in Multilateral Negotiations," paper presented to 1987 Meeting, American Political Science Association.

14. Friedheim, "Parliamentary Diplomacy—A Survey," Memorandum 76:0046.10 (Arlington, Va.: Center for Naval Analyses, 1976).

15. The literature on U.N. General Assembly and conference bargaining is large. The most important works are Chadwick F. Alger, "Negotiation, Regional Groups, Interaction and Public Debate in the Development of Consensus in the United Nations General Assembly," in James Rosenau and Maurice East, eds., *The Analysis of International Politics* (New York: Free Press, 1972), pp. 278–298, and "Research on Research: A Decade of Quantitative and Field Research on International Organizations," *International Organization* 24, no. 3 (1970): 414–450; John Hadwin and Johann Kaufman, *How United Nations Decisions Are Made* (Leyden: Sythoff, 1960); Johann Kaufman, *Conference Diplomacy* (Dobbs Ferry, N.Y.: Oceana, 1970); Phillip Jessup, "Parliamentary Diplomacy," *Recueil Des Cours* 89 (1956): 181–320, and "International Negotiation Under Parliamentary Procedure" in *Lectures on International Law and the United Nations* (Ann Arbor: University of Michigan Law School, 1957); Dean Rusk, "Parliamentary Diplomacy—Debate vs. Negotiation," *World Affairs Interpreter* 26 (Summer 1955): 123–138; and Friedheim, "Politics of the Sea." The following works describe newer developments in parliamentary diplomacy: S. Jayakumar and T. T. B. Koh, "The Negotiating Process of the Third United Nations Conference on the Law of the Sea" in Myron Nordquist, ed., *United Nations Conference on the Law of the Sea, 1982*, vol. 1 (Dordrecht: Nijhoff, 1985), pp. 29–68; Barry Buzan, "United We Stand . . . Informal Negotiating Groups at UNCLOS III," *Marine Policy* (July 1980), pp. 183–204; Barry Buzan, "Negotiating by Consensus: Developments in Techniques at the United Nations Conference on the Law of the Sea," *American Journal of International Law* 752 (1981): 324–436; Robert D. Eustis, "Procedures and Techniques of Multilateral Negotiation: The LOS III Model," *Virginia Journal of International Law* 17, no. 2 (1977); Edward Miles, "A Research Design for Analyzing

Structure and Process in the Emerging International Decision System for Ocean Exploration and Exploitation,'' paper presented to the Annual Convention of the Eastern Sociological Association, April 1970, and ''The Structure and Effects of the Decision Process in the Seabed Committee and the Third United Nations Conference on the Law of the Sea,'' *International Organization* 31, no. 2 (1977): 159–234.

16. Zartman, *The 50% Solution* (Garden City, N.Y.: Anchor, 1976), p. 8.

17. See Zartman, *50% Solution,* pp. 7–8; Jeffrey Z. Rubin and Bert R. Brown, *The Social Psychology of Bargaining and Negotiation* (New York: Academic Press, 1975), pp. 1–18.

18. Axelrod, *Conflict of Interest* (Chicago: Markham, 1970), pp. 158–162.

19. James K. Sebenius, *Negotiating the Law of the Sea* (Cambridge: Harvard University Press, 1984), pp. 50–55.

20. Richard E. Walton and Robert B. McKersie, *A Behavioral Theory of Labor Negotiations* (New York: McGraw-Hill, 1965).

21. Zartman, ''Many Are Called.''

22. I do not mean strategic in the sense of forecasting the best move from a repertory of available moves in a situation of strategic interaction. While the LOS Study group did not attempt to forecast the ''outguessing regress,'' it did provide data to assess the general pattern of the overall negotiation and its most important component parts. There, the work was conducted at the strategic *level,* even though strategic analysis was not conducted. See Young, *Bargaining: Formal Theories of Negotiation* (Urbana: University of Illinois Press, 1975), p. 13.

23. I do not agree with Robert Jervis that analysts must reduce multilateral negotiations to their bilateral dimension to understand them. Robert Jervis, (1986), in Zartman, ''Many Are Called.''

24. Zartman, ''Many Are Called.''

25. See Friedheim et al., *Forecasting Outcomes* [CRC 291], vols. 1–2, for the protocols established for the collection, recording, and manipulation of data. In addition to data derived from the official U.N. record, data were also extracted from the U.S. diplomatic cables related to the Conference. This work uses only the data derived from the U.N. records.

26. For a detailed description of the content analysis technique, see Friedheim et al., *Forecasting Outcomes,* [CRC 291].

27. See Ole Holsti, *Content Analysis for the Social Sciences and Humanities* (Reading, Mass.: Addison-Wesley, 1969); Phillip J. Stone et al., *The General Inquirer: A Computer Approach to Content Analysis* (Cambridge: MIT Press, 1966).

28. See William J. Durch, ''Information Processing and Outcome Forecasting for Multilateral Negotiations: Testing Our Approach,'' paper prepared for delivery at the 18th Annual Convention of the International Studies Association, St. Louis, March 1977.

29. See Lincoln E. Moses et al., ''Scaling Data on Inter-Nation Action,'' *Science* 156:3778 (May 26, 1967), pp. 1,054–1,059.

30. See Friedheim et al., *Forecasting Outcomes* [CRC 291], vol. 1, pp. 16–17.

31. The national score was computed:

$$\text{National Score} = \frac{\text{THEMES (Rank of Theme)} \times \text{(Number of Mentions)}}{\text{Total Number of Mentions}}$$

32. The following regression model was used:

$$Y = b_1X_1 + b_2X_2 + b_3X_3 + \ldots + b_nX_n$$

Where Y = Rank of the Theme Mentioned

$b_{1\ldots n}$ = Beta Coefficients

$X_{1\ldots n}$ = Group Affiliations and Interests

33. The preferred position model was computed:

$$\text{Number of PREFERRED POSITION} = \frac{\text{National Score Remarks + Estimate}}{\text{Number of Remarks + 1}}$$

34. See Robin Farquharson, *Theory of Voting* (New Haven: Yale University Press, 1969). Other important works on voting in legislative-like organizations are Duncan Black, *Theory of Committees and Elections* (Cambridge: Cambridge University Press, 1958); and Buchanan and Tullock, *Calculus of Consent*.

35. At times, during the most active period of the project, I would provide unlabeled histograms to the clients and ask *them* to interpret them. They almost always could do so correctly. This sometimes made the clients unhappy since, sometimes, the peaks they interpreted as probable winners represented their opponents' position on the issue. Friedheim, "Research Utilization Problems."

36. Fred Charles Ikle, *How Nations Negotiate* (New York: Harper & Row, 1964), pp. 59–75.

37. Zartman, "Negotiation: Theory and Reality," *Journal of International Affairs* 9, no. 1 (Spring 1975): 71.

38. Zartman, "Negotiations: Theory and Reality," p. 71.

39. For the view that modern multilateral negotiations is a process of mutual learning because of the need "to create a structure out of a large mass of information," see Gilbert Winham, "Negotiation as a Management Process," *World Politics* 30, no. 1 (October 1977): 89.

40. See Zartman and Berman, *Practical Negotiator*, chaps. 3–5.

41. Although the movement of all known groups was calculated and plotted on all 25 major issues, tables and figures showing these data usually were omitted from chapters 4–7 because the enormous amount of data would have overwhelmed most readers. However, these materials will be kept available for interested readers who request them from the author within two years of the date of publication of this work.

42. The following utility model was used:

$$\text{Utility Score} = U_j = (M_j - V_A)^2 - (M_j - V_B)^2$$

Where M_j = Preferred Position of country j

V_A = Rank of Proposal A

V_B = Rank of Proposal B

43. The packaging model is shown below:

$$U_j = \frac{\sum_{i=1}^{n} S_{ij} (\Delta_{ij1} - \Delta_{ij2})}{\sum_{i=1}^{n} S_{ij}}$$

44. We went further and asked ourselves the question, What if some of the negotiators wanted to identify and work toward the optimal package? What advice could we give them? Dr. Joseph Kadane developed an interesting maximization technique that could be applied to this problem. See Friedheim et al., *Forecasting Outcomes* [CRC 291], vol. 1, appendix C, pp. C1–C8.

Chapter 4: Committee II: Attempting to Create "Agreement in the Large" via Trade-offs

1. Raiffa, *Art and Science of Negotiation*, pp. 155–160.
2. Zartman, *50% solution*, p. 10.
3. The phrase "agreement in the large" is borrowed from Sebenius, *Negotiating the Law of the Sea*.
4. Grotius, *Freedom of the Seas*.
5. See Jonathan I. Charney, "Technology and International Negotiations," *American Journal of International Law* 76, no. 1 (1982): 78–118.
6. See Eckert, *Enclosure of Ocean Resources*, pp. 3–20.
7. See Richard J. Sweeney et al., "Market Failure, The Common Pool Problem, and Ocean Resource Exploitation," 179–192.
8. See Pearson, *International Marine Environmental Policy*, pp. 4–7.
9. See Alan G. Friedman, "U.S. Law of the Sea Policy," *Marine Policy* (October 1978), pp. 304–320; Hollick, "Seabeds Make Strange Politics," *Foreign Policy* 9 (1972–73): 148–170.
10. For the positions of the stakeholders of the late 1960s and early 1970s, see Robert Osgood et al., *Toward a National Ocean Policy*, pp. 87–198.
11. Breckner et al., *The Navy and the Common Sea*, pp. 191–212.
12. The attack on the regime's rules by Third World states did not begin at UNCLOS III, but rather at UNCLOS I. See Friedheim, "The 'Satisfied' and 'Dissatisfied' States Negotiate International Law," pp. 20–41.
13. See Garcia-Amador, "The Origins of the Concept of an Exclusive Economic Zone: Latin American Practice and Legislation," in Vicuña, ed., *The Exclusive Economic Zone: A Latin American Perspective*, pp. 7–26; Thomas A. Clingan, Jr., "The Emerging Law of the Sea: The Economic Zone Dilemma," *San Diego Law Review* 14, no. 3 (1977): 538–541; and Oxman, "An Analysis of the Exclusive Economic Zone as Formulated in the Informal Composite Negotiating Text," *Law of the Sea: State Practice in Zones of Special Jurisdiction*, ed. by Thomas A. Clingan, Jr. (Honolulu: University of Hawaii Law of the Sea Institute, 1982), p. 77.

14. For the concept of imposed regimes, see Young, *Resource Regimes*, pp. 98–99.

15. See James Cable, *Gunboat Diplomacy, 1919–1979*, 2d ed. (New York: St. Martin's Press, 1986); Ken Booth, *Law, Force and Diplomacy at Sea* (London: George Allen & Unwin, 1985), pp. 47–49.

16. On mixed motives in bargaining, see Zartman, *50% Solution*, p. 9.

17. On earlier attempts in the twentieth century to bargain over ocean issues, see Friedheim, "Politics of the Sea," pp. 29–93; and Hollick, *U.S. Foreign Policy and the Law of the Sea*, pp. 127–159.

18. John R. Stevenson and Bernard H. Oxman, "The Preparations for the Law of the Sea Conference," *American Journal of International Law* 68, no. 1 (1974): 9–13.

19. See Jessup, *Law of Territorial Waters and Maritime Jurisdiction*.

20. On the importance of innocent passage before UNCLOS III, see "The Fourth Dimension of Seapower: Special Issue," *The JAG Journal* 22, no. 2 (1967): 22–51; E. D. Brown, "The Legal Regime of Inner Space: Military Aspects," *Current Legal Problems* 22 (1969): 183–185.

21. This is still a matter of concern. See Bruce Harlow, *Mission Impossible? Preservation of U.S. Maritime Freedoms*, McKernan Lecture in Marine Policy (Seattle: Washington Sea Grant, 1985), pp. 8–12.

22. See Bureau of Intelligence and Research, U.S. Department of State, *Sovereignty of the Sea*, Geographic Bulletin no. 3 (1965).

23. For the traditional ocean law position of the Soviet Union, see William Butler, *The Law of Soviet Territorial Waters* (New York: Praeger, 1967); for an analysis of the Soviet Union's bargaining at UNCLOS I and II, see Friedheim, "Factor Analysis as a Tool," pp. 47–70.

24. P. D. Barabolya et al., *Manual of International Maritime Law*, pts. 1–2 (Washington, D.C.: Commerce Clearinghouse, 1968).

25. See Friedheim, "Factor Analysis As a Tool," pp. 56–67.

26. See Friedheim, "Politics of the Sea," pp. 29–93; Hollick, *U.S. Foreign Policy and the Law of the Sea*, pp. 127–159.

27. Akaha, *Japan in Global Ocean Politics*, p. 117.

28. Oxman, *From Cooperation to Conflict: The Soviet Union and the United States at the Third U.N. Conference on the Law of the Sea* (Seattle: Washington Sea Grant, 1984), pp. 7–8.

29. U.S. Congress, Senate, Committee on Commerce, Science and Transportation, *The Third U.N. Law of the Sea Conference*, 95th Congress, 2d Session, p. 28.

30. See Barry B. L. Auguste, *The Continental Shelf: The Practice and Policy of the Latin American States, with Special Reference to Chile, Ecuador, and Peru* (Geneva: Droz, 1960); Loring, "The United States–Peruvian 'Fisheries' Dispute," pp. 391–453.

31. Our data confirm the observations of Stevenson and Oxman, in "The Preparations for the Law of the Sea Conference," pp. 9–13.

32. This is a matter of current concern, especially since many of the defenders of the Convention from the Third World would deny rights under the Convention to nonsignatories, principally the United States. However, as signatories, they may

choose to ignore some of the Convention's provisions. See Caminos and Molitor, "Progressive Development of International Law and the Package Deal," pp. 871–890.

33. Oxman, "From Cooperation to Conflict," pp. 7–8; Robert L. Friedheim and Mary Jehn, "The Soviet Position at the Third U.N. Law of the Sea Conference" in *Soviet Naval Policy: Objectives and Constraints,* ed. M. McGwire, K. Booth, and J. McDonnell (New York: Praeger, 1975), pp. 341–362.

34. See Harlow, "Mission Impossible?"

35. V. Manchits and Y. Markov, "Legal Regime of International Straits," *Morskoy Sbornik* 9 (1985): 95.

36. See W. Michael Reisman, "The Regime of Straits and National Security: An Appraisal of International Lawmaking," *American Journal of International Law* 74, no. 1 (1980): 48–76; John Norton Moore, "The Regime of Straits and the Third Nations Conference on the Law of the Sea," *American Journal of International Law* 74, no. 1 (1980): 77–121.

37. Committee on Commerce, *The Third United Nations Law of the Sea Conference,* p. 28; also see Robert W. Smith, "An Analysis of the Strategic Attributes of International Straits," *Maritime Studies Management* 2, no. 2 (1974): 88–101.

38. Haruhiro Fukui, "How Japan Handled UNCLOS Issues: Does Japan Have an Ocean Policy?" and Tsuneo Akaha, "A Cybernetic Analysis of Japan's Fishery Policy Process," in Friedheim et al., *Japan and the New Ocean Regime,* pp. 22–24; 36–44; 191–192.

39. See Oceanographer of the Navy, *An Assessment of the Contribution to Coastal Pollution by Transiting Ships in Selected International Straits* (Washington, D.C.: unpublished, 1972); Oxman, "The Third United Nations Conference on the Law of the Sea: The 1977 New York Session," p. 64; George Kent and Mark Valencia, eds., *Marine Policy in Southeast Asia* (Berkeley: University of California Press, 1985), pp. 26; 223–225; 379–381.

40. Willard Hanna, "Nationalizing the Straits of Malacca," *American Field Staff Reports, Southeast Asia Series* 21, no. 8 (1973): 1–9.

41. On "choke points," see Booth, *Law, Force, and Diplomacy at Sea,* chap. 5.

42. The Montreau Convention is reprinted in Barabolya, *Manual of International Maritime Law,* pt. 1, pp. 148–161.

43. Scandinavian states are still sensitive to unauthorized submarine incursions through their straits. See Kjell Goldmann, "The Challenge To Sweden," in Sverre Jerrel and Kare Nyblom, eds., *The Military Buildup in the High North* (Lanham, Md.: Harvard University Center for International Affairs, and University Press of America, 1986), pp. 107–124.

44. See Alfred T. Mahan, *The Influence of Seapower Upon History, 1660–1783* (Boston: Little, Brown, 1890); James J. Tritten, "Benefits of Seapower: Mahan was more than a mercantilist," *Journal of the Australian Naval Institute* 9, no. 2 (May 1983): 19–20; John B. Hattendorf, "Some Concepts in American Naval Strategic Thought, 1940–70," in Joyce Bartell, ed., *The Yankee Mariner and Seapower:*

America's Challenge of Ocean Space (Los Angeles: University of Southern California Press, 1982), pp. 93–109.

45. Oxman, *From Cooperation to Conflict,* pp. 20–21.

46. The metaphor harked back to the supposed ruination of trade in medieval Europe caused by landholders on the banks of the Rhine stretching a chain across the river, and demanding ruinously high tariffs to lift it. This notion was bruited about in U.S. Government agencies in the late 1960s–early 1970s.

47. Article 1 of the 1944 Chicago Convention on International Civil Aviation, *Final Act and Related Documents of the International Civil Aviation Conference,* Department of State Publication no. 2282.

48. Article 14[6] of the 1958 Convention on the Territorial Sea, as reprinted in Plotzoder and Vitzthum, eds., *Seerecht,* p. 22.

49. Maureen T. Franssen, "The Archipelagic Principle," *Oceanus* 12 (1973): pp. 15–17.

50. Osgood, "U.S. Security Interests in Ocean Law," *Ocean Development and International Law* 2, no. 1 (1974): 11–15.

51. Leslie Gelb, "U.S. Jets for Israel Took Route around Some Allies," *New York Times* (October 24, 1973), p. 1.

52. Cable, *Gunboat Diplomacy,* p. 8. Also see: Edward N. Luttwak, *The Political Uses of Sea Power* (Baltimore: Johns Hopkins University Press, 1974), pp. 1–38.

53. See Bureau of Public Affairs, U.S. Department of State, "Address of Ambassador John R. Stevenson, Special Representative of the President and United States Representative to the Law of the Sea Conference before the Plenary Session at Caracas, Venezuela," News Release, July 11, 1974.

54. Caminos and Molitor do not cite a single statement by an official representative of the United States Government accepting the package deal. Caminos and Molitor, "Progressive Development of International Law," pp. 871–890. Many statements, including those of the John R. Stevenson, head of the U.S. delegation at the time the package deal was made, deny explicitly that an arrangement relating to the deep seabed was part of the package deal. See *Ocean Science News* (May 1990), p. 5.

55. For a discussion of "imposed" regimes, see Young, *Resource Regimes,* pp. 98–99.

56. Hollick, *U.S. Foreign Policy and the Law of the Sea,* p. 236.

57. As noted in chapter 3, at note 41, in order to keep the length of this work manageable, detailed discussions of the time-series analyses performed have been omitted.

58. See Ruth Lapidoth, "The Strait of Tiran, the Gulf of Aquaba, and the 1979 Treaty of Peace," *American Journal of International Law* 77, no. 1 (1983): 84–108.

59. See Donat Pharand, "The Northwest Passage in International Law," *Canadian Yearbook of International Law* 17 (1979): 99–133; Donat Pharand, *The Waters of the Canadian Archipelago in International Law* (Cambridge: Cambridge University

Press, 1986). For a review of the legal and political problems of the United States and Canada in the Arctic, see papers by D. L. VanderZwaag, C. Lamson, W. E. Westermeyer, V. Goyal, D. M. McRae, and R. L. Friedheim in the "U.S.–Canada Arctic Policy Forum," *Arctic* 39, no. 4 (1986): 327–367.

60. See D. M. McRae and D. J. Goudry, "Environmental Jurisdiction in Arctic Waters: The Extent of Article 234," *University of British Columbia Law Review* 16 (1982): 197–228.

61. Nordquist and Park, eds., *Reports of the U.S. Delegation,* p. 97.

62. For example, in 1976, the United States unilaterally declared a 200-mile "Fishing Conservation Zone," within which it enforced most of the coastal-state rights associated with an economic zone. The United States adopted a full economic zone in 1983. See President of the United States, "Exclusive Economic Zone of the United States of America," White House Press Release, 10 March 1983.

63. See, for example, David A. Colson, "The Arctic: Geopolitics and the Law of the Sea," a paper delivered at the 11th Annual Seminar of the Center for Ocean Law and Policy, University of Virginia, March 27, 1987.

64. See Caminos and Molitor, "Progressive Development of International Law"; p. 875 Tommy T. B. Koh, "Should the United States Ratify the New Law of the Sea Treaty?" *Seward Johnson Lecture in Marine Policy* (Falmouth: Woods Hole Oceanographic Institution, 1980).

65. See Jean Bodin, *Six Books Concerning the State,* reprinted in *Readings in Political Philosophy,* ed. by Francis Coker (New York: Macmillan, 1938), pp. 370–381; and George Sabine, *History of Political Thought* (New York: Henry Holt, 1937), pp. 399–414.

66. The 200-mile EEZ began as the "patrimonial sea," a concept put forward by a number of Latin American states who sympathized with aspects of the 200-mile territorial sea claims made by the so-called C-E-P states (Chile-Ecuador-Peru), but who were, for a variety of reasons, reluctant to go as far as their regional colleagues. What they had in mind for the "patrimonial sea" is described in Vicuña, ed., *The Exclusive Economic Zone: A Latin American Perspective,* and Andres M. Aquilar, "The Patrimonial Sea or Economic Zone Concept," *San Diego Law Review* 11, no. 3 (1974): 579–602.

67. Landlocked states wanted to limit coastal states to control of 200 meters depth of water, or 40 nautical miles, whichever was further, with an additional requirement of preferential right for landlocked states citizens in those zones of their coastal neighbors. Stevenson and Oxman, "Preparations for the Law of the Sea Conference," p. 16.

68. Indeed, this was the advice I was giving during that era as a member of a study group working for the U.S. Navy doing preparatory work for UNCLOS III. See Breckner et al., *The Navy and the Common Sea,* pt. 3, pp. 135–225.

69. Hollick, "United States Ocean Politics," *San Diego Law Review* 10, no. 3 (1973): p. 469.

70. See Law of the Sea Study Group, "The Landlocked and Shelf-locked States in the Law of the Sea Negotiations," Center for Naval Analyses, Memorandum 01-

74, 31 January 1974; and Friedheim, "Law of the Sea Briefing for P^3 Advisory Committee," Center for Naval Analyses, Memorandum, 01598-74, 3 October 1974.

71. Nordquist and Park, eds., *Reports of the U.S. Delegation*, p. 102.

72. For a small sample of early and late statements see Committee on the Peaceful Uses of the Seabed and Ocean Floor Beyond the Limits of National Jurisdiction, *Summary Records*, (A/C.138/SR. 17–28), November 1970, pp. 17, 31, 49; Third United Nations Conference on the Law of the Sea, *Provisional Summary Records* (A/CONF. 62/SR. 162), April 1982, pp. 19, 28, 30.

73. Committee on Commerce, *Third U.N. Law of the Sea Conference*, p. 41.

74. Standard deviations tightened, indicating that members of all groups moved toward coherent group positions. This is to be expected on an issue on which there was a near-consensus outcome.

75. See Hollick, *U.S. Foreign Policy and the Law of the Sea*, pp. 75–80.

76. Nordquist and Park, eds., *Reports of the U.S. Delegation*, p. 87.

77. See Robert Bowen, "The Landlocked and Geographically Disadvantaged States and the Law of the Sea," *Political Geography Quarterly* 5, no. 1 (1986): 63–69.

78. The results of a pairs analysis, showing the failure of consensus to emerge, has been omitted for reasons of space.

79. Article 2, "Convention on the High Seas (1958)," reprinted in Platzoder and Vitzthum, eds., *Seerecht*, p. 28. See the references in notes 19–20 for the traditional interpretation of high-seas rights.

80. Nordquist and Park, eds., *Reports of the U.S. Delegation*, pp. 67, 105, 128–129. The Soviet Union also was concerned about the question of whether the waters of the EEZ would be subject to high-seas rights. F. Kovalyov, "The Economic Zone and Its Legal Status," *International Affairs (USSR)* 2 (1979): 62.

81. Clingan, "The Emerging Law of the Sea: The Economic Zone Dilemma," p. 541.

82. See Tullio Treves, "Military Installations, Structures, and Devices on the Seabed," *American Journal of International Law* 744 (1980): 808–857.

83. Oxman, "The Third United Nations Conference on the Law of the Sea: the Ninth Session (1980)," p. 235.

84. For a discussion of Zartman's "framework to details" conceptual scheme, see chapter 3 of this work, or Zartman and Berman, *Practical Negotiator*, chaps. 4–5, pp. 87–202.

85. Nordquist and Park, eds., *Reports of the U.S. Delegation*, p. 68.

86. David A. Ross, *Opportunities and Uses of the Ocean* (New York: Springer-Verlag, 1978), pp. 11–17.

87. "Proclamation of President Truman of 28 September 1945 on Policy of the United States with Respect of the Natural Resources of the Subsoil and Seabed of the Continental Shelf," reprinted in Platzoder and Vitzthum, eds., *Seerecht*, pp. 475–476. For a more extended discussion of the Truman Proclamations, see chapter 1.

88. Ross, *Introduction to Oceanography*, 4th ed. (Englewood Cliffs, N.J.: Prentice-Hall, 1988), p. 101.

89. See Breckner et al., *The Navy and the Common Sea*, pp. 155–160.

90. See, for example, Hollick, *U.S. Foreign Policy and the Law of the Sea,* pp. 67–95.

91. "Convention on the Continental Shelf (1958)," reprinted in Platzoder and Vitzthum, eds., *Seerecht,* pp. 58–63. For a discussion of all four conventions produced by the First United Nations Conference on the Law of the Sea, see chapter 1.

92. An American proposal to limit the claim to jurisdiction was defeated by the assembled states. See the vote on the Indian proposal to convert the language from exclusive to sovereign. United Nations Conference on the Law of the Sea, *Official Records,* vol. 2, *Plenary Meetings* (A/Conf.13/38), p. 14.

93. See Slouka, *International Custom and the Continental Shelf.*

94. See Eckert, *Enclosure of Ocean Resources,* pp. 47–58.

95. Ross, *Introduction to Oceanography,* p. 100.

96. U.N. General Assembly, "Draft United Nations Convention on the International Seabed Area," Report of the Committee on the Peaceful Uses of the Seabed and the Ocean Floor Beyond the Limits of National Jurisdiction, *Official Records* 25th Sess., Supplement no. 21 (A/8021), 1970, pp. 130–190.

97. The notion of cross-cutting cleavages was borrowed from Axelrod, *Conflict of Interest,* pp. 158–164.

98. Buzan, "United We Stand," p. 185; S. Jayakumar and T. T. B. Koh, *The Negotiating Process of the Third United Nations Conference on the Law of the Sea.* (March 1980), mimeo, p. 36.

99. See Hollis Hedberg, "Boundary Reforms of the Proposed Law of the Sea and Recommended U.S. Action," *Oil and Gas Journal* (February 15, 1982), pp. 175–189, and "A Critique of Boundary Provisions in the Proposed Law of the Sea," *Ocean Science News: On Station* (August 24, 1981).

100. See Choon-ho Park, *East Asia and the Law of the Sea* (Seoul: National University Press, 1983), pp. 1–52; Masayuki Takeyama, "Japan's Foreign Negotiations over Offshore Oil Development," in Friedheim et al., *Japan and the New Ocean Regime,* pp. 276–313.

101. For reasons of space, a display of the confirming data has been omitted.

102. Article 62, Part II, SNT.

103. Zartman, "Conclusions: Importance of North-South Negotiations," in Zartman, ed., *Positive Sum: Improving North-South Negotiations* (New Brunswick, N.J.: Transaction, 1987), p. 292.

104. Article 68, Part II, SNT.

105. Article 64, Part II, RSNT.

106. Article 76, ICNT.

107. Article 70, Part II, RSNT.

108. Article 82, ICNT.

109. Bernard Oxman provides a useful chart of the provisions demonstrating what he thought the proposers meant by the language of Article 76. "The Third United Nations Conference on the Law of the Sea: Ninth Session (1980)," p. 229.

110. See Hedberg, "Geomorphic Basis for National-International Boundaries on the Ocean Floor," *AAPG Studies in Geology no. 2* (1981), pp. 441–464, and "Ocean Floor Boundaries," *Science* (April 13, 1979), pp. 135–144.

111. Pardo, "Law of the Sea Conference—What Went Wrong," in Friedheim, ed., *Managing Ocean Resources*, pp. 144–148, and "The Convention on the Law of the Sea—A Preliminary Appraisal," *San Diego Law Review* 20, no. 2 (1983): 492.

112. Oxman, *From Cooperation to Conflict*, p. 17.

113. Park, *East Asia and the Law of the Sea;* Kent and Valencia, eds., *Marine Policy in Southeast Asia.*

114. Thomas A. Clingan, Jr., *The 1982 Law of the Sea Treaty: One Observer's Assessment of the Conference, the Treaty, and Beyond*, McKernan Lectures in Marine Affairs (Seattle: University of Washington Sea Grant Program, 1986), p. 15.

Chapter 5: Terminating the Common Wealth in Ocean Fisheries

1. For descriptions of arguments concerning closed and open seas, see White, *Seven Great Statesmen in the Warfare of Humanity with Unreason*, pp. 62–63; Knight, *Life and Works of Hugo Grotius*, pp. 108–109.

2. Human intervention can affect the reproduction of wild animals as a result of predation, especially at a vulnerable time in the animals' life cycle, such as a spawning period.

3. See National Oceanic and Atmospheric Administration, *Antarctic Marine Living Resources: Directed Research, Program Plan Update, 1988–90*, March 1987, p. 14; World Resources Institute and International Institute for Environment and Development, *Resources 1988–89* (New York: Basic Books, 1988), pp. 194–197.

4. See Krasner, "Structural Causes and Regime Consequences," p. 185; Young, "International Regimes: Problems of Concept Formation," *World Politics* 32 (April 1980): 331–356; and Robert Keohane and Joseph Nye, *Power and Interdependence* (Boston: Little, Brown, 1977), pp. 38–42.

5. See Albert W. Koers, *International Regulation of Marine Fisheries* (London: Fishing News, 1973), pp. 17–19.

6. Friedheim, "The Political, Economic, and Legal Ocean," in Friedheim, ed., *Managing Ocean Resources*, p. 28.

7. Fenwick, *International Law*, 4th ed., pp. 404–408.

8. See C. P. Idyll, *The Sea Against Hunger* (New York: Crowell, 1978), pp. 10–14; 145–161.

9. Hardin, "The Tragedy of the Commons," in Hardin and Baden, eds., *Managing the Commons* (San Francisco: Freeman, 1977), pp. 16–30.

10. There has been a recent attempt to correct the errors of Garrett Hardin who used the enclosure of the English Commons as the example of his "tragedy." Hardin's example concerned enclosure of *communal* land. By definition, the land was owned by the community, which could both exclude outsiders (and therefore there was no open entry) and impose use rules on members to prevent overexploitation. Contrary to Hardin's view, enclosure of the English Commons occurred because of economic greed, rather than the inexorable working of things. I believe those who demonstrated Hardin's misinterpretation of the events of the eighteenth century are correct. The incentives that promote tragedy are found when resources are unowned and indivisible, not when owned by individual or group. However, I am not ready to abandon the term "commons" to the critics, since one of its meanings as a word

is "pertaining to all," or common. I argue this point in "Managing the Second Phase of Enclosure," *Ocean and Coastal Management*, 17 (1992): 223–25. Among the notable critiques of Hardin are F. Berkes et al., "The Benefits of the Commons," *Nature* 340 (13 July 1989): 91–93; Fikret Berkes and David Feeny, "Paradigms Lost," *Alternatives* 17, no. 2 (1990): 48–55; Daniel W. Bromley, "The Commons, Property, and Common Property Regimes," paper presented at the First Annual Meeting of the International Association for the Study of Common Property, Duke University, 27–30 September 1990; and Susan Hanna, "The Eighteenth-Century English Commons: A Model for Ocean Management," *Journal of Ocean and Shoreline Management* 14, no. 3 (1990): 155–172.

11. I am grateful to Francis T. Christy, Jr., for pointing out the differences between the two types of overfishing, in his letter to me of 21 August 1990.

12. See Paul A. Driver, "International Fisheries," in R. P. Barston and Patricia Birnie, *The Maritime Dimension* (London: Allen & Unwin, 1980), pp. 35–36.

13. Wilbert Chapman, "The Theory and Practice of International Fishery Development-Management," *San Diego Law Review* 7 (1970), pp. 445–446.

14. Christy, letter to Friedheim, 21 August 1990.

15. See J. Scharfe, "Interrelations between Fishing Technology and the Coming International Fishery Regime," in Christy et al., *Law of the Sea: Caracas and Beyond* (Cambridge, Mass.: Ballinger, 1975), pp. 259–264.

16. See Committee on Commerce, U. S. Senate, "The Soviet Fishing Fleet," *Soviet Oceans Development*, 94th Cong., 2d Sess., pp. 377–478.

17. Vladimir Kaczynski, *Controversies in Strategy of Marine Fisheries Development between Eastern and Western Countries* (Seattle: University of Washington Institute for Marine Studies, 1977).

18. Roy Jackson, "Extended Fisheries Jurisdiction: Palliative or Panacea?" Donald L. McKernon Lecture in Marine Affairs (Seattle: University of Washington Sea Grant Program, 1981), p. 25.

19. For an interesting view of the fight over tuna from the point of view of the U.S. tuna industry, see August Felando, "Tuna and UNCLOS III," unpublished manuscript, October 1982, p. 60.

20. See Hollick, *U.S. Foreign Policy and the Law of the Sea*, pp. 75–95.

21. For the literature on the prisoner's dilemma, see Axelrod, *Evolution of Cooperation*.

22. Friedheim, "International Organizations and the Uses of the Oceans" in Robert Jordan, ed., *Multinational Cooperation* (New York: Oxford University Press, 1972), pp. 236–251.

23. Friedheim and Akaha, "Antarctic Resources and International Law: Japan and United States and the Future of Antarctica," *Ecology Law Quarterly* 16, no. 1 (1989): 1,413–1,414. However, as a consequence of refusing to lift the moratorium on commercial whaling at the IWC meeting in Reykjavik (May 1991), Iceland has formally announced its withdrawal from the Commission. Norway, Japan, and others may follow. Bold action without consensus has its costs. *Marine Mammal News* 17, no. 5 (May 1991).

24. See Koers, *International Regulation of Marine Fisheries*, pp. 77–228.

25. Pardo, "Law of the Sea Conference–What Went Wrong," in Friedheim, ed. *Managing Ocean Resources*, pp. 139–140.

26. Pardo, "Speech before the General Assembly," (mimeo).

27. Friedheim, "Understanding the Debate on Ocean Resources," University of Denver *Monograph Series in World Affairs* 6, no. 3 (1969): 7–8.

28. Hollick, *U.S. Foreign Policy and the Law of the Sea*, pp. 75–77, n. 65.

29. "It is now recognized almost universally, particularly since the FAO World Conference on Fisheries Management and Development held in Rome, June–July 1984, that where there is open access to resources for nationals, there is little incentive for individual fishermen to conserve the stocks." Chris Newton, "A Review of Management Schemes in Developing Countries," in *Fishery Access Control Programs Worldwide*, Alaska Sea Grant Report No. 86-4 (Fairbanks: Alaska Sea Grant, 1986), p. 360.

30. This phenomenon has occurred widely around the world. I investigated the attempt by the Japanese Government and a regional electric power company to construct a nuclear power plant in the coastal village of Onagawa. Even though generous compensation was offered to the local fishermen's cooperative, many members fought the plant vigorously. When the plant was authorized and compensation was paid, it was quickly spent by many fishermen, who were left with no cash and no livelihood. Friedheim, "Coastal Management and Nuclear Power," in Friedheim et al., *Japan and the New Ocean Regime*, pp. 314–352.

31. Hollick, *U.S. Foreign Policy and the Law of the Sea*, pp. 19–22.

32. Proclamation 2667, "Policy of the United States With Respect to the Natural Resources of the Subsoil and Seabed of the Continental Shelf," *Federal Register*, vol. 10 (28 September 1945), p. 12,303.

33. Proclamation 2668, "Policy of the United States With Respect to Coastal Fisheries in Certain Areas of the High Seas," *Federal Register*, vol. 10 (28 September 1945), p. 12,304.

34. See Vicuña, ed., *The Exclusive Economic Zone: A Latin American Perspective*.

35. Hearnshaw, "Grotius and the Reign of Law," in *Some Great Political Idealists of the Christian Era*, pp. 85–86.

36. Eckert, *Enclosure of Ocean Resources*, p. 116.

37. Friedheim, "The Politics of the Sea."

38. See Akaha, *Japan in Global Ocean Politics*, pp. 85–100.

39. On the concept of cross-cutting pressures and cleavages, see Axelrod, *Conflict of Interest*.

40. For the interesting argument that the so-called C-E-P states (Chile, Ecuador, and Peru), thought to have been claiming general jurisdiction or sovereignty, really meant all along what was later defined as an EEZ, see Garcia-Amador, "The Origins of the Concept of an Exclusive Economic Zone," in Vicuña, ed., *The Exclusive Economic Zone: A Latin American Perspective*, pp. 7–26.

41. Under the traditional U.N. voting system, two-thirds of states present and voting can pass a measure. Therefore to block, one-third plus one votes are needed. See,

for example, Rules 35, 36, "Rules of Procedure, United Nations Conference on the Law of the Sea," *Official Records,* vol. 2, Plenary Meetings (A/Conf.13/38), p. xxxiii. Hereinafter UNCLOS I.

42. Law of the Sea Study Group, "The View from the Beginning of the Conference: Projected Outcomes on Seven Major Law of the Sea Issues," Center for Naval Analyses, Memorandum 01011-74, 26 June 1974.

43. Felando, "Tuna and UNCLOS III," p. 14.

44. See, for example, the statement of the head of the U.S. Delegation, John R. Stevenson, "of the critical importance for a successful conference of adequate guarantees of transit in straits," Stevenson and Oxman, "Preparations for the Law of the Sea Conference," p. 12.

45. Article 55, *Official Text of the United Nations Convention on the Law of the Sea with Annexes and Index* (New York: United Nations, 1983), p. 18. Hereinafter UNCLOS III Convention.

46. Article 57, UNCLOS III Convention.

47. Article 56, paras. 1 (a) (b), UNCLOS III Convention.

48. Article 58, para. 1, UNCLOS III Convention.

49. For example, the United States gained sovereign rights over 3.9 billion acres. The land area of the United States and its territories encompasses only 2.3 billion acres. "Introduction: The Exclusive Economic Zone, Special Issue," *Oceanus* 27, no. 4 (Winter 1984/85): p. 3.

50. The grandfather clause as a device for including or excluding particular claimants was invented during the Reconstruction Period after the U.S. Civil War to avoid giving newly enfranchised black citizens the right to vote by restricting the right to vote only to those citizens whose grandfathers voted.

51. See, for example Gordon R. Munro, "The Optimal Management of Transboundary Renewable Resources," *Canadian Journal of Economics* (1979) 12, no. 3: 335–376, and "The Management of Shared Fishery Resources under Extended Jurisdiction," *Marine Resource Economics* 3, no. 4 (1986): 276–287; T. Kawasaki, "The 200-mile regime and the management of the transboundary and high seas stocks," *Ocean Management* 9, nos. 1–2 (July 1984): 7–20.

52. See George Taft, "The Third U.N. Law of the Sea Conference: Unresolved Fisheries Issues," *Columbia Journal of Transnational Law* 14, no. 1 (1975): 113–114.

53. Article 50(1), Informal Single Negotiating Text, May 7, 1975 (U.N. Doc. A/Conf.62/WP.8).

54. I am grateful to Ross D. Eckert for making this point in his comments to me of 22 April 1990.

55. It was precisely the coastal state's power to "deprive other States of the right to participate in determining how their interests would be defined and protected" that was the subject of concern to the head of the U.S. Delegation, John Stevenson, in 1971. Quoted approvingly in Felando, "Tuna and UNCLOS III," p. 59.

56. William G. Gordon and Richard E. Gutting, Jr., "The Coastal Fishing Industry and the EEZ," *Oceanus* 27, no. 4 (Winter 1984/85): 35–40.

57. Susan Ferguson, "UNCLOS III: Last Chance For Land-Locked States?," *San Diego Law Review* 14, no. 3 (April 1977): 637.
58. On the interests of landlocked states, see Lewis Alexander and Robert Hodgson, "The Role of the Geographically Disadvantaged States in the Law of the Sea," *San Diego Law Review* 13, no. 3 (1976): 558–582; Lewis Alexander, "The Disadvantaged States and the Law of the Sea," *Marine Policy* 5, no. 3 (1981): 185–193.
59. For analyses of the political behavior of the landlocked at UNCLOS I and II, see Bowen, "The Geographically Disadvantaged States and the Law of the Sea: A Study in Coalition Formation, 1967–75," (Ph.D. diss., Los Angeles: University of Southern California, 1983), and Friedheim, "The Politics of the Sea."
60. Article 3, Convention on the High Seas, UNCLOS I.
61. Article 4, High Seas Convention, UNCLOS I.
62. Article 14, Convention on the Territorial Sea, UNCLOS I.
63. See Part X, UNCLOS III Convention.
64. Article 125 (2), UNCLOS III Convention.
65. Article 140 (1), 148, 161 (1) (d), 161 (2) (a), UNCLOS III Convention.
66. For definitions of these groups and statistics concerning the attributes of their members, see Alexander and Hodgson, "The Role of Geographically Disadvantaged States in the Law of the Sea." For statistical data concerning the interests of these states, see Karen Goudreau and William J. Durch, *Forecasting Outcomes of Multilateral Negotiations: Methodology: Codebook* [CRC 291] vol. 2 (Alexandria, Va.: Center for Naval Analyses, 1977), pp. 195–212.
67. Nordquist and Park, eds., *Reports of the U.S. Delegation,* p. 30.
68. Mr. Jens Evensen, Minister for Law of the Sea Questions, Statement to the Storting on questions related to fishery limits and the Law of the Sea on 28 May 1976, (mimeo), p. 6.
69. SNT.
70. Since this issue concerns the efforts of a known number of caucusing groups acting as stakeholders to force the majority to retreat, and we have described the behavior of these groups, we will omit the formal analysis of caucusing groups on this issue. It merely confirms what has already been described.
71. Robert E. Bowen came to essentially the same conclusion in "The land-locked and geographically disadvantaged states and the law of the sea," *Political Geography Quarterly* 5, no. 1 (January 1986): 68
72. James Joseph, "The Management of Highly Migratory Species—Some Concepts," *Marine Policy* 1, no. 4 (October 1977): 275–288.
73. The principal North-North quarrel on anadromous species was between Japan and the United States. See Akaha, *Japan in Global Ocean Politics,* p. 72.
74. Article 66 (1), UNCLOS III Convention.
75. Article 66 (3) (a), UNCLOS III Convention.
76. William T. Burke, "U.S. Fishery Management and the New Law of the Sea," *American Journal of International Law* 761 (1982): 46.
77. Hollick, *U.S. Foreign Policy and the Law of the Sea,* pp. 67–95.

78. Friedheim, "International Organizations and the Uses of the Ocean," in Robert S. Jordan, ed. *Multinational Cooperation: Economic, Social, and Scientific Development*, pp. 243–251.

79. Fishermen's Protective Act, PL 680, 27 August 1954 in U.S. *Statutes at Large*, 89th Cong., vol. 79, 1965, p. 660.

80. Felando, "Tuna and UNCLOS III," p. 60.

81. Fukui, "How Japan Handled UNCLOS Issues: Does Japan Have an Ocean Policy," in Friedheim et al., *Japan and the New Ocean Regime*, p. 23.

82. Article 64 (1), UNCLOS III Convention.

Chapter 6: Committee III: Making the EEZ Work and Scientists Pay

1. See Chapter 1, R. Michael M'Gonigle and Mark W. Zacher, *Pollution, Politics and International Law: Tankers at Sea* (Berkeley: University of California Press, 1979), pp. 3–38.

2. The use of foreign vessels in cabotage is prohibited by the United States in Section 27 of the Merchant Marine Act of 1920 (Jones Act). Samuel A. Lawrence, *United States Merchant Shipping Policies and Politics* (Washington, D.C.: Brookings, 1980), p. 35.

3. See Boleslaw A. Boczek, *Flags of Convenience: An International Legal Study* (Cambridge: Harvard University Press, 1962); H. Meisers, *The Nationality of Ships* (The Hague: Nijhoff, 1967).

4. This is not the first time that ocean negotiations were used for this purpose. It began with UNCLOS I. See Friedheim, "The 'Satisfied' and 'Dissatisfied' States Negotiate International Law," pp. 20–41.

5. U.S. GOSP Interagency Working Group, *The U.S. Global Ocean Program: A Strategy for Understanding the Role of the Ocean in Global Change* (Washington, D.C.: U.S. GOSP Interagency Working Group, 1987), p. 8; Dennis Pirages, *Global Technopolitics: The International Politics of Technology and Resources* (Pacific Grove, Calif.: Brooks/Cole, 1989), pp. 125–139.

6. World Resources Institute and International Institute for Environment and Development, *World Resources 1988–89*, pp. 163–202; Andrew Goudie, *The Human Impact on the Natural Environment*, 2d ed. (Cambridge: MIT Press, 1986), pp. 247–283.

7. For a useful summary, see Ross, chapter 6, "Ocean Pollution," *Opportunities and Uses of the Ocean*, pp. 194–230.

8. For the general economic argument concerning pollution management, see Eckert, *Enclosure of Ocean Resources*, pp. 160–166.

9. Pearson, *International Marine Environment Policy*, p. 3–7; 18–23, 38.

10. Rapoport and Chammah, *Prisoner's Dilemma*; and Axelrod, *Evolution of Cooperation*.

11. Friedheim, "Ocean Ecology and the World Political System," in John Lawrence Hargrove, ed., *Who Protects the Ocean?* (St. Paul, Minn.: West, 1975), p. 170.

12. For a discussion of a holistic framework for "political ecology," see Anna Bramwell, *Ecology in the 20th Century* (New Haven: Yale University Press, 1989), pp. 39–63.

13. See E. F. Schmacher, *Small is Beautiful* (New York: Harper & Row, 1953); Richard A. Falk, "Toward a World Order Respectful of the Global Ecosystem," *Environmental Affairs* 1, no. 2 (1971): 251–265.

14. See, for example, Jeremy Rifkin, *Entropy: A World View* (New York: Bantam, 1981), pp. 185–187.

15. Jean Bodin, *Six Books of the Republic*, vol. 1, as quoted in W. A. Dunning, *A History of Political Theories: From Luther to Montesquieu* (New York: Macmillan, 1905), p. 96.

16. See Friedheim, "International Organizations and the Uses of the Oceans," in Jordan, ed., *Multinational Cooperation* pp. 223–281; J. D. Kingham and D. M. McRae, "Competent International Organizations and the Law of the Sea," *Marine Policy* (April 1979): 106–132.

17. A useful summary of the arguments can be found in Berhard J. Abrahamsson, *International Ocean Shipping: Current Concepts and Practices* (Boulder, Colo.: Westview, 1980), pp. 124–127.

18. Edgar Gold, *Maritime Transport: The Evolution of International Marine Policy and Shipping Law* (Lexington, Ma.: Lexington Books, 1981), pp. 346–349; Lawrence Juda, "World Shipping, UNCTAD, and the New International Economic Order," *International Organization* 35, no. 3 (1981): 493–516.

19. Friedheim and Kadane, "Ocean Science in the U.N. Political Arena," *Journal of Maritime Law and Commerce* 3, no. 3 (1972): 473–502.

20. Michael Brenner, "The Intergovernmental Oceanographic Commission and the Stockholm Conference: A Case of Institutional Non-Adaption," *International Organization* 29, no. 3 (1975): 771–804.

21. M'Gonigle and Zacher, *Pollution, Politics, and International Law*, p. 15; Lester R. Brown, *Building A Sustainable Society* (New York: Norton, 1981), pp. 58–81; Roy Neresian, *Ships and Shipping* (Tulsa, Okla.: PennWell, 1981), p. 18.

22. See Berhard Abrahamsson and Joseph L. Strickler, *Strategic Aspects of Seaborne Oil* (Beverly Hills, Calif.: Sage, 1973).

23. Most of these data were collected from the meetings of the General Assembly, the Ad Hoc and Permanent Seabed Committees, and the first three sessions of UNCLOS III.

24. Nordquist and Park, eds., *Reports of the U.S. Delegation*, pp. 48–49; Friedheim, "Ocean Ecology and the World Political System," p. 177.

25. Nordquist and Park, eds., *Reports of the U.S. Delegation*, p. 73.

26. Nordquist and Park, eds., *Reports of the U.S. Delegation*, p. 131.

27. *The Law of the Sea: Official Text of the United Nations Convention on the Law of the Sea* (New York: United Nations, 1983), Part XII. Hereinafter UNCLOS III Convention.

28. Article 207, UNCLOS III Convention.

29. Article 208, UNCLOS III Convention.

30. Article 212, UNCLOS III Convention.
31. Article 194, UNCLOS III Convention.
32. Article 197, UNCLOS III Convention.
33. Article 204, UNCLOS III Convention.
34. Article 193, UNCLOS III Convention.
35. Article 203, UNCLOS III Convention.
36. Article 202, UNCLOS III Convention.
37. Young, *Management at the International Level: The Case of the North Pacific* (New York: Nichols, 1977), p. 45.
38. Article 21(5), Part III, Revised Single Negotiating Text (Document A/CONF./ 62/WP. 8/Rev. 1). Hereinafter RSNT.
39. For an account of UNCLOS III from a Canadian perspective, see Clyde Sanger, *Ordering the Oceans: The Making of the Law of the Sea* (Toronto: University of Toronto Press, 1987).
40. Arctic Waters Pollution Prevention Act, *Elizabeth II*, Chapter 47, pp. 653–676.
41. The literature on U.S.–Canada Arctic problems is now large. Two publications provide useful introductions: a Special Section of an issue of *Arctic* 39, no. 4 (December 1986): 327–367. Included are papers by David Vanderzwaag and Cynthia Lamson, William Westermeyer and Vinod Goyal, D. M. McRae, and Robert Friedheim; Franklyn Griffiths, ed., *The Politics of the Northwest Passage* (Montreal: McGill-Queen's Press, 1987). Other aspects of U.S.–Canada Arctic relations are analyzed in: Robert L. Friedheim, "The Regime of the Arctic—Distributional or Integrative Bargaining?" *Ocean Development and International Law* 19 (1989): 493–510.
42. Article 234, UNCLOS III Convention.
43. The data in figure 8.2 were made available to members of the U.S. delegation in the form of forecasts from 1969 to 1975. Many papers were provided, and specific issues analyzed. However, given the general history of the use of these materials, it is doubtful that our forecasts influenced U.S. delegation perception of where matters stood in 1973–1974. On how our work was, and was not used, see Friedheim, "Research Utilization Problems," in Hennessey, ed., *Formulating Marine Policy;* Otho Eskin, *Law of the Sea and the Management of Multilateral Diplomacy* (Charlottesville: University of Virginia Center for Oceans Law and Policy, 1978), pp. 31–33.
44. Nordquist and Park, eds., *Reports of the U.S. Delegation,* p. 74.
45. Nordquist and Park, eds., *Reports of the U.S. Delegation,* p. 132.
46. Article 20(1), Informal Single Negotiating Text, (U. N. Doc. A/Conf.62/WP.8). Hereinafter SNT.
47. Article 219, Composite Single Negotiating Text (A/CONF.62/WP.10/Corr.1). Hereinafter ICNT.
48. Article 212(5), ICNT.
49. Robert Hage, "Canada and the Law of the Sea," *Marine Policy* 8, no. 1 (1984): 8.
50. The Canadian delegation wanted to exclude passages that threatened pollution as not innocent in the definition of innocent passage.

51. Article 26, Part III, SNT.
52. Article 27(2), Part III, SNT.
53. Article 28, Part III, SNT.
54. Article 31, Part III, SNT.
55. Article 35, Part III, SNT.
56. Article 27, Part III, RSNT; Article 218, ICNT; Article 217, UNCLOS III Convention.
57. Article 38, Part III, RSNT; Article 229, ICNT; Article 228, UNCLOS III Convention.
58. Article 219, ICNT; Article 218, UNCLOS III Convention.
59. Article 220(6), UNCLOS III Convention.
60. Descriptive, analytic, and argumentative pieces include Daniel S. Cheever, "Marine Science and Ocean Politics," *Bulletin of the Atomic Scientists* 26, no. 2 (February 1970): 29–34; George Cadwalader, "Freedom for Science in the Oceans," *Science* 182 (5 October 1973): 15–20; John Knauss, "Developing the Freedom of Scientific Research Issue of the Law of the Sea Conference," *Ocean Development and International Law Journal* 1, no. 1 (1973): 93–110; Deborah Shapley, "Oceanography: Albatross of Diplomacy Haunts Seafaring Scientists," *Science* 180 (1973): p. 1,036–1,039; Warren Wooster, "Scientific Aspects of Maritime Sovereignty Claims," *Ocean Development and International Law Journal* 1, no. 1 (1973): 13–20; W. Burger, "Treaty Provisions Concerning Marine Science Research," *Ocean Development and International Law Journal* 1, no. 2 (1973): 159–184; William Burke, "Scientific Research Articles in the Law of the Sea Informal Single Negotiating Text," *Occasional Paper no. 25* (Kingston, R.I.: Law of the Sea Institute, 1975); Manik Talwani, "Marine Research and the Law of the Sea," *Columbia Journal of World Business* 14, no. 4 (1980): pp. 84–91; Ad Hoc Committee of the Freedom of Ocean Science Task Group, Ocean Policy Committee, National Research Council, *Bilateral Agreements for Marine Science* (Washington, D.C.: National Academy Press, 1981); David Ross, "Marine Science and the Law of the Sea," *EOS Journal* 62, no. 35 (1981): 650–652; Warren Wooster, "Ocean Research under Foreign Jurisdiction," *Science* 212, no. 4496 (1981): pp. 754–755; Bowen, "Law of the Sea Threatens Research," *Nature* 317, no. 123 (1985); William L. Sullivan, Jr., "Freedom of Fisheries Research in the U.S. in the Best Interest of the United States," *San Diego Law Review* 22, no. 4 (1985): 793–800; C. Barry Raleigh, "Commentary: The Internationalism of Ocean Science vs. International Politics," *Marine Technology Society Journal* 23, no. 1 (March 1989): 44–47.
61. Article 5(8), Convention on the Continental Shelf, reprinted in Platzoder and Vitzthum, eds., *Seerecht*, p. 60.
62. The early history of the issue was documented in Friedheim and Kadane, "Ocean Science in the U.N. Political Arena," p. 475.
63. Friedheim and Kadane, "Ocean Science in the U.N. Political Arena."
64. Nordquist and Park, eds., *Reports of the U.S. Delegation*, p. 75.
65. Nordquist and Park, eds., *Reports of the U.S. Delegation*, p. 111.

66. Article 25(2), Part III, SNT.
67. Article 68, Part III, RSNT.
68. Article 10, Part I, RSNT.
69. Article 143, ICNT.
70. Articles 143, 257, UNCLOS III Convention.
71. *The U.S. Proposals for Amendment to the Draft Convention on the Law of the Sea (Green Book)*.
72. Joseph Kadane and I published such a prediction in 1972: "But we believe this means that unless states change their views, there is little chance that a requisite majority of the Delegates to the 1973 conference can be induced to vote *for* a sweeping endorsement of the principle of freedom of ocean science research. We think that the odds are even poorer for endorsement of science rights which could be seen by some states as a prima facie infringement of their sovereign rights. This would doom any chance of international acceptance [of a proposal] that would allow scientific research (including fisheries research) to be conducted with only prior notification and without permission in the territorial waters, exclusive fisheries zone, or continental shelf of signatory states." Friedheim and Kadane, "Ocean Science in the U.N. Political Area," p. 500.
73. Giulio Pontecorvo and Maurice Wilkerson, "From Cornucopia to Scarcity: The Current Status of Ocean Resource Use," *Ocean Development and International Law* 5, nos. 2–3 (1978): 395.
74. "Proclamation of an Exclusive Economic Zone of the United States of America" (Proclamation 5030, 10 March 1983) and "Statement by the President on United States Ocean Policy," reprinted in Platzoder and Vitzthum, eds., *Seerecht*, p. 500.
75. This requirement was especially troubling to the U.S. delegation. National Ocean Policy Study, Committee on Commerce, Science and Transportation, *The Third U.N. Law of the Sea Conference*, 95th Congress, 2d Session (June 1978), p. 83.
76. National Ocean Policy Study, *The Third U.N. Law of the Sea Conference*, p. 60.
77. Article 15, Part III, SNT.
78. Article 18, Part III, SNT.
79. Article 21, Part III, SNT.
80. Article 58, Chapter 2, Part III, SNT.
81. Article 60, Chapter 2, Part III, RSNT.
82. Article 61, Chapter 2, Part III, RSNT.
83. Article 247(3), ICNT.
84. Nordquist and Park, eds., *Reports of the U.S. Delegation*, pp. 340–343.
85. Nordquist and Park, eds., *Reports of the U.S. Delegation*, p. 443.
86. Nordquist and Park, eds., *Reports of the U.S. Delegation*, p. 181.
87. Nordquist and Park, eds., *Reports of the U.S. Delegation*, p. 221.
88. Nordquist and Park, eds., *Reports of the U.S. Delegation*, p. 357.
89. Article 246(3), UNCLOS III Convention.
90. For Latin American views, see Vicuña, ed., *The Exclusive Economic Zone: A Latin American Perspective*, pp. 86, 90, 93, 100, 103, 106, 108, 112, 115 (n. 24), 120 (n. 40), 127, 128, 131, 132, 141.

91. Supporting data have been omitted for reasons of space.
92. See, in particular, the views of Wooster, "Ocean Research under Foreign Jurisdiction," note 60; and John A. Knauss, *Marine Research—A Casualty of Law of the Sea,* A McKernan Lecture in Marine Affairs (Seattle: Washington Sea Grant Program, 1988).

Chapter 7: Committee I: Seabed Mineral Exploitation and "Disagreement in the Large"

1. Article 136, UNCLOS III Convention.
2. Pardo, "Law of the Sea Conference—What Went Wrong," in Friedheim, ed., *Managing Ocean Resources,* pp. 137–148, and "An Opportunity Lost," in B. H. Oxman, D. D. Caron, and C. L. O. Buderi, eds., *Law of the Sea: U.S. Policy Dilemma* (San Francisco: ICS Press, 1983), pp. 13–26.
3. For a definition of the concept of "physical commons" see Friedheim, "Managing the Second Phase of Enclosure," *Ocean and Coastal Management* 17 (1992): 217–36.
4. I have addressed these issues in Friedheim and Durch, "The International Seabed Resources Agency Negotiations," pp. 343–384; and Friedheim, "The Third United Nations Conference on the Law of the Sea: North–South Bargaining on Ocean Issues," in Zartman, ed., *Positive Sum: Improving North–South Negotiations,* pp. 73–114. For works on the broader context of the New International Economic Order, consult Krasner, *Structural Conflict* (Berkeley: University of California Press, 1985); Robert O. Keohane and Joseph S. Nye, *Power and Interdependence,* 2d. ed. (Glenville, Ill.: Scott, Foresman, 1989), pp. 35–36; Jeffrey A. Hart, *The New International Economic Order: Conflict Negotiations, 1964–1984* (New York: St. Martin's Press, 1986); Craig Murphy, *The Emergence of the NIEO Ideology* (Boulder, Colo.: Westview, 1983); Thomas G. Weiss, *Multilateral Development Diplomacy in UNCTAD: the Lessons of Group Negotiations, 1964–1984* (New York: St. Martin's Press, 1986).
5. GNP data for the period of 1967–1975 can be found in: Karen W. Goudreau and William J. Durch, *Forecasting Outcomes of Multilateral Negotiations: Methodology: Codebook* [CRC 291] vol. 2 (Arlington, Va.: Center for Naval Analyses, January 1977), pp. 195–214. For current GNP data, see a recent edition of World Resources Institute, *World Resources 1988–89* (New York: Basic Books, 1988), pp. 236–237.
6. If this was an assumption of key Third World leaders at the United Nations, it was proved wrong some years later when the representatives of the infant industry had little trouble persuading a sympathetic new administration in Washington, D.C., to strenuously oppose all NIEO features of the draft treaty.
7. See figure 1, Friedheim and Durch, "The International Seabed Resources Agency Negotiations," p. 354, for an attempt to scale these approaches.
8. For a defense of U.S. enjoyment of rights as a third party, see Luke T. Lee, "The Law of the Sea Convention and Third States," *American Journal of International Law* 77, no. 3 (1983): 541–568.

9. See, for example, Hugo Caminos and Michael R. Molitor, "Progressive Development of International Law," p. 875. In this comprehensive statement of the position
of those who deny the U.S. can enjoy any rights under the Convention, all quotes
of U.S. officials link navigation with EEZ only. For a more general statement of the
linkage between navigation and resource rights, see Richardson, "Power, Mobility
and the Law of the Sea," *Foreign Affairs* 58 (1980): 902–919.

10. Sebenius, *Negotiating the Law of the Sea,* pp. 80–81. Sebenius noted elsewhere
that the supposed trade-off between navigation interests and seabed-mining interests was "implicit." Sebenius, "Deep Ocean Mineral Resources," in Gardner M.
Brown, Jr., and James A. Crutchfield, eds., *Economics of Ocean Resources: A Research Agenda* (Seattle: Washington Sea Grant, 1982), p. 80.

11. Stevenson and Oxman, "The Third United Nations Conference on the Law of the
Sea: The 1975 Geneva Session," *American Journal of International Law* 69 (1975):
767–769.

12. Clingan, *The 1982 Law of the Sea Treaty: One Observer's Assessment,* p. 6.

13. With much trepidation, our study group provided the data and some of the analysis
requested by the U.S. delegation member who attempted an experiment in rational
persuasion. We were convinced that what the U.S. delegate was trying to do was
poor politics. We were neutral concerning his economic argument: "The policies
are more likely to be perverse in the sense that industrially developed land-based
mineral producers are those protected, with mineral consumers, especially those in
developing countries being most in jeopardy." James L. Johnston, "The Economics of the Common Heritage of Mankind," *Marine Technology Society Journal* 136
(December 1979–January 1980): 26.

14. The U.S. delegation reported after the Third Session in 1975: "The crucial question remains as to whether there is a widespread genuine will to reach accommodation. . . . The point has now been reached when a majority of States must make
an assessment in the interim period before the next session as to whether a timely
conclusion of an overall treaty is in their interests." Nordquist and Park, eds., *Reports of the U.S. Delegation,* p. 82.

15. Moritaka Hayashi, "Registration of the First Group of Pioneer Investors by the
Preparatory Commission for the International Sea-Bed Authority and for the Inter-
national Tribunal for the Law of the Sea," *Ocean Development and International
Law* 20 (1989): 1–33.

16. Bowen, Guest Editor, "Special Issue: Preparatory Commission of the International Sea-Bed Authority: Progress and Prospects," *Journal of Ocean and Shoreline Management* 14, no. 4 (1990): 239–317.

17. Sebenius, *Negotiating the Law of the Sea.*

18. An excellent summary of what is known about deep-ocean mineral resources can
be found in Ross, *Opportunities and Uses of the Ocean,* pp. 132–155.

19. John L. Mero, *The Mineral Resources of the Sea* (New York: Elsevier, 1965).

20. This term was developed by Vincent McKelvey (himself a U.S. delegate to
UNCLOS III). "Reserve base" is defined as "part of an identified source that
meets the economic, chemical, and physical requirements that would allow it to be

mined." Quoted in Office of Technology Assessment, U.S. Congress, *The Antarctic Minerals Convention: A New Treaty for the Southern Continent* (draft) (Washington, D.C.: OTA, n.d.).

21. Although a considerable fuss was made about the constituents of the polymetallic nodules as "strategic minerals," especially during the first Reagan election campaign and early years in office, the constituent elements were not scarce on the contemporary world market. Moreover, they were probably not useful for political blackmail purposes. Substitution, pricing policies, and stockpiling could have taken care of supply problems. One author even recommended stockpiling only berylium, chromium, and columbium. See Rae Weston, *Strategic Materials: A World Survey* (London: Croom Helm, 1984).

22. They were Kennecott Consortium (members: Kennecott Copper, Rio-Tinto-Zinc, Consolidated Gold Fields, Mitsubishi, Noranda Mines, and British Petroleum); Ocean Mining Associates (members: U.S. Steel, Union Minière, Sun Company, Samim); Ocean Mining, Inc. (members: International Nickel of both U.S. and Canada, AMR Group, 23 Japanese companies, and SEDCO); and Ocean Minerals Company (members: Lockheed Missile and Space, Billiton International Metals BV, BKW Minerals BV, Amoco Minerals). Subcommittee on Oceanography, Committee on Merchant Marine and Fisheries, House of Representatives, *Hearings: Law of the Sea,* 97th Cong., Serial No. 97-29, pp. 70–71.

23. Raiffa defines this as "the very maximum [a negotiator] will settle for." Raiffa, *The Art and Science of Negotiation,* p. 45.

24. I dealt, in some detail, with the liberal internationalists interest in the oceans in Friedheim, "Understanding the Debate on Ocean Resources," University of Denver, *Monograph Series in World Affairs* 6, no. 3 (1969): 27–30.

25. Friedheim and Durch, "The International Seabed Resources Agency Negotiations," p. 352.

26. United Nations General Assembly, Doc. A/9021, supplement No. 21 (New York: United Nations, 1973), p. 3. For commentaries on the moratorium, see Committee on Commerce, Science, and Transportation, *The Third U.N. Law of the Sea Conference,* 95th Cong., 2d Sess., p. 11; Hollick, *U. S. Foreign Policy and the Law of the Sea,* pp. 224–226.

27. For this reason, we present only the data for T-1 here. The distribution in T-2 is essentially the same, although the median moved to the higher end of the spectrum.

28. Said Mahmoudi, "Deep Seabed Mining and the Nordic States," *Marine Policy Reports* (Center for the Study of Marine Policy, University of Delaware) 10, no. 4 (September 1988): 1–5.

29. These proposals were related by scaling in Friedheim and Durch, "The International Seabed Resources Agency Negotiations," p. 354.

30. For an analysis of registry proposals, see Breckner, et al., *The Navy and the Common Sea,* pp. 180–184.

31. For an excellent assessment of the process of making the decision to promulgate the Draft Treaty, see Hollick, *U. S. Foreign Policy and the Law of the Sea,* pp.

226–234. The Draft Treaty is reprinted in *Journal of Maritime Law and Commerce* 2, no. 2 (January 1971): 451–480.

32. As Ann Hollick noted, Kissinger's interest arose out of "a broader concern to intervene visibly in the North–South debate. Thus the policy concessions he offered the Group of 77 . . . were not evolved within the Delegation." Hollick, *U. S. Foreign Policy and the Law of the Sea*, p. 352.

33. Raiffa, *The Art and Science of Negotiation*, p. 23.

34. Nordquist and Park, eds., *Reports of the U.S. Delegation*, pp. 82–86.

35. Article 22 (1)(2), SNT.

36. Hollick, *United States Foreign Policy and the Law of the Sea*, p. 302.

37. "The central tendency on this question would appear to be support for a system of joint ventures . . . ," Law of the Sea Study Group, "The View from the Beginning of the Conference: Projected Outcomes on Seven Major Law of the Sea Issues," Center for Naval Analyses, Memorandum (produced under State Department Contract No. 1722 420062), June 1974.

38. Article 22(1), RSNT.

39. Annex I, RSNT.

40. Article 151, ICNT.

41. Article 151, UNCLOS III Convention.

42. Quoted in Oxman, "The Third United Nation's Conference On The Law Of The Sea: The 1977 New York Session," pp. 59–60.

43. Richardson, "Seabed Mining and the Law of the Sea," *Department of State Bulletin* 80 (December 1980) p. 60.

44. Sebenius, *Negotiating the Law of the Sea*, p. 71.

45. The change in the position of the Department of Defense was significant. Previously, the Navy and the Department of Defense wanted U.S. participation in the Convention to protect its right of transit through straits used for international navigation, and to lock states into acceptance of a relatively narrow territorial sea (12 nautical miles). For the views of the then-Secretary of the Navy, see John F. Lehman, "National Interest and the Law of the Sea," *World Affairs Journal* 1, no. 1 (Spring 1982), pp. 9–15. For the traditional Department of Defense view, see Bruce Harlow, *Mission Impossible: Preservation of U.S. Maritime Freedoms*, McKernan Lecture in Marine Affairs (Seattle: Washington Sea Grant, 1985).

46. Otho E. Eskin, "U.S. Administration Views on the Law of the Sea," Edward L. Miles and Scott Allen, eds., *The Law of the Sea and Ocean Development: Issues in the Pacific Basin* (Honolulu: University of Hawaii Law of the Sea Institute, 1983), pp. 277–281.

47. Statement of Ambassador James L. Malone Before the House Merchant Marine and Fisheries Committee (mimeo), February 23, 1982.

48. Article 153(1), Green Book (n.p., n.d.).

49. Article 153(2)(b), Green Book.

50. Article 153(4)(a), Green Book.

51. Article 153(4)(b), Green Book.

52. Sebenius, *Negotiating the Law of the Sea*, pp. 71–109.

53. Rateiner, "The Law of the Sea: A Crossroads for American Foreign Policy," *Foreign Affairs* 60, no. 5 (Summer 1982): 1,007–1,021.

54. Young, "The Politics of International Regime Formation," A revised version of a paper prepared for presentation at the Annual Meeting of the International Studies Association, St. Louis, 29 March—1 April 1988, p. 36.

55. Young, "The Politics of International Regime Formation," p. 37.

56. Before the Convention was adopted, Finn Laursen estimated, using a 2 × 2 matrix, that the United States was in a win-win position whether it took a unilateral position or chose to return to the negotiation. "Security Versus Access to Resources: Explaining a Decade of U.S. Ocean Policy," *World Politics* 34 (2 January 1982): 227–229.

57. For the importance of a "shadow of the future" for engendering cooperation, particularly in prisoner's dilemma situations, see Axelrod, *Evolution of Cooperation*, pp. 12–19.

58. Malta's presence among those skeptical about production controls was due to Dr. Arvid Pardo's desire not to make the developed states feel the system was inequitable and defect. Without their participation, he thought that no funds would become available for a new international agency. As of 1992, he was correct.

59. Sebenius, "Deep Ocean Mineral Resources," in Brown and Crutchfield, eds., *Economics of Ocean Resources*, p. 84.

60. Article 9(1)(b), SNT.

61. Article 28(1)(xi), SNT.

62. Article 9(4)(ii), RSNT.

63. Article 9(4)(i), RSNT.

64. Article 9(4)(iii), RSNT.

65. Article 150(1)(a).

66. Article 150(1)(B)(iv), ICNT.

67. Article 150(1)(d), ICNT.

68. Lance N. Antrim and James K. Sebenius, "Incentives for Ocean Mining under the Convention," in Oxman, Caron, and Buderi, eds., *Law of the Sea: U.S. Policy Dilemma*, p. 89. Also see Article 151, UNCLOS III Convention.

69. Article 151(4)(b)(i), UNCLOS III Convention.

70. The text of Kissinger's speech to the Foreign Policy Association, 8 April 1976, was reprinted in U.S. Congress, Senate *Congressional Record* 1976, S.5223–S.5226.

71. Article 151, Green Book.

72. See, for example, W. Scott Burke and Frank S. Brokow, "Ideology and the Law of the Sea," and Robert A. Godwin, " 'Common Sense' vs. 'The Common Heritage' " in Oxman, Caron, Buderi, eds., *Law of the Sea: U.S. Policy Dilemma*, pp. 43–58; 59–78.

73. For example, F. G. Adams claimed, based upon a model of future seabed-mining efforts, that seabed mining would convert producer net benefit into consumer net benefit. For developed market economies that are both producers and consumers, the net transfer is positive. But for developing producer countries, the transfer

would result in a loss of $1.5 billion per year. Cited in Per Magnus Wijkman, "UNCLOS and the Redistribution of Ocean Wealth," *Journal of World Trade Law* 16, no. 1 (January–February 1982): 40.

74. Article 160(2)(f)(i), UNCLOS III Convention.

75. Article 160(1), UNCLOS III Convention.

76. According to the records of the Law of the Sea Study Group, 150 states participated in UNCLOS III bargaining to 1975. Of these, 110 were affiliated with the Group of 77, or 73 percent of the total.

77. Friedheim and Durch, "The International Seabed Resources Agency Negotiations," p. 364.

78. Article 161, (1),(8)(c), Article 162,(2)(j), UNCLOS III Convention.

79. Article 27(1) SNT.

80. "Introductory Note," Part I, RSNT, p. 10.

81. Article 157, ICNT.

82. Quoted in Oxman, "The Third United Nations Conference on the Law of the Sea: The Tenth Session (1981)," *American Journal of International Law* 76, no. 1 (1982): 11.

83. Article 161 (1)(a), Green Book.

84. Article 161 (1)(b), Green Book.

85. Article 161 (7)(c), Green Book.

86. Article 161 (7)(d), Green Book.

87. Krasner, *Structural Conflict*, p. 307.

Chapter 8: UNCLOS III—The Regime Negotiated

1. Although Krasner treats an "obligation" as a "norm," it is mentioned explicitly here as a critical part of a legal regime because international lawyers treat state obligations as such.

2. Krasner, "Structural Causes and Regime Consequences," *International Organization* 36, no. 2 (Spring 1982): 186.

3. I shrank from using the term "interdependent" to avoid the connotation that Susan Strange identifies of "highly asymmetrical and uneven dependence or vulnerability," Strange, *"Cave! Hic dragones,"* p. 485.

4. Keohane, "The Demand for International Regimes," *International Organization* 36, no. 2 (Spring 1982): 325–355, and *After Hegemony*, p. 79.

5. Young, *International Cooperation*, p. 5.

6. Young, *International Cooperation*, pp. 84–89.

7. For an exponent of this view, see Eckert, *Enclosure of Ocean Resources*.

8. Young, *International Cooperation*, p. 95.

9. McDougal, "International Law and the Law of the Sea," in Alexander, ed., *The Law of the Sea: Offshore Boundaries and Zones*, p. 15.

10. R. M. MacIver, *The Web of Government* (New York: Macmillan, 1947), pp. 39–60.

11. Friedheim and Durch, "The International Seabed Resources Agency and the New International Economic Order," *International Organization* 31, no. 2 (Spring 1977): 343–384; Krasner, *Structural Conflict*, pp. 227–250.

12. I also argue, in chapter 7, that deep-seabed minerals was a symbolic issue, useful precisely because it had little practical worth. My position is similar to Giulio Pontecorvo's: "We have enjoyed—and the end is not in sight—the privilege of watching intelligent, well-meaning diplomats diligently and laboriously create an elaborate institutional structure and a set of rules that permit them to impose an optimal levy on a fantasy. Surely these episodes are the raw materials for the talents of Jonathan Swift or Gilbert and Sullivan." Pontecorvo, "Musing About Seabed Mining, or Why What We Don't Know Can Hurt Us," *Ocean Development and International Law* 21, no. 1 (1990): 117.

13. Pardo, "Law of the Sea Conference—What Went Wrong," in Friedheim, ed., *Managing Ocean Resources,* pp. 137–148, and "The Evolving Law of the Sea: A Critique of the Informal Composite Negotiating Text (1977)," in E. M. Borgese and N. Ginsburg, eds., *Ocean Yearbook I* (Chicago: University of Chicago Press, 1978), pp. 9–37; Arvid Pardo and Carl Q. Christol, "The Common Interest: Tension between the Whole and the Parts," in R. St. J. MacDonald and D. M. Johnston, eds., *The Structure and Process of International Law* (The Hague: Nijhoff, 1983), pp. 647–655; Elizabeth Borgese, "Law of the Sea: Crossroads Again," *International Perspectives* (July–August 1986), pp. 12–14.

14. Grotius, *Freedom of the Seas.*

15. Grotius, *De Jure Belli Ac Pacis Libri Tres,* vol. 2, no. 3 (Oxford: Clarendon Press, 1925).

16. R. M. MacIver, *The Web of Government,* p. 364.

17. Dunning, *A History of Political Theories,* pp. 81–123.

18. Hearnshaw, "Grotius and the Reign of Law," in *Some Great Political Idealists of the Christian Era,* p. 91. Also see Charles R. Beitz, *Political Theory and International Relations* (Princeton: Princeton University Press, 1979), p. 65.

19. F. J. C. Hearnshaw, "Grotius and the Reign of Law," p. 95.

20. Young, *Resource Regimes,* p. 92, and *International Cooperation,* p. 81.

21. Although no formal measure is used in the following sections to judge the adequacy of the new ocean regime, a number of attributes drawn from the regime literature were the basis for the assessments performed. Since the new ocean regime was an explicit, negotiated regime, it was assumed not to be necessary to demonstrate the explicitness of the commitment, nor its attempt to create a regularized pattern of behavior. These were givens. However, the attributes below were considered, albeit that the categories are not independent of each other:

    1. Did UNCLOS III relate to an agreed international order?
    2. Did it establish rights, rules, and obligations?
    3. Did it create a right to allocate—did it clarify *who* might get *what?*
    4. Did it clarify lines of authority?
    5. Did it resolve questions of distribution, redistribution, and equity satisfactorily?
    6. Were technically appropriate solutions agreed to? Were they "efficient"?
    7. Was the language sufficiently precise to reduce interpretation problem to an acceptable level?
    8. Will the agreed arrangements be enforceable at low cost?

9. Does the agreement provide for conflict management mechanisms, both prevention and cure?

10. Are the measures agreed to likely to be stable over time?

The above factors are drawn from a variety of sources the most useful of which are Krasner, ed., "International Regimes," *International Organization* 36, no. 2 (Spring 1982): 185–510; Stephen Haggard and Beth A. Simmons, "Theories of International Regimes," *International Organization* 41, no. 3 (Summer 1987): 491–517; Nicholas Onuf and Frank F. Klink, "Anarchy, Authority, Rule," *International Studies Quarterly* 33, no. 2 (June 1989): 149–173; Young, *International Cooperation*, and *Resource Regimes*.

22. Vicuña, ed., *The Exclusive Economic Zone: A Latin American Perspective*.

23. Breckner et al., *The Navy and the Common Sea*, pp. 174–175.

24. Dante, *On World Government or De Monarchia* (Indianapolis: Bobbs-Merrill, 1949), p. 39.

25. Young, *International Cooperation*, p. 22.

26. See chapter 4 for a discussion of the package deal and its components, the territorial sea, transit passage through straits used for international navigation, and the EEZ.

27. For an analysis of fisheries related issues, see chapter 5.

28. Young, *Natural Resources and the State* (Berkeley: University of California Press, 1981), pp. 5–13.

29. See chapter 6 for analysis of the bargaining over scientific rights in the coastal and open ocean.

30. C. Barry Raleigh, "Commentary: The Internationalism of Ocean Science vs. International Politics," *Marine Technology Society Journal* 23, no. 1 (March 1989): 44–47.

31. For example, it is critically important for management to associate whales (predator) with krill (prey of whales and predator of plankton), plankton, and the oceanographic conditions associated with plankton blooms. The ecosystem approach has been implemented in the Convention on the Conservation of Antarctic Marine Living Resources (CCAMLR), and in cooperation with the International Whaling Commission. Friedheim and Akaha, "Antarctic Resources and International Law: Japan, the United States and the Future of Antarctica," *Ecology Law Quarterly* 16, no. 1 (1989): 119–154.

32. See chapter 4 for a discussion of the debate surrounding the "Hedberg Proposal."

33. *New York Times*, September 23, 1989, p. 23. Also see Samuel LaBudde, *Stripmining the Seas: A Global Perspective on Driftnet Fisheries* (Honolulu: Earthtrust, 1988).

34. See Douglas M. Johnston, "The Driftnetting Problem in the Pacific Ocean: Legal Considerations and Diplomatic Options," *Ocean Development and International Law* 21, no. 1 (1990): 5–40.

35. See chapter 6 for a discussion of the bargaining over vessel-source pollution.

36. For analysis of the deep-seabed negotiations that took place in the First Committee, see chapter 7.

37. For accounts of a number of North–South encounters in multilateral fora, see: Zartman, ed., *Positive Sum*.
38. Jose Luis Jesus (Chairman, Preparatory Commission) "Statement on the Issue of the Universality of the Convention," Council on Ocean Law, *Special Report* (July 1990).
39. *Ocean Policy News* (May 1990), pp. 6–8.
40. Nandan, "The 1982 United Nations Convention on the Law of the Sea: At A Cross-Road," pp. 4–7.
41. The assumption stated is a clue that what will follow will be a rational choice model. Since we know that strong subordinate stakeholders often do dominate decisions even if an analysis shows they represent only a minority of "the national interest", we admit that rational choice models are flawed. Therefore, caution must be exercised in interpreting the results of the use of such models.
42. This basic fact shaped the manner in which I used or, as some will conclude, abused multiattribute utility analysis. The stakeholders probably would not have cooperated with an attempt to assess their utilities. Moreover, even if they were cooperative, resource constraints probably would have been prohibitive. The second-best option—to ask a panel of representative citizens or experts from some of the stakeholders to stand in for the actual stakeholders—also was not tried because of resource constraints. However, this will be attempted in a future project. I would like to thank Professor Ward Edwards, Director of the Social Science Research Institute, and "guru" of Multiattribute Utility analysis for his assistance and patience with my violations of the carefully developed details of his method. However, I hope I have remained within the spirit of his work. Naturally, despite his best efforts, the remaining errors are mine.
43. See Ward Edwards and J. Robert Newman, *Multiattribute Evaluation* (Beverly Hills, Calif.: Sage, 1982); Ward Edwards and Detlof von Winterfeldt, "Public Values in Risk Debates," *Risk Analysis* 7, no. 2 (1987): 141–158, and "Public Disputes about Risky Technologies: Stakeholders and Arenas," in V. Covello, J. Menkes, and J. Mumpower, eds., *Risk Evaluation and Management* (New York: Plenum, 1986); Ralph L. Keeney and Howard Raiffa, *Decisions With Multiple Objectives: Preferences and Value Trade-offs* (New York: Wiley, 1976).
44. Since the author was role-playing for each of the stakeholders, the analysis inevitably reveals not only the author's expertise, or lack thereof, but also his biases. I cannot rid myself of these biases, but I can put their results on display. That is what the table of value dimensions does. Each cell displays a judgment which I am prepared to defend. Unfortunately space limitations preclude me from doing so here. However, readers have available in the tables the basis for understanding my judgments, and can pinpoint where and why we disagree. Indeed, readers are invited to use the same model to help them summarize their perceptions.
45. This is similar to the salience measure used in the multilateral bargaining model. See chapter 3.
46. To posit an "imposed" regime means, for the sake of analysis, that the cost of the regime is assumed not to be prohibitive.

47. It was difficult to make these estimates. Since I have observed governments experiencing difficulties with short-term chaos, when all states act individually in their self-interest on ocean problems, it is difficult for me to see when uncoordinated actions will result in the adjustments that reduce the chaos to manageability. Therefore, I might have overestimated the short-term difficulties of a spontaneous regime, and not seen the longer run benefits.

48. See Thomas Hovet, Jr., *Bloc Politics in the United Nations* (Cambridge: Harvard University Press, 1960).

49. The White House, Office of the Secretary, *Fact Sheet: United States Ocean Policy* (March 10, 1983); "The Exclusive Economic Zone," *Oceanus* 27, no. 4 (1984–1985): 3; National Advisory Committee on Oceans and Atmosphere, *The Exclusive Economic Zone of the United States: Some Immediate Policy Issues* (Washington: n.p., 1984), p. 1.

50. Friedheim, "The Regime of the Arctic—Distributional or Integrative Bargaining?" *Ocean Development and International Law* 19 (1988): 493–510.

51. They include (1) a Grotian capture claim to resources brought up from rich oceanic nodule beds; (2) an extension of coastal jurisdiction to absorb polymetallic sulfide crusts and smokers lying just beyond 200-mile EEZs; and, (3) if the problem of Part XI is not resolved relatively soon, a national lakes-type claim to a large swath of deep seabed. On the last option, see Mark W. Zacher and James G. McConnell, "Down to the Sea with Stakes: The Evolving Law of the Sea and the Future of the Deep Seabed Regime," *Ocean Development and International Law* 21, no. 1 (1990): 71–104.

Chapter 9: Negotiation of the Regime—Lessons Learned

1. See, for example, Eckert, "United States Policy and the Law of the Sea Conference, 1969–82: A Case Study of Multilateral Negotiations," in Thomas D. Willett and Roland Vaubel, eds., *The Political Economy of International Organizations* (Boulder, Colo.: Westview, forthcoming).

2. Young, *International Cooperation*, pp. 120–123, 131, 140, 226–227.

3. For a definition of transaction costs as applied to ocean problems, see Eckert, *Enclosure of Ocean Resources*, pp. 54–56.

4. The calculation was very rough. It included only direct costs of transportation, per diem, hall use, document productions, etc. It did not include the salary of officials, nor the costs of participation by nongovernment observers. No inflation factor over the 15 years was used.

5. For examples of an array of opportunity-cost considerations in public policy, see Douglass C. North and Roger Leroy Miller, *The Economics of Public Issues* (New York: Harper & Row, 1971).

6. See epigraph at beginning of chapter 1.

7. See Buchanan and Tullock, *Calculus of Consent*; Douglas Rae, "The Limits of Consensual Decision," *American Political Science Review* 69, no. 4 (1975): 40–56; Mancur Olson, *The Logic of Collective Action* (Cambridge: Harvard University

Press, 1965); Robert Abrams, *Foundations of Political Analysis: An Introduction to the Theory of Collective Choice* (New York: Columbia University Press, 1980); John Bonner, *Introduction to the Theory of Social Choice* (Baltimore: Johns Hopkins University Press, 1986).

8. Rule 37(1), *Rules of Procedure*, United Nations, Third Conference on the Law of the Sea (A/Conf.62/36), 2 July 1971. However, in an appendix, a declaration incorporating the "gentleman's agreement" stated: "The Conference should make every effort to reach agreement on substantive matters by way of consensus and there should be no voting on such matters until all efforts at consensus have been exhausted."

9. R. P. Barston has noted that consensus as an "exhaustive search for widely acceptable solutions" has been used in the U.N. Disarmament Commission and Conference on Security and Cooperation in Europe (CSCE), and combined with voting in the United Nations Conference on Aid, Trade and Development (UNCTAD). *Modern Diplomacy* (London: Longman, 1988), p. 117.

10. Cf. Kenneth Arrow: "By consensus I understand any reasonable and accepted means of aggregating individual interests. As is well known, there are deep paradoxes connected with any form of consensus mechanism, such as majority rule, short of the situation where unanimity obtains." *The Limits of Organization* (New York: Norton, 1974), p. 69.

11. Cf. Chie Nakane: "The process is not necessarily logical. They will talk about this and that, often with much indulgence toward any individual feelings at stake. A meeting may be adjourned if a deadlock is reached, and will be resumed later in a fresh mood. In the course of time dissension decreases, and consent increases. When a point is reached where support comes from about seventy percent of the members, this is a sign that consensus is near. In the final stage the minority makes a concession, saying 'I will join you, since all of you have agreed. Though I dissent in this particular issue, I am very ready to cooperate with you, and at any rate I have been able to say all that I wanted to say." *Japanese Society* (Harmondsworth, U.K.: Penguin, 1974), p. 150.

12. We should note that, at times, some commentators have overstated the case of consensus decision-making in Japan. Ezra Vogel and colleagues have provided a useful corrective in Ezra F. Vogel, ed., *Japanese Organization and Decision-Making* (Berkeley: University of California Press, 1975). Moreover, the flip-side of consensus decision-making is a right of rebellion, used often by the Japanese throughout their history. See Hugh Borton, *Japan's Modern Century* (New York: Ronald, 1955).

13. Zartman, *Positive Sum*, pp. 6–7, and *50% Solution*, pp. 20ff.

14. For more detail on the development of the model, see preface and chapter 3 of this volume.

15. See Zartman and Berman, *Practical Negotiator*.

16. Zartman and Berman, *Practical Negotiator*, pp. 42–202; Zartman, "Many Are Called but Few Choose"; and "Negotiation: Theory and Reality," *Journal of International Affairs* 9, no. 1 (1975): 69–77; William Mark Habeeb, *Power and*

Tactics in International Negotiation (Baltimore: Johns Hopkins University Press, 1988).

17. Zartman and Berman, *Practical Negotiator*, p. 98; Zartman, "Negotiation: Theory and Reality," pp. 69–77.

18. Gilbert R. Winham, "Negotiation as a Management Process," *World Politics* 30, no. 1 (October 1977): 100; G. Matthew Bonham et al., "Cognition and International Negotiation: The Historical Recovery of Discursive Space," *Cooperation and Conflict* 22, no. 1 (1987): 5.

19. Stevenson and Oxman, "The Third United Nations Conference on the Law of the Sea: The 1975 Geneva Session," *American Journal of International Law* 67 (1975): 764.

20. S. Jayakumar and T. T. B. Koh, *The Negotiating Process of the Third United Nations Conference on the Law of the Sea*, n.p., n.d., p. 64.

21. Cf. "Dealing with details is often the most complex part of the process of negotiation . . . ." Zartman and Berman, *Practical Negotiator*, p. 148.

22. Zartman and Berman, *Practical Negotiator*, p. 134, 147.

23. Gilbert R. Winham and H. Eugene Bovis, "Agreement and Breakdown in Negotiation: Report on a State Department Training Simulation," *Journal of Peace Research* 15, no. 4 (1978): 296.

24. All patterns shown are actual histograms. None are "smoothed" or idealized.

25. Raiffa and Sebenius, "Synthesizing Themes of the U.S.-PIN Program," in Francis Mautner-Markhof, ed., *Processes of International Negotiations* (Boulder, Colo.: Westview, 1989), p. 295.

26. Sebenius, *Negotiating the Law of the Sea*, pp. 61–69.

27. Jayakumar and Koh, *The Negotiating Process*, p. 126.

28. Buzan, " 'United We Stand . . . ,' " p. 195.

29. Friedheim and Durch, "The International Seabed Resources Agency Negotiations," pp. 343–384; Krasner, *Structural Conflict*, p. 241.

30. Jayakumar and Koh, *The Negotiating Process of the Third United Nations Conference on the Law of the Sea*, pp. 104–124; Miles, *Global Ocean Politics*, pp. 136–150; Buzan, " 'United We Stand,' " pp. 183–204; and Sanger, *Ordering the Oceans*, pp. 23–39.

31. Article 3, Convention on the High Seas (1958), in Platzoder and Vitzthum, eds., *Seerecht*, p. 25.

32. Friedheim et al., "The Landlocked and Shelf-locked States in the Law of the Sea Negotiations," Center for Naval Analyses, Memorandum 01-74 (31 January 1974).

33. Axelrod, *Conflict of Interest*, pp. 158–163.

34. Miles, *Global Ocean Politics: The Decision Process at the Third United Nations Conference on the Law of the Sea, 1973–1982* manuscript, pp. 133–142.

35. Habeeb, *Power and Tactics in International Negotiation*, p. 132.

36. Sanger, *Ordering the Oceans*, pp. 25, 31.

37. W. Lang, "Multilateral Negotiations: The Role of Presiding Officers," in Francis Mautner-Markhof, ed., *Processes of International Negotiations* (Boulder, Colo.: Westview, 1989), pp. 23–42.

38. Nordquist and Park, eds., *Reports of the U.S. Delegation*, p. 83.

39. Jayakumar and Koh, *The Negotiating Process*, p. 89.

40. Sanger, *Ordering the Oceans*, p. 31.

41. Guy Olivier Faure, "The Mediator as a Third Negotiator," in Mautner-Markhof, ed., *Process of International Negotiations*, pp. 415–426.

42. Raiffa, *The Art and Science of Negotiation*, pp. 23–24.

43. Sebenius, "The Computer as Mediator: Law of the Sea and Beyond," *Journal of Policy Analysis and Management* 1, no. 1 (1981): 92; Sebenius, *Negotiating the Law of the Sea*, pp. 24–48.

44. This is in contrast to "instrumental" behavior. Cited in David Baldwin, *Economic Statecraft* (New York: Columbia University Press, 1985), pp. 96–101.

45. Murray Edelman, *The Symbolic Uses of Politics* (Urbana: University of Illinois Press, 1967), pp. 130–151.

46. Daniel Bell, *The End of Ideology* (New York: Collier, 1961), pp. 16, 394–395.

47. Karl Manheim, *Ideology and Utopia* (New York: Harcourt, Brace and World, 1936), pp. 56–58.

48. Clingan, *The 1982 Law of the Sea Treaty: One Observer's Assessment*, p. 6.

49. This is consistent with Sebenius's conclusion "that the real precedent set by the treaty is one of NIEO rhetoric overlaying a system that is generally compatible with conventional economic operation." *Negotiating the Law of the Sea*, p. 104.

50. Roger Fischer and Scott Brown, *Getting Together: Building Relationships As We Negotiate* (New York: Penguin, 1989), p. 43.

51. Axelrod, *Evolution of Cooperation*, pp. 8–15; Rapoport and Chammah, *Prisoner's Dilemma*.

52. "Distributive bargaining is the process by which each party attempts to maximize his own share in the context of fixed-sum payoffs. Integrative bargaining is the process by which the parties attempt to increase the size of the joint gain without respect to the division of the payoffs." Walton and McKersie, *A Behavioral Theory of Labor Negotiations*, p. 13; Dean G. Pruitt, *Negotiation Behavior*, (New York: Academic Press, 1981), pp. 71–135.

53. Pruitt, *Negotiation Behavior*, p. 162.

54. Nicholas Onuf, *World of Our Making: Rules and Rule in Social Theory and International Relations* (Columbia: University of South Carolina Press, 1989), p. 140.

55. For a review of studies using a cognitive perspective to analyze bargaining on international trade issues, see John Odell, "Understanding International Trade Policies: An Emerging Synthesis," *World Politics* 43, no. 1 (October 1990): 149–152.

56. Pardo, "Law of the Sea Conference—What Went Wrong," in Friedheim, ed., *Managing Ocean Resources*, pp. 137–148.

57. Jose Luis Jesus, "The Completion of the Work of the Preparatory Commission and the Universality of the Convention," *International Challenges* 10, no. 3 (1990): 6–17.

58. Marvin S. Soroos, *Beyond Sovereignty: The Challenge of Global Policy* (Columbia: University of South Carolina Press, 1986), pp. 33–74.

59. Kilaparti Ramakrishna, "Third World Countries in the Policy Response to Global Climate Change," in Jeremy Leggett, ed., *Global Warming: The Greenpeace Report* (Oxford: Oxford University Press, 1990), p. 423.
60. Sebenius, "Crafting a Winning Coalition: Negotiating a Regime to Control Global Warming," in Richard Elliot Benedick et al., *Greenhouse Warming: Negotiating A Global Regime* (Washington: World Resources Institute, 1991), p. 71.
61. Young, *International Cooperation*, pp. 81–89.
62. For example, a new shipping regime is emerging which requires that to be an active participant in international trade, a state must have capital-intensive ships or port facilities even though, at present, many developing states believe they would do better in the short run with reliance upon labor-intensive ships and facilities. I doubt if the development of these practices was the result of a conspiracy. Rather it was a matter of convenience for the developed states that had spillover effects. See Amy Friedheim, "Puerto Quetzal, Guatemala: Container Cranes or Stevedores?" *Oceanus* 32, no. 3 (Fall 1989): 74–78.

Index